WORDS

OVERFLOWN

BY STARS

WRITER'S DIGEST BOOKS
Cincinnati, Ohio
www.writersdigest.com

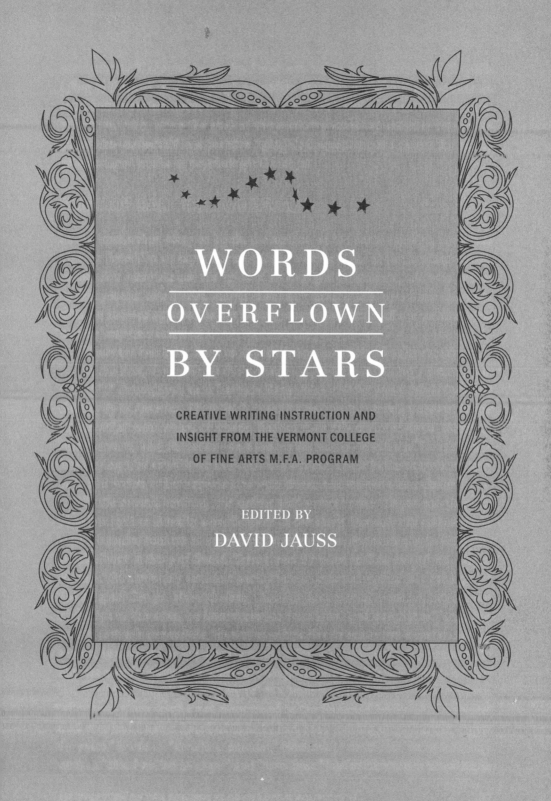

WORDS

OVERFLOWN

BY STARS

CREATIVE WRITING INSTRUCTION AND
INSIGHT FROM THE VERMONT COLLEGE
OF FINE ARTS M.F.A. PROGRAM

EDITED BY

DAVID JAUSS

For more resources for writers, visit www.writersdigest.com/books. To receive a free weekly e-mail newsletter delivering tips and updates about writing and about Writer's Digest products, register at http://newsletters.fwpublications.com.

13 12 11 10 09   5 4 3 2 1

Distributed in Canada by Fraser Direct
100 Armstrong Avenue
Georgetown, Ontario, Canada L7G 5S4
Tel: (905) 877-4411

Distributed in the U.K. and Europe by David & Charles
Brunel House, Newton Abbot, Devon, TQ12 4PU, England
Tel: (+44) 1626-323200, Fax: (+44) 1626-323319
E-mail: postmaster@davidandcharles.co.uk

Distributed in Australia by Capricorn Link
P.O. Box 704, Windsor, NSW 2756 Australia
Tel: (02) 4577-3555

Library of Congress Cataloging-in-Publication Data

Words overflown by stars : creative writing instruction and insight from the Vermont College of Fine Arts M.F.A. program / edited by David Jauss. -- 1st ed.
    p. cm.
  Includes index.
  ISBN 978-1-58297-540-5 (pbk. : alk. paper)
  1. English language--Rhetoric--Study and teaching (Higher)--United States. 2. Creative writing (Higher education)--United States. 3. Fiction--Authorship--Study and teaching (Higher)--United States. 4. Poetry--Authorship--Study and teaching (Higher)--United States. I. Jauss, David. II. Vermont College of Fine Arts.
  PE1405.U6W66 2009
  808'.0420711--dc22   2008034582

Edited by Kelly Nickell
Designed by Terri Woesner
Production coordinated by Mark Griffin

media

... the word overflown by stars,
drenched by the seas.
To each the word.

—Paul Celan, "Argumentum e Silentio"

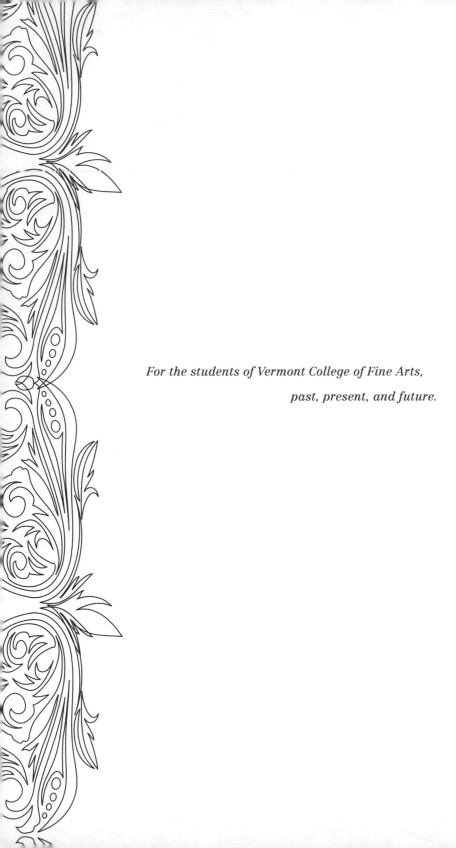

For the students of Vermont College of Fine Arts,

past, present, and future.

Table of Contents

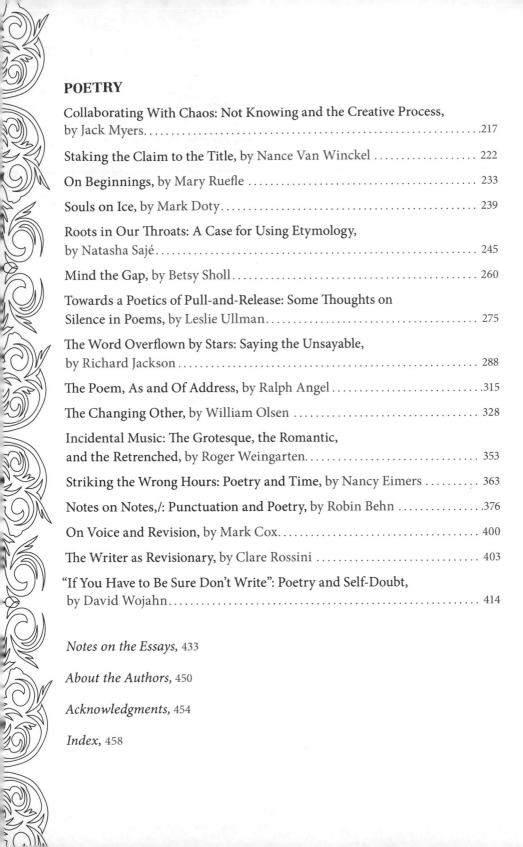

POETRY

PREFACE

In his contributor's note to this volume, Mark Doty says, "I ... consider my time teaching in the [Vermont College of Fine Arts M.F.A. in Writing] program to have been my own second graduate education." I've heard many of my colleagues say the same thing over the years, and I second the sentiment wholeheartedly. Although I earned graduate degrees from the writing programs of two exceptional universities, Syracuse University and the University of Iowa, in many ways my most valuable education as a writer began nearly twenty years later, in 1999, when I began teaching in the low-residency M.F.A. in Writing Program at Vermont College, as it was then known. (In 2008, the college became Vermont College of Fine Arts, an independent institution that is the first college in the nation devoted solely to M.F.A. programs.) While I had several brilliant teachers at Syracuse and Iowa—including perhaps the finest writing teacher I've ever known, the late Frederick Busch—at Vermont College I found myself surrounded by brilliant teachers, all of whom delivered lectures during ten-day residencies at the program's beautiful hilltop campus in Montpelier, Vermont. These lectures weren't the casual, impromptu riffs I was used to hearing in workshops; they were carefully thought-out and exquisitely written lectures informed by reading that was both deep and wide, and they were chockfull of both thought-provoking aesthetic observations and sound, practical advice. Time and again, I left Vermont both exhausted from the intensive residencies and energized by the insights I'd gained from the lectures by my colleagues (and, I'm happy to admit, from those by our graduating students as well).

This anthology contains a sampling of essays, virtually all of which were originally presented as lectures at Vermont College of Fine Arts, by some of the distinguished writers who have served on the faculty of the program over the past quarter century. Of the thirty-two essays included here, half focus predominately on fiction and creative nonfiction and half predominately on poetry, but many of them also address more than one genre. For example, both Laurie Alberts's "Showing *and* Telling" and Robin Hemley's "Painful Howls From Places That Undoubtedly Exist: A Primer of Deceit" discuss the shifting, tenuous borders between fiction and nonfiction, and Cynthia Huntington's "Poetic Technique in Nonfiction Writing" and Sydney Lea's "'I Recognize Thy Glory': On the American Nature Essay and Lyric Poetry" discuss the intersections of creative nonfiction and lyric poetry, as does Sue William Silverman's section on the lyric essay in "The Meandering River: An Overview of the Subgenres of

Creative Nonfiction." Natasha Sajé's "Roots in Our Throats: A Case for Using Etymology" refers not only to poetry, its principal subject, but also to fiction and nonfiction. Even those essays that don't overtly address more than one genre apply to other genres as well. As François Camoin notes in "The Textures of Fiction: An Inquiry," what he says about fiction applies equally to nonfiction. And Nance Van Winckel's advice about titles, Mark Cox's thoughts about voice and revision, and David Wojahn's ruminations on the relation of self-doubt to creativity—to name just three of the essays—apply to all three genres. Finally, Jack Myers's "Collaborating With Chaos: Not Knowing and the Creative Process" discusses the creative process that underlies all of these genres. In short, the anthology offers an abundance of craft advice to writers of any or all three genres.

One note of caution, however. As valuable as these essays are, it is important to remember what William Olsen says in his essay about the craft of poetry (though he could be talking about any of the genres included here): "To appreciate craft you have to experience craft; in poetry this means you have to hear it done and learn how to hear it be done rather than learn handbooks and be content with their excerpts and principles: You have to encounter another poem, not the one you would write from your own life but one from another existence than yours. It is in this shared place that craft happens."

I hope this anthology helps you find your way to that shared place.

—*David Jauss*

PROSE

BEFORE WE GET STARTED

By Bret Lott

Let me begin this essay on the nature and aim of words by saying that I won't be talking about those glamour words we all get to use now and again, the ones that set our pride spinning at our actually using in a sentence. *Abrogate* was one of those words I used that, once I'd actually employed it correctly in a sentence, made me lean back and put my hands behind my head, kick my feet up on the desk, and beam at my intelligence. Another one I love is the word *limn*, which I've used a number of times for what I hope was good effect. Once, in a review of a perfectly dreadful novel that centered on hidden incestuous relationships, I had the great good fortune of putting together the phrase "the most Byzantine jamboree of family flesh possible." That was a glorious occasion, I remember, and I remember, too, me smiling at the monitor for a good five minutes about that. *Byzantine jamboree.* That was fun.

But I won't be talking about those words here. The kind of words I'm talking about are those trench warfare words, those grunt-work words we oftentimes don't give a second thought because we traffic in them day in and day out, truck them in and offload them like they were so many yards of gravel being used to rough pave the road for the brilliant parade of paper floats our ideas and ambitions and intellect will be once this story is done.

Byzantine jamboree. Man, that was fun.

No. I'll be talking about *a*, *the*, and *this*. Those few small words we couldn't care less about because they are, like the poor, always with us.

But before I begin holding forth on even that much—those three numbingly nondescript syllables that together only use up three vowels and three consonants—I need to tell you about how I used to live behind a guy who used the term *no-brainer* way too often. He was a doctor—a gastroenterologist—and because doctors know everything precisely because they are doctors, it was never any surprise to me that everything he encountered was a "no-brainer."

And because he used it so often in our everyday exchanges—from the "no-brainer" it was for him to buy a two-year-old Lexus instead of a new one, to the "no-brainer" it was deciding to scope a patient complaining of blood in his phlegm—slowly the term crept into my own lexicon, until for a while I was walking around saying it just as much as he was. It's a fun term, I found out, infectious for its sharp little shorthand expressing your own acumen and eloquence at once.

"Can I get a transverse Mohawk?" my older son Zeb once asked me. Really.

"That's a no-brainer," I told him. Meaning, I hoped he understood, no.

"That's a no-brainer," I said when Jacob asked if he could ride his bike alone to Wendy's for lunch one Saturday back when he was in the third or fourth grade. He'd have to cross Highway 17 where Mathis Ferry Road intersected it, six lanes without a crosswalk.

But I've since kicked the habit—or almost. Because, finally, I hate that term. There's something about it that smacks of condescension, something in it that implies everyone else is an idiot who can't assess and discuss things as quickly and accurately as you.

Which leads to how I'd like to begin this essay: with a moment a few semesters ago when I almost blurted out "That's a no-brainer" to a student in class.

This was toward the beginning of things, during the critique of one of the first student stories, all of us doing the old workshop shuffle: what you like, what you don't, what works, what doesn't, what's at stake, what's missing, blah blah blah, all in the hopes not just to put a Band-Aid on the story at hand but to try to speak of the larger notion of writing fiction. There was a particular point I wanted to make about the way the student used a proper noun, and how its usage called into question the verisimilitude of the entire story, because it called into question the authority of the writer herself.

Within one page of a story told in the first person, the narrator had referred to her mother as "Mom," "Momma," and "Mother." I pointed this out to the class as being a matter of consistency of both point of view and of voice—that is, in order to get a first-person narrator nailed down so that the reader can begin to get to know the character and thereby come to whatever experience the story might offer, the writer needs to use language consistently, in this case decide whether the narrator calls her mother "Mom," "Momma," or "Mother." Of course there are lots of different considerations that go into making such a blanket statement: What if the narrator is fragmented herself, is unreliable and so does not in fact know any kind of consistency in her own voice? What if her mother is to her three persons at once, a kind of matriarchal holy trinity? What if she calls her "Momma" in dialogue, but thinks of her as "Mother" when relating the story here on the page? What if what if what if? Certainly extenuating, qualifying circumstances are always at work. But the story we were reading carried with it none of those free passes to arguing with the teacher.

I made this point about the proper noun, and made it pretty well, I thought. Hey, I'd been doing this for a long time. I'd made this little speech enough times before. They're getting it, I thought.

And then I glanced to my left to see a student with her nose wrinkled up, as though smelling something false. She wasn't one of those kinds of belligerent students, either, those sorts who think they know something going in and so rebut everything that comes out of your mouth in order to hold together the sad and tattered last shreds of the nomad's tent their understanding of writing has become. Those students you hope and pray will not darken your door because when they do, the semester can stretch out before you like the Hundred Years War. No, she was a fine writer, seemed sensible, and so I asked her, "What's wrong?"

"I don't see why that matters," she said, and shrugged, still with her nose wrinkled up.

This was when I very nearly said, "This is a no-brainer." Instead, I caught myself, and went on to beat her and the rest of the class about the ears with the blunt instrument of my further instruction, as I am wont to do when somebody doesn't get what I want them to get.

I'm going to pause a moment or two here to quote a little piece of a lecture I gave the first residency I spent teaching in the low-residency M.F.A. program at Vermont College, back in 1994, this in the hopes of illuminating why this particular moment in my teaching life—an undergrad's pooh-poohing my point about a proper noun—was one that carried a bit more weight than it might otherwise seem.

The lecture was on the architecture of Jayne Anne Phillips's *Machine Dreams*. But the section I'm going to quote doesn't have anything to do with her book; instead, it's a passage I hope will relate the sort of self-deluding snobbery bred by looking at words as though their examination one by one were beneath us. Or at least beneath me.

> When I was in grad school at UMass-Amherst I took a seminar in Virginia Woolf from Lee Edwards. There were about ten or eleven of us in there, and it just so happened that that semester there was a centennial celebration of Woolf's birthday down at Pembroke, a three-day shindig at which plenty of papers would be presented on what was becoming, in no small part due to Lee Edwards's teaching capabilities, our favorite writer. We decided to go down there for a day of the festivities, and piled in two cars, drove all the way to Providence. We got lost once in town, finally found the right building, and walked in, all of us, on a panel already in progress. I don't remember who the heck the presenter was talking up there, but it soon became obvious to each of us that we had no clue what she was saying, only that it had to do with *The Waves*. When she finished, the crowded room applauded enthusiastically, and we all sort of looked at one another, shrugged.
>
> The next presenter stood, and began reading her own paper, this one about the use of personal pronouns in *To the Lighthouse.*
>
> That was when we stood as a group, and filed out. Once in the hallway, we shook our heads, perplexed at the lifeblood being sucked out of books we loved happening just inside the closed doors behind us. We found a pub down one or another street, and all sat at a table, and talked about the books we'd been reading for class, why we loved them, why not. Then, disillusioned at the proceedings but glad for each other's company, all that talk, we piled back in the cars, drove on home to western Mass.
>
> The talk, of course, let me and each of the others simply come to know more fully those books, and how and why and when they moved our hearts. Hearts moving, by the way, the reason any of us ought to write.

Well, okay. I'll give myself that last line. It seems true enough, these many years later, that moving the heart is the reason we ought to write. But I can't help but think how smug I sounded, and how unwilling to learn I was, not just back in 1983 when we did all that, but as near to now in my own history as when I gave that lecture in 1994. Because the longer I write—and this is the one sure thing I know about writing—the harder it gets, and the more I hold close the truth that I know nothing.

I can't help but think of how smug I was to very nearly blurt out to that student, "That's a no-brainer."

Because, if you want to write, there really is no such thing as a no-brainer. Flannery O'Connor wrote, "There's a grain of stupidity that the writer of fiction can hardly do without, and this is the quality of having to stare, of not getting the point at once." I think what she's saying is that if one begins to see the world and its dilemmas and desires and questions and heartbreaks and, yes, personal pronouns and proper nouns as being no-brainers, one has begun to lose the necessary wonder at and reverence for what is eternally unfolding around us that it takes to be one "upon whom nothing is lost," as Henry James exhorted writers to be.

Wonder and *reverence*, I want to say before I get started, are the twin dynamos that generate the art of writing.

To look at something without wonder and reverence—to see things as being no-brainers—is to dismiss *deliberation*; dismissing deliberation eliminates the possibility for *reflection*; to eliminate reflection is simply and fully and sadly to reject the possibility of *discovery*. Of course the difference between *a* and *the* and *this* is a vast one. Of course words matter. Of course we must choose carefully.

But why is there such a vast difference? And given the endless valley of bones the same old words used again and again and again by writers far superior to ourselves truly is, we writers no more than buzzards picking over the same words used by Faulkner and Melville and O'Connor and Hawthorne and Welty and Baldwin and all of them—given all those words, and our pitiful little attempts at recycling them in the hopes we might create our own Holden Caulfields or Lily Briscoes or Boo Radleys, attempts that most often result not in literature but in the same sort of recycling that goes on in the lower intestines of those same buzzards—well, given the same words as always, why must we be so careful?

Why do words matter so?

And in thinking about the why, I have been led deeper and deeper into this whole thing called writing, and deeper and deeper into what it means to be a writer altogether, until I have arrived here, now, writing this thing down for you and me both, discovering as I sit here that there is, finally, too much to say about this topic. Before I get started here, I want to say that everything—everything—regarding writing gets right down to the difference between *a* and *the* and *this*. The more I think about it the more I am convinced that there really is *nothing else* to talk about.

Because all things are informed by the word one writes next, and the one after that, and the one after that. All things come down to the difference between one word and another. All things: point of view, tone, characterization, body language, setting, dialogue, theme, symbols.

Meaning.

Let me start with saying the word means everything.

But first, let's get back to *Mom, Momma,* and *Mother.*

Here I was, making a case for the importance of the use of a proper noun in a story, when in my own life I'd walked out of a similar talk on one of my favorite writers because I in my ignorance believed myself to be superior, to be above these matters of pronouns, talk of which I asserted was sucking out the lifeblood of the work of Virginia Woolf, when I in my ignorance did not know that in fact the use of the personal pronoun was the lifeblood itself. The use of the word is the lifeblood. All this brought home to me, the teacher, nearly twenty years later by a student story in which proper nouns were used willy-nilly. *Mom,* or *Momma,* or *Mother* matters, and the wrinkling of a nose by an undergrad sniffing out the ponderous notion of such a statement reminded me of none other than me, standing and filing out of a lecture hall at Pembroke with a disdainful posse of young writers bent on making certain they—we—I—knew what was important about writing: bar talk. Not the use of pronouns.

And it just so happened that in that particular class meeting we had just finished talking about "Kiss Away," a Charles Baxter story from the collection *Believers,* one of the standards I use for my classes. For some reason there came to me a sentence from that story that exhibited precisely the importance of what I mean when I say the difference is vast between *the* and *a* and *this.*

Here's the sentence: "She had worn a rather formal white ruffled blouse with the palm tree pin, and a dark blue suit, and she had a semi-matching blue purse, at the sight of which Walton had announced that Jodie had 'starched notions of elegance,' a phrase he didn't care to explain."

The sentence seems innocuous enough in and of itself, and describes what she has worn to her first job interview since meeting Walton, a strange and sort of mystic character she spots from the sleeping porch of the house she's living in at the beginning of the story. It is my hope you have read or will read the story, and so I won't say much more about this or any of the other stories I will mention in terms of intricacies of plot. Suffice it to say she has dwelt inside a kind of lethargic sense of self that, until meeting Walton, seemed destined for paralysis.

Then here is this word *the* before the words *palm tree pin*.

The rest of her attire is brought to us courtesy of the lonely and shivering indefinite article *a*, but the palm tree pin is delivered by the confident, even cocksure definite article *the*.

Here, in this single word, is the fulcrum of the story, the moment in which the story takes its turn toward its fruition, its revelation, its meaning. We have neither seen the palm tree pin before this nor see it again afterward, yet in her selecting the pálm tree pin, an object made intimate by its being labeled with the definite article and not the indefinite, we see that in fact there is something deeply at stake in her choosing to get a job, or at least choosing to get out of the house in order to pursue one. The palm tree pin signals us that the pin has some kind of importance to Jodie and hence is a sign of hope in her heart, however small, that her life will improve.

She doesn't get that job. She doesn't get the next, or the next, but finally lands one. Getting a job is not the key to the story, and her gainful employment is not what finally brings her to love and security in the midst of a dangerous world, the same world, in fact, she inhabits at the beginning of the story.

But it is the *the* here that ushers in the security she finds only after making herself vulnerable to an indefinite article of a world, that cold and anonymous world she has inhabited just before the *the* appears.

This story, I submit, relies on *the*.

I talked to Mr. Baxter just now—Friday, June 23, 2000, at 5:35 P.M.—to see if I were on the right track in all this. He is my favorite living writer, I do not hesitate to say, and has been a friend for many years—I even had the privilege of shoveling his driveway of snow one February afternoon while I was a guest at his house, just so I could impress my readers in some future essay by writing, "I shoveled Charlie Baxter's driveway of snow one February afternoon"—and so I figured I would go to the source, just in case I was making too much of this all. I shot the breeze with him for a while, then presented to him what I have said here, to which he responded, "Whatever you tell those people, you tell them I said, "Bret, my friend, you are right as rain." So there.

But he also went on, because in fact understanding words and their meanings does matter to writers, to say that when he wrote that sentence he was using the pin "as a means to show her increasing identification with the objects of her own life, and so her increasing identification with herself in light of this new relationship with Walton." That is, in the pin she is coming to see herself, to know herself again. She is coming to life.

So, you may be wondering, what does this example have to do with my assertion that everything in a story has to do with the difference between *a* and *the* and *this*? To begin with, there is plot: This day she chooses a pin that has meaning to her, and in choosing that pin she is making herself vulnerable to defeat, to not getting a job, but she goes forward regardless; as for character development, she is increasingly identifying herself in relationship to the objects she owns, thereby showing us the growth in her character; as for how this informs point of view, because this word *the* carries no associations with it that would reveal the pin's actual history to us—where she got it and how—we see we are so deeply embedded in her point of view that in fact there is no need for associations. Just as when one walks into one's bedroom and looks at the dresser for the keys or tube of Chapstick or half-roll of Cherry Lifesavers before walking out of the house, one doesn't in that moment necessarily stand in silent pontification upon the memories and histories all the objects littered across the dresser might elicit at some other point. We are instead in her point of view, and in deep: This pin means something.

I could have gone on with that story for the rest of the class period, but there came to me, in the blessed way things sometimes come to teachers in the trench of fighting the good fight getting your students to see can and always will be, the fact we'd just recently read Flannery O'Connor's story "A Good Man Is Hard to Find," and—and you can believe or not believe this came to me, too—a usage of the indefinite article *a* that, I believe, serves as a fulcrum as well. There's a place in the story, I remembered, where that single letter exists as a dagger to the base of the spine in what it shows not only of the reality of death, but also a transcendence—or, depending on your interpretation, debasement—of the grandmother's soul.

This is one of my favorite stories ever; its presence is never far from mind whenever I'm talking about short stories. There is contained in it humor, tragedy, physical comedy and the play of words, notions of Grace and Jesus and the stark truth of how close we all are to our own mortality not just of body, but more importantly of soul.

But before I got to all that with this group of young writers impatient to get back to the student's story being critiqued, and with me fully aware of the necessary breach of protocol leaving a story splayed open there in the middle of the room was, I pointed out a few images, and the point of view taking them in.

The first moment occurs immediately after the accident precipitated by the grandmother's cat erupting from the basket, where she has secreted it away. To draw attention away from the fact this whole damn thing is all her fault, the grandmother says, "I believe I have an injured organ." Then O'Connor writes, "Bailey's teeth were clattering. He had on a yellow sport shirt with bright blue parrots designed in it and his face was as yellow as the shirt."

Here we have, pretty late in the story, the first mention of this ghastly yellow shirt, its color inextricably tied to the fear and anger and perplexity and simple surprise of adrenaline of this moment. The second mention comes after the grandmother, who can't keep her mouth shut, identifies The Misfit, thereby making it inevitable that she and the rest of the family will be killed.

O'Connor writes, "'Listen,' Bailey began, 'we're in a terrible predicament! Nobody realizes what this is,' and his voice cracked. His eyes were as blue and intense as the parrots in his shirt and he remained perfectly still."

Here we are brought through the shirt not anger or exasperation, but dead, paralyzed, panicked fear, fear so deep and so intense that the head of the household cannot finish his sentence. He knows what is coming. He knows.

A few lines later arrive the grandmother's last moments of pleading lucidity in the world she inhabits before what will surely come to pass, a world shattered by the single pistol shot in the woods followed closely by another, a world of sin and depravity she thinks will be solved by the simple act of prayer.

But The Misfit will have none of it, and then this:

> Bobby Lee and Hiram came ambling back from the woods. Bobby Lee was dragging a yellow shirt with bright blue parrots in it.
> "Throw me that shirt, Bobby Lee," The Misfit said. The shirt came flying at him and landed on his shoulder and he put it on. The grandmother couldn't name what the shirt reminded her of.

A yellow shirt.

That single letter *a* serves double duty here. In the first place, the chilling effect of its being unnamed and unknown—it is only *a* shirt—when in reality it was worn by her son only moments before serves, I hold, as that dagger at the base of the spine: Prior to this moment the violence of this all has existed first in the abstract—the escaped convicts arrive, are identified, words are passed by the son as to the possibility of what might happen, offstage the pistol reports shout from the woods—only to have that violence brought front and center, no argument or doubt or relief from its impending presence in the grandmother's life about it: Her son's shirt is now *a* shirt. No one's.

This letter *a* also reveals her character in that we see this all through her eyes, through her sensibilities, the indefinite article illuminating who she has become in this moment that tests, finally and utterly, her faith in and understanding of Grace, a test, it seems to me, she fails. There is no longer any recognition, no longer any evidence before her of her son's life. And here is where I believe that transcendence—or debasement—of her soul occurs: She now replaces her son with The Misfit himself.

All this pinnable on that letter *a*.

And finally, in this particular classroom on this particular day at the end of what had seemed a particularly unremarkable workshop, I remembered yet one more instance of the importance of these small words, this from another story we had all read: Raymond Carver's "Where I'm Calling From."

I could have spent that entire long afternoon simply talking about the craft of this story, the way the point-of-view character—never named—tells JP's story as though inhabiting it were a means to avoid the reality of his own sorry life. I could have talked, too, about the use of the single personal pronoun, *me*, uttered only three times in the story.

The word appears twice near the end of the story, when the narrator, still and always nameless, finally engages himself in a memory—a good one—from his past life, a moment when, sober and naked, he stands before the landlord outside his bedroom of a Sunday morning, the landlord setting out to paint the house before the day gets too hot, the narrator's wife laughing and calling the narrator back to bed. Carver writes, "And at that minute a wave of happiness comes over me that I'm not him—that I'm me and that I'm inside this bedroom with my wife." This usage of the word *me* is a precursor to the last word of the story, when the nameless narrator finally knows who he is: "It's me," he says, and lays claim to his own life, the reality of it and the need for his own moving, however tentatively, out into it. He doesn't call either his girlfriend or his wife, please note. He doesn't actually do anything here. He only recognizes himself.

But there is also an intriguing and, again, fulcrumatic, if I may invent such a word, use of one of those grunt-work words I've been talking about, this time the word *this*.

"Imagine this kid!" the narrator exhorts us at one point in the story in describing the loudmouth son of his girlfriend. That word *this* carries with it no value whatsoever, the word existing in this context and throughout the story only as a kind of unceremonious shorthand adjective for virtually everything and everyone in the story, from Roxie who "plants this kiss" on his lips to the fact of Tiny's seizures haunting his own waking life with the possibility of lost control: "So every time this little flitter starts up anywhere, I draw some breath and wait to find myself on my back, looking up, somebody's fingers in my mouth."

Yet in that same last paragraph as the narrator's declaration of identity, there is a strange and wonderful turn from the loose change that word *this* is used for throughout, when suddenly, in identifying himself, the narrator says, "There's no way to make a joke out of this."

Suddenly and without warning, the familiar inarticulate adjective becomes the entire noun of his present life, a noun—a life—that is unforeseeable at this particular moment of light, but which is a noun nonetheless. The word *this* precipitates, then, his ability simply to lay claim to being *me*, and moving forward into whatever gray world he sees he has no choice but to move into next.

This is the *me* of who he is *now*.

And so, for all these reasons, I'd like to start this essay with the suggestion we be careful with the word, no matter how "small." I propose that in caring for the word, in all its light and texture and density and purpose, we see ourselves as the servants to the word we are called to be as writers. I would like to begin by suggesting that even the single letter *a* is worthy of our carrying, through the long and arduous and fulfilling and ill-attended parade our writing lives will be, as though it were a golden crown on a tufted velvet pillow, and not so many yards of gravel dumped on a roadbed. Our ideas, our ambitions, our intellect truly are, after all, nothing more than paper floats. The word came before us, and will live on after us, whether that word be a single timorous letter or a polysyllabic fiesta.

But should the sheer weight even the word *a* can carry daunt us? Should we now hold up each use of every word to the cold light of all of literature before we even put it to pen, or at least commit it to the electronic impulses trafficking in the yes and no language of our computers, 1, 0, 1, 0, 1?

Well, 1, and 0. Yes, and no.

Because though I have pointed out these instances of what might seem micromanagement of the word by the author, I do not for an instant believe that these writers spent much time in the moment of creation, that moment of passion and joy and sorrow and opacity and understanding that is the moment of creation. I may be wrong, but I am willing to venture that it was through their faith in the indescribable and unteachable moment of inspiration—and by this I mean both that moment of divine guidance or influence exerted directly on the mind and soul of humankind, and the act of drawing air into the lungs—that these writers proceeded, as carefully and thoughtlessly as we each of us breathe in and breathe out, with the words chosen, seeing those characters they had created no longer through a glass darkly, but in the firm and brilliant light of truth. They saw these characters in their own moments of truth, and let reach the page the smallest scratches of meaningful ink: *a, the, this.*

Regardless to whom one may ascribe those moments of inspiration, inspiration they will be, and unteachable they will remain.

But the weight of words should not—cannot—be reason enough to cease carrying them. Nor should the fact they have been used, and used better, by so many great writers paralyze us. Faced with that endless valley of bones we have available to us, we must do what Ezekiel did: We must bring those bones to life. Ezekiel's vision can teach us a lot about writing, though I've never seen it on any creative writing course's reading list. Here are his words:

> The hand of the Lord came upon me and brought me out in the Spirit of the Lord, and set me down in the midst of the valley; and it was full of bones. Then He caused me to pass by them all around, and behold, there were very many in the open valley; and indeed they were very dry. And He said to me, "Son of man, can these bones live?" So I answered, "O Lord God, You know." Again He said to me, "Prophesy to these bones, and say to them, 'O dry bones, hear the word of the Lord! Thus says the Lord God to these bones: "Surely I will cause breath to enter into you, and you shall live. I will put sinews on you and bring flesh upon

you, cover you with skin and put breath in you; and you shall live. Then you shall know that I am the Lord."'" So I prophesied as I was commanded; and as I prophesied, there was a noise, and suddenly a rattling; and the bones came together, bone to bone. Indeed, as I looked, the sinews and the flesh came upon them, and the skin covered them over; but there was no breath in them. Also He said to me, "Prophesy to the breath, prophesy, son of man, and say to the breath, 'Thus says the Lord God: "Come from the four winds, O breath, and breathe on these slain, that they may live."'" So I prophesied as He commanded me, and breath came into them, and they lived, and stood upon their feet, an exceedingly great army. Then He said to me, "Son of man, these bones are the whole house of Israel. They indeed say, 'Our bones are dry, our hope is lost, and we ourselves are cut off!' Therefore prophesy and say to them, 'Thus says the Lord God: "Behold, O My people, I will open your graves and cause you to come up from your graves, and bring you into the land of Israel. Then you shall know that I am the Lord, when I have opened your graves, O My people, and brought you up from your graves. I will put My Spirit in you, and you shall live, and I will place you in your own land. Then you shall know that I, the Lord, have spoken it and performed it," says the Lord.'" (37:1-14)

One can only imagine Ezekiel standing there and being questioned by God as to God's power, and I don't think it would be too far from the truth to imagine that Ezekiel, knees trembling before the despair of so many bones and God breathing down his neck for an answer, thought fleetingly, dangerously, *There's no way. Bones to life? Nope.*

But it is a testament to his wisdom, and I think perhaps an indictment of his skepticism as well, that his answer is one of reflection: "O Lord God, You know." He doesn't say, *You bet.* He doesn't say, *Don't think so.* He leaves it to God, and then proceeds—and here is the most important moment—*to speak the prophesy he has been called to speak*, whether he believes it or not, and not knowing as well what that prophesy means. He speaks, because he has been called to, and not because he knows what will be the outcome.

And then these dry bones come to life.

And then, in the writer's answer to whatever has called him to write, and in his willingness to look at each word with fear and trepidation coupled with faith that speaking it will be an act in obedience to what has called him to speak it, those words will line up, will breathe, will become the vast army of sentences that will take up residence in the new Israel every story, novel, essay, and poem ought to be.

Finally, I'd like to start this essay by saying that in the beginning was the Word, and that in the original Greek the Gospel of John was written in, the word *Word* was *logos*, which translated also means "reason."

The old cliché is that, in the best scenario a teacher can encounter, the teacher will learn from the student. That's a no-brainer, I want to say before I get started. And such was the case on an otherwise procedural day in an undergrad creative writing class when a sensible student wrinkled her nose at an assertion I made.

I want to begin by saying words matter, so pick them carefully.

So. Let's begin.

THE GIRL I WAS, THE WOMAN I HAVE BECOME:

Fiction's Reminiscent Narrators

By Ellen Lesser

I started to ponder the nature of reminiscent narration after a certain M.F.A. short-story workshop, during which the question *To reminiscence or not to reminisce?* arose in discussion after discussion. All workshop veterans have witnessed these uncanny overlaps: the group where a statistically unaccountable percentage of pieces feature, say, the death of an animal, or a spousal affair. Yet this seemed like more than one of those coincidental recurrences of motif or plot device; seemed to cut deeper, revealing an issue at the heart of our craft as writers of fiction. About half the submissions cried out for some added insight, of the sort a retrospective stance on their events could provide. The other half were set up as remembrances but never made particular use of that vantage point; some even appeared to forget, a few pages or paragraphs in, that their protagonists were gazing backward. It struck me that our developing writers had agonized over whether to narrate in past or present tense, in first or third person, but they'd approached this other crucial decision—the point in time from which the story gets told—at best casually, with little reflection.

Around the same era, I began to toy with the idea for a novel inspired by a trip I'd taken at nineteen. I had reached my mid-thirties, so the choice of whether to recount the journey as it unfolded or from some mature remove presented itself rather graphically as the start-up, technical key to locating the narrative. When I queried my colleagues for pertinent reading suggestions, one sent me an "In Brief" notice from *The New York Times Book Review*, which opened with this pronouncement: "Sometimes writers seem to set their stories in flashback because they don't trust the story itself to move us, relying instead on the sentiment that memory creates." As you can probably guess, what followed wasn't a glowing assessment. I never read the novel in question, and in fact the photocopied review has long since disappeared from my archives. And yet this notion of a suspect reliance on "the sentiment that memory creates"—a kind of false inflation of story through memory's cachet—stayed with me, implying as it does a useful test for reminiscent narration in general.

What *is* the writer's impetus for casting a story in retrospect? Is he or she merely aiming to cash in on this special aura, the heightened emotional currency, which recollection seems to impart? Or can we identify more substantive motives that bear on the fiction's significance? Does hindsight supply a dimension of meaning which wouldn't arise if an event were told from within the thick of experience, with the necessarily limited understanding that position entails? Is such an expanded or altered perspective the sole *raison d'être* of reminiscence? Or might authors have other, legitimate reasons for adopting this angle of vision?

The term *reminiscence* tends to conjure a mood of gentle nostalgia, stirred by fond musings on a bygone era. But in its understated, insidious way, Kazuo Ishiguro's novel *The Remains of the Day* attests to the potentially treacherous nature of gazing backward.

Ishiguro's narrator, Stevens (we never learn his first name), rarely abandons his post at Darlington Hall, where he served for many years as head butler to the influential Lord Darlington. When circumstances conspire to send him on a motoring tour of the English countryside, Stevens keeps a travel diary, though the trip itself is a rather low-key affair. Our old-style manservant sees a couple of lovely views; his radiator overheats; major crisis: He runs out of petrol once. Indeed, Ishiguro dishes up a present narrative where virtually nothing happens. The real drama lies elsewhere, as Stevens's days of tooling along in his now-deceased master's classic Ford provide the occasion for him to rethink his theory of what makes a great butler and to relive his career in Lord Darlington's service.

At first, Stevens's reflections unfurl in a decorous and apparently harmless fashion. By attending Lord Darlington, he believes himself to have stood at the hub of great events, coming as close as possible for a man of his station to accomplishing something significant for humanity. And yet, as the revelations about Lord Darlington's well-meaning but misguided diplomatic efforts during the years between the two world wars gather speed, Stevens's past gets progressively undermined and eventually completely discredited. If Lord Darlington proved a failure, a dupe, then Stevens must rate as one also, since his butler's ethic irrevocably tied his own fate and worth to that of his master.

The present narrative does feature one important event—Stevens's rendezvous with Miss Kenton, Darlington's former head housekeeper. Interestingly enough, Ishiguro opts to replay the meeting out of chronological sequence. The diary suddenly jumps from "Day Four" to "Day Six," skipping over the date with Miss Kenton, this crucial encounter toward which we've been motoring and building tension. Only at the close of the novel do we return to it. Though he gains just a couple of days' perspective, Stevens in effect reminisces about this meeting as well, requiring that margin of distance from the pivotal moment.

The rendezvous with Miss Kenton puts the final nail in the coffin of Stevens's revised understanding. In the light of this meeting, the butler recognizes what the reader has long suspected: that the reserve and repression bred by his calling have robbed him of his one true chance at his own life and happiness in the form of a romantic relationship with Miss Kenton. For Stevens, the act of reminiscence proves dynamic, transformative, appreciably altering the way he interprets past events. A man who all along has viewed his life one way now comes, through this act of remembering, to see it entirely differently.

Outwardly, the novel's climactic present event is anything but explosive; it's simply a quiet if resonant chat between two former colleagues. Neither would most of what Stevens remembers register very high on a Richter scale for overt drama. The butler focuses on tiny tremors of a magnitude that might not be dwelled upon or dissected at all in a *non*reminiscent narration. In the process, he offers a meditation on how we construe dramatic significance. Stevens has been looking back at the time when he insisted on breaking off his customary evening conferences with Miss Kenton, during which their professional communication had begun to bleed into something more intimate.

> Naturally—and why should I not admit this—I have occasionally wondered to myself how things might have turned out in the long run had I not been so determined over the issue of our evening meetings; that is to say, had I relented on those several occasions over the weeks that followed when Miss Kenton suggested we reinstitute them. I only speculate over this now because in the light of subsequent events, it could well be argued that in

making my decision to end those evening meetings once and for all, I was perhaps not entirely aware of the full implications of what I was doing. Indeed, it might even be said that this small decision of mine constituted something of a key turning point; that that decision set things on an inevitable course toward what eventually happened ...

But what is the sense in forever speculating what might have happened had such and such a moment turned out differently: One could presumably drive oneself to distraction in this way. In any case, while it is all very well to talk of turning points, one can surely only recognize such moments in retrospect. Naturally, when one looks back to such instances today, they may indeed take on the appearance of being crucial, precious moments in one's life; but of course, at the time, this was not the impression one had. Rather, it was as though one had available a never-ending number ... of further opportunities in which to remedy the effect of this or that misunderstanding. There was surely nothing to indicate at the time that such evidently small incidents would render whole dreams forever irredeemable.

From this passage of restrained heartbreak we can distill a virtual manifesto of reminiscence: by his own admission, Stevens needed the filter of hindsight to apprehend the arc and significance of what occurred. Through his poignantly, maddeningly reticent and myopic narrator, Ishiguro signals us that without this perspective, we in fact would not have a story—to the extent that the very notion of story implies discerning a shape within the seemingly amorphous flow of events as perceived from the vantage point of the moment. Only in the context of the residue of loss and waste from contemplating Stevens's whole lifetime do the novel's "small incidents" achieve their full stature.

In Alice McDermott's *That Night*, the past likewise only acquires its final shape in the light an older narrator shines backward. Here, the character does not review a whole lifetime, but rather circles obsessively back to a single incident that took place on her Long Island block on a summer evening when she was ten: the night—*that night*—when a teenager named Rick, with the help of three carloads of his "hood" buddies, came to claim his girlfriend, the narrator's neighbor, Sheryl, who'd already been packed off to relatives in Ohio after her mother learned of her unwanted pregnancy. As the narrator re-creates the events of that night, and the world of 1950s suburban childhood that formed the stage for them, we repeatedly shift between the youngster's limited observations and the broader grasp of the adult remembering. This rhythmic alternation between girl and woman, then and now, plays through the novel like a refrain: "I once thought … but now I wonder …" "I know now … but then …" "Even at that age we knew …" "It occurs to me now …" On practically every page, you can find an explicit flagging of *now* or *then*—those distinct zones of perception and interpretation.

Though McDermott draws more attention to it than many writers, this polarity is fairly typical of fictional retrospect. Typical, also, is the fact that the narrator's present situation fosters her desire to relive the events of that earlier era. Her marriage is falling apart, she's come back to the old neighborhood to supervise the sale of her parents' house, and the grown-up Rick arrives for a tour with the realtor. This present-day encounter triggers the memory of that night, though we only discover this on page 168 of a narrative that totals 184 pages. And though the specific occasion for memory enters at the eleventh hour, almost as an aside, the narrator's current reality clearly motivates her retelling.

What's more unusual, even audacious, about *That Night* is the speculative nature of this retelling, which allows the "I" to enter into and even appropriate other characters' experience. Not only do we see what the young girl saw, and how that vision gets filtered through her adult sensibility, we also relive in intimate, convincing detail the way it was for the star-crossed lovers, including during the period before and after that night—information which our narrator, then or now, could not possibly access. This element of imaginative reconstruction supports and actually enriches the retrospective stance of the novel, reinforcing that level on which reminiscence itself entails an act of speculation and extrapolation: the adult filling in not only other people's, but her own past experience—piecing together the entire mirror, if you will, from what may only survive as a few shards of memory.

Not surprisingly, the sensibility and needs of the reminiscing adult guide the speculative re-creation. Toward the end of *That Night*, the narrator muses:

> Enough, too much, has been said about the cowardly incompetence of memory, how it can be pushed around by time, bullied by desire, worked over by our intractable ability to see what we want to see. Even children know you cannot separate the tale from the teller.

Here, the teller stands at a point of transition and loss in her own romantic life as an adult; from that juncture, she extracts a very particular vision of love from the teenagers' drama. In this version, Sheryl runs away from the house of her relatives. She slits her wrists in a gas-station restroom somewhere between Ohio and home but gets found in time. Later, once Sheryl has given birth to her baby, to be put up for adoption, she rides back to the aunt and uncle's from the hospital, with one of her cousin's kids on her lap. Through the speculative lens of the narrator, McDermott offers this redemptive take on that moment, in what comprises the novel's penultimate paragraph:

> The miracle, then, was not the door banging open and filling the small bloody room with hot sunlight, bringing her more life; the miracle was that, despite all she had lost, despite all she knew was no longer true—her love alone was not enough, it would always, eventually, come to nothing—still, there was the blind, insistent longing, stirred now by the child in her arms, that this emptiness be filled again.

This may or may not have been Sheryl's experience—either the facts themselves or their emotional coloration. The accuracy of the passage lies, instead, in its projection of the *narrator's* truth—her own undaunted longing in the face of loss and disillusionment.

This longing, then, shades the narrator's reinvention of past events. Part two of the novel opens with this rumination: "It is only after a certain age, twenty-five or so, when the distance between the child you were and the adult you have become has grown great enough to breed wistfulness …" That air of wistfulness suffuses the novel's evocation of suburban upbringing. Shortly after that night, the neighborhood men, who've done battle with their baseball bats and snow shovels against the hoods and their chains, gather to talk about how they'd fight to defend their own daughters from the tragedy and violence of love: "Our fathers. They were still dark-haired then, and handsome. Their bruised arms were still strong under their rolled shirt sleeves, their chests still broad under their T-shirts." Note the unmistakable tonal quality McDermott affects in these simple sentences, through the pointed use of *then*, the repetition of *still*, so the knowledge of subsequent change, of the fall from that state of grace, permeates the description, turns it bittersweet and achingly tender.

Where else but in a remembrance do we find this particular shade of sentiment? *That Night* doesn't just take an easy route to gravity and significance, though the relative thinness of its plot might certainly lead a lesser artist to seek false means of inflating it. For a novelist of McDermott's caliber, to capture memory's special aura is not to take a cheap shot but rather to tap into the deep root of the impulse to reminiscence.

Lynne Sharon Schwartz's short novel *Leaving Brooklyn* tells a tale of two boroughs as its narrator, Audrey, recalls growing up in Brooklyn during and after World War II, and her sexual initiation at the hands of a Manhattan eye doctor. Eyes are central to *Leaving Brooklyn*. The novel begins, "This is the story of an eye and how it came into its own." Through some mysterious injury in the minutes after her birth, Audrey has suffered a deformation of her right eye. Legally, that eye is blind, but in actuality, it's not blind at all. Instead, the wandering eye has its own type of vision.

> Its world was a Seurat painting, with the bonds hooking the molecules all severed, so that no object really cohered; the separate atoms were lined up next to one another, their union voluntary, not fated. This made the world, through my right eye, a tenuous place where the common, reasonable laws of physics did not apply ... I could tease and tempt the world, squinting my left eye shut and watching things disintegrate, and when I was alone my delight was to play with the visible world this way, breaking it down and putting it back together. I had secret vision and knowledge of ... the volatile nature of things before they congeal, of the tenuousness and vulnerability of all things, unknown to those with common binary vision ...

Schwartz builds out of Audrey's physical idiosyncrasy a metaphor for different kinds of sight: the tediously conventional vision of Brooklyn as opposed to the freer, more penetrating brand the girl seeks to cultivate, and which her secret experience with the optometrist—occurring, naturally, across the river—advances.

Just as Audrey's bad eye takes objects apart, Schwartz deconstructs the notion of reminiscence, weaving through the story of Audrey's girlhood and precocious erotic adventure a treatise on the nature of retrospection. Like *That Night*, the novel contains an ongoing series of references to its two levels of experience, perception and narration. Yet more than a simple shift in temporal distance, between "then" and "now," the byplay in *Leaving Brooklyn* involves two distinct selves: "the girl I was" and "the woman I have become." And the relationship between these two is far more complex than a linear, ignorance-to-understanding progression would posit.

Schwartz's first-person adult narrator doesn't see herself as merely an older, wiser version of the young, marooned Audrey; she perceives a more radical split. So great a split, in fact, that she speaks of this girl she once was in third person.

> And so the girl I was, the girl I would like to reincarnate here, possessed double vision. Not simultaneous. Alternate. Her world was veiled and then, when she shut the ordinary eye and allowed the other free play, it was unveiled; the act of learning anything was not absorbing or digging out or encountering, but removing a veil, and it was the most dramatic act imaginable. From the start she had a taste for drama, self-dramatization, and her themes, naturally, were secrecy and hiding and revelation, the doling out and manipulation of information. She thought that she too could be unveiled in similar fashion, that like an ocean, she was surface and depths, and she feared this unveiling without knowing what would be revealed or why it might be dangerous. Perhaps it was simply the secret of her double vision that she feared would be exposed, for as her childhood moved along its dual paths she sensed she wasn't supposed to be seeing what she saw.

For whole stretches of the novel, the text slips into this third-person stance, until the reader almost forgets it's really an "I" talking about herself in that earlier incarnation. The narrator goes on to propose that the act of reminiscence—the revelation of that "she," the girl—is a challenge more daunting than a mere act of memory.

> Telling about her is an attempt at unveiling her, an act of self-sabotage, if one assumes that the woman I am today is that girl worked over and layered by time. The common wisdom holds that the process of growing older involves a toughening of the skin. But it may be the opposite, a gradual removal of layers, a peeling process. The girl has been stripped by time to produce me. I suspect I was there all along, though she is so very tough and layered that when I focus my vision to see her I can scarcely glimpse myself beneath. Before she vanishes altogether from memory ... I want to make her transparent. I want to expose the

mystery of change and recall, peel her story off her the way some
people can peel an orange, in one exquisite unbroken spiral.

Measured against this ideal of the single, unbroken spiral, the story the narrator actually delivers is rather fragmented and faltering, because the adult can't always sort out in the telling who she was from who she's become. During a recap of Audrey's teenage years, we learn that she's pledged for a high-school sorority.

That I agreed to pledge is hard for me to believe: it does not fit with the girl I think I was, or the girl I am attempting to reconstitute in the telling, who is perhaps turning out to be not the girl I really was. I am confused about who I was: why else would I need to tell this story of my eye? The confusion is that I seem to have grown up into someone who could not have been me as a child. Yet in the telling the girl grows to sound more and more like the woman I became. The voice overcomes her. The real girl with her layers concealing me becomes more elusive the more I tell. She has been superseded, but I am sure she existed. As I try to find her in me, I keep finding me in her.

This confusion about the "real girl" as distinct from the girl the woman would seek to reconstitute reaches its peak in the episode with the eye doctor. The doctor is a pioneer in primitive contact lenses, and Audrey is getting one for her wandering eye: not to correct the vision—that technology doesn't exist yet—but to make it look more normal, to please her parents. Fifteen now, she rides the subway the first couple of times with her mother, but once the lens has been fitted, she travels alone, dressed up and with a forbidden makeup job, so she won't "feel as out of place on Park Avenue." During her first solo visit, the doctor presses his leg against hers more than necessary, it fleetingly dawns on her, to examine her eye. The next time, he places his hand on her leg, then runs it up and down, as if testing her.

As though in a dream, as though it were not a conscious act, I reached out and touched him. I touched him where I knew he would want to be touched. I know that I—she—was not the kind of girl who could do that. ... Even as I recall it, record it, I suspect I really didn't do such an outrageous thing and memory is falsifying, inventing what I wish I could have done or imagining it from what I have since become capable of doing.

Indeed this is the point at which memory may be at its least trustworthy. ... It would seem much more likely that he didn't put his hand to her leg, that she only wished and feared he would. Or if he did ... it seems more likely that she didn't reach out and touch him but instead stood up slowly ... then picked up her school bag and walked to the door. ... At home she would have told her parents fretfully that she didn't want the lens after all. It hurt. It violated her values—you can imagine by now the sorts of high-minded arguments she would have used. In the end she would have prevailed, yet felt abashed and disgusted with herself, knowing that the arguments were irrelevant, that it was only fear that kept her away.

In case that was the way it was, if she was thwarted by her fear, I must let her have it now, do it for her, since it is right that it should have happened. It suits the person I became. So I can only repeat that I did do it, unlikely as it seems. I was taken over by my bad eye, wandering.

And so, at the end of this protracted round of skepticism and speculation, ambivalence and rationalization, this movement from "I" to "she" and then "I" again, we loop back to the action: The eye doctor touched her and she touched him back, and the affair proceeds from that moment.

All of this significantly complicates the notion of perspective in reminiscence. Yes, the adult has a different vantage point. The woman she's become is distinct from the girl she was—in fact so distinct that her hindsight re-creation changes not only the spin that gets put on the story, the residue of meaning left at the end, but the story itself, to the point where the character's memory itself must be construed as a fiction.

Combing through the text of a reminiscent narrative, we can tease apart the disparate strands—the passages where the narrator slips back in time to the earlier experience, and those where she returns to shed light from the adult viewpoint. But on a deeper, metaphysical level, we can't always separate the two selves whose collaboration gives rise to the story. Significantly, at the moment of epiphany for young Audrey, the last time she makes love with the eye doctor, the two sensibilities, girl and woman, merge: "She was me, at that moment. She already knew what I know." Again, at the close of the novel, the dual identities fuse.

Perhaps I haven't succeeded in finding the girl I was, but only in fabricating the girl I might have been, would have liked

> to be, looking backwards from the woman I have become … It
> hardly matters by this time. By this time the border between
> seeing straight on and seeing round the corners of solid objects,
> between the world as smooth and coherent and the world as
> dissociated skinless particles, is thoroughly blurred. No longer a
> case of double vision, but of two separate eyes whose separate
> visions—what happened and what might have happened—come
> together in what we call the past, which we see with hindsight.

Not all reminiscences are so explicit about their collaborative dimension or self-conscious about the nature of memory, and I suppose we can be grateful for that. As McDermott's narrator suggests, enough has already been said on the subject. So now I want to consider a retrospective narration that operates without all of this overt metaphysical and metafictional baggage—one that never even announces itself as a reminiscence, per se, but simply goes about its business of unpeeling the layers of experience that separate the girl from the woman.

The very title of Edna O'Brien's *Returning* heralds a revisitation, in both fact and memory. In characteristic fashion, the lead story, "The Connor Girls," focuses on a set of people and events from the narrator's girlhood in rural Ireland, from the vantage point of her subsequent escape. Ireland functions for O'Brien's adult expatriates much as Brooklyn does for Audrey: To paraphrase from Schwartz's novel, it's the place they have left but leave again every day, because it never leaves them. At the end of another tale in this volume, "Ghosts," O'Brien's narrator says of the people she's remembering: "I still can't imagine any of them dead. They live on. They are fixed in that faroff region called childhood, where nothing ever dies, not even oneself." The sense of the past as undying, continuous, dictates the form of O'Brien's reminiscences.

When we set off with "The Connor Girls," we find none of the usual signposts of looking back—the sort of "that time … that place" orientation we get upon entering *Leaving Brooklyn*. Instead, we launch directly into the experience of the past as if it were eminently present, ongoing: "To know them would be to enter an exalted world. To open the stiff green iron gate, to go up their shaded avenue, and to knock on their white hall door was a journey I yearned to make." In this first section, the narrator's fascination with the older Connor daughters, Miss Amy and Miss Lucy, is presented uncritically, not complicated by adult perspective. When the sisters decline her mother's invitation to tea, the hurt the narrator feels, and her innocent hope that someday they might accept, comes across without any buffer of irony or tempering hindsight.

> ... I saw them shake their heads a couple of times, and long be-
> fore she had come back into the house I knew that the Connor
> girls had refused our invitation and that the table which we had
> laid with such ceremony was a taunt and downright mockery. ...
>
> "They didn't come," I said stupidly, being curious to know
> how the Connor girls had worded their refusal.
>
> "They never eat between meals," Mama said, quoting their
> exact phrase in an injured, sarcastic voice.
>
> "Maybe they'll come later on," I said.

Of course, the adult narrator knows they won't come later on, but the story is not, at least on the surface, filtered through that understanding: O'Brien just gives us the girl's reaction. The tale proceeds in this fashion, running with the tide of gossipy details about the Connors, in particular Miss Amy. When the Protestant Miss Amy becomes engaged to a bank clerk who turns out to be a lapsed Catholic, the narrator and her parents present Amy with a gift and they enjoy an amiable exchange, prompting this rush of girlish feeling in the narrator: "I loved her then, and wanted to know her and wished with all my heart that I could have gone across the fields with her and become her confidante, but I was ten and she was thirty or thirty-five."

Bit by bit the story progresses into the future, through Miss Amy's disappearance, the wedding's cancellation, and Major Connor's death. Then Miss Amy returns and undergoes a drunken decline, a recovery. All the while the girl the narrator was keeps growing older. Toward the close of the penultimate section, she has the tête-à-tête with Miss Amy of which she's long dreamed. Amy gives her a going-away present for boarding school and invites her on a walk. And then, in that section's closing paragraph, the narrator fast-forwards us away from Miss Amy, away from the whole provincial childhood that so far has been our focus:

> In September I went to boarding school and got involved with
> nuns and various girl friends, and in time the people in our par-
> ish, even the Connor girls, almost disappeared from my memory.
> I never dreamed of them anymore, and I had no ambitions to
> go cycling with them or to visit their house. Later when I went
> to university in Dublin I learned quite by chance that Miss Amy

had worked in a beauty parlor in Stephens Green, had drunk heavily, and had joined a golf club. By then the stories of how she teetered on high heels, or wore unmatching stockings or smiled idiotically and took ages to say what she intended to say, had no interest for me.

In the story's next and final section, we take another large leap, to the point where suddenly we're looking back on the narrator's entire young womanhood.

Somewhat precipitately and unknown to my parents I had become engaged to a man who was not of our religion. Defying threats of severing bonds, I married him and incurred the wrath of family and relatives, just as Miss Amy had done, except that I was not there to bear the brunt of it.

The phrase, "just as Miss Amy had done," supplies the critical link, by which we're given to understand, if only retroactively, why the story of Miss Amy occupies the reminiscence to start with. Whether the narrator is self-conscious or not, we still can't separate the tale from the teller.

The narrator stays in exile for several years, but then, late in the story, returns to visit her family. O'Brien's choice of verb tense is noteworthy. The narrator still hasn't reached the present time from which the story gets told; she's still recollecting: "I shall never forget the sense of awkwardness, sadness, and dismay when I stepped out of my husband's car and saw the large gaunt cut-stone house with thistles in the front garden."

The narrator's mother announces that the Connors plan to ask the narrator to tea, which for the mother still symbolizes a victory—social and religious—for both her daughter and herself. The next day, the group heads off to a fair in the village, where they run into Amy and Lucy. The narrator's husband—not a Catholic but an atheist, a comparable liability in this setting—snubs the aging sisters and leads the narrator and their young son away.

'They were going to ask us to tea,' I said to my husband as we walked downhill. I could hear the suction of his galoshes in the soggy ground.

'Don't think we missed much,' he said, and at that moment I realized that by choosing his world I had said goodbye to my own and to those in it.

Even at this point of epiphany, the tense hasn't shifted. We still have yet to arrive at the present from which the narrative issues.

If we're going to get there, O'Brien had better work quickly, since only one sentence remains. Sure enough, in the crowning utterance, we achieve the current perspective: "By such choices we gradually become exiles, until at last we are quite alone." We never learn precisely how far this narrative present lies from the realization at the "gymkana"; it could be fifteen years, or forty. But in its flash we understand that this choice to pull away with the husband forms part of a broader pattern of subsequent, exiling choices; that the pattern, as revealed in retrospect, is what gives the individual incident its significance, what justifies elevating the memory into an occasion for narrative. Both the message and mood of that final clause—"until at last we are quite alone"—tell us that this narrator, like McDermott's, is viewing her past from a vantage point of present loss and alienation. And that haunting final line—the only one that gives full voice to the woman she has become—then casts its shadow back over the narrative, darkens and deepens it, imbuing the story's events with a quality of yearning and poignancy they would not otherwise possess.

In his story "What Peter Saw," W.D. Wetherell explicitly signals our entry into reminiscent terrain with this introductory sentence: "The first timeless thing Peter ever saw was on August 29, 1968, at two o'clock on a humid Friday afternoon." Jumping off from this oddly, arrestingly specific location in time, the opening paragraph expands on the idea of the event's timelessness:

> Remembering, the 1968 part faded away, and it could just as easily have been a moment in the 1940s somewhere, or 1914 in the last twilight of the Edwardian summer, or even further back, back beyond all his history books, back to the days when Greece was taking boys with no malice in them and sticking spears in their hands and shipping them off to Troy.

Pretty neat trick: taking us from the absolutely anchored coordinates of mundane, recent time and sliding us back into this vast and fluid zone of historical, even mythic resonance. The second paragraph works the same sleight of hand with place, zooming out from the summer home on Cape Cod to posit a dimension of universality, emphasizing those features "that linked it with all the other places in the country." As we move into the reminiscence proper, this archetypal context fades into the background; the narrative doesn't continue to insist on its universality, which might quickly grow tedious, self-inflating. And yet the mythic quality persists in coloring our sense of Peter's experience, even as the telling plunges headlong into the details of that concrete, time-bound moment.

> It was the summer he turned twelve—old enough to get serious about two pressing ambitions. The first was to row the family's skiff all the way to Martha's Vineyard and not just the breakwater where the pond opened. The second ... was to see a girl without any clothes on.

Peter's equipment list for the rowing excursion maintains this balance between the timeless and the contemporary:

> Two one-gallon cans of Hawaiian Punch, to be drunk when neces-sary, then stowed away beneath the bow seat to serve as sea anchors in case of storm or water wings in cast of swamping. An orange beach umbrella to keep the sun off his neck. A fishing line to use if the current carried him out to sea and he was starving. A bottle of ketchup to drown out the fishy taste. ...

On one level this passage reflects the twelve-year-old's experience, delivered in all the seriousness with which it takes itself. And yet it carries a tone—a gentle, teasing irony—which we sense but can't exactly pinpoint in the text. Is it the sort of irony that sometimes rises out of a child narrative, where the author is in effect winking at the reader over the young speaker's shoulder? Or is it an irony more proper to reminiscence—the adult, simultaneously wistful and wry, conveying the earnestness of his or her younger self's efforts? In "What Peter Saw," that dance of the two selves, boy and man, is so agile and seamless we can't readily distinguish between them.

For much of the story, we don't appear to be viewing experience through an adult lens; instead, our information is drawn exclusively from the youth-ful Peter's circumscribed understanding. In truth, during major segments of "What Peter Saw," Wetherell resists adult interpretation to the point where, if he hadn't waved the flag of "Remembering ..." in his first paragraph, we might almost miss the reminiscent character of the narration. The fact that this story, unlike the others, is cast in third instead of first person contributes to this shadowy aspect of the reminiscing self: Beyond that early cue of "Remember-ing ...," the adult Peter exists in the text largely by implication.

Peter's family's distant relations, the Gerards, arrive for the day, along with two strangers, Danny and Doreen—a young soldier about to ship off to Vietnam and his wife of recent duration. Peter's mother and his aunt Alice conspire on behalf of the couple, trying to maneuver them into a bedroom on this hot Cape Cod afternoon.

> "A nap?" His mother's eyes met Alice's and something was exchanged there too quickly for Peter to tell what. "There's Peter's room. They can have that, I suppose. We haven't gotten around to insulating the ceiling yet. This time of day it's hotter than an oven."
>
> "Oh, that's okay," Alice said. "They just want to take a nap, just a short one."
>
> The conversation was normal enough, but both women seemed relieved when it was over. Alice went back and said something to Danny; Danny turned and said something to Doreen. A moment later they disappeared through the screen door into the house, holding hands with each other but differently than before, tighter somehow, higher.

The reader knows why they're holding hands differently, what they're fixing to do—as would the older, remembering Peter. But Wetherell doesn't explicitly speak from that stance; instead, he just relies on the basic convention of child narrative: that the reader's grasp exceeds that of the viewpoint character.

We proceed through that strangely charged afternoon until we arrive at the payoff—the intimate scene Peter spies when he sneaks a look through his bedroom window. But like Ishiguro skipping over Stevens's date with Miss Kenton, Wetherell cagily withholds that prize, keeping us in suspense as he recounts the rest of that day and evening. Before he makes good on this narrative "IOU" in the final paragraph, he returns us to that heightened, portentous mode of the story's beginning. Peter walks out to the water and spots a swan swimming across a band of moonlight.

> Peter stared at it as he had never stared at anything before, trying to make the seeing so hard and so permanent it would never leave him. He knew, without anyone telling him, it was the most beautiful sight he had ever seen.
>
> It didn't last long. By the time he really saw it the swan was past the band into the darkness. As it disappeared—in the

regret of the moment's passing—he felt a chill settle across his shoulders and his intuition take a sudden leap ahead. All summer long his knowing had butted itself against the secret, unreadable blankness of things, and now suddenly here it was past them, skipping ahead the way a twelve-year-old's imagination sometimes will, so that the truths that come then are often the most lasting. He knew—

For the second time we get these words, "He knew," insisting on the epiphany that the boy had then, in that moment, not what the recollecting adult has realized.

He knew, watching the swan glide off, that whatever else happened in the future, life would continue to present itself to him in that same shimmery, ungraspable way—that behind distant islands and distant girls' camps and lowered flags and adult silences was nothing he could isolate and give answers to, nothing concrete, but only these intertwined, bewildering strands of beauty and sadness and mystery combined.

Only then does Wetherell deliver the *coup de grâce*, rewinding the day's chronology to show us what the peeping Peter glimpsed through his window:

Doreen, that is, on her knees by the side of the bed, her hair stroked by a Danny who is crying. Doreen on her knees resting her cheek against the side of Danny's leg, crying likewise. Doreen with her chewing gum reaching down to tie with inexpressible tenderness the laces of her husband's boots.

It's not the tableau that at least this reader's inner voyeur was expecting, especially after the set-up of Doreen "on her knees." And yet it makes a fitting reward for Peter's stubborn pursuit of life's mysteries. After all, it's not in the prurient sight of naked bodies or sexual mechanics where beauty resides but rather in love's "inexpressible tenderness." That's the "timeless thing" Peter spied, made all the more lovely and poignant for its marriage with gritty timeliness, thanks to the inclusion of "chewing gum" in that final gesture.

Unlike Ishiguro's butler, who needed hindsight to recognize crucial turning points, Peter perceived the momentous, enduring quality of his experience "even then." This precocious vision is akin to that intuitive leap Schwartz's

Audrey makes in the eye doctor's office, when the girl becomes the woman; knows all that the woman will come to know. Why, then, does Peter's tale require a reminiscent perspective? Does the insistence on timelessness, on the transcendent, mythic quality of what Peter saw, betray a lack of confidence in the event's ability to pull its own weight? Would the piece be just as effective without the remembering "I" that Wetherell embeds in his close third-person narration?

I trust that readers of the full story would reply in the negative, if only for reasons of tone—this air beyond the particulars of perception or interpretation that suffuses the narrative.

How can we define that quality? McDermott's returning "I" called it wistfulness. We find a marvelous image for it right here in Wetherell's final sequence: "nothing concrete, but only these intertwined, bewildering strands of beauty and sadness combined." That idea of bewilderment sends me back to a passage from Jane Smiley's novella, "Ordinary Love," whose narrator speaks about an event that took place decades earlier: "When I remember that time, twenty years ago now, the light around me seems to have been blinding. ... It cannot be understood, really, only re-experienced unexpectedly."

Even if there can be no understanding, no twenty-twenty hindsight, we have that sudden, "blinding" illumination. We have the volatile, pointillistic vision of Audrey's right eye. We have the "shimmery, ungraspable way" life presents itself, those "intertwined, bewildering strands of beauty and sadness and mystery." To the extent that this complex interweaving, this special vision, this dazzling light, are part and parcel of the sentiment recollection evokes, then we as writers of fiction do well to trust not only our stories themselves, but that slippery, self-serving teller of tales we call memory.

FROM LONG SHOTS TO X-RAYS:

Distance and Point of View in Fiction

By David Jauss

1.

Point of view is arguably the most important element of fiction writing, for it is inextricably linked to characterization, style, and theme, yet it is perhaps the least understood of all aspects of fiction. This lack of understanding is due in part to the fact that the term *point of view* has several different meanings. In common usage, of course, it refers to an opinion (as in, "That's just your point of view"), but in literary discussions, it refers to three not necessarily related things: the narrator's person (first, second, or third), the narrative techniques he employs (omniscience, stream of consciousness, and so forth), and the locus of perception (the character whose perspective is presented, whether or not that character is narrating). Since there is no necessary connection between person, technique, and locus of perception, discussions of point of view in fiction almost inevitably read like relay races in which one definition passes off the baton to the next, and the result is confusion about what, exactly, constitutes the point of view of a particular work. The lack of understanding about point of view is also due to the tendency of the authors of creative writing and literature textbooks to write prescriptively rather than descriptively about point of view, asserting that certain techniques are available only to certain types of narrators and that a work's point of view should be consistent. In this essay I will attempt to present a more accurate conception of point of view by closely examining the actual practice of authors and explaining how they use point of view to manipulate the degree of emotional, intellectual, and moral distance between a character and a reader.

Let's begin with Ernest Hemingway's "Hills Like White Elephants." In this story, Hemingway seats us at a table outside a train station in Spain. Sitting at a table near us are a man and a woman who are waiting for the train to arrive, and for the bulk of the story we eavesdrop on their conversation, just as we might in real life. And also just as in real life, we cannot enter into their minds; we can only hear what they say and see what they do. This objective point of view is commonly called "dramatic," for it imitates the conventions of drama, which does not reveal thoughts, only words and deeds.

Like a play, Hemingway's story consists largely of dialogue. At first, the dialogue is the smallest of small talk—the man and the woman discuss what they should drink, etc.—but it's clear there's some tension between them, something unmentioned that's lurking beneath their trivial conversation, and our interest is piqued. Two pages into this five-page story, the man finally broaches, however indirectly, the subject that is causing their tension: The woman is pregnant, and she wants to have the baby but he doesn't. Though the man repeatedly says that he's "perfectly willing" to go through with the pregnancy, it's clear he's doing his best to pressure her into having an abortion. Eventually, his protestations of selfless concern for her wear out her patience, and she asks him to "please please please please please please stop talking." The conversation over, he picks up their suitcases and carries them to the other side of the station, and we follow him there.

At this point, Hemingway momentarily abandons the dramatic point of view for only the second time in the story (the first time occurs when he says that the woman "saw the river through the trees") and tells us that the man "looked up the tracks but could not see the train." In this sentence, Hemingway reveals something that cannot be externally observed—what the man was *unable* to see—and so moves us a little way into his mind, reducing the distance between us and him ever so slightly. And two sentences later, Hemingway completes the segue that sentence begins, taking us even farther inside the character and reducing the distance significantly. He writes that the man "drank an Anis at the bar and looked at the people. They were all waiting reasonably for the train." Notice that word *reasonably*. This word violates the objective, dramatic point of view even more than the statement that the man did not see the train, for it tells us not just what the man sees—or, in this case, fails to see—but the man's *opinion* about what he sees. Just as Hemingway could have written "He looked up the tracks" without going on to tell us whether the man saw the train, so he could have written "They were all waiting for the train" without conveying the man's opinion that they were all waiting "reasonably."

If Hemingway had done these things, he would have maintained consistency of point of view, and according to virtually every discussion of the subject I've ever read or heard, consistency of point of view is an essential element of good fiction writing. But for my money, the word *reasonably* is the most important word in the story and Hemingway's point-of-view shift is the single smartest move in a story full of smart moves. In the context of their argument over the abortion, this word implies that the man considers the woman *un*reasonable, unlike these people in the bar—and, of course, unlike him. This implication complicates the story considerably, for if the man didn't believe he was being reasonable, we would see him as a relatively simple villain, someone who consciously manipulates the woman into doing what he wants—all the while absolving himself of any responsibility for the decision—and we would see the woman, who agrees to have the abortion, as a victim (albeit a knowing one) of his manipulation. The story would therefore veer in the direction of melodrama, which thrives on the simple, knee-jerk emotions that result from villains' mistreatment of victims. But if the man truly believes what he's saying, then he is a relatively complex character, someone whose behavior stems from self-delusion, not one-dimensional villainy, and the story immediately becomes too complex to evoke the simple responses of melodrama. It is essential, then, that the reader know what the man thinks about himself and the woman. If Hemingway had maintained the same point of view throughout the story, as most commentators on point of view would recommend, we'd never know whether the man was a conscious, Machiavellian villain or merely a self-deluded person. But Hemingway wisely shifts his point of view, twice moving in from outside to reveal, with increasing depth, the man's thoughts. In my opinion, this is a brilliant example of how a writer can use the technical resources of point of view to manipulate distance between narrator and character, and therefore between character and reader, in order to achieve the effect he desires.

Similarly, Anton Chekhov violates the so-called "rule" against shifting point of view in his story "A Trifle From Real Life" in order to manipulate distance and achieve the effect he desires. For all but two sentences of this story, the unidentified first-person narrator reports the thoughts and feelings of only one character, Nikolai Belayeff, who discovers during a conversation with his lover's eight-year-old son Aliosha that the boy has been secretly seeing his father against his mother's wishes. Although Nikolai promises not to reveal this secret to the boy's mother, as soon as she returns home, he does. Distraught, Aliosha's mother turns to her son and asks him if what Nikolai has said is true. At this point, Chekhov steps slightly closer to the boy's mind for a moment, telling us that Aliosha "did not hear her," then he immediately returns to Nikolai's point of view. It isn't until the story's final sentence that Chekhov closes the distance between his narrator and Aliosha enough to tell us the boy's thoughts: "This was the first time in his life that he had come roughly face to face with deceit; he had never imagined till now that there were things in this world besides pastries and watches and sweet pears, things for which no name could be found in the vocabulary of childhood."

As this sentence suggests, the true protagonist of this story is Aliosha, not Nikolai, for he is the character who undergoes a completed process of change. Yet, except for the two sentences I've mentioned, the story restricts itself to Nikolai's point of view. Why does Chekhov shine the spotlight of point of view on a minor character rather than on his protagonist? The answer, I believe, is that by focusing on Nikolai, Chekhov forces us to make the same mistake Nikolai does: the mistake of assuming that it's the adult's experience that is important, not the child's. By abruptly shifting to Aliosha's point of view, Chekhov reveals that the story is not really about Nikolai and his trifling grievance but about Aliosha and his devastating discovery of an adult's capacity for duplicity and betrayal. This revelation allows Chekhov to complicate our response to Nikolai's despicable act by making us "accomplices" of sorts—for we, too, have been guilty of underestimating the importance of this "trifle from real life" to Aliosha. In a way, then, by abruptly reducing the *narrative* distance between Aliosha and us at the end of the story, Chekhov reduces the *moral* distance between Nikolai and us, and a potentially "trifling" story becomes a serious and complex one.

As these two examples suggest, perhaps the most important purpose of point of view is to manipulate the degree of distance between the characters and the reader in order to achieve the emotional, intellectual, and moral responses the author desires. Outside of Wayne C. Booth, who makes this argument persuasively in his book *The Rhetoric of Fiction*, few writers have stressed this aspect of point of view. Of the creative writing textbooks I know, only two discuss the issue of narrative distance at any length—Janet Burroway's *Writing Fiction* and Richard Cohen's *Writer's Mind: Crafting Fiction*—and neither one goes into much depth about the subject. Generally, textbook authors define point of view in terms of "person," focusing on the *angle* of perception—who's telling the story—instead of the various degrees of depth available within that angle. Even Richard Cohen, who does go on to discuss narrative distance briefly, defines point of view this simplistically. "There is no mystery about point of view," he says. "There are basically two of them: first person ('I') or third person ('he, she')." (He says "basically two" because there are relatively few works of fiction written in second person—examples include Carlos Fuentes's *Aura*, Jay McInerney's *Bright Lights, Big City*, and some of the stories in Lorrie Moore's *Self-Help*.) The more complex discussions of point of view, like Burroway's, go on to divide each of Cohen's two basic points of view into various types: First person is usually divided into "first-person central" and "first-person peripheral," depending on whether the narrator is the main character or a secondary one; and third person is divided into "omniscient," "limited omniscient," and "dramatic," depending on whether the narrator tells us the thoughts and feelings of several characters, just one character, or none.

In my opinion, classifying works of fiction according to their person tells us virtually nothing about either the specific works or point of view in general. If we think all we need to do to define the point of view of a work is identify its person, we're missing not only the boat but also the ocean. As Booth has said, "We can hardly expect to find useful criteria in a distinction that would throw all fiction into two, or at most three, heaps." Furthermore, as Christian Paul Casparis has noted, "The 'I' is a 'she' to the reader" and hence "[w]hole novels are read without leaving any particular impact as to whether they are written in the first or third person." Booth again: "To say that a story is told in the first or the third person … will tell us nothing of importance unless we … describe how the particular qualities of the narrators relate to specific desired effects." In other words, we need to focus on the *techniques* a narrator uses, not the *person* he uses. And as Booth has pointed out, *all* narrative techniques are found in "both first- and third-person narration alike." For example, both first- and third-person narrators can, and do, tell us the thoughts and feelings of other characters. We may call this technique "omniscience" when a third-person narrator uses it, or "inference" or "speculation" when a first-person narrator uses it, but the terminology cannot hide the fact that the technique is the same: In each case, the narrator assumes what Booth calls "privilege," the right to inform the reader of the contents of a character's heart and mind. While I'd like to see us abandon the term *omniscient* and replace it with *privileged*, I know that word would cause at least as many problems as it'd solve, so I'll continue to use the conventional word *omniscient* throughout this essay. But please be aware that when I talk about "omniscience," I'm not referring to its ostensible meaning—"all-knowing" and "truthful"—but to the narrative technique of reporting—*whether accurately or not*—characters' thoughts and feelings. It seems to me that we cannot begin to understand how point of view actually works in fiction until we put more emphasis on technique than we do on Truth.

In short, despite what the textbooks tell us, the technique of omniscience is not the sole property of third-person narrators. As Booth tells us, "There is a curious ambiguity in the term 'omniscience.' Many modern works that we usually classify as narrated dramatically, with everything relayed to us through the limited views of the characters, postulate fully as much omniscience" as we find in third-person works. The only difference between first- and third-person omniscience (and it can of course be a *crucial* difference) is not in the narrator's technique but in the reader's response: We never question the truth of a third-person narrator's statement, but sometimes we do question a first-person narrator's statement.

Sometimes, but not always. Often, we respond to a first-person narrator's omniscience exactly as we do to a third-person narrator's omniscience—with complete trust. Chekhov's "A Trifle From Real Life" is one example. Conrad's *Heart of Darkness* is another. In it, Conrad's principal narrator, Charlie Marlow, tells us not only the thoughts and feelings of Kurtz and other characters but also the thoughts and feelings of the *jungle*. If that's not omniscience, I don't know what is. And though we certainly may question some of Marlow's editorial comments on the nature of women and so forth, we do not question the accuracy of his omniscient statements about other characters' thoughts.

Madame Bovary is another work whose first-person omniscience we accept without question. Flaubert's narrator, who identifies himself as one of Charles Bovary's former classmates, enters as fully into the minds of both Charles and Emma as any third-person narrator could, telling us about thoughts and events he could not have known anything about, and yet at no point do we question his omniscience. Because we have been taught—erroneously—that omniscience is the sole province of third-person narrators, readers tend to consider first-person omniscience a "mistake" on the part of the author. A scholar I know once had the audacity to claim that Flaubert—possibly the most fanatically meticulous artist who ever lived   simply *forgot* that he was writing in first person and began writing from a third-person omniscient perspective. (If he was afflicted with authorial amnesia, it apparently vanished from time to time, for the first-person point of view recurs in all three parts of the novel.) Mario Vargas Llosa's explanation isn't much different, I'm afraid. In *The Perpetual Orgy: Flaubert and Madame Bovary,* he explains the co-existence of a first-person narrator and omniscient narration by asserting that the novel actually has two separate narrators: the "character-narrator" who narrates in first-person plural and the "omniscient narrator" who uses third-person singular and "witnesses and recounts with equal ease what takes place in the outside world and in the heart of hearts of the characters." In Vargas Llosa's view, these narrators take turns narrating the first chapter, and then from that point on, the character-narrator "disappears, never to return" and the omniscient narrator takes over for the remainder of the novel. (In fact, as I mentioned above, the first-person plural point of view recurs throughout the novel. While it's most evident in chapter one, it also appears two more times in part one, twice in part two, and four times in part three.) Unlike the character-narrator, Vargas Llosa continues, the omniscient narrator exists apart from the fictional world he describes and so is "invisible." But at times, he admits, this "invisible" narrator "manifests himself ... in the form of intrusions which betray ... the existence of a being who is a stranger to the fictitious reality." These intrusive comments range from such trivial opinions as "It is here that the worst Neufchâtel cheeses of the entire district are made" to such philosophical observations as "every notary carries within himself the remains of a poet." Vargas Llosa considers these intrusions mistakes—"involuntary ... lapses"—in Flaubert's handling of the point of view. Well, if they're mistakes, Flaubert certainly made a lot of them: although Vargas Llosa says there are "no more than fifty" of these "involuntary lapses" in the novel, in fact the number is at least double that amount. The effect of these "mistakes," Vargas Llosa argues, is to create yet another narrator: the "philosopher-narrator." I submit that there's a much less convoluted and far more logical way to explain these intrusions than by positing the use of a third narrator: they are the comments of the first-person narrator, who "disappears" only insofar as he stops referring to himself as overtly and regularly as he does in the first chapter. Furthermore, I submit that the first-person narrator and the omniscient narrator are also one and the same. In short, the novel has only one narrator, not two or three. The narrator's *techniques* may change, but the narrator himself does not.

Vargas Llosa's assumption is, sadly, a common one: that first-person narration and omniscience are mutually exclusive. At the heart of this assumption is the notion that since individuals are not omniscient in life, they cannot be omniscient in fiction. It's particularly ironic that Vargas Llosa would subscribe to this view, since he says in his *Letters to a Young Novelist* that "Life as described in fiction ... is never just life as it was lived ... but rather ... what [authors] were obliged to fabricate because they weren't able to live it in reality." One of the things we can't do in reality is know what other people are thinking; in fiction, however, we can.

To those who, like Vargas Llosa, would maintain that first-person omniscience violates the most basic of all "rules" about point of view, I would point out that there isn't, and never was, such a rule. An abundance of first-person omniscience can be found in every period of literature. We see it in the oldest-known collection of stories, the Egyptian *Tales of the Magicians*, which was written between 5000 and 2000 B.C.E.; we see it in such medieval works as the *Gesta Romanorum* and Boccaccio's *Decameron*; we see it in such early novels as Cervantes's *Don Quixote*, Fielding's *Tom Jones*, Defoe's *Moll Flanders*, Sterne's *Tristram Shandy*, Thackeray's *Vanity Fair*, Eliot's *Middlemarch*, and we see it in Melville's *Moby-Dick*, Hawthorne's *The House of the Seven Gables*, Hugo's *Les Miserables*, Dostoevsky's *The Devils*, Gogol's "The Overcoat," and James's *The Turn of the Screw*. And first-person omniscience isn't just some "old-fashioned narrative liberty" we've outgrown; it's still very much with us today. Among the many contemporary writers who have used it to superb effect are John Barth, Samuel Beckett, Jorge Luis Borges, Frederick Busch, Junot Díaz, Jeffrey Eugenides, Gabriel García Márquez, Günter Grass, Milan Kundera, Alice Munro, Tim O'Brien, Alain Robbe-Grillet, Marilynne Robinson, Salman Rushdie, Alexander Solzhenitsyn, and Eudora Welty. First-person omniscience has a long and noble pedigree; the prejudice against it is of more recent birth. If this attitude persists, I'm afraid we fiction writers will be deprived not only of a narrative technique that has served the masters well for centuries but also of the complex effects it can achieve.

Our misunderstanding of first-person omniscience is not the only problem that results from defining point of view primarily in terms of person rather than technique. Because it is generally a bad idea to shift person in a work of fiction—to have a first-person narrator suddenly morph into a third-person narrator, for example—we leap to the conclusion that point of view should be singular and consistent. In fact, however singular and consistent the *person* of a story may be, the techniques that truly constitute point of view are inevitably multiple and shifting. For example, the point of view we call third-person omniscience may be consistently third person but it is not consistently omniscient, for the narrator must of necessity shift from omniscience to the dramatic point of view whenever he deals with a character whose mind he does not enter.

Defining point of view largely in terms of person ignores the fact that whenever a third-person narrator presents a character who is telling a story, that character in effect takes over as narrator, if only briefly. (Consider, for example, the many first-person narrators who combine to tell the story of Thomas Sutpen and his descendents in Faulkner's third-person novel *Absalom, Absalom!*) Defining point of view in terms of person also ignores the fact that first-person narrators, when they talk about other characters, use *third* person. And it ignores the fact that sometimes a first-person narrator uses third person to talk about *himself.* (Examples include Thackeray's *Henry Esmond*, Günter Grass's *The Tin Drum*, Charles Baxter's "Media Event," and Kevin Brockmeier's "These Hands," the last of which opens, "The protagonist of this story is named Lewis Winters. He is also its narrator, and he is also me.") How, then, are we to classify these narratives? First person? Third person? Both? Clearly, defining a work's person doesn't tell us much about its point of view.

I agree with Booth that the term *point of view* should be understood to refer not only to person but also to the various techniques that allow fiction writers to manipulate the degree of distance between characters and readers. Some of these techniques have the effect of long shots in a film—they keep us very distant from the characters—and others resemble close-ups. Still others are like X-rays: They take us all the way inside characters, so we're thinking and feeling with their central nervous systems. For most of "Hills Like White Elephants," for example, we watch Hemingway's protagonist with the distance and detachment of a surveillance camera, then Hemingway zooms in for a close-up of the man and, finally, a quick one-word X-ray of his soul. Chekhov follows this same pattern with Aliosha in "A Trifle From Real Life." (In terms of technique, these two stories are virtually identical, though one is written in third person and the other in first.) Good fiction writers, like good filmmakers, know how to use these techniques to manipulate the reader's distance from the characters, sometimes moving in for a close-up and other times moving back for a panoramic view. And, often, going where the camera can't, into the mind and heart and soul of a character.

2.

What I want to do now is define, and provide examples of, the principal techniques we can use in our fiction to manipulate narrative distance. Though we don't have enough space to discuss how each point of view, and each shift from one point of view to another, can affect the reader's response to a story, please remember that directing the reader's response is the ultimate purpose of these techniques, as I hope my comments on "Hills Like White Elephants" and "A Trifle From Real Life" have demonstrated.

Most, if not all, of the techniques that constitute point of view will be familiar. What may not be familiar is the fact that all of these techniques are available to any narrator, whether that narrator uses first, second, or third person. Since second-person narrators are rare, we'll focus here on first- and third-person narrators. And we'll look at the techniques these narrators use in order of decreasing distance—from long shots to X-rays. As we'll see, some of the resulting points of view keep us entirely outside the characters; some allow us to be simultaneously outside and inside; and others take us all the way in. We'll also see that point of view is more a matter of where the language is coming from than it is of person. The points of view that keep us outside a character require the narrator to use *his* language, not his character's, whereas the points of view that allow us to be inside a character require the narrator to use the *character's* language, at least some of the time.

OUTSIDE

Dramatic

There is only one point of view that remains outside all of the characters, and that's the dramatic point of view, the point of view Hemingway uses almost exclusively in "Hills Like White Elephants." In this point of view, the narrator assumes maximum distance from the characters he describes and writes about them in language appropriate to him but not necessarily to them. We are so distant from Hemingway's characters, for example, that we don't even know their names—they're simply "the man" and "the girl." As James Joyce says in *A Portrait of the Artist as a Young Man*, a writer who uses the dramatic point of view is "like the God of the creation": He is "within or behind or beyond or above His handiwork, invisible, refined out of existence, indifferent, paring His fingernails." The narrator who uses this point of view imitates the conventions of drama, restricting himself to presenting dialogue, action, and description but not thoughts. The excerpt from "Hills Like White Elephants" that follows is a good example. Like a play, it consists solely of dialogue and "stage directions."

> "It's really an awfully simple operation, Jig," the man said.
> "It's not really an operation at all."
> The girl looked at the ground the table legs rested on.

"I know you wouldn't mind it, Jig. It's really not anything. It's just to let the air in."

The girl did not say anything.

"I'll go with you and I'll stay with you all the time. They just let the air in and then it's all perfectly natural."

The girl looked at the ground the table legs rested on.

"Then what will we do afterward?"

"We'll be fine afterward. Just like we were before."

"What makes you think so?"

"That's the only thing that bothers us. It's the only thing that's made us unhappy."

"The girl look at the bead curtains, put her hand out and took hold of two of the strings of beads.

"And you think then we'll be all right and be happy?"

"I know we will. You don't have to be afraid. I've known lots of people that have done it."

"So have I," said the girl. "And afterward they were all so happy."

"Hills Like White Elephants" is written in third person, but Hemingway also uses the dramatic point of view extensively in some of his first-person stories. In the following excerpt from "The Light of the World," Nick Adams, the narrator, reports action and dialogue but no thoughts, either his own or those of any other character.

When he saw us come in the door the bartender looked up and then reached over and put the glass covers on the two free-lunch bowls.

"Give me a beer," I said. He drew it, cut the top off with the spatula and then held the glass in his hand. I put the nickel on the wood and he slid the beer toward me.

"What's yours?" he said to Tom.

"Beer."

He drew that beer and cut it off and when he saw the money he pushed the beer across to Tom.

"What's the matter?" Tom asked.

The bartender didn't answer him. He just looked over our heads and said, "What's yours?" to a man who'd come in.

Because the dramatic point of view allows the narrator to report only the externals of a story, it requires a mastery of what T.S. Eliot called the "objective correlative," an objective, sensory detail or action that correlates to a character's subjective thought or feeling. (In "Hills Like White Elephants," for example, we know that the woman doesn't want to discuss having an abortion because she looks at the ground instead of responding to the man. And in "The Light of the World," we know that the bartender thinks Nick and Tom don't have much money because he covers the free-lunch bowls and waits to see the nickels before he gives them their beers.) When an author is a master of this technique, as Hemingway is, the story that results is inevitably subtle. Careless or inexperienced readers will often be confused by stories employing this point of view.

OUTSIDE AND INSIDE

There are two points of view that allow the narrator to be simultaneously outside and inside a character to various degrees: omniscience and indirect interior monologue.

Omniscience

Most textbooks distinguish between two kinds of omniscience: "limited" and "regular." In limited omniscience, the narrator relates the thoughts and feelings of only one character whereas in regular omniscience, he relates the thoughts and feelings of at least two and usually more. I don't believe dividing omniscience into "limited" and "regular" tells us anything remotely useful. The technique in both cases is identical; it's merely applied to a different number of characters. And as I see it, all omniscience is "limited": I don't know of any work of fiction that goes into the minds of *all* of its characters. Although we call the point of view of *War and Peace* "omniscient" rather than "limited omniscient," Tolstoy stays outside of far more minds—hundreds, in fact—than he enters. So I propose that we use the term *omniscience* to describe the point of view used when the narrator reports, in *his* language, the thoughts of any number of characters. The fact that the narrator retains his own language keeps him "outside" while the fact that he reports a character's thoughts allows him to go "inside"; hence this point of view allows the narrator, and the reader, to be simultaneously outside and inside a character.

Let's start by looking at two relatively simple examples of omniscience, one in third person and the other in first. The following passage is from Dostoevsky's third-person novel, *Crime and Punishment*:

> The triumphant sense of security, of deliverance from overwhelming danger, that was what filled his whole soul that moment without thought for the future, without analysis, without suppositions or surmises, without doubts and without questioning. It was an instant of full, direct, purely instinctive joy.

As I suggested earlier, "where the language is coming from" is one of the most important issues in point of view. The language here clearly belongs to the novel's third-person narrator. At this particular moment, Raskolnikov would not have used these rational, abstract, insightful words to describe his "purely instinctive joy"—in fact, he *could not* have used them because the moment was "without thought" and "without analysis." For Raskolnikov, the moment was "purely instinctive," not reflective, as the passage is. And if these are supposed to be his thoughts, they amount to the absurdly contradictory thought "I'm not thinking." If Raskolnikov is not thinking and analyzing at this moment, then, these thoughts and analyses—and the language that conveys them—must be the narrator's. As a result, we are conscious of someone outside the character peering into his soul and telling us what he sees. We are therefore both inside and outside Raskolnikov at the same time—inside in the sense that we witness his feelings, and outside in the sense that we are conscious that those feelings are being defined and articulated by an omniscient observer. In omniscience, then, the narrative perspective is still external to the character, as in the dramatic point of view, but we have moved, if only tentatively, into his mind and heart.

The next example is from Fitzgerald's *The Great Gatsby*, in which the first-person narrator, Nick Carraway, occasionally assumes an omniscient understanding of Gatsby.

> One autumn night, five years before, they [Gatsby and Daisy] had been walking down the street when the leaves were falling, and they came to a place where there were no trees and the sidewalk was white with moonlight. They stopped here and turned to each other. Now it was a cool night with that mysterious excitement in it which comes at the two changes of the year. The quiet lights in the houses were humming out into the darkness and there was a stir and bustle among the stars. Out of the corner of his eye Gatsby saw that the blocks of the sidewalks really formed a ladder and mounted to a secret place above the

> trees—he could climb to it, if he climbed alone, and once there
> he could suck on the pap of life, gulp down the incomparable
> milk of wonder.
>
> His heart beat faster and faster as Daisy's white face
> came up to his own. He knew that when he kissed this girl, and
> forever wed his unutterable visions to her perishable breath,
> his mind would never romp again like the mind of God. So he
> waited, listening for a moment longer to the tuning-fork that
> had been struck upon a star. Then he kissed her. At his lips'
> touch she blossomed for him like a flower and the incarnation
> was complete.

Like the example from *Crime and Punishment*, this passage employs the language of the narrator, not of the character the narrator is discussing. Whereas Carraway's style is often lyrical and poetic, Gatsby's is nothing if not laconic, though he dresses it up with his affected use of British expressions like "old sport." Can you imagine him saying, "So I waited, listening for a moment longer to the tuning fork that had been struck upon a star, old sport"? Me, neither. Clearly, Carraway is translating Gatsby's overwhelming, inchoate feelings into language that conveys what his own could not. Technically, then, both Dostoevsky's and Fitzgerald's passages employ the same point of view, though one is in third person and the other is in first person. Indeed, if we didn't know the excerpt from *The Great Gatsby* was narrated by one of the novel's characters, we would almost certainly assume it was another example of conventional third-person omniscience. That fact alone should indicate that we need to pay more attention to technique than to person.

Now let's look at two examples of omniscience that are a little more complex, one from Tolstoy's third-person novel *War and Peace* and another from Delmore Schwartz's first-person story "In Dreams Begin Responsibilities."

> When Boris came into the Rostovs' drawing room, Natasha was
> up in her room. Hearing of his arrival she almost ran down to
> the drawing-room, red in the face and radiant with a more than
> friendly smile.
>
> Boris was still thinking of the little Natasha he had known four
> years ago dressed in a short frock, with brilliant black eyes darting
> out from under her curls, all wild whoops and girlish giggles, so
> when he saw a totally different Natasha coming into the room he

was quite taken aback, and the surprise and delight showed on his face. Natasha was thrilled to see him looking like that.

"Well, do you recognize your little playmate and sweetheart?" said the countess.

Finally my mother comes downstairs, all dressed up, and my father being engaged in conversation with my grandfather becomes uneasy, not knowing whether to greet my mother or continue the conversation. He gets up from the chair clumsily and says "hello" gruffly. My grandfather watches, examining their congruence, such as it is, with a critical eye, and meanwhile rubbing his bearded cheek roughly, as he always does when he reflects. He is worried; he is afraid that my father will not make a good husband for his oldest daughter.

If we define the points of view of these passages in the conventional, person-oriented way, the passage from Tolstoy is an example of "regular omniscience" (despite the fact that its omniscience is limited to two of its three characters) and the passage from Schwartz is an example of "first-person central." But classifying these passages according to person can only mislead the reader into thinking that they are diametric opposites when in fact their techniques are essentially identical. Both Tolstoy's third-person narrator and Schwartz's first-person narrator omnisciently enter the minds of two characters (Boris and Natasha, the father and grandfather) while presenting a third character (Countess Rostov, the mother) dramatically, reporting only her actions or dialogue, not her thoughts or feelings. In terms of technique, then, there is virtually no difference between these two passages, yet most scholars would put them into two separate categories, based on person.

These two passages not only illustrate that all omniscience is limited to some extent but also that point of view is inevitably multiple and shifting, not singular and consistent. Unless the omniscient narrator enters the mind of *every* character, he will of necessity use the dramatic point of view for one or more characters. Imagine, for example, a hypothetical short story containing five characters. If the narrator—whether first- or third-person—uses the omniscient point of view for one character, he would have to use the dramatic point of view for the remaining four. And if he uses omniscience for two characters, he'd have to treat the remaining three from the dramatic point of view. And so forth.

It is of course theoretically possible for a story to employ only one point of view, but I can't think of a single example that does. More than any other story I know, "Hills Like White Elephants" consistently employs one point of view, but even it departs from that point of view three times, as we've noted. Since the major function of point of view is to manipulate the degree of distance between reader and character, it shouldn't surprise us that writers use more than one point of view in a story: How else can they create different degrees of distance between the reader and the various characters? And how else can they keep the story from feeling static? Imagine a film in which the camera stays the same distance from the characters, never moving back or in. Boring, right? The same is true for fiction.

Indirect Interior Monologue

The second technique that allows the narrator and reader to be simultaneously outside and inside a character is indirect interior monologue. This technique was invented by Flaubert, who uses it extensively in *Madame Bovary*, and it has become ubiquitous in twentieth- and twenty-first-century fiction. Indirect interior monologue—or, as the French call it, *style indirect libre*—differs from omniscience in one very important way: Whereas the omniscient point of view requires the narrator to translate the character's thoughts and feelings into his own language, indirect interior monologue allows him to use his character's language. As a result, the character becomes a kind of "co-narrator," even though he is not, properly speaking, narrating at all. Henry James called this kind of character a "reflector," for indirect interior monologue functions like a mirror that reflects a character's thoughts. But just as mirrors distort what they reflect, inverting left and right, so indirect interior monologue distorts what it reflects. A narrator using this technique doesn't report a character's thoughts verbatim. Take, for example, that sentence from "Hills Like White Elephants" we discussed earlier: What the man is actually thinking is "They **are** all waiting reasonably for the train" but Hemingway's third-person narrator says "They **were** all waiting reasonably for the train." As this example reveals, indirect interior monologue involves altering the *tense* of a character's thought. Further, it often involves transforming the *person* of the thought from first to third. These alterations make us aware that the narrator is outside the character, reflecting the character's thoughts. In this point of view, then, we witness the character's interior monologue, but we do so *indirectly*, through the narrator's alterations. The result is, as Vargas

Llosa has said, "an ambiguous form of narration," one in which "the narrator tells what he is recounting from a viewpoint so close to the character's that the reader at times has the impression that it is the character himself who is speaking." Like omniscience, indirect interior monologue allows the narrator to be simultaneously outside and inside a character, but because he is giving us the character's thoughts in the character's language, not his own, he is farther inside than in the other points of view we've examined so far.

The following passage from *Madame Bovary* demonstrates this technique. In it, Emma is recalling the romantic afternoons she spent in a garden with her former lover Léon. I have italicized the passages that employ indirect interior monologue.

> With his head bare he would read aloud as he sat on a footstool of dried sticks. The fresh breeze from the meadow would blow on the pages and on the nasturtiums in the arbor. *And now he was gone, the one pleasure of her life, the one possible hope for happiness. Why hadn't she seized this happiness when it first appeared? Why hadn't she held him back with her hands or by begging on her knees when he wanted to leave?* She cursed herself for not having loved him.

Clearly, the italicized sentences are not the narrator's thoughts and questions; they're Emma's, reflected via indirect interior monologue. If they were presented directly, they would read as follows: "And now he **is** gone, the one pleasure of **my** life, the one possible hope for happiness. Why **didn't I seize** this happiness when it first appeared? Why **didn't I hold** him back with **my** hands or by begging on **my** knees when he wanted to leave?" Because Emma's thoughts are presented indirectly, through alterations in their tense and person, when we read them we feel as if the narrator and character are somehow talking to us at the same time. As the distinction between narrator and character blurs, the distance between them shrinks, and so does the distance between the reader and character. In no other point of view is the boundary line between narrator and character as thin as it is in indirect interior monologue.

While indirect interior monologue is most often employed by third-person narrators reflecting a character's thoughts, it can also be used by first-person narrators reflecting the thoughts of another character. In *Midnight's Children*, for example, Saleem, Salman Rushdie's narrator, uses this technique to reflect the thoughts his grandfather Aziz had when he visited the holy city of Amritsar before Saleem was even born: "Aziz stood at the window, inhaling the city. The spire of the Golden Temple gleamed in the sun. But his nose itched: something was not right here." What Aziz actually thought, of course, was "something **is** not right here." First-person narrators also use indirect interior monologue to reflect their own *prior* thoughts. In such cases, the first-person narrator treats his previous self as if it were a separate character. In *Heart of Darkness*, for example, Charlie Marlow uses indirect interior monologue to present thoughts he had during his voyage up the Congo River: "I turned my shoulder to him [the manager of the Central Station] in sign of my appreciation and looked into the fog," he says, then adds, "How long would it last?" Marlow is not asking *now*, at the moment he's narrating the story, how long the fog would last; rather, he's reflecting the thought he had at that time, the thought "How long **will** it last?" Clearly, he is reflecting his previous self's interior monologue just as a third-person narrator would reflect a character's.

Jeffrey Eugenides' *Middlesex* also offers excellent examples of first-person indirect interior monologue. In the following example, his hermaphroditic narrator, Cal/Calliope, reflects the thoughts she had twenty-seven years earlier, when she discovered she was genetically male, not female, and had her long hair cut in a male's style:

> Ed the barber put a comb in my long hair. He lifted it experimentally, making snipping sounds with his scissors. The blades weren't touching my hair. The snipping was only a kind of mental barbering, a limbering up. This gave me time for second thoughts. What was I doing? What if Dr. Luce was right? What if that girl in the mirror really *was* me? How did I think I could defect to the other side so easily? What did I know about boys, about men? I didn't even like them that much.

Cal/Calliope is not asking herself these questions, now, as she narrates; she's reflecting, through the change in tense, the "second thoughts" she had all those years ago, the thoughts, "What **am** I doing? What if Dr. Luce **is** right? What if that girl in the mirror really *is* me?" and so forth.

As the preceding examples of indirect interior monologue suggest, a narrator using this point of view reflects not only the diction of the character's thoughts but also the grammar, syntax, and associational movement of those thoughts. In passages employing indirect interior monologue, we frequently find rhetorical questions, exclamations, sentence fragments, and associational leaps as well as diction appropriate to the character rather than the narrator. The following example is from Joyce's *A Portrait of the Artist as a Young Man*. It portrays Stephen Dedalus, Joyce's protagonist, well before he became the young man of the title—at this point in the novel, he's a young boy, a student in a boarding school.

> It pained him that he did not know well what politics meant and that he did not know where the universe ended. He felt small and weak. When would he be like the fellows in poetry and rhetoric? They had big voices and big boots and they studied trigonometry. That was very far away. First came the vacation and then the next term and then vacation again and then again another term and then again the vacation. It was like a train going in and out of tunnels and that was like the noise of the boys eating in the refectory when you opened and closed the flaps of your ears. Term, vacation; tunnel, out; noise, stop. How far away it was! It was better to go to bed to sleep. Only prayers in the chapel and then bed. He shivered and yawned.

Clearly, the adult narrator of Joyce's novel is not asking the question "When **would he** be like the fellows in poetry and rhetoric?" Rather, he is reflecting the child's question "When **will I** be like the fellows in poetry and rhetoric?" Similarly, the adult narrator would not characterize the young boys Stephen looks up to as having "big voices and big boots": Those words come from the character, not the narrator. And the narrator, whose sense of time is certainly more sophisticated than young Stephen's, wouldn't measure it in vacations and school terms, nor would he think the year or two that separates Stephen from the older boys he admires is an extraordinary amount of time. The exclamation "How far away it **was**!" is not the narrator's thought, therefore; it's a reflection of Stephen's thought, "How far away it **is**!" And of course it's Stephen, not the narrator, who associates the alternation between term and vacation with a train going in and out of tunnels and the noise of the boys eating in the refectory. As this example shows, the change in person and tense allows the narrator to remain outside the character while simultaneously reporting, *almost* verbatim, the language, grammar, syntax, and associational movement of a character's interior monologue.

This example also illustrates the extremely important but rarely acknowledged fact that narrators often shift points of view not only within a story or novel but also within a single paragraph. The first two sentences, which summarize Stephen's thoughts in the narrator's diction, employ omniscience. The next nine reflect Stephen's thoughts indirectly, by changing their tense and person, and are therefore examples of indirect interior monologue. And the final sentence, which reports action only, uses the dramatic point of view. If we were to graph the point of view of this paragraph, we'd see that it begins on the outside edge of Stephen's consciousness, then goes deeper and deeper inside, and finally retreats to being completely outside.

As I hope this example suggests, handling point of view is much more than a matter of picking a person or a narrative technique and sticking with it; rather, it involves carefully manipulating the distance between narrator and character, moving closer one minute, then farther away the next, so as to achieve the desired response from the reader. In this case, Joyce manipulates the distance to allow the reader to enter into the psychological drama of what, on the surface, might appear to be a moment of extreme boredom. If he had employed only the omniscient point of view, our sense of this drama would be significantly diminished. As evidence, here's a purely omniscient rendering of the paragraph's opening sentences: "It pained him that he did not know well what politics meant and that he did not know where the universe ended. He felt small and weak. He wanted to be like the older boys at the school, who studied poetry, rhetoric, and trigonometry, but several terms and vacation would have to pass before he was their age. That seemed like a long time to him."

Or, worse yet, imagine how the moment's drama would utterly disappear if Joyce had used only the dramatic point of view. This entire paragraph would shrink to the simple and unevocative sentence, "Stephen shivered and yawned."

INSIDE

There are two points of view that to differing degrees eliminate the distance between character and reader and take us all the way inside, abandoning either temporarily or permanently the mind and diction of the narrator. They are direct interior monologue and stream of consciousness.

Direct Interior Monologue

In direct interior monologue, the character's thoughts are not just "reflected," they are presented *directly*, without altering person or tense. As a result, the external narrator disappears, if only for a moment, and the character takes over as "narrator." Unlike a conventional first-person narrator, however, the character is not consciously narrating. Elizabeth Bowen's story "The Demon Lover" provides an example of this point of view:

> As a woman whose utter dependability was the keystone of her family life she was not willing to return to the country, to her husband, her little boys, and her sister, without the objects she had come up to fetch. Resuming work at the chest she set about making up a number of parcels in a rapid, fumbling-decisive way. These, with her shopping parcels, would be too much to carry; these meant a taxi—at the thought of the taxi her heart went up and her normal breathing resumed. I will ring up the taxi now; the taxi cannot come too soon: I shall hear the taxi out there running its engine, till I walk calmly down to it through the hall. I'll ring up— But no: the telephone is cut off ... She tugged at a knot she had tied wrong.

Like the excerpt from Joyce we looked at a moment ago, this passage demonstrates how a great writer can manipulate distance within a brief paragraph. The first two sentences here are examples of omniscience. The third sentence slides into indirect interior monologue, altering the thoughts "These **will** be too much to carry" and "these **mean** a taxi" to "These **would** be too much to carry" and "these **meant** a taxi," then the sentence shifts back to omniscience. The next three sentences are direct interior monologue—her actual thoughts presented without alteration, comment, or even attribution by the narrator—and the final sentence is dramatic.

Sometimes the transition from external third-person narration to direct interior monologue is even more abrupt than in this passage. In the following sentence from *Ulysses*, Joyce leaps from a description of Leopold Bloom's external behavior to the thought that accompanies it with the aid of nothing more than a colon: "He sighed down his nose: they never understand." Jean-Paul Sartre uses the same technique in his short story "Intimacy," though he uses a comma more often than a colon to separate the external from the internal. And sometimes he makes the transition into direct interior monologue without any punctuation at all, as in this sentence: "She didn't even take the time to comb her hair, she was in such a hurry and the people who'll see me won't know that I'm naked under my grey coat."

As with indirect interior monologue, direct interior monologue is most common in third-person narration, but it is sometimes used by first-person narrators also. Again, Conrad's Charlie Marlow provides an example when he says, "I caught sight of a V-shaped ripple on the water ahead. What? Another snag!" The last two sentences report directly, without altering person or tense, the thoughts that occurred to him *then*, not thoughts he's having *now*, as he tells his story to his shipmates. Another example of this technique occurs in Hemingway's *A Farewell to Arms*:

> At a quarter to five I kissed Catherine good-by and went into the bathroom to dress. Knotting my tie and looking in the glass I looked strange to myself in the civilian clothes. I must remember to buy some more shirts and socks.

Frederic Henry is clearly not reminding himself now, as he narrates the novel, to buy some shirts and socks; instead, he's reporting the thought he had at a quarter to five on that now-distant day.

Stream of Consciousness

The other point of view that takes us completely inside a character is stream of consciousness. The term comes from William James, who coined it in his book *The Principles of Psychology* to describe the incessant, associational movement of our thoughts. Writers and critics have adopted this term as the name for a point of view that, as Burroway puts it, "tries to suggest the process as well as the content of the mind." Like direct interior monologue, stream of consciousness presents a character's thoughts and feelings directly, without transforming either their person or tense, but unlike direct interior monologue, it presents those thoughts as they exist before the character's mind has "edited" them or arranged them into complete sentences. Because our thoughts are continually moving, each one rippling into another, writers who want to convey the process as well as the content of a character's mind often eschew punctuation. But sometimes writers use a kind of "shorthand" approach to the character's constantly flowing thoughts, giving us brief fragments from the stream of associations. Joyce does this regularly throughout *Ulysses*. In the following example, he sandwiches nineteen fragments from Leopold Bloom's stream of consciousness between two sentences of external action:

> He walked on. Where is my hat, by the way? Must have put it back on the peg. Or hanging up on the floor. Funny, I don't remember that. Hallstand too full. Four umbrellas, her raincloak.

Picking up the letters. Drago's shopbell ringing. Queer I was just thinking that moment. Brown brilliantined hair over his collar. Just had a wash and brushup. Wonder have I time for a bath this morning. Tara street. Chap in the paybox there got away James Stephens they say. O'Brien.

Deep voice that fellow Dlugaacz has. Agenda what is it? Now, my miss. Enthusiast.

He kicked open the crazy door of the jakes.

In the final chapter of *Ulysses*, Joyce uses the "longhand" version of the stream of consciousness technique. By telling us everything Molly Bloom thinks, without interrupting for so much as a comma, he takes us as far inside her mind as an X-ray takes us inside a body. The chapter, which consists of forty-some pages of Molly's unpunctuated thoughts as she falls asleep, opens with the following words:

> Yes because he never did a thing like that before as ask to get his breakfast in bed with a couple of eggs since the City Arms hotel when he used to be pretending to be laid up with a sick voice doing his highness to make himself interesting to that old faggot Mrs Riordan that he thought he had a great leg of and she never left us a farthing all for masses for herself and her soul greatest miser ever was actually afraid to lay out 4d for her methylated spirit telling me all her ailments she had too much old chat in her about politics and earthquakes and the end of the world let us have a bit of fun first God help the world if all the women were her sort down on bathingsuits and lownecks of course nobody wanted her to wear I suppose she was pious because no man would look at her twice I hope I'll never be like her a wonder she didn't want us to cover our faces ...

If we define point of view solely in terms of person, stream of consciousness is "first-person point of view." But there's an enormous difference between stream of consciousness and your garden-variety first-person narration, and that difference stems from the all-important fact that in stream of consciousness the character is not conscious of narrating. As Chuck Rosenthal has said, "Consciousness does not narrate itself. It's exposed to us by a narrator" whose presence is implied but not overtly revealed, either through self-reference or the use of third person. What's more, this implied narrator stakes claim to the ultimate form of omniscience, the ability to know, and present verbatim, absolutely every thought that passes through his character's mind. Other points of view *report*, in the *narrator's* language, a character's conscious thoughts, or they *reflect*, in the *character's* language, that character's conscious thoughts. But this point of view *presents*, directly and without any apparent mediation, a character's conscious—even, sometimes, *unconscious*—thoughts. In a way, then, this point of view resembles its diametric opposite, the dramatic point of view, which remains completely outside a character's mind. As with that point of view, the author is—to quote Joyce once more—"like the God of creation": "within or behind or beyond or above His handiwork, invisible, refined out of existence, indifferent, paring His fingernails."

The last chapter of *Ulysses* uses only stream of consciousness, but sometimes a narrator will mix stream of consciousness into passages that employ other points of view. In the second chapter of *The Sound and the Fury*, for example, Faulkner inserts brief italicized passages of stream of consciousness into Quentin Compson's first-person narration of his conscious thoughts and actions as he walks through the streets of Boston. Here is a representative passage:

> *The street lamps would go down the hill then rise toward town* I walked upon the belly of my shadow. I could extend my hand beyond it. *feeling Father behind me beyond the rasping darkness of summer and August the street lamps* Father and I protect women from one another from themselves our women *Women are like that they dont acquire knowledge of people we are for that they are just born with a practical fertility of suspicion that makes a crop every so often and usually right they have an affinity for evil for supplying whatever the evil lacks in itself for drawing it about them instinctively as you do bed-clothing in slumber fertilising the mind for it until the evil has served its purpose whether it ever existed or no* He [the deacon] was coming along between a couple of freshmen. He hadn't quite recovered from the parade, for he gave me a salute, a very superior-officerish kind.

Within the stream of consciousness point of view, as within every other point of view, there are various degrees of depth possible. Most passages of stream of consciousness go only as deep as conscious thought, but in this passage Faulkner gives us two levels of Quentin's mind, both his conscious thoughts and those that lie just beneath them. In *Light in August*, he goes even deeper, giving us *three* levels of a character's mind:

> "I dont even know what they are saying to her," he thought, thinking *I dont even know that what they are saying to her is something that men do not say to a passing child* believing *I do not know yet that in the instant of sleep the eyelid closing prisons within the eye's self her face demure, pensive* ...

As Dorrit Cohn has noted in *Transparent Minds: Narrative Modes for Presenting Consciousness in Fiction*, "A sort of stratification of Joe Christmas's consciousness is suggested here, with each successive mental verb ("he thought, thinking ... believing") descending into lower depth, less clear articulation, and more associative imagery." In short, Faulkner quotes Joe Christmas's *conscious* thought and then, in italics, presents first a *semiconscious* thought that exists simultaneously with it and then the *unconscious* thought that underlies them both.

3.

These, then, are the basic techniques fiction writers may use to manipulate distance between the reader and the characters. It's important to note, however, that there are other ways that writers manipulate distance, and a more complex description of point of view would have to take them into account. Consider, for example, the question of a narrator's reliability. Both Melville's *Moby-Dick* and Grass's *The Tin Drum* are first-person novels that employ omniscience, but we feel substantially "closer" morally, intellectually, and emotionally to Ishmael than we do to Oskar Matzerath because Ishmael is clearly a reliable narrator—even when he reports thoughts Ahab has when he's alone, we never question the truth of what he says—and Oskar is an unreliable one—he is an inmate in a mental institution, after all, and he credits his omniscience to his toy drum, which he claims "tells him" about people and events he never witnessed. (There are degrees in our response to a narrator's unreliability, of course: We feel much closer to Oskar than we do to, say, the narrator of Ring Lardner's "Haircut," who thinks destroying someone's life with a practical joke is great fun.)

And just as we feel closer to a character in a play who breaks through the "fourth wall"—that imaginary wall that separates us from the actors—and speaks directly to us, so we feel closer to narrators who are conscious of addressing an audience. Both Twain's *The Adventures of Huckleberry Finn* and Hemingway's *A Farewell to Arms* are first-person novels that focus on the thoughts, feelings, and experiences of their narrators, but we feel closer to Huck, whose very first word is *You* and who addresses us throughout his narration, than we do to Frederic Henry, who tells his story as if the fourth wall were reality, not metaphor. I do not mean to suggest that Twain succeeded where Hemingway failed—far from it. Each author created the kind of distance that best directs our response to his protagonist. We are supposed to feel an affinity to Huck, who behaves nobly while thinking he's behaving badly, and we are supposed to feel some distance from Frederic Henry, who sometimes behaves badly while thinking he's behaving nobly.

When we think about point of view in our fiction, then, we should pay attention not only to the person we're using but to all the techniques that manipulate our narrator's distance from the characters. And if we remember that manipulating distance is the primary purpose of point of view, we'll write stories and novels that take fuller advantage of this all-important narrative resource.

BREAKING THE "RULES"
OF STORY STRUCTURE

By Diane Lefer

When I first started teaching, I worked with a creative writing student who produced stylish, astute literary criticism but kept turning in conventionally plotted stories that clunked their way to pat conclusions. Finally I confronted him. "What happens to all your sophistication when you sit down to write fiction?" He explained he'd once been told to pack it away until he'd mastered the so-called basics: "You have to learn to write a traditional story before you begin to experiment." To me that's like saying a musical person with great fingers but no breath control has to master the trumpet before playing the piano.

There's a mistaken premise here: The "basics" to me include attention to language, convincing characterizations, a sense of discovery and surprise, insights that make the reader stop and marvel, prose that lives and tells the truth.

QUESTIONING THE TRADITIONAL STORY

There's nothing second-rate about a traditional story. Lots of people write great ones and millions of people love to read them. For some writers, though, the form itself may feel unnatural, not suited to portraying the complexities of a world marked by ambiguity and dislocation, chaos and incongruities, where answers are suspect and bizarre juxtapositions a part of daily life.

- Do you want to go beyond telling what happened and re-create the feeling?

- Are you as interested in inner life as in outward action?

- As a reader, are you as curious to find out what an author is going to say or think next as in what the character will do?

- Do you take pleasure in what the narrator of Kafka's story "The Burrow" calls "the mind reveling in its own keenness"?

- Do you pay attention to language itself and judge stories—including your own—not just on how they read on the page, but out loud?

- Do you often discover what you're writing about only in the process of writing?

- Do you tend to order events by their emotional or psychological links rather than their chronology?

- Do you think we can best approach Truth through intuition, through hints and suggestions, that Truth flees at any direct approach?

If you answered yes to many of these questions, you probably find traditional structure confining, an obstacle to expression instead of a helpful guide. You're not alone. Consider some of the writers and readers who have questioned the premises many of us take for granted.

The traditional story revolves around a conflict—a requirement Ursula K. Le Guin disparages as the "gladiatorial view of fiction." When we're taught to focus our stories on a central struggle, we seem to choose by default to base all our plots on the clash of opposing forces. We limit our vision to a single aspect of existence and overlook much of the richness and complexity of our lives, just the stuff that makes a work of fiction memorable.

The movement of the story progresses from rising action to climax to the falling off of the denouement. Hmm, say the feminist literary critics. As poet Eloise Klein Healy pointed out to me, that sounds suspiciously like male sexual response. Which is *not*, she notes, the only way to satisfy a reader.

This doesn't mean for a moment that only women will reject the standard progression. In a *Paris Review* interview, William Goyen compared his writing process to creating the individual medallions of a quilt—"all separate and perfect as I can make them." For him, the challenge came in discovering the relationship of the parts without faking the connections, in "graft[ing] the living pieces to one another so that they finally become a living whole." Kafka began *The Metamorphosis* with the most dramatic event: "As Gregor Samsa awoke one morning from uneasy dreams he found himself transformed in his bed into a gigantic insect." I can just imagine a modern-day workshop leader telling Kafka that this transformation must happen near the *end*. But Kafka—like many contemporary writers who wonder how ordinary life goes on after great trauma and what may be revealed about us and those close to us—is not concerned with the hows and whys of the unthinkable cataclysmic event, but rather its aftermath.

In modern fiction, it's strange to talk about story climax anyway when so many stories offer a subtle realization or epiphany rather than rockets going off. As a result, the edgy juxtapositions and pulsing rhythms of an unconventional story may actually be more engaging to readers than the traditional structure in which, these days, the buildup often leads not to a bang but a whimper.

A main character must undergo a change. I like to imagine Kafka walking out of that imaginary workshop: "You want change?" he mutters. "All right, I'll give you change!" My objection to this "rule" is that experience teaches us an equally dramatic (if frustrating) truth: In spite of conflict, confrontation and crisis, people often don't, can't, or won't change.

SOME ALTERNATIVE METAPHORS

Critics have compared Amy Hempel's stories to *mosaics*: She provides scenes and information in bits and pieces until the whole picture comes together. I would go further and say she strategically leaves out a few key scenes so the reader must participate in the creation of meaning. In her powerful story "In the Cemetery Where Al Jolson Is Buried," the narrator recalls her visit to a dying friend and her inability to give all the desired support. We never see a confrontation between the two young women; though we know it happens, there's no account of the death; there's no funeral. Can't you just hear the workshop complaint: *Amy, you're avoiding the emotion.* Well, yes. The reader must fill in the incidents too painful for the narrator to recount. The story ends with a series of memories and anecdotes through which Hempel communicates a sense of the narrator's emotions without ever naming them.

I've heard author William Least Heat-Moon use the metaphor of a *wheel* to describe Native American storytelling. The heart of the story is the hub of the wheel. The storyteller moves around the circumference a bit, then down one of the spokes to touch the hub, then back to the circumference, approaching the heart again and again from different points. As with Hempel's mosaic, the listener or reader shares in the effort of creation until every spoke leads to the hub and the wheel is whole.

A story that seems to work this way is "The Water-Faucet Vision" by Gish Jen. The hub is the desire to find comfort for the pains of life. The circumference is represented through narrator Callie's life history as she grows up in a turbulent Chinese-American family, attends Catholic school and longs to be a martyred miracle-working saint, reaches adulthood, and mourns her mother's death. The narrative jumps around in time—all over the outer rim of the wheel—but whatever its starting point, every anecdote and every memory becomes another spoke leading to the desire for comfort in the face of pain. Every moment connects to the hub, the heart which is the yearning for a time when—in the story's closing words—"one had only to direct the hand of the Almighty and say, just here, Lord, we hurt here—and here, and here, and here."

A jazz musician may seem to go all over the place in a *musical improvisation*, but there's always an underlying structure to refer to and return to. The sense of liberating spontaneity is exhilarating when paired with technical proficiency and control. That's the feeling I get from Sandra Cisneros's collection, *Woman Hollering Creek and Other Stories*, a series of Mexican-American vernacular solos of such immediacy they feel effortless, though the careful crafting and choice of language and image make it clear they were not. In many of these short short stories—some no more than a page or two—Cisneros states an idea or image in the first sentence, flies away with it, and returns to the same image—the way a musician returns to a chord—to ground the story in the end. One story opens and closes with language reminiscent of a nostalgic ballad; another reads like a ranchera-style love song in paragraphs instead of stanzas. Some stories in the collection are longer, more traditional and sustained. Some are like overheard gossip sessions. The overall effect made me think of attending a concert in a plaza while watching the people around me and listening to their chatter in between songs. Cisneros even ends the book with a brass instrument flourish:

tan TÁN

¡tan TÁN!

Tim O'Brien's "How to Tell a True War Story" makes devastating use of *instant replay*. O'Brien holds up to view the memory of a terrible event in Vietnam: A man is blown up by a landmine. At such times, O'Brien writes,

"The angles of vision are skewed. ... The pictures get jumbled; you tend to miss a lot," and so he tells it again and again, differently each time, obsessed by the incident and by trying to tell it truthfully. The story's unconventional structure—replay, authorial commentary, replay, commentary—evokes the post-traumatic response while forcing the horrified and fascinated reader to face the relentless intensity and impossible-to-resolve contradictions of war.

M. NourbeSe Philip's "Burn Sugar" is a *process* story. The action is simple: The narrator, a Caribbean-born woman now living in Canada, bakes a cake from a family recipe while remembering her mother's kitchen. She describes the beating hand, the batter stiffening in resistance, the disappearance and blending of ingredients. At the same time, the language of the narrative switches between Caribbean and Canadian English. The very process of baking the cake is metaphoric on different levels, all having to do with cultural transformation and survival as well as the conflicted relationship between mother and daughter. The process bridges cultures, past and present, mother and daughter. That doesn't happen *in* the story, but rather *through* it.

If a story that rises to a climax and then falls off is "male," what sort of story would illustrate *female* textual/sexual response? Could it be a story that peaks again and again, in which waves of excitement and satisfaction are diffused throughout the text instead of being focused on a single moment near the end? Is it a story in which individual themes and incidents connect to create a sense of union or unity instead of resulting in a clear-cut choice or change?

What "happens" in Kate Braverman's chillingly seductive story "Winter Blues" is deceptively simple. The protagonist, Erica, works on a college paper about contemporary American poets while her bored daughter demands attention. As far as plot goes, that's it. But what really happens is that Braverman weaves together several themes and makes them cohere into a frightening vision of a self-destructive civilization. The Chernobyl nuclear accident hangs like a threat over the story; the poets Erica writes about are suicidal; shocking memories of life with her drug-addicted husband surface as Erica tries to keep her young child distracted. The elements of the story are not related through logic or cause and effect but through image and incantatory, almost hallucinogenic prose. Poets wear "their diseases like garlands"; the blood of Los Angeles is "a red neon wash, a kind of sea of autistic traffic lights"; the Hawaiian sky is the "pink of irradiated flamingos," and children are taught not to touch flame: "Then we touch it."

WHY LOOK FOR METAPHOR?

Obviously the alternative metaphors I've cited overlap and are not the only possibilities. And be forewarned: In reliance on metaphor, sound and rhythm, careful and evocative word choice, intuitive links, unexpected juxtapositions, and suggestion instead of statement, the unconventional story has much in common with poetry, an art form many people in our society, alas, disdain. If you choose this route, you'll have to expect a specific kind of rejection on occasion: the stodgy editor who sniffs and says, "This isn't a story, it's a prose poem," as if poetic effect diminishes a story rather than enriches it.

Why do I look for metaphors and invent labels? Isn't that just as arbitrary and rule-bound as following conventional form?

Our brains are wired so that thinking often takes the path of least resistance, the most worn path. (I suspect that's one reason why we may end up with pat predictable stories when we follow the most traditional structure. We may shunt our most original insights and deepest intuition off onto unused branch lines as we barrel down the familiar track.) Once alternative structures have been brought into conscious awareness—something metaphor can do in a suggestive rather than dogmatic way—they become internalized, part of our psychic inventory. We can intuitively select the best form for our material without always falling back on the same old scheme.

IT HAPPENS BECAUSE IT HAS TO

I don't sit down and think I'm going to write a male story today, or a female story. (Anyway, I think most great stories are hermaphroditic, with both "male" and "female" attributes.) An alternative structure usually appears naturally as a story develops—as long as I don't fight against it—because it *has* to. I may not even recognize the controlling metaphor until I start revising. Then I can keep the model in mind as I shape the story and make the elements cohere, to lessen the danger that my intuitively written story will end up too scattered, random, and meaningless to anyone other than me. For example, in a mosaic story, I'll try to see that each constituent piece, which has its own boundaries, its own shape, is juxtaposed with pieces that complement it, make it resonate. I may alternate dramatic incidents with digressions, meditations, or sections that explore the inner workings of a character's mind, but throughout, I will attempt to ensure that the same search or question or metaphor connects all of the sections, like—to use another metaphor—a thread through the hearts of many beads.

CONTINUITY VS. CHANGE

Consider one of history's great transformations, when Saul, the persecutor of Christians, became Paul, who practically created Christianity as an institution and church. But it's not unreasonable to interpret Paul's story this way: that he was vigorous, zealous, and single-minded both before and after the transformative experience. So much for change!

Still, if fictional characters appear the same at beginning and end, they're likely to seem sculpted rather than alive, and that can make a story static. But if there has to be a turning point, why not make it a shift in the *reader*? What if the *reader* changes and comes to see a character or situation in a new light?

One day I shocked myself by joining in a conversation complaining about the younger generation. When I was an adolescent, I swore I'd never forget what it was like to be a kid and would never judge teenagers cruelly or put them down, but there I was, doing just that. I reacted to my treachery by writing my story "What She Stood For." I started out by intentionally repeating and illustrating all the common negative stereotypes I had attributed to today's teens, saddling my protagonist, Kendra, with her shallow shopping mall mentality, her apparent lack of values, her flirtation with violence, her emotionally disconnected sexuality. But as I wrote, I tried to see her point of view, and found myself bringing her environment to life with all its contradictions and hypocrisy, its background of terrible but half-understood world events and troubled adults. In the course of the story, Kendra began to look almost heroic to me, striving and yearning for something better, sometimes choosing self-defeating paths because she hadn't yet been able to see any others. Kendra didn't so much change as show her shifting shape—formed by the interplay of her own intrinsic qualities and outside forces—and her possibilities. I'd begun by dismissing, despising, and satirizing her. I hope that readers changed their views as I did: first separating themselves from Kendra, laughing bitterly and shaking their heads, but eventually identifying with her struggle for self, fervently wishing her a better future.

CREATING OUT OF A PERSONAL VISION

There's a serious omission in this discussion. Where are the truly experimental writers? I haven't discussed the work of such authors as Nobel Laureate Samuel Beckett; Robert Kelly, whose "Russian Tales" are "experiments in telling," based on intuitive responses to a chart of Russian-language roots; and

Diane Williams with her postmodern broken disjunctions in *Some Sexual Success Stories and Other Stories in Which God Might Choose to Appear*. The authors I did use as examples may be unconventional, but their works are also widely read—and not just by literary sophisticates. I chose them to make a point: You can explore many possibilities in structure and form and still be entirely accessible.

All the same, I won't deny that if you hope to be a popular author and even make a living at it, you probably stand a better chance if you can write like Stephen King rather than Virginia Woolf. But I don't believe that's a matter of choice. Most writers create out of a personal vision; we each have a particular way of seeing the world.

I began this essay by telling of a student who kept struggling with traditional form. By trying to fit himself into some arbitrary category, this talented writer was unintentionally denying and deforming his gift. When he broke the "rules" for the first time and told his story as he felt it needed to be told, he produced a remarkable piece of fiction that was promptly accepted by a prestigious journal and nominated for a Pushcart Prize.

I can't promise you the same outcome if you break the rules. But if those rules hold you back, I invite you to claim your freedom.

NOTES ON NOVEL STRUCTURE

By Douglas Glover

The following is a synopsis of a lecture I have given dozens of times on how to put a novel together. I always deliver the lecture extemporaneously. It is never the same twice. And when I have tried to write it out, it goes dead at my fingertips. I've come to think of it as oral lore, not meant to be fixed on the page. But I have, over the years, managed to write a short summary of the lecture to send out to students when they need their memories refreshed. The disadvantage of this summary is that it is too concise and didactic, a bit of a sketch. It reads like a prescription: Take two of these, and a novel will pop out of you in a week. I wish it were that easy. The advantage of it is that I deal with structures the craft books and the literary critics never tell aspiring writers about: How to construct a point of view. How to construct a subplot. How to think up a theme. How to construct an image pattern. How characters in a novel think. How all these elements relate to one another.

In any case, readers should try to ignore the prescriptive language and imagine, first of all, that I am telling them how to read a novel. Then they should go to a novel they love and try to read it for the structures I have suggested are basic to the writing of novels. The beauty of form is its infinite variability. Experimental novels tend to take some of the structures I talk about and invert them or emphasize them differently than a conventional novel. But the structures remain roughly the same. Some novelists use very little image patterning. Sometimes the subplot gets confined to an amazingly tiny amount of text. Sometimes backfill expands to form a plot parallel to the main plot. Occasionally, an author will invent a device that does the job of, say, a subplot but isn't exactly a subplot. Tim O'Brien does this in his novel *In the Lake of* the *Woods*, where, instead of a subplot, he writes multiple speculative versions of the main plot. Obviously, my model is based on a simplest-case scenario: single character first- or third-person narrative. But the reader won't have to think too hard to figure out how what I say about point of view plays in a third-person multiple narrative or a first-person reminiscent narrative.

I break down the novel into six major structures: point of view, plot, novel thought, subplot, theme, and image patterning. In any actual novel, these structures are intricately folded together to form an organic unity. Teasing them apart for the purpose of discussing them separately in this present context creates an artificial impression of distinctness. Also it is important to realize that a novel is an illusion. A narrative seems to flow through time when, in fact, it is made up of a number of static structures: scenes, events, event sequences, reflective devices, repetitions, all of which are nothing but words fixed on the page. The first time we read a novel we read to experience the flow of time; it is only on rereading the book over and over that we begin to see the static structures that give the illusion of life.

POINT OF VIEW

Point of view is the mental modus operandi of the person who is telling or experiencing the story—most often this is the protagonist. This mental modus operandi is located in a fairly simple construct involving desire, significant history, and language overlay. The writer generally tries to announce the desire, goal, or need of the primary character as quickly as possible. The key here is to make this desire concrete and simple. In Tolstoy's *Anna Karenina*, Anna wants to be with Vronsky. In Joyce Cary's *The Horse's Mouth*, Gulley Jimson wants to paint pictures. In Kingsley Amis's *Lucky Jim*, Jim wants to keep his teaching job. Concrete simplicity at the outset can yield to generalization down the line if only because, with a thematic sentence here and there, any particular desire can be tweaked into standing for all human striving and aspiration. The important thing to remember: The novel is a machine of desire.

Significant history is background material that tells the story of how the main character arrives at the beginning of the novel wanting what he wants. Its significance derives from its relationship to the character's concrete desire and current situation. History that does not relate directly to this desire is not always helpful. It often makes the narrative turn flabby or worse—boring (the reader yawns, loses concentration). The key thing to remember is that significant history can be kept brief but needs to be repeated (via references, expansions, variations). These repetitions begin to give the novel a rhythm and a memory. Unless you have a really good reason for doing so, make sure that the character is passionately engaged with his desire and current situation. Don't give someone, say, a job that doesn't mean anything—a job, social station, and life circumstances should connect with desire in a significant way. Keep things passionate (love, obviously, but don't forget the negative passions—hatred and anger and fear). Once you have the desire and significant history in place, then you'll have a fairly clear idea how your character will react as new situations arise—hence the modus operandi idea.

The device of language overlay involves diction, syntax, and figurative language: Your character needs to talk and think in terms that reflect his passionate attachment to life (desire and significant history). For example, in my novel *Precious* the protagonist is a newspaperman; on the first page of the novel, a tavern hides across a street "like an overlooked misprint between jutting office towers." At another point, the protagonist starts thinking in newspaper headlines. Conversely, it would have been a faux pas to have him start thinking in sailing metaphors. Here is Gulley Jimson, a passionate painter, describing the Thames in *The Horse's Mouth*:

> Sun all in a blaze. Lost its shape. Tide pouring up from London as bright as bottled ale. Full of bubbles and every bubble flashing its own electric torch. Mist breaking into round fat shapes, china white on Dresden blue. Dutch angels by Rubens della Robbia. Big one on top curled up with her knees to her nose like the little marble woman Dobson did for Courtauld. A beauty.

The diction and figurative language are drawn straight from the heart of the perceiving subject.

PLOT

Plot is rather complicated and to discuss it we need to break it down into smaller issues. It also helps to use a diagram. I like to draw what I call railroad track diagrams (an exercise that can be tried at any point in the writing process—at the beginning or after several drafts). By "railroad track diagrams" I mean train tracks as they are often represented on maps: a single line with perpendicular crossbars at regular intervals. If you draw this as a semicircular arch, it brings to mind an "arc of action." Later, as you develop scenes, events, sequences of events, and/or plot steps. you can attach little balloons with text to the perpendicular crossbars and the train track becomes a plot diagram. But start by putting an *A* at one end and a *B* at the other. *A* needs to be a question. Generally this question relates to the concrete desire of the protagonist: Will he get what he wants? It's very simple. The end of the novel then becomes equally simple. *B* will be an answer to the question: yes or no. Answering yes or no doesn't limit you as to tone or degree of closure. You can immediately add a structural *but*-construction to shade this simple answer. For example, Bill wants to marry Sue, Bill gets to marry Sue, but he discovers he is gay and locked in a loveless marriage. In *Lucky Jim*, Jim wants to keep his job teaching at a third-rate English university. By the end of the novel, he has lost his job but found a much better one. In *Anna Karenina*, Anna wants to be with Vronsky. By the end of the novel, she has gotten her wish, but the reality of life with Vronsky drives her to despair and suicide. In *The Horse's Mouth*, Gulley finally gets to paint his masterpiece, but the wall he is painting it on is demolished and he ends up in hospital. But—this is a double *but* ending—he is happy. In any case, deciding how the question will be answered gives you the general direction of the book.

Next you begin to fill in between *A* and *B* with events, plot steps, or scenes. (In a novel, scenes don't always correspond to plot steps—at least to my way of thinking. An event or a plot step might involve a sequence of scenes and summary. I tend to use terms like *plot step* or *event* or *event sequence* so that students don't jump straight to the idea of "scene." Part of this is a question of level as well. At a certain level, a novel plot might consist of six large actions—call them events or event sequences or plot steps, but each of these might be broken down into a number of smaller events, sequences of events, plot steps, or scenes, and so on.) Sometimes you have a few events in your head or a collection of characters and an ending. Sometimes you already have a whole novel draft to work with. In any case, you now begin to fill in those little balloons attached to the train tracks in the diagram with notes about events. You try to put them in order, arrange a rough sequence and a climax. Then you keep doing versions of this as you add more events and as you reconstruct events based on certain other structural principles that need to be taken into consideration.

For example, you need to think of the novel as a dramatic action: intention (desire, question)–resistance (conflict)–climax. The key here is to develop a consistent resistance, the force pushing against the achievement of the concrete desire. The novel as a whole will have a dramatic structure (you get to decide where on the railroad diagram you want to put your climax), but each event along the way to the climax needs also to have a dramatic structure that is a smaller version of the larger dramatic structure. The main character will go into each event or plot step or scene wanting something, usually something that will help her attain that concrete goal, and then she encounters resistance. You can think of every scene or event as a win-lose situation and you decide (and this is a decision of tone—light or dark—and a decision of structure—will the character achieve her goal?) how close or how far from winning the character comes in each scene.

Then, finally, you need to construct your sequence of events and scenes so that each leads logically into the next. I say "logically" where a lot of how-to writers say "causally"—both words evade the essential issue. In each scene, you have a situation and a conflict and a win or loss at the end; and at the end of each scene you need to get into the shoes of your primary character and "feel" what he wants to do next. The key here is to realize that what I call ordinary human motivation is the causal factor moving the plot from one event to another. Just keep asking yourself: Given what's happened and what my character wants, what does he do next (this can be as simple as deciding where he points his feet when he takes his next step)? You then need to test your sequence of events on this what-would-he-do-next? line.

This should give you a fairly solid plot—and, of course, you'll probably be writing the novel as you produce these successive train track models. It's important to realize that this kind of experiment with scene and sequence and event is not exactly an outline. Rather it's a process of thinking about plot. It's not the sort of thing one does once and never has to return to again. It's an evolving project. In every novel I have written, I have found sequences that needed to be re-plotted again and again, either taking out or putting in steps. This is partly because writing is driven by sentences; sentences you write at the beginning of a novel can have drastic effects, even at the level of plot, as the novel develops.

NOVEL THOUGHT

In connection with plot, creating plot, and plot continuity, novelists use what I call novel thought to sew the novel together. Novel thought is very stylized and systematic, unlike real thought. It functions by concentrating on time and motive. Characters are always doing three things:

1. Looking back, remembering where they have been and why they have come to where they are. This happens over and over, obsessively, as it were,

so that the reader is forever being reminded of the character's past or earlier events in the novel as seen from the character's perspective as well as the character's current motivation. For example, here is Gulley Jimson in *The Horse's Mouth* thinking at the end of a scene in which he has telephoned his old patron Hickson and tried to extract more money from him, this after just being released from jail for harassing the same man. Gulley suffers from what we now call poor impulse control.

> In fact, I realized that I had been getting upset. I hadn't meant to say anything about burning Hickson's house down. Now, when I say anything like that, about shooting a man or cutting his tripes out, even in a joke, I often get angry with him. And anything like bad temper is bad for me. It spoils my equanimity. It blocks up my imagination. It makes me stupid so that I can't see straight. But luckily I noticed it in time. Cool off, I said to myself. Don't get rattled off your centre. Remember that Hickson is an old man. He's nervous and tired of worry. That's his trouble, worry. Poor old chap, it's ruining any happiness he's got left. He simply don't know what to do. He sends you to jug and it makes him miserable, and as soon as you come out you start on him again. And he's afraid that if he gives you any money, you'll come after him more than ever and fairly worry him to death.

2. Assessing where they are now: What am I doing? Why am I doing it? Why is that other character doing what he is doing? What does this look like? What does it remind me of? (Thought is action. Characters don't necessarily have to be right in their assessments; they just have to be true to themselves in the context of what's gone before.) Here is Jim Dixon thinking in *Lucky Jim*. He's at a dance party with a set of awful phonies, but he is hoping to meet up with a girl who turns out to be his major love interest. He steps outside to wait. Note the run of rhetorical questions, a classic device of novel thought.

> Feeling less hot, Dixon heard the band break into a tune he knew and liked; he had the notion that the tune was going to help out this scene and fix it permanently in his memory; he felt romantically excited. But he'd got no business to feel that, had he? What was he doing here, after all? Where was it all going to lead? Whatever it was leading towards, it was certainly leading away from the course his life had been pursuing for the last eight

months, and this thought justified his excitement and filled him with reassurance and hope. All positive change was good; standing still, growing to the spot, was always bad. He remembered somebody once showing him a poem which ended something like "Accepting dearth, the shadow of death." That was right, not "experiencing dearth," which happened to everybody. The one indispensable answer to an environment bristling with people and things one thought were bad was to go on finding out new ways in which one could think they were bad. The reason why Prometheus couldn't get away from his vulture was that he was keen on it, and not the other way around.

3. Looking ahead: Given what's just happened, what do I want to do next? What plan can I make? What do I think the other character(s) will do next? How will I react to that? Here is Jim Dixon again, planning a lecture on which his academic career depends.

Avoiding thinking about Margaret, and for some reason not wanting to think about Christine, he found his thoughts turning toward his lecture. Early the previous evening he'd tried working his notes for it up into a script. The first page of notes had yielded a page and three lines of script. At that rate he'd be able to talk for eleven and a half minutes as his notes now stood. Some sort of pabulum for a further forty-eight and a half minutes was evidently required, with perhaps another minute off for being introduced to the audience, another minute for water-drinking, coughing, and page-turning, and nothing for applause or curtain calls. Where was he going to find this supplementary pabulum? The only answer to this question seemed to be ... Yes, that's right, where? Ah, wait a minute; he'd get Barclay to find him a book on medieval music. Twenty minutes at least on that, with an apology for "having let my interest run away with me." Welch would absolutely eat that. He blew bubbles for a moment with the milk in his spoon at the thought of having to transcribe so many hateful facts, then cheered up at the thought of being able to do himself so much good without having to think at all. "It may perhaps be thought," he muttered to himself, "that the character of an age, a nation, a class, would be but poorly revealed in anything so apparently divorced from ordinary habits of thought as its music, as its musical culture." He leant forward impressively over the cruet. "Nothing could be further from the truth."

These various kinds of thought, their temporal modes (call them recapitulative, grounding, and anticipatory), should be in the text continuously. Characters should always be connecting events in their own heads (so the reader can remember and see the connection). Every chapter, event, plot step, or scene should have some memory of or reference to earlier events—that is, every movement forward in the text needs to include a glance back. And every chapter, event, plot step, or scene should look ahead—that is, have reference to what's coming up (in the form of a plan or an expression of desire or fear, etc.). All these references occur in the point-of-view character's mind, in novel thought.

Over and over in novels you'll find a pattern. The chapter opens, then there will be a tiny bit of backfill connecting this chapter to the last one, maybe a summary of events or plot steps leading to this point, and a clear sense of what the character plans to get out of the coming scene(s). Then, as the chapter closes, you will find a section of reflection on what has just happened and a moment of decision or planning—Where do I turn next? A novel is always making connections with itself in the form of novel thought; novel thought links events by reminding the reader of what's already happened in the text and, crucially, by establishing motivation for what's to come. (A corollary of this principle is that if you can't write a piece of novel thought that logically connects one event with the next, then you almost certainly have a plot problem.)

Finally, it's important to see how novel thought connects with the device of point of view, the narrating consciousness of the novel, or the modus operandi of this narrating consciousness. I talked earlier about point of view in terms of concrete desire, significant history, and language overlay. Now add to this the idea that novel thought must be an expression of the point-of-view complex. It's important for any novelist to invent a point of view that can perceive the world of the novel adequately. By "adequately," I mean the point of view needs to be able to filter for the reader all the facets, complications, interrelationships, histories, ironies, and nuances the novelist wishes to get across. Many beginning novelists mistakenly limit themselves by faulty invention of point of view, that is, they invent a point of view too stupid or inarticulate or psychologically limited to see the world of the novel properly. Here is Henry James, in his preface to *The Golden Bowl*, writing about his point-of-view structure:

The Prince, in the first half of the book, virtually sees and knows and makes out, virtually represents to himself everything that concerns us ... Having a consciousness highly susceptible of registration, he thus makes us see the things that may most interest us reflected in it ... and yet after all never a whit to the prejudice of his being just as consistently a foredoomed, entangled, embarrassed agent in the general imbroglio, actor in the given play. The function of the Princess, in the remainder, matches exactly with his; the register of *her* consciousness is as closely kept—as closely, say, not only as his own, but as that (to cite examples) either of the intelligent but quite unindividualised witness of the destruction of "The Aspern Papers," or of the all-noting heroine of "The Spoils of Poynton," highly individualised *though* highly intelligent; the Princess, in fine, in addition to feeling everything she has to, and to playing her part just in that proportion, duplicates, as it were, her value and becomes a compositional resource, and of the finest order, as well as a value intrinsic.

SUBPLOT

You need to have a clear idea of your plot structure in order to construct an appropriate subplot. A subplot or subplot-like device is a distinguishing characteristic of the novel as opposed to the short story; you need at least one for a novel (of course, there are exceptions, but they are usually very short novels), whereas in short stories you can do without them. In its simplest and most direct form the subplot is another plot, involving another set of characters, weaving through the novel (obviously, characters can and do act on both plot and subplot lines). Sometimes a subplot expands to about the same amount of text as the main plot and becomes a parallel plot.

As I say, you have to know how the main plot works in order to construct the subplot because the subplot has to bear a particular relationship to the main plot: It has to be congruent or antithetical. In *Anna Karenina*, for example, the main plot is about Anna's adulterous and tragic affair with Vronsky. The subplot, bulked up in terms of the amount of text to a parallel plot, is about Levin's dutiful and successful marriage. The plot and subplot are opposites (and there is a third plot—the Oblonsky plot, also a story of adultery—which is congruent with the main plot). I know I make this sound a bit geometrical.

Aldous Huxley in *Point Counter Point* has his novel-writing character describe it slightly differently: "A novelist modulates by reduplicating situations and characters. He shows several people falling in love, or dying, or praying in different ways—dissimilars solving the same problem. Or, *vice versa*, similar people confronted with dissimilar problems."

If the subplot bears the proper relation to the main plot, then you get the resonating or echoing effect that you want. To my mind, this subplot resonance is the key to what we call the "aliveness" of a novel—contrary to popular opinion, which seems to hold that aliveness comes from verisimilitude. Subplot resonance is also one of the ways of giving a novel the sense of being about a world teeming with people, when it will most often be about a small group of characters. In an essay on *King Lear*, W.B. Yeats called the effect of subplotting "the emotion of multitude."

> The Shakespearian drama gets the emotion of multitude out of the subplot which copies the main plot, much as a shadow upon the wall copies one's body in the firelight ... Lear's shadow is in Gloucester, who also has ungrateful children, and the mind goes on imagining shadows, shadow beyond shadow, till it has pictured the world. In *Hamlet*, one hardly notices, so subtly is the web woven, that the murder of Hamlet's father and the sorrow of Hamlet are shadowed in the lives of Fortinbras and Ophelia and Laertes, whose fathers, too, have been killed.

Generally, subplots involve a second or third set of characters who are closely related to the main set of characters. Tolstoy, in his letters, said he always used other family members as subplot characters. In *Anna Karenina*, the main plot is between Anna and Vronsky, the parallel plot is between Levin and Kitty, and the smaller subplot is between Oblonsky (Anna's brother) and his wife (Kitty's sister). Anne Tyler also uses family members for subplot characters in her novel *The Accidental Tourist* (main plot—Macon and the dog trainer; subplot—Macon's sister and his editor; lesser subplot—Macon's brothers). But there is also the upstairs-downstairs novel, in which the plot and subplot are distributed among social classes (*Don Quixote* is a good example—Quixote and his servant Sancho Panza have parallel plots with divergent outcomes; Tobias Smollett followed Cervantes—see his novel *Humphry Clinker*, where the contrast is between Squire Bramble and his sister and their servants; a good modern instance is John Fowles's *The French Lieutenant's Woman*). And a group of friends or schoolmates or army buddies can provide the same opportunities (e.g., Mary McCarthy's *The Group*). The advantage of the near relations between characters on plot and subplot lines is that they can interact with and observe one another naturally. This mutual awareness creates opportunities for thematic commentary that cuts both ways.

There is one interesting variation on the subplot that gives some people trouble. This is the structure sometimes called first-person biographical narrative. Examples include Conrad's *Heart of Darkness*, Fitzgerald's *The Great Gatsby*, and John le Carré's *The Russia House*. In these texts, the first-person narrator (Marlow, Nick Carraway, and George Smiley, respectively) is telling someone else's story. But in each case, the first-person narrator, the point-of-view character, has a story also, and this story is related to the main plot as a subplot. But there is an interesting element of gradation here. The subplot characters are not as passionately given to their desires as their main plot counterparts, not as driven to extremes. Thus Nick Carraway admires Daisy but will never achieve Gatsby's fatal obsessiveness (and seems diminished for it); Marlow follows Kurtz into the jungle but his common sense prevents him from falling for the seductions of power (at the end, having flown too close to the sun, Kurtz dies; Marlow almost dies); and while his agent risks his life in Soviet Russia to rescue the woman he loves, George Smiley, safe in England, can't summon the passion to save his own marriage. The inner story and the outer story resonate with each other because they have similar structures. This element of gradation is a fairly common aspect of the relationship between plot and subplot.

In any case, writing a novel involves weaving back and forth between plot and subplot. You can invent more than one subplot. You can have more or less text devoted to a subplot. You can and should probably have direct contacts between people in the plot and people in the subplot., etc. For learning about subplot, I send people to Tolstoy, or to *Wuthering Heights*, or to *The Accidental Tourist*. It's important when teaching yourself (by reading) how to handle subplots to find the exact points at which main plot text shifts to subplot text and back again. Only in this way will you become aware of the range of variation in the subplot structure.

THEME

I define theme as a general usable statement of the author's belief about the world and human nature. A theme is usable if it incorporates a statement of human desire and a further statement about how the world works to thwart or interfere with that desire. A phrase like "the conflict between men and women" is not a thematic statement because it doesn't talk about yearning and resistance. There is a sense in which talking about theme this way always takes me back to Freud and his mythic conception of the struggle between the Pleasure Principle and the Reality Principle. In a sense, every novel, at its thematic base, is the story of a human infant encountering the grim reality of other wills, scarcity, work, choice, loss, and evil. Every plot focuses on the disconnect between the self and the world.

There are many ways of arriving at a theme. You can buy one off the rack, which is basically what you do when you choose to write a genre novel. Or you can find something topical in the journalistic sociology of the day. Often authors who do this write novels without ever thinking about theme. But it seems to me the best themes evolve out of deeply held personal beliefs. One generally arrives at theme over a period of time and thought, usually focused on the material the author has chosen to work with, that is, the novel itself. Sometimes theme doesn't become clear for several drafts. To arrive at your theme (if you're not lucky enough to figure out what you are doing right away), you need to ask yourself over and over: What does this material illustrate to me about what I believe to be the way the world works? The key here is that you have to arrive at some rock-bottom belief of your own—it doesn't have to be right, to agree with modern therapeutic or sociological theory or be politically or statistically correct or jibe with what your mother told you when you were three. It just has to be something you believe, rather than something you've been taught or told to believe.

You then enunciate your theme in the text of your novel and repeat it over and over—not verbatim but in various forms and from different points of view. Obviously, the plot/subplot structure of the novel gives plenty of opportunity for this in dialogue or in novel thought: characters thinking about their own situations, characters observing and commenting on characters on other plot lines. And obviously, it helps if you have invented a narrating consciousness that is capable of enunciating the theme without sounding out of voice. The passage of novel thought from *Lucky Jim* quoted earlier is a fair example of novel thought rising to the level of a thematic statement. Here is a lively thematic moment from Saul Bellow's *Henderson the Rain King*. Notice the essential temporal plasticity of novel thought. Henderson is wandering among the tribes of Africa, but part of this moment is remembering and reinterpreting a much earlier scene in the novel with his wife.

I put my fist to my face and looked at the sky, giving a short laugh and thinking, Christ! What a person to meet at this distance from home. Yes, travel is advisable. And, believe me, the world is a mind. Travel is mental travel. I had always suspected this. What we call reality is nothing but pedantry. I need not have had that quarrel with Lily, standing over her in our matrimonial bed and shouting until Ricey took fright and escaped with the child. I proclaimed I was on better terms with the real than she was. Yes, yes, yes. The world of facts is real, all right, and not to be altered. The physical is all there, and it belongs to science. But then there is the noumenal department, and there we create and create and create. As we tread our anxious ways, we think we know what is real. And I was telling the truth to Lily after a fashion. I knew it better, all right, but I knew it because it was mine—filled, flowing, and floating with my resemblances; as hers was with *her* resemblances. Oh, what a revelation! Truth spoke to me. To *me*, Henderson!

The general human desire of the theme should be connected clearly with the specific concrete desire of the main character, that is, the concrete desire of the main character (who, in the simplest model, is also the point-of-view character) should be a particular instance of the general desire. The concrete desire defines the plot question that begins the novel and structures its plot arc. The structure of the plot arc is repeated or contrasted in the subplots. In this way, the novel, with its desire, question, plot, thought, and subplot(s) in proper relation, will throughout reflect a consistent pattern of ideas or theme. It will have unity, coherence, focus, and resonance.

IMAGE PATTERNING

Now add to this some sense of how image patterning works. An image is something available to sensory apprehension that can be inserted into a piece of writing in the form of a word or words. (The structure I describe also extends to idea patterning—e.g., the ideas of lightness and heaviness in Milan Kundera's *The Unbearable Lightness of Being*—or word patterning in which the words refer to concepts instead of sensory details—e.g., in her novel *The Quest for Christa T.*, Christa Wolf constructs an elaborate pattern based on words such as *measure* and *sickness*.) An image pattern is a pattern of words and/or meanings created by the repetition of an image. The image can be manipulated or "loaded" to extend the pattern by: 1) adding a piece of significant history, 2) associating and/or juxtaposing, and 3) ramifying or "splintering" and "tying-in." "Splintering" means splitting off some secondary image associated with the main or root image and repeating it as well. "Tying-in" means to write sentences in which you bring the root and the split-off image back together again.

Some authors get very good at this. I've managed to bring as many as three and even four patterns back together again in the same sentence. For example, on the last page of *The Life and Times of Captain N.*, my character Oskar writes: "Sometimes I dream there are only the Masks. I walk in a Forest of Trees carved with Masks, a Forest of Masks. Then a roaring, gibbering, whirling Wind comes & sweeps them away." The running patterns are mask, forest, whirl, and wind. In my novel *Elle*, I wrote: "I pack meat in a rolled-up sealskin, along with Itslk's stone knife, skin drum, lamp and bear statue, a tinder box and Leon's tennis ball, throw on my feather bags, fasten the bearskin over my shoulders with a couple of bone pins, and strap two tennis racquets to my feet, for the snow is still deep among the trees." This sentence ties in three major running patterns—bear, tennis ball, tennis racquets—as well as a couple of lesser ones.

Image patterning gives a novel: 1) a sense of "strangeness" that works against verisimilitude and is a factor in the so-called "poetry" of the piece; 2) an echo effect, a repetitive quality that creates a kind of "story memory," which, like the structural repetition in subplotting, helps give the reader the sense that the book is a coherent world; 3) a rhythm; and 4) a root effect that promotes organic unity (the threads connecting the pattern in the text are like the roots of a tree holding the soil together). A boss image is a species or subset of repeating image in which a single overarching image controls the meaning of the story. Margaret Atwood's novel *Cat's Eye* is a good example of this. Elaine Risley's cat's-eye marble is the root image that controls the figurative meaning of the novel. Symbols are simply images that have been loaded with meaning. By loading, again, I mean the process by which a writer adds to and extends the meaning of the bare image. An image that is not repeated and/or loaded is mere incidental description. But in great writing, there is very little that can be classed as mere description. Image patterning, loading, and repetition are basic principles in the generation and control of narrative material.

For a quick example of how point of view, plot, subplot, point of view, theme, and image pattern function in a particular work, look at my Revolutionary War novel *The Life and Times of Captain N.* It is constructed by weaving together three parallel plots (a variation of the plot/subplot structure), each with a different point of view: the Loyalist Captain Hendrick Nellis, his son Oskar, and a girl named Mary Hunsacker. The concrete desire of all three is to go home (they have been displaced by the American Revolution). The question of the novel is: Will they get home? The answer for Hendrick is no, but he'll build a copy, an imitation home in Canada, which is what he's doing when he dies. The answer for Oskar is no; he'll reluctantly end up in Canada after the Revolution. The answer for Mary is yes; she makes a new home for herself among the Mississauga Indians in Canada, but then loses that as well.

The theme of the book is that contact with the Other (race, language, gender) creates a zone of marginality in which the rules by which we identify ourselves become confused—hence, it is a zone of freedom and loss. The natural human reaction is to want to retreat to identity (represented by the concrete image "home"). But there is also part of us that yearns for that zone of confusion, for difference and otherness, for love and freedom. The theme is conveyed through the actions of the characters as the war forces them out of their homes into the inter-zone of the forest, where they live among Indians. In their thoughts (novel thought) the characters mull over what's happened to them and what they plan to do, but the three points of view are quite distinct—each approaches the thematic material from a different angle. Angry at the betrayals of history, Hendrick finds he likes Indians better than his own people and embraces the painful passage into Otherness on his deathbed. Oskar, who wants to be a modern American and writes chatty letters to George Washington, registers panic and discomfort but is the primary narrator, the writer of all the words. And Mary falls in love with the Indian boy who tries to kill her with his death maul; becoming someone new is not so difficult for her. Novel thought also extends into a fourth narrative element, a series of essay fragments titled "from Oskar's Book about Indians," which are more or less lengthy aphorisms contrasting white European culture and Native American culture. (Once you understand the basic principles of novel thought, the structure can be expanded in all sorts of ways.)

Finally the theme is also bodied forth in a cluster of images and concepts—border, frontier, margin, translation—that spread throughout the book. The root image pattern of the novel is the Whirlwind Mask, an ancient Iroquois mask which is divided down the middle, one side painted black, the other red. A picture of the mask painted on a rock is the first thing Hendrick sees at the beginning of the novel. He recognizes it immediately as the image of the migraine headaches he suffers, which he ties (in novel thought) directly to the multiplicity of languages (the otherness) in his head and the chaos of the war. Everyone in the novel ends up with some version of this split superimposed on his or her face. And the image splinters and ramifies into multiple ongoing lines: whirlwind, whirl, wind, mask, face (the Iroquois word for *death* means "without a face"), shadow, forest (a character carves a series of masks into living trees), and split, among others.

The final picture of the novel, when all these devices are working together, is an organized unity, a kind of total awareness within the novel itself of its own agenda, its parts, its themes and structures and patterns which are woven back and forth through its fabric.

WAKE UP AND GO TO SLEEP:

Dreams and Writing Fiction

By Philip Graham

It is not true, it is not true
that we come to this earth to live.
We come only to sleep, to dream.
—Aztec philosopher, quoted in
Miguel Léon-Portilla's
Aztec Thought and Culture

To read is to dream, guided by
someone else's hand.
—Fernando Pessoa,
The Book of Disquiet

Sleep can (or should, if we're lucky enough to get close to the eight hours a night we deserve) occupy a third of our lives. In other words, any person who makes it to the ripe old age of sixty has likely been asleep for twenty of those years. Asleep, but not necessarily unaware, because this vast sleepscape has, as its capital city, the dream.

Dreaming, however, remains an elusive territory of the human experience: We can forget our dreams soon after waking, or never remember them at all. And if we remember, our dreams may seem anomalous, confusing excursions that fade before our pressing daily lives. This might explain why, when a fiction writer's characters go to sleep in a story or a novel, the writer seems to go to sleep as well. Why do we as writers not wonder more at the relative lack of dreams in the fictions we read, and write, a lack so out of proportion to the amount of time we spend dreaming in our lives? Why, so long after Freud and Jung, is the dreamworld still largely uncharted territory?

There's certainly no lack of drama in the dream world, as can be seen from this excerpt from John Updike's novel, *Couples*:

> The luxurious plane of his dream was gliding as if motionless through the sky; the backs of heads and hands receded tranquilly down the length of aqua-carpeted aisle. The pilot's voice ... jubilantly announced over the loudspeaker system, "I think we've slipped it, folks!" and through his little rubber-sealed porthole Piet saw a wall of gray cloud, tendrilous and writhing, slowly drift backward, revealing blue sky. They had evaded a storm. Then the plane rocked and jerked in the bumpy air currents; it sank flatly through a gap in the atmosphere, grabbed for something, missed, slipped, tilted. The angle of tilt increased; the plane began to plunge. The huge hull rushed toward earth. The delicately engineered details—the luminously stenciled seat numbers, the chrome rivets holding the tinted head napkins—stayed weirdly static amid the rising scream of the dive. Far down the aisle, a stewardess, her ginger hair in a high stiff coiffure, gripped the seats for support, and there was no acknowledgment of the horror, no outcry.

Though Updike signals from the start that this passage is a dream, we are soon caught in the scene's tension. Its logic grabs us, and we're swept along, because we've all had this experience in our own private night worlds, of following a narrative to its seemingly inevitable conclusion. Surely we can invite more of the dramas we dream into our fiction.

Drawing on current research as well as examples from fiction, I hope to demystify the fluid nature of dreaming by examining the connections between the structure and inventiveness of dreams and their connection to the persistent imaginings of waking life, and to the process of writing.

In our culture, the sentence "It was only a dream" is a commonly accepted dismissal of our experiences while asleep. In other societies, however, the sentence would be nonsensical. A seminal anthology, *Dreaming: Anthropological and Psychological Interpretations*, offers numerous examples: In northern Mexico, for example, the Rarámuri Indians believe that dreaming is a time of danger, when their souls might encounter malevolent spirits; Rastafarians refer to both dreams and daydreams as visions; a good part of Moroccan life is devoted to trying to distinguish between "God-given" dreams and "deceitful" dreams outside of Islamic tradition; and the Sambia people of Papua New Guinea believe dreams are narratives of actual events that happened to their souls.

However remote these beliefs may be from the "common knowledge" of our culture, it's still shocking to read these words of Richard Ford, from his interview with Naomi Epel in the anthology *Writers Dreaming*: "I have never in my life been as bored as I have been by my friends telling me their dreams. ... I can't think of any reason I should tell a dream to anybody that could be anything more to someone else than watching cartoons on Saturday morning." Happily, Ford's is a lonely voice discounting dreams in this excellent anthology, yet even those interviewed writers most enamored of the power of dreams (John Barth, Isabel Allende, Amy Tan, and Charles Johnson among them) speak more of how their dreams have inspired breakthroughs in their writing, and much less about if and how they include dreams in their fictions. If dreams can so influence the creative act, it seems odd that we as writers don't allow ourselves to explore more often our characters' inner lives when sleeping, or allow our characters' dreams to influence their waking lives.

Certainly dreams can be confoundingly difficult to write about. This difficulty reminds me of how hard it is to write about coincidences—another common feature in our lives. We all experience coincidences—some are minor curiosities in a busy day, while others can have a profound effect on the trajectory of our lives. But a dramatized coincidence can be the death of a story, particularly if that coincidence too easily unties a dramatic knot. In such a case, the writer appears to be coasting to an easy resolution. However, a reader will more likely accept a coincidence if its arrival in a story complicates the narrative, deepens its possibilities. Ah, this feels more like life: trouble that appears from an unexpected corner.

In a similar fashion, a dream whose symbolism too obviously serves as a story's subtext, or explains what's not being explained elsewhere in the story, will make the writer appear lazy. The writer will also run the risk of looking ignorant, because readers know that dreams often confound as much as they illuminate. Even the wisest dreams can remain elusive, and a fictional dream will have a better chance of being accepted by a reader if it combines clarity and insight with ambiguity and mystery. Of course it's not easy to do this: Writing about dreams will always be fraught with false paths and unforeseen traps. But why would any writer wish to avoid taking on what is difficult, especially when embracing that difficulty could lead to more compelling characterization and a richer fictional world?

While dreams may be terrain that could challenge even the fittest writer, their place in our experience is also so common that they can be shockingly easy to overlook. And yet so bracingly welcome when revealed. Andrew Allegretti certainly provides a moment of recognition when he begins his short novel, *A Fool's Game*, with the sentence, "The doctor and the doctor's wife lay close in their close bed, their bodies stirring with restless dreams." First Allegretti allows us access to the doctor's dream, which changes from an unfamiliar street to a coffeehouse, then to an expanse of high hills, where the doctor's dream self realizes that he's searching for a young man with whom he had an erotic encounter more than twenty years ago. When the doctor wakes, he's aroused, though he is not sure for whom. Beside him his wife still sleeps. Allegretti then provides the reader with her dream, an encounter with her husband, who "opens his shirt, shows her a gaping wound there in his chest, not red, but blue—a cavity filled with sunlight and sky and tiny, drifting white clouds." She wakes, her dream gone, but she somehow knows that "something is missing. Something has been misplaced."

These dreams resolve nothing in their relationship; upon waking the couple soon go about their morning rituals, the truths of their separate dreams left behind. Though one almost never reads of parallel dreamscapes, these twinned interior states play themselves out within couples who lie beside each other in bed millions, billions of times around the world every night. It's one of the most common features of human existence, far more common than those same couples having sex that night, or having breakfast together the next morning.

Perhaps another difficulty in writing about dreams is that our Western-based culture constructs a gulf between the dreaming and the waking state, blinding many of us to their very real connections. Consider, for example, the Portuguese poet Fernando Pessoa, who writes in his prose masterpiece, *The Book of Disquiet*, "I'm almost convinced that I'm never awake. I'm not sure if I'm not in fact dreaming when I live, and living when I dream, or if dreaming and living are for me intersected, intermingled things that together form my conscious self." Most of us, I suspect, at least secretly feel this process at work within ourselves, and it is, after all, common two-way traffic for any writer or poet. But the anthropologist Barbara Tedlock reminds us that in 1900 the French psychiatrist Theodore Flournoy postulated that some part of the unconscious continually made fictions, day and night, and this professional hunch has been borne out by recent research about the structure of the brain.

Dr. Rudolfo Llinas, chief of physiology and neuroscience at the New York University School of Medicine, has spent forty years studying brain cells. As reported by Philip J. Hilts in *The New York Times*, Llinas has made two extraordinary discoveries. The first is the discovery of a "small knot of cells" in the brain (called, charmingly, the inferior olive), which apparently serves as a movement "pacemaker for the cells in the cerebellum … It turns out that the cells are actually 'walking' all the time; that is, they are active and producing tiny tremor-like movements of the muscles continuously." In other words, human beings never completely shut down, no matter how still our bodies may be. Our ignition, you might say, is never turned off; even when parked, the engine of our physical movement idles, ready to go.

Dr. Llinas's second and related discovery is a second "pacemaker" in the brain (called, much less charmingly, the intralaminar nucleus), and this one appears to set the rhythm for conscious thinking: "an active internal state—like walking for the cerebellum—which is then modulated by the senses." Llinas says, "If you are asleep, it is called dreaming. If you happen to be awake, and it's very strong, it is called daydreaming. If you are aware of what is happening outside at the same time, it is called thinking." Essentially, Llinas claims that the brain is a dreaming instrument, which, like the body, sometimes is idling, sometimes is more active. The brain at night, "in the absence of sensory input … is free to be as crazy as it wants to be" and in the day, "it dreams in a more limited fashion because the senses serve to limit the types of images you can generate."

If the difference between what we imagine and fantasize about during the day and what we dream about at night is only a matter of degree, then the act of dreaming as an imaginative process becomes less mysterious. That's certainly the conclusion of the sociologist John L. Caughey. In his remarkable book *Imaginary Social Worlds*, he examines the internal social experiences all of us have, our fantasy interactions with other people who are not actually present. Caughey was initially inspired to write his book because of two public events: the death of John Lennon at the hands of Mark David Chapman, who for more than fifteen years had nurtured an obsessive identification with Lennon that began to obscure his own identity; and John

Hinckley Jr.'s assassination attempt on Ronald Reagan, which was a failed attempt to strengthen his fantasy relationship with Jodie Foster.

Caughey quickly realized while conducting his research that one doesn't have to be insane or homicidal to participate in fantasy relationships. Think of your own experience. When you walk down the street, part of you maintains the physical movement of your legs (your "inferior olive" takes control: left foot, right foot, left foot …) while your mind (paced by the intralaminar nucleus) roams free. Then, when you arrive at your destination, you realize that you have no specific memory of how you got there. That's because, more than likely, you were having a drama in your mind with someone: a conversation or argument with a parent or a sibling, a spouse or a co-worker. We rehash the past, or model in advance the words we want or need to say to others, even those words we know we'll never speak but try out in our minds anyway. A young woman passing by in a mall, with a faraway look in her eyes, could be, for all anyone might know, imagining herself in conversation with her absent father. In many ways each of us is, in the words of the Mozambican writer Mia Couto, "a sleepwalker strolling through fire."

We slip into these imaginary conversations or scenarios so often that we barely notice the transitions, but our fantasy life often takes up a good deal of our time—the majority of our day, Caughey claims, and sometimes our improvised inner worlds can separate us from the world in which we live. In Dan Chaon's short story "Big Me," Andrew, the narrator, confesses the internal life he's led since he was a child: "Back then I spent a lot of time in my mind, building a city … I don't know how many of my childhood years existed in this imaginary city. Already by the age of eight I had become a Detective, and shortly thereafter I began drawing maps of the metropolis." Andrew's private obsession became so powerful it overwhelmed his other relationships. "My family thought of me as a certain person, a figure I knew well enough to act out on occasion. Now that they are far away, it sometimes hurts to think that we knew so little of one another." Andrew is deceiving himself, however, if he thinks his emotional distance is part of the past—it's also affecting his current "normal life" with his wife and daughters.

And yet, a certain amount of *everyone's* normal life includes being "away," as Caughey says in the following passage:

> We do not live only in the objective world of external objects
> and activities. On the contrary, much of our experience is inner
> experience. Each day we pass through multiple realities—we

phase in and out, back and forth, between the actual world and imaginary realms. We awake in the morning after spending six or seven hours entangled in the phantasmagorical world of dreams. During our early morning routines, we regularly drift off … As we dress, our attention wanders, we experience moments from the past, imaginatively engage in scenes of the day ahead, and silently converse to ourselves about these non-present worlds. At breakfast we may sleepily talk to our families but then, picking up the morning newspaper, we are off again, caught up in the political machinations of Washington and the doings of the sports worlds and comic strip characters. Driving to work, we are only partly aware of the familiar route. Much of the time we are "away," lost in anticipations of the hours or years ahead or in fantasies about how things might otherwise be … and so on throughout the day, hour after hour, day after day.

But *is* the world of dreams, as Caughey describes it, really all that "phantasmagorical"? This deeply held assumption of strangeness is, I think, another reason why writers too often avoid dreams in their fiction: They fear the imagery is too fantastic, too personal, for any literary reconstruction to readily engage a reader. I would argue that while a closer look at one's daily fantasy life reveals much to be found that's similar to dreaming, much that pushes the envelope of what would be considered "realism," at the same time a closer look at the bizarre twists and turns of dreams will reveal that they have their own hidden normality.

Bert O. States, in his book *Dreams and Storytelling*, claims that the bizarre is overrated in dreams: "Should a dream image suddenly break out into an impossibility—a double-headed man, a giant, a talking plant—that is simply one of the probabilities of dream transformation, like anger or fear suddenly breaking out of temperate human behavior." Indeed, we can surprise ourselves with our daily behavior, our flashes of emotion casting strange new light upon us. Dream imagery simply makes metaphoric what we suspect or fear or hope to be true—not only about ourselves, but about others as well. States says that when he dreams of his friend Paul, the dream figure is not actually his friend, but instead, "possibilities of Paul." In much the same way, fictional characters are often composites of the people they're modeled upon. As writers, we're using (just as States says we employ the figures who inhabit our dreams) "real people, or scraps of real people, as the instruments of hypothetical acts."

A version of States's "double-headed man" can be found in this passage from Leo Tolstoy's *Anna Karenina*:

> In her dreams, when [Anna] had no control over her thoughts, her position appeared to her in all its shocking nakedness. One dream she had almost every night. She dreamt that both [Alexey and Vronsky] at once were her husbands, and lavished their caresses on her. Alexey ... wept, kissing her hands, saying "How beautiful it is now!" and ... Vronsky was there too, and he also was her husband. And she was surprised that formerly this had seemed impossible to her, and laughingly explained to them how much simpler it really was, and that they were both now contented and happy. But this dream weighed on her like a nightmare, and she woke from it filled with horror.

A beautifully written, unsettling dream, but its strangeness isn't so far from what can occur in a daydream. Think of how, while walking, say, through a park, the imaginary conversation you're having with a female friend can suddenly segue into an imaginary argument with your mother—as if the one person has suddenly become the other—and this fraught scene then abruptly shifts to a moment in the past you still gnaw at like a bone. These transformations contain their own logic—an offhanded gesture typical of your friend reminds you of your mother, who then appears as if unbidden and ready to engage in an argument that had its origins in an event that occurred ten years earlier.

These instantaneous scene changes that take place inside us (by day and by night) resemble the edited crosscuts of film, where a scene can change from the desert to the streets of London in an instant, with an emotional logic that an audience has no problem following. The great film editor Walter Murch, in his book *In the Blink of an Eye*, postulates that the reason audiences accept such abrupt shifts is that they remind us of the primal leaps of dream imagery. Of course writers and poets engage in instant transitions all the time on the page: the switching of place, or narrative perspective, or the metaphoric leaps of language.

There's a further, deeper connection between dreams and writing as well. States makes, I believe, a convincing case that dreams are actually organized along very clear storytelling structures, which he says are "the brain's pervasive attempt to make sense of experience." He speculates that dreams must have been the template for the invention of storytelling—all the various fictions humans have been creating for thousands of years—because "the kinds of stories lived in dreams are lived in life as well."

A dream is a complete world, and entirely created: What we can call the actors in the dream, and the script, stagecraft, lighting, and direction, all are being created each moment—improvised—by the dreamer. How could it be otherwise, since no one else dreams our dreams? Every writer daily attempts to take responsibility for each detail in his or her fiction. Where in our lives is the template for this? Long before any of us wrote, we dreamt.

Finally, Dr. Llinas's research provides us with what I believe is one of the best reasons for writers to take dreamtime more seriously in our narratives. Because throughout the day and night the brain is "actively making both facts and fantasies," Llinas states that "our mental maps get so elaborate we get lost in them, or we hide from even ourselves. Humans are probably the only self-delusional animal." We live in the physical world, but we navigate that world with fallible inner charts of our own creation. All any writer has to do is write two simple words— "He thought," or "She imagined," or "I dreamt" —and those inner worlds open for exploration. What better subject could there be for a writer than to examine how much interior world-building and world-destruction goes on within us all, what greater challenge than to chart our uncertain inner turns, which can have such fateful repercussions in the outside world?

It's true that we have no idea what the people standing next to us in a hallway might be daydreaming, or what the people sleeping beside us are dreaming. But we can imagine, and offer that imagining with others. Then we might be able to say, as the aboriginal Australian Napangarti has said, "This is a good country; we are good dreamers."

KEEPING OPEN THE WOUNDS OF POSSIBILITY:

The Marvelous, the Uncanny, and the Fantastic in Fiction

By Christopher Noël

"Sometimes fairy stories may say
best what's to be said."
—C.S. Lewis

"A lady," writes C.S. Lewis, "… had been talking about a dreariness which seemed to be creeping over her life, the drying up in her of the power to feel pleasure, an aridity of her mental landscape. … I asked, 'Have you any taste for fantasies and fairy tales?' I shall never forget how her muscles tightened, her hands clenched themselves, her eyes started as if with horror, and her voice changed, as she hissed out, 'I *loathe* them.' … On the other side," he continues, "I know from my own experience that those who like [fantasies] like [them] with almost equal intensity. The two phenomena, taken together, should at least dispose of the theory that [this] is something trivial. It would seem … that [we're dealing with] a mode of imagination which does something to us at a deep level, [though] I am not sure that anyone has satisfactorily explained the keen, lasting, and solemn pleasure which such stories can give."

We can make some headway toward an explanation by looking at a few of the strategies and motivations involved in this species of fiction, to see what's available to us as writers, and why we might wish to push back our boundaries and embrace a greater sweep of what's possible.

I should confess right up front to a certain affinity with Lewis's "lady"; my own skin crawls not with fright but with prospective boredom at the very mention of swords and sorcery, of anything medieval (knights, wizards, etc.). And then there are fairies, dragons, witches, warlocks, vampires; even most ghosts leave me cold, and not in the good sense. Plus, we have the usual treatments of the *future*—"Captain Russell entered the chamber and sat down across from The Ohm. 'You think the Jarts will oppose us?'"—or airy New Age tales, with mist, rainbows, soft light, transcendence everywhere you look.

Our topic here, on the other hand, is what I'll call "grounded fantasy," with the emphasis on the *grounded*. Philip Van Doren Stern writes:

> Depart too far from the norm of human experience and you bore the … reader, who will no longer care what happens to your characters once they have stepped through a dozen dimensions of time and are consorting with twelve-sided green monsters somewhere in interstellar space. The true artist, who knows how to deal with elusive material, is more likely to work his tricks right in your living room, where the reality of familiar things lends strangeness to whatever he may conjure up.

Or, if it *is* a world other than "your living room," then this world must be constructed with scrupulous attention to detail, all the more so because it departs from what is generally accepted as reality. Also, the sort of fantasy I want to focus on here does not rest upon old spooky conventions; instead, it's the sheer unprecedentedness of its inventions that forms the core of its excitement, though they may spring from the same source that originally *produced* fairies, witches, vampires, and ghosts.

Back to C.S. Lewis. In his autobiography, *Surprised by Joy*, he tells of certain rare moments in his life, moments when, fleetingly, he's stabbed by what he calls "Joy." One summer day, when he was a child, standing beside a flowering currant bush, he suddenly remembered being given a miniature garden by his older brother, who had filled the lid of a biscuit tin with moss and tiny growing things. Other such moments, modest in their magic, came to him over the years from reading Norse Sagas and fantasy stories—moments of perception, of incongruity or otherness that seem to offer quick glimpses into another world; and this sheer evanescence, the *glimpse* quality, is for him part of the point. Curiosity is awakened but not quenched. This is "an experience whose quality is that of an unsatisfied desire which is itself more desirable than any other satisfaction. I call it Joy, which is here ... sharply distinguished both from Happiness and from Pleasure ... [because it is a "*stab*" that] might almost equally well be called a particular kind of unhappiness or grief. I doubt whether anyone who has tasted it would ever ... exchange it for all the pleasures in the world."

This experience maps onto the at-root-evasiveness or inconclusiveness of all genuine fantasy; even if presented in a direct and lucid manner (as in Kafka), its conceptions retain a certain opacity by virtue of their strangeness, heartier because oblique, refusing any would-be domesticating, circumscribing consciousness. Could we say that Lewis's garden in the tiny biscuit tin turned its trick by seeming to capture nature but stylizing it, defamiliarizing it through the admixture of artifice, parodying a certain dream of rational containment?

Gabriel García Márquez, too, received a joyful jolt very early in his career. "At the university in Bogota," he says in his *Paris Review* interview,

> I started making new friends and acquaintances who introduced me to contemporary writers. One night, a friend lent me a book of short stories by Franz Kafka. I went back to the pension where I was staying and began to read "The Metamorphosis." The first line almost knocked me off the bed. I was so surprised. The first line reads, "As Gregor Samsa awoke one morning from uneasy dreams he found himself transformed in his bed into a gigantic insect." When I read that line, I thought to myself that I didn't know anyone was *allowed* to write things like that. If I had known, I would have started writing a long time ago. So I immediately started writing ...

One of his first stories, "A Very Old Man with Enormous Wings," opens this way:

> On the third day of rain they had killed so many crabs inside the house that Pelayo had to cross his drenched courtyard and throw them into the sea, because the newborn child had a temperature all night and they thought it was due to the stench. The world had been sad since Tuesday. Sea and sky were a single ash-gray thing and the sands of the beach, which on March nights glimmered like powdered light, had become a stew of mud and rotten shellfish. The light was so weak at noon that when Pelayo was coming back to the house after throwing away the crabs, it was

hard for him to see what it was that was moving and groaning in the rear of the courtyard. He had to go very close to see that it was an old man, a very old man, lying face down in the mud, who, in spite of his tremendous efforts, couldn't get up, impeded by his enormous wings.

Notice how this paragraph subtly tenderizes our outlook, readying us for the startling final image by means of descriptions already at odds with our conventional way of thinking: crabs inside a house; illness potentially produced by a smell; the world itself possessing human emotion. The elements of the world, too, are melding, distinctions rubbed out, sea and sky, sparkly beach and muddy stew, becoming one, night and day homogenized by a light that is too "weak" to maintain the categories.

The story goes on to recount what Pelayo and Elisenda do with this "flesh-and-blood angel": They lock him in a chicken coop and start charging the townspeople five cents admission to see him. In the tradition of Kafka's "The Metamorphosis," García Márquez grounds the fantasy via specific sensory details—the mud, the hens pecking at his feathers, trying to find "stellar parasites," cripples pulling out feathers "to touch their defective parts with," and so forth. There's nothing airy or fairy-like about this angel—or rather, *almost* nothing. And it's exactly this "nothing" *and* this "almost," held each in its purity, that turns the trick, I think, that brings the joy. This creature is maybe ninety percent earthbound, pathetic, *non*transcendent. The remaining ten percent corresponds to Lewis's "fleeting" transcendence, to his "unsatisfied desire." García Márquez keeps strict pressure on himself to maintain this ratio till the very end, so that we may be thrilled and saddened all the more when the angel suddenly returns to the sky. Up till then, we could say, perhaps, that of this ten percent, five percent is due to the sheer fact of the wings themselves, and that the other five percent is accomplished subtly by means of language: "stellar parasites"; "chicken dung and lunar dust." Such phrases act as little bridges between our world of mud and shit and the other, celestial world. (As in metaphor, this is a yoking of dissimilars; "meta-phor" means "to carry across or beyond"; hence Nietzsche's comment, "Metaphor is a desire to be elsewhere.") In the story, we're never once permitted to outright cross over; that would disturb the steep and essential asymmetry; we're planted in *this* world, where the supernatural can only be suggested by verbal gesture and by snapshots showing the two realms intersecting, but so humbly as never to leap out at the reader. At another place in the story, a simple reference to the sun provides just a glint of a heavenly beyond: "He was lying in a corner drying his wings in the sunlight among the fruit peels and breakfast leftovers that the early risers had thrown him."

Another literary virtue we find in this story is one that's fundamental for fantasy writing per se—the matter-of-fact presentation of extraordinary material. When García Márquez has the doctor note "the logic of the wings [which] seemed so natural on that completely human organism," we believe implicitly, without having to be shown this logic directly; the doctor's is a surrogate expertise, so that merely stating that "he couldn't understand why other men didn't have them too" hits us harder than would elaborate anatomical details. Say the truth as concisely, as unflinchingly as possible, and the reader's imagination will generally rush in to fill any gaps.

García Márquez discusses just this in his *Paris Review* interview:

> [My approach] was based on the way my grandmother used to tell her stories. She told things that sounded supernatural and fantastic, but she told them with complete naturalness. ... She did not change her expression at all when telling her stories, and everyone was surprised. In [the earliest] attempts to write *One Hundred Years of Solitude*, I tried to tell the story without believing in it. I discovered that what I had to do was ... write it with the same expression with which my grandmother told hers: with a brick face.

Now let's look at Kafka's brick face. "It was no dream," he writes of Gregor Samsa's transformation into a dung beetle, and nowhere in "The Metamorphosis" are we given the slightest reason to doubt this plain narrative assurance.

> He was lying on his hard, as it were armor-plated, back and when he lifted his head a little he could see his domelike brown belly divided into stiff arched segments on top of which the bed quilt could hardly keep in position and was about to slide off completely. His numerous legs, which were pitifully thin compared to the rest of his bulk, waved helplessly before his eyes. ...
> It was no dream.

And now we witness a very similar sort of bridging between worlds employed, many years later, by García Márquez, although here of course the direction out of the everyday is toward the subhuman rather than the superhuman.

His room, a regular human bedroom, only rather too small, lay quiet between the four familiar walls. ... Gregor's eyes turned ... to the window, and the overcast sky— one could hear raindrops beating on the window gutter—made him quite melancholy. What about sleeping a little longer and forgetting all this nonsense, he thought, but it could not be done, for he was accustomed to sleep on his right side and in his present condition he could not turn himself over. However violently he forced himself toward his right side he always rolled onto his back again. He tried at least a hundred times, shutting his eyes to keep from seeing his struggling legs ...

Since we're in the mind of the monster this time, and since nothing about his body appears human, the mixture of ordinary and extraordinary is much more thorough than in the García Márquez story. What links the two approaches, however, is their careful grounding of the abnormal element, both physically and logistically. Once we accept the opening premise, which we do quite readily, everything else in "The Metamorphosis" proceeds without straining our credulity. The rules of this universe are set right away and then adhered to loyally; Gregor is a big insect and never changes back; ostracized from the fold of humanity, from his own family within the rooms of their apartment, he gets sick and gradually fades into death. Every moment of his thinking and acting seems entirely appropriate to this situation, and therefore, this situation can be accepted as allegorical—Gregor is the more deeply human, somehow, for being an appalling bug. That is, Kafka captures aspects of being a person that could not have been captured so well otherwise. "Sometimes fairy stories may say best what's to be said," wrote C.S. Lewis. Gregor is hardly a "fairy," except in the broadest sense of the term. James Thurber quotes psychologist Morton Prince: "Far from being mere freaks, monstrosities of consciousness, [authentic inventions] are in fact ... a manifestation of the very constitution of life."

To flesh out this point, here are four ways in which Gregor lets us come nearer to our humanness. The root of the word *monster*, the Latin *montrare*, means "to show," as in the word *demonstrate*.

First, identity is a tenuous thing, even a little so from moment to moment, and just tenuous enough from day to day that when we look in the mirror in the morning we take a secret breath of relief. Kafka's "what if?" pries at this fissure in our personal edifice.

Second, one's relationship with oneself is endlessly fraught and mysterious, with constant gulfs and self-retaliations. Kafka once said, "What have I in common with the Jews? Better to ask, what have I in common with *myself*?" To the extent that we identify with this protagonist—an alarming extent—Gregor's estrangement from Gregor solidifies this trouble in us, throws it into glaring relief, and thus, our own opaqueness to ourself can, itself, shine out.

Third, Gregor's hideous form further polarizes the ever-problematic duality between inside and outside, essence and appearance, "real self" and the figure one cuts through the world.

Lastly, we're finite, small and alone, sealed off from others. Emerson uses the image of an individual as a sphere that can come into contact with another sphere at one point only. Gregor's younger sister, Grete, whose violin playing he's always fostered, helps him for a while, feeding him and cleaning his room, trying to treat this nauseating vermin as none other than her dear brother; but even she never addresses him directly and eventually abandons him to the solitude of his room, which fills with dust and garbage and the family's unwanted furniture. It's the heartbreaking particularities of Gregor's ousting from the warm circle of life in the apartment that opens apertures for us to glimpse our own continual ouster, which lies beneath or alongside our ruddier sense of belonging in the world. For instance, after the family has returned to a relative normalcy, Gregor takes to peeking out the door of his dark room at his parents and sister in their lit living room. One night, Grete plays her violin and "Gregor, attracted by the playing, ventured to move forward a little until his head was actually inside the living room. ... Fluff and hair and remnants of food trailed with him, caught on his back and along his sides. ... He felt as if the way were opening before him to the unknown nourishment he craved. He was determined to push forward till he reached his sister, to pull at her skirt and so let her know that she was to come into his room with her violin, for no one here appreciated her playing ..." They spot him, the violin falls silent, then hits the floor with "a resonant note," and Grete says, "My dear parents ... I won't utter my brother's name in the presence of this creature, and so all I say is: we must try to get rid of it."

Kafka and García Márquez help us to see that we are detachable from our names, that each of us is both angel and junk, a thing to be prized and a thing to be cast away.

You know that state of being halfway between waking and sleep, when our thoughts get fluid, wildly associative and yet intensely plausible, sketchy and vivid at once. We love that, and most of us try to set up our lives so that we can be in that state as much as possible, so we can have our mind show us ridiculous things, tell us outlandish little tales, and all, so to speak, with "a brick face."

What emerges from us naturally at these moments usually fades when we get up, drink coffee, sit down to write. Fantasy writers try to battle this fading, discounting nothing. "Writing fantasy has given me more personal joy than anything I have done before," says Lloyd Alexander in his essay "Wishful Thinking—Or Hopeful Dreaming."

> I have never been so caught up in a work ... [though] I am not altogether sure why this should be so. ... First, on the very surface of it, [there is] the sheer delight of "let's pretend" and the eager suspension of disbelief. ... Still, this is only the surface. ... Below the surface, fantasy must draw on ... deeper resources ... [like] its ability to work on our emotions with the same vividness as a dream. ... Reading a fantasy, we are never disinterested bystanders. To get the most from it, we have to, in the best sense of the phrase, "lose our cool."

This is all to the good, if we remember that as writers we must, also, *retain* a level of "cool." Alexander continues, "You may set your own ground rules and, in the beginning, decree as many laws as you like—though in practice the fewer departures from the 'real' world the better."

Eleanor Cameron expands on this point in *The Green and Burning Tree*.

> The fantasist must create an inner logic for his story and ... draw boundary lines outside of which his fantasy may not wander. ... In good fantasy, anything does *not* go.

Some authors make the point that to write fantasy is to be, in a sense, actually *more* realistic than to traffic in conventional "realism," inasmuch as we are expanding into a truer relationship with existence in the broadest sense. Jorge Luis Borges told an interviewer, "I wonder if you *can* define [fantasy]. I think it's rather an intention in a writer. Really, nobody knows whether the world is realistic or fantastic, that is to say, whether the world is a natural process or whether it's a kind of dream, a dream that we may or may not share with others." And Brian W. Aldiss, writer and friend of C.S. Lewis: "'Actual life' may be a fantasy too. It's many centuries since Chuang Tzu woke from a dream that he was a butterfly to ponder whether he was a man who had dreamed he was a butterfly or a butterfly who now dreamed he was a man."

On the other hand, though, doesn't thinking like this too easily conflate two realms, smudge what feels like a fundamental dividing line? For certainly a large part of the joy depends upon the distinction between worlds, between our familiar place here and the "invented" realm. It's the difference between fact and fantasy, the friction, that generates the sparks and the heat. Fantasy, J.R.R. Tolkien says, "is founded upon the hard recognition that things are so in the world as it appears under the sun; on a recognition of fact, but not a slavery to it. ... If [we] really could not distinguish between frogs and men, fairy-stories about frog-kings would not have arisen."

All right, now we're getting somewhere; we can better look around at the terrain. But doesn't Tolkien's clarity also oddly domesticate this terrain, and us inside of it?

So let's turn back to literature, to the thing itself, briefly, before returning to C.S. Lewis, making a fascinating complaint.

In Randall Jarrell's *The Bat-Poet*, a chipmunk asks the bat to recite the following poem about an owl:

> A shadow is floating through the moonlight.
> Its wings don't make a sound
> Its claws are long, its beak is bright.
> Its eyes try all the corners of the night.
>
> It calls and calls: all the air swells and heaves
> And washes up and down like water.
> The ear that listens to the owl believes
> In death. The bat beneath the eaves,
>
> The moss beside the stones are still as death—
> The owl's air washes them like water.
> The owl goes back and forth inside the night,
> And the night holds its breath.

After the bat recites the poem, the chipmunk says, "It makes me shiver. Why do I like it if it makes me shiver?" And the bat answers, "I don't know. I see why the owl would like it, but I don't see why we like it."

The bat's good question seems to me more illuminating than most good answers. This character has *composed* this poem about the owl, yet the deadly figure retains its potency, its otherness. And yet again, there is something in the shivering that nourishes both writer and listener, that brings them to life. At the risk of muffling this "life," again, with abstraction, one could go to the concept of "psychic distance," that aesthetic phenomenon whereby the viewer of the art work—and the artist herself is also in this sense a viewer—is at one and the same time in intimate contact with and at a safe distance from what's being represented, moved by and re-moved from the drama. There's always a protective frame. For the artist, this frame is her medium; it dutifully mediates.

Now this idea sounds plausible, but it also doesn't feel quite right, does it? Maybe *it's* too framed, not immediate enough, and so tames the experience. After all, the bat and the chipmunk are anything *but* safe even as they do poetry in the forest, and yet they can love this rendering of dark danger. *We* are not safe either—shivering like bat and chipmunk—when Kafka reveals to us our constant, low-lying peril; we somehow spring to life thanks to this peril; the shivering depletes as it replenishes. Does the secret of delight hide inside the nature of being "caught"? Animals shiver when they're caught, because they're about to be eaten. We shiver when we're caught, if well caught, because we're about to be guessed, treated to a particularly emancipating exposure, determined in a tightening that loosens, takes us outside our suffocating sphere and the endless inconclusive drift of our own small subjectivity; it's a disburdenment from *mere* selfhood. On our own, we can never quite fix our position, never quite land. Of course, *any* good art, good fiction, helps us in this way, but authentic fantasy lets us stand outside not only our individual self but also the extension—our shared conventions of reality, similarly constricting. Now of course C.S. Lewis famously believed in God, and yet even he felt constricted here on Earth, never lost his longing for other worlds, his need to invent them. We yearn for ec-stacy (literally: "standing outside oneself"); without perspective, how can we recognize and embrace our own spot on the map, put our finger on it ("I am here")? Once caught out, we can plunge back *in*, as if for the first time.

A frog turns into a king; a man turns in his sleep into a gigantic cockroach; a couple discovers a winged old man stuck in the mud. We could call such occurrences true "marvels," and this is how theorist Tzvetan Todorov categorizes such fiction—"the marvelous." But in his book on extraordinary fiction, *The Fantastic*, Todorov is more interested in two other categories, "the uncanny" and "the fantastic," and to these we now turn.

Something weird takes place in a piece of fiction. We the curious readers try to determine what's really going on from evidence within the text. If everything pushes us toward a literal interpretation, we settle here, squarely inside the marvelous: In an Aesop's fable, the fox actually talks, no doubt about it. Dracula bites a woman's neck, sucks her blood, and perpetuates his immortality, no problem. In a tale by Scheherazade, the flying carpet really flies. Questions of credibility simply do not arise; ambiguity isn't welcome within these bright, magical confines.

But now suppose that ambiguity does leak in; suppose our vision of the case becomes partly obscured and we can't tell whether or not the "something weird" is to be taken as real, within the fictive world. There's a species of delight in this *un*knowing. In Ron Hansen's *Mariette in Ecstasy*, the reader is never sure whether the young woman's wounds on her hands and side are truly the result of a transcendent participation in Christ's passion or a hysterical reaction, brought on by Mariette's extreme mental state. The pleasure comes from the fact that we see vivid evidence for *both* interpretations, that what Kierkegaard called "the wounds of possibility" are scrupulously held open through to the end of the book. We're familiar with the distinction between authentic mystery on the one hand and, on the other, mere vagueness or confusion. Fruitful ambiguity provides two or more possibilities for understanding what's really going on, and gives good ground for each reading; in bad ambiguity, all's a muddle, wherein none of the options strongly compels our eye. Here, Todorov is talking about productive ambiguity:

> The fantastic ... lasts only as long as a certain hesitation: a hesitation common [in most cases] to reader and character, who must decide whether or not what they perceive derives from "reality" as it exists in the common opinion. ... "*I nearly reached the point of believing*": that is the formula which sums up the spirit of the fantastic. Either total faith or total incredulity would lead us beyond the fantastic: it is the hesitation which sustains its life. ... In the fantastic story, there is an important integration of the reader into the world of the character(s); that world is defined by the reader's own ambiguous perception of the events narrated. ... If ... he decides that new laws of nature must be entertained to account for the phenomena described, we enter the genre of the marvelous. If, on the other hand, the reader decides that the laws of reality remain intact and permit

an explanation of the phenomena, we say that the work belongs
to another genre: the uncanny.

Why the term *uncanny*? In everyday parlance, it is used broadly to mean "very strange," but for the sake of discussion, let's adopt Todorov's narrower definition: a strange occurrence that may be rationally understood as arising from the consciousness of a perceiver, rather than being externally, objectively real. Thus, the uncanny lies at the other end of the spectrum from the marvelous, and can exist within present laws of nature, which already include a flexible concept of the human senses as susceptible to illusion and, more deeply, of the mind as capable of even highly unconventional perception.

So, we have before us two poles, two very different genres of the strange, and we remember that within the fantastic, in Todorov's scheme, the reader hangs in between them, hesitant, breathless, intellectual faculties at play, tested against the rich texture of the text. In order to best position ourselves to encounter this suspended state of charged ambiguity—and given that we've spent time considering the marvelous—let's first complete the picture of the outer edges by taking a closer look for a while at the uncanny.

In German, the word is *unheimlich*. Freud's 1919 essay, "The Uncanny," was an influential treatment. It won't surprise you to hear that he places this category within the context of the given individual's psychosexual history—arresting images or visions that arise (for a patient or a fictional character) represent "the return of the repressed."

This is, of course, a rich vein to mine, but I want to zero in on what I find most intriguing within Freud's essay, his discussion of the single, central word, which reverberates throughout the essay. He says, "The German word *unheimlich* ['uncanny'] is [apparently] the opposite of *heimlich*, *heimisch*, meaning 'familiar,' 'native,' 'belonging to the home'; and we are tempted to conclude that what is 'uncanny' is frightening precisely because it is *not* known."

But then he takes a closer look and notes that *heimlich*'s secondary meaning is "Concealed, kept from sight, so that others do not get to know about it, withheld from others, cf. *geheim* [secret]. … To do something *heimlich*, i.e., behind someone's back; to steal away *heimlich*; to behave *heimlich*, as though there were something to conceal; *heimlich* love, love-affair, sin, *heimlich* places (which good manners oblige us to conceal)."

Freud concludes: "What interests us most in this … is to find that among its different shades of meaning, the word *heimlich* exhibits one which is identical to its opposite, *unheimlich*. … Schelling says that everything is uncanny that ought to have remained hidden and secret, and yet comes to light."

In Charlotte Perkins Gilman's 1913 story "The Yellow Wallpaper," an unstable young woman is confined by her husband and her doctor to her bedroom, for a "rest cure." As the story unfolds, we are treated to a constant oscillation between the meanings of *heimlich* and *unheimlich*, the polarities of familiar and unfamiliar. On the familiar side, this woman is getting to live in a beautiful colonial mansion, to spend her days reclining in her "airy and comfortable" room, where she sleeps each night with a "careful and loving" husband, John, who is a reasonable man of science with only her best interests at heart and who takes her "in his arms and call[s her] a blessed little goose." He protects her, keeps her, like a child, disburdened of all responsibility for herself. Quite condescending, we think; but still, the situation seems homey, safe. Out her bedroom window she can see "a lovely country ... full of great elms and velvet meadows." All is well.

At first glance. The closer we look, the more a shadow side emerges. The bedroom windows are barred; John's high degree of control is gradually revealed. He's stripped her of her work (reading and writing), and even her *child*—"such a dear baby! And yet I cannot be with him, it makes me too nervous." She's compliant, early on, but increasingly John's prohibitions against "giving way to fancy," against any "stimulations" whatsoever, begin to weigh on her, to squeeze and overheat her already heated imagination, forcing it to retaliate the only way it can, through subversive industry, returning feverish complexity for oppression. She stares day and night at the yellow wallpaper: "I get positively angry with the impertinence of it and the everlastingness. Up and down and sideways [the tendrils] crawl, and those absurd, unblinking eyes are everywhere. ... This wallpaper has a kind of sub-pattern in a different shade, a particularly irritating one, for you can only see it in certain lights, and not clearly then ... I can see a strange, provoking, formless sort of figure ..."—an *unheimlich* apparition, something "that ought to have remained hidden and secret, and yet comes to light."

But at this point, an astonishing further flip takes place, in which our narrator changes this horrifying strangeness *back* into a soothing familiarity, as *she* comes to set the terms, appropriating the situation, making it her own: "I'm becoming really fond of the room in spite of the wallpaper. Perhaps because of the wallpaper." The figure behind the front-pattern shows itself to be a woman imprisoned there, and *our* woman feels a powerful kinship with her, an odd sort of at-homeness, and conceives a mission to *free* her. Now any effort John makes to pry his fanciful little "goose" away from her obsession is futile; she has made a virtue of the necessity he's imposed, converted the experience of being treated like a child into a feral rage, an autonomy of judgment and action—getting up at night while John sleeps peacefully, *heimlich* in his bed, and creeping alongside the woman in the wall, making a groove in the paper and peeling off lengths of it. The room has become her domain, familiar to her, ghastly only to us and John and the doctor. Her prison cell has turned into free space; the shadowy woman has gained great prowess:

> I think that woman gets out in the daytime!
> And I'll tell you why—privately—I've seen her!
> I can see her out of every one of my windows!
> It is the same woman, I know, for she is always creeping, and most women do not creep by daylight.
> I see her on that long road under the trees, creeping along, and when a carriage comes she hides under the blackberry vines.
> I often wonder if I could see her out of all my windows at once.
> But, turn as fast as I can, I can only see her out of one at a time. ... she *may* be able to creep faster than I can turn!
> I have watched her sometimes away off in the open country, creeping as fast as a cloud shadow in a high wind.

This breaking loose puts us back in touch with Freud's "return of the repressed"; John's wife comes out on top, we might say, when he rushes in. "'What is the matter?' he cried. 'For God's sake, what are you doing!' I kept on creeping just the same, but I looked at him over my shoulder. 'I've got out at last,' said I, 'in spite of you. ... And I've pulled off most of the paper, so you can't put me back!' Now why should that man have fainted? But he did, and right across my path by the wall, so that I had to creep over him every time."

As we read "The Yellow Wallpaper," it becomes increasingly evident that we are dealing with a mind being pushed over the brink into insanity, albeit a comprehensible and compelling insanity. Thus, we are operating squarely within the uncanny. We don't leave these pages wondering whether perhaps in fact this other woman actually exists; this story just isn't that sort of animal. The joy of reading it comes, then, not from our being played off between explanations, but in the very fluidity and blaze of the hallucinations themselves, their rightness, their justice. *And* in their fleetingness, their obliqueness, their refusal to hold still for longer than a glimpse and be nailed down.

Recall C.S. Lewis's notion of "Joy" in relation to the writing of fantasy fiction, that it possesses "the quality ... of an unsatisfied desire which is itself more desirable than any other satisfaction." When I read Gilman's line, "I have watched her sometimes away off in the open country, creeping as fast as a cloud shadow in a high wind," I get chills, because of the clash between my "unsatisfied desire" to grasp this apparition and my love for her absolute elusiveness.

One day in 1989, in Dublin, Ireland, a friend and I wandered into an exhibit of paintings by Francis Bacon. On a little card was an excerpt from his journal that addresses this paradoxical response to the uncanny nature of reality:

> To me, the mystery of painting is how can appearance be made. I know it can be illustrated, I know it can be photographed. But how can this thing be made so that you catch the mystery of appearance within the mystery of the making? Van Gogh speaks of the need to make changes in reality, which become lies that are truer than the literal truth. This is the only possible way the painter can bring back the intensity of reality. ... He has to reinvent realism ... to wash realism back onto the nervous system by his invention. ... We nearly always live through screens—a screened existence. And sometimes I think, when people say my work looks violent, that perhaps I have from time to time been able to clear away one or two of the veils or screens.

It seems to me that great fiction does this, too—it makes present, as if for the first time. And the particular kind of fiction that we're talking about here reaches places, clears veils, in ways that strictly realistic, straightforward fiction cannot.

Two years before Freud wrote "The Uncanny," in 1917, Viktor Shklovsky asserted that "the essential purpose of art is to overcome the deadening effects of habit by representing familiar things in unfamiliar ways. ... Art exists that one may recover the sensation of life; it exists to make one feel things, to make the stone *stony*." To describe this process of defamiliarization, Shklovsky coined the term *enstrangement*.

In Elizabeth Jane Howard's 1951 story "Three Miles Up," we enter the realm of "the fantastic." Here, two characters are trying to feel "at home" aboard a little houseboat ... and yet circumstances quickly become radically slanted, "enstranged," and we find ourselves confronted with a version of reality that comes to feel as true as it does unprecedented.

Clifford and John, spending their holiday cruising along the canals of England, are "typical men," proud of their map-reading abilities, their mechanical prowess, and their spirit of adventure. Yet their trip is a shambles until they find a young woman named Sharon to organize things and cook for them. Sharon seems perfect: agreeable, anticipating their every need, leaving them free to forge ahead. After spending time with her, Clifford reflects upon "how little Sharon had actually said. She listened to everything and occasionally … made some small composed remark. … 'She has an elusive quality of freshness about her,' he thought, 'which is neither naive nor stupid nor dull, and she invokes no responsibility. She does not want us to know what she was, or why we found her as we did, and curiously, I, at least, do not want to know. She is what women ought to be,' he concluded with sudden pleasure; and slept."

They first found this little gem "[l]ying face downwards quite still on the ground, with her arms clasping the trunk of a large tree …" Though one could posit a link between Sharon and a mythological figure like Diana, goddess of the forest and of fertility, what's so interesting about this story here and throughout is its recalcitrance before analysis. But we can at least associate her with nature, think of her as primal, elemental, since she's lying in the mud, grasping a tree, and since she seems to have no possessions (when asked about her things she says, "My things?"), much less any home ("You could be happy anywhere, couldn't you?" John asks her, to which she replies, "I could *be* anywhere"), and yet oddly at one with her surroundings, whether domestic or meteorological: "'I like it when the whole sky is red and burning and it begins to be cold.' '*Are* you cold,' said John. 'Oh, no. I am never cold.'"

The journey soon reaches a crucial point at which the guys must decide whether to follow a safe canal that's clearly marked on the map, or proceed off-map into one that seems much wilder. The desire to "explore" wins out, and they turn into uncharted waters, attempting to master the unknown. There are no guideposts or even trees near enough for mooring. Around them is "half wilderness, half marsh, dank and grey and still, with single trees bare of their leaves; clumps of hawthorn … and, in the distance, hills and an occasional wood: these were all one could see, beyond the lines of rushes which edged the canal winding ahead." One evening, they find a village, but the next morning, it is gone.

As the men progressively lose their grip, they come all the more to admire and depend upon Sharon's preternatural helpfulness:

> "How can you see to cook?" asked John eyeing his
> plate ravenously.

> "There is a candle."
>
> "Yes, but we've selfishly appropriated that."
>
> "Should I need more light?"
>
> "There's no should about it. I just don't know how you do it, that's all. Chips exactly the right colour, and you never drop anything. It's marvelous."

Oh, John only *wishes* he could simply define it so. In fact, he seems almost to have been reading Todorov (and he'd evidently much rather be a reader of than a character in such a story): "'I must be mad, or else the whole place is haunted.' ... These two possibilities seemed to relieve him of any further anxiety in the matter, as he ate a huge breakfast and set about greasing the engine." Alas, he is given sanctuary in neither interpretation, neither the uncanny nor the marvelous, proper. Nor can *we* ever know for sure whether Sharon is a projection of their desires—entailing its own shadow—or an independent and scheming agent endowed with some sort of extraordinary power. John's misery is our delight, though, because our "unsatisfied desire" to know the true state of affairs is, in C.S. Lewis's phrase, again, "more desirable than any other satisfaction." From the reader's viewpoint, there is much vibration or shimmering between the stances of *heimlich/unheimlich*. Sharon's classic female behavior is indeed familiar turf to the men, but in its very conformity, its inescapable exactness, it becomes eerie, and strangeness rises from the familiar, the foreign from the domestic, like smoke. We have no idea what, at bottom, is going on here, but we do get the sneaking suspicion that we are being granted, in some sense, a glimpse of "the other side of the tapestry," as Henry James put it.

In the science fiction novel *Perelandra*, C.S. Lewis has a passage which feels appropriate here, too.

> I felt sure that the creature was what we call "good," but I wasn't sure whether I liked "goodness" so much as I had supposed. This is a very terrible experience. As long as what you are afraid of is something evil, you may still hope that the good may come to your rescue. But suppose you struggle through to the good and find that it also is dreadful? How if food itself turns out to be the very thing you can't eat, and home the very place you can't live, and your very comforter the person who makes you uncomfortable? Then, indeed, there is no rescue possible: the last card has been played.

Back to our story. Though Sharon herself is dispassionate, both men fall hopelessly in love with her and she even does manage with spooky efficiency to rise to absorb Clifford's passion.

> Sharon ... lay on the *floor* [emphasis added] beside him. Immediately he was filled with a sudden and most violent desire for her, even to touch her. ... "Sharon," he whispered; "Sharon, Sharon," and stretched down his fingers to her in the dark. Instantly her hand was in his, each smooth and separate finger warmly clasped. She did not move or speak, but [therefore?!] his relief was indescribable and for a long while he lay in an ecstacy of delight, until his mind slipped imperceptibly with her fingers into oblivion.

So, the next morning, a second village, spotted the night before, has vanished, like Clifford's mind and fingers. He links this latest defeat of reason with an *increased* familiarity with Sharon herself.

> "It doesn't surprise you about the village at all, does it? Do you love me?"
> She glanced at him quickly, a little shocked, and said quietly: "Don't you know?" then added: "It doesn't surprise me."

This rather opaque reply gives Clifford nothing to go on, of course. It occurs very near the end, but what's led them forward, in addition to their remaining will, are two brief encounters with male guides on the bank of the canal. The first is an old man, who is cutting rushes with a scythe. Yes, the symbolism here suddenly isn't so shy. We can link this man's appearance with a reading of Sharon's name as Charon, the ferryman who conducted the souls of the dead across the river Styx into Hades. All right, but does this make the overall meaning any less ambiguous? The man says there's a village "three miles up," but distance has ceased to make sense, even to Clifford—Mr. Maps and Measures himself—who responds to this, "Three miles! That might mean anything."

After continuing for what seems forever, they pass a boy, who is dressed, just like the old man, in corduroy, though he holds a fishing rod instead of a scythe, and who says he has *told* them already that there is a village "three miles up." So it's the same man, having grown six or seven decades younger? That's hard to align with Sharon as Charon and the old man as Grim Reaper, since they would take us across the *end* of our life, not back to and perhaps beyond the beginning.

At some level, we know that Sharon and the two male figures are monsters. And we recall that *monster*'s root, *monstrare*, means "to show." So what are these monsters showing? If this is an emergency, what's *emerging*?

Here comes another startling turn of events—Sharon appears on deck and the boy "gave a sudden little shriek of fear, dropped the rod, and turned to run down the bank the way they had come"—in other words, back in the direction of himself as an old man. Sharon says, "He was a very foolish little boy," and now reveals emotion for the first time, seeming "really angry, white and trembling"—momentarily, more conventionally monstrous.

And again, what's she showing us? Precious little that we can cash in. But neither is the mystery fuzzy or confusing in the weak sense. We're supplied with a flash of insight into some scheme to which we are never to be privy, which the boy has perhaps nearly exposed. We get to clearly see the mask slip, for an instant, from Sharon's face; to this extent, the mystery, as well, is clear. It's only the solution that eludes us, even while we're granted means of speculation.

Finally, we circle back to Sharon as primal force. We've witnessed her systematically dismantling the machinations, upending the pretentions, quietly and deliberately absorbing, dissolving the hubris, of the men. After all, it's mentioned with peculiar frequency that Sharon is tending to the "primus," which ostensibly means "cookstove" but also, of course, suggests that she has supplanted the *priority* of the two men.

As long as we are thinking of Sharon this way, maybe we'd like to try seeing this fateful canal as the *birth* canal, back along which she's drawing these overgrown children, to their beginnings, before they separated from the great plasma pool and differentiated into masculine poses setting themselves over against nature, seeking to navigate and appropriate it both in the form of land and in that of woman. Just as grasping at her in the middle of the night brought Clifford into "oblivion," so here at the end, having overreached, overpenetrated, has ushered them into the same placeless place, inviting them to lose themselves.

As my father once said of a film, "the plot promises more than it delivers, but I love the promising." Recall how disappointing, how reductive, *delivery* can often be, taking the pressure off, closing up shop, collapsing a fiction down onto the easy flatland of explaining. "Three Miles Up" gapes at us with a suggestive openness that is itself as shocking as or more so than anything that occurs within it, as expansive and opaque as the "sheet, [the] infinity, of water" into which our boys are finally released: "oily, silent, as far as the eye could see, with no country edging it, nothing but water to the low grey sky above it." Behind them, they can see "no canal at all, no inlet, but grasping and

close to the stern of the boat, the reeds and rushes or marshy waste close in …"
Now, having lost even their meager context, they find "no sign of Sharon at all,"
she who has organized and oriented them right off the map, ushered them so
genially over the edge of the known world.

And yet, what if one does not wish to engage in such radical imagining? I
must remind you that the word *radical* means "of the root." But all right, fair
enough; probably only a small percentage of writers will be drawn quite so
far down this pathway.

To the rest I want to suggest that the subtler or more modest end of this
same path holds its own riches. In an article in *Poets & Writers Magazine*,
David Long speaks to this issue:

> For writers, accepting the mandate to produce "strange
> work" can be haunting, paralyzing. It's necessary to remember
> that there are many ways … that most works progress *toward*
> strangeness during revision. Even if the design of your story isn't
> so willfully "different" [and even if events aren't overtly unreal],
> you can be guided by the same impulse, to catch the reader—to
> catch *yourself*—off guard, by trusting your attraction to the odd
> fact, the odd image, to go where it leads, and not down the same
> old cowpath. … The strange need not come forth in a blaze of
> glory. It can accumulate through a thousand small choices. …
> Strangeness comes to those writers who crank the material one
> more crank. … It's like watching light on the surface of a lake,
> then suddenly seeing through to the rocks on the bottom.

HOW DO WE MEAN WHAT WE DO NOT SAY:

The Uses of Omission in Fiction

By Victoria Redel

I have worn glasses or contacts since I was seven years old. My myopia makes it impossible for me without correction to read any print—even ridiculously large print—unless the letters are centimeters from my face. So when the guy at the optician's needed to do an overnight repair on my glasses, I was nervous. I was also a little excited to navigate my way the fifteen blocks home to my apartment. What was surprising for me on the walk was that without seeing any precise details, simply a human gesture, the gait of a walk, a length of color, I was able to discern things about people. I found that while I could not have told you any specific details—I could not have told you exactly what a person was wearing—I was able through very little to glean a surprisingly full sense of the street and the individual people walking on it. And most intensely, from a block away, from a distance where the world looked like an overworked finger painting, I recognized my sister from a kind of slant or crooked motion. We can say this is because for all these years I have managed every day with the aid of corrective lens to read the world in detail. Being on the street, while discombobulating that day, was still informed by all the years of sightedness. I was making associational leaps, reading the street with a sense of history. We do this with texts. That is why when the author renders the obvious and not exact, selected images, we grow impatient. We come to the text with all that we know. And while we perhaps want to recognize the world in the text, we want to do it by making associational connections, by leaping.

A fiction is—to take a word from Nelson Goodman—"worldmaking." To make this world we might assume we need all the landmarks, the place names, the millions of titles and details by which we know a world and those that inhabit it. In response to this there is a tendency to fill the fiction with the news—a kind of agreeable clutter to provide an aura of reality. But for the most part these fictions feel thin and seeming fictions rather than necessary fictions. The jumble of details—that John is a young man in his late twenties at a New Haven firm taking the 5:55 down to New York City where Deborah is late getting away from her copyediting desk at *Mirabella*—gives us little more than a mediocre pedigree, a false sense of place and class.

We would like to believe that the most truthful stories are those in which everything has been written down. Give all the details, as many as possible, and the reader will feel exactly what happened. Simple. Seems like these should be the best stories. And yet, as a general rule, nothing could be less true. We all have the friend who—in telling the you-won't-believe-what-happened-to-me story—gets so lost in digressions, in the "essential" backstory, that we as listeners are bored even while watching the storyteller thrilled by the accumulation of facts and things she's got to tell us in order for us to really get the importance of what has happened.

Fiction is about the selection of details, not the accumulation of them, and every detail, even the most seemingly random or improbable, must accrue, must finally as the details thread and weave through the fiction become imbued with larger meaning. The worldmaking we seek on the page is not the reality of the news account or the sociologist's essay or social worker's report. Instead, this worldmaking in all of its strange unknowable texture must not have meaning layered over it but itself must bear meaning.

As writers, we are in a state of constant and brutal negotiation with ourselves and the details of the world. What to include. What not to include. All this to make an effect. Which is the task of making fictions. Creating an effect. Creating an effect to move a reader. To break a reader's heart. To make a reader believe. Or simply, just to keep a reader reading your pages instead of drifting to sleep, or going to the kitchen or, God forbid, to another writer's pages.

I love the questions about how these effects are made because they involve the largest formal concerns and also the itsy-bitsy ways we manipulate language on the page.

Manipulate.

Negotiate.

Sounds, suddenly, like a crass thing we're engaged in. So false. So dishonest. When what we've wanted to believe is that this act of writing is about truth. And yet, truth in writing seems to me to be like my Jewish God—unknowable, unfair, jealous, punitive, and, finally, surprising.

And the truth depends on the reader's participation in the worldmaking. Fictions chuggy-jammed with everything fail, I believe, because they give the reader no chance to be a participant. And for the reader to have that flash of truth, she has to do some work, take some risks herself. How do we propel the reader into participation? How do we engage the reader sentence by sentence in a necessary act so that together, by the end of the fiction, it seems both writer and reader have achieved that sublime finish together?

We do it through the details we include, yes, but just as importantly, we do it through the details we omit.

Let's look at three contemporary fictions that achieve powerful effects through their use of omission: Christine Schutt's "You Drive," Amy Hempel's "In the Cemetery Where Al Jolson Is Buried," and Shirley Jackson's "The Lottery." Two of these stories are told in third person and the other in first person. But all of them resonate because of what does not get told.

Schutt starts her story with a long knockout of a sentence. I'm going to deliver that sentence in little bits and pieces so that we can see what we as readers know and don't know or sort of kind of think we know as we read the sentence.

> She brought him what she had promised, ...

Let's stop here. What do we know so far actually and what do we know because our mind is already making its leaps? There is a "she," there is a "he," and there is something being delivered from her to him. What have we already thought it might be? Who have we already considered he and she might be and be to one another? Let's continue.

> She brought him what she had promised, and they did it in his car, on the top floor of the car park, looking down onto the black flat roofs of buildings, and she said, or she thought she said, "I like your skin,"

By now we have a place—transient, grimy. And this thing delivered is done. So what are we thinking? Are they having lunch? Is she bringing papers to sign? Are they doing drugs? Have you thought that sex might be the thing being promised and delivered? What does Schutt gain so far from not telling? She gains ambiguity. She gains mystery. These are major gains. She forces us as readers into activity, and in trying to decode we become participants in the fiction. This is good. This is especially effective, as you'll see by the swerve in the next adverbial clause.

> She brought him what she had promised, and they did it in his car, on the top floor of the car park, looking down onto the black flat roofs of buildings, and she said, or she thought she said, "I like your skin," when what she really liked was the color of her father's skin, the mottled white of his arms and the clay color at the roots of the hairs along his arms.

Now we feel turned around. Now we have the willies. He is a father. Not just any father. He is *her* father. And our thinking seems all the more forbidden for that. We as participants can't help but want to backtrack and think, maybe it really was a deli sandwich, maybe she just brought a ham and cheese sandwich on rye bread for her dad.

Many things are at play in this sentence. Postponement. *She, he, it*: we do not learn quickly who and what these things are. We never really learn what the *it* is explicitly throughout the story. There is also postponement built into the syntax of the sentence, which delays telling us the relationship of "he" and "she" till the last part of the sentence. Still, in the end, what do we know? That they are father and daughter. It feels shocking, that word *father*—not because anything has happened that we can claim as overtly wrong—but because we have somehow become part of this shady activity. We are grimy and tainted. The writer has made us complicit. As the father says at the paragraph's end, "What a dirty place this is. … That poor dog should be ashamed of himself."

But what they have done, what she has brought him—these are still unknown.

The use of *it* and *thing* is worth our lingering over and following though the fiction. Here by unspecifying, by refusing to name, the *it* shifts, keeps changing, grows in its possibility. A few examples: "… they did it in his car." "'Honest,' she said, but T didn't believe her, and put his hand in under her skirt to prove it." "T said, 'Even your mother wants it,' and she was surprised." "'But do you like it?' she asked her father."

Schutt is a writer well aware of the tricks she's up to. Throughout the story she refuses to make the definition of *it* easy for her reader. Is the story about father/daughter incest? Or something less absolute? Back to that short opening section. The father takes his daughter's hands. The father puts his hand on her leg. These are activities that could be entirely nonsexual. And perhaps playing that boundary, the boundary of now it is/now it isn't, Schutt gains access to a murky and true terrain—the covertly sexualized. But mystery intensifies the "what is happening"—the fragmentation, the stoned quality, the vague eroticism and longing between the father and daughter. With this mystery, Schutt forces us to think about the longing, the way these estranged beings have come together late in life to try to know one another.

Another way Schutt creates mystery is by omitting the temporal relationships between parts of her story. The fragmentation of the story underscores the strange dilation of time in this fiction. Is it happening over months, days, a few afternoons? I'm not sure. Schutt keeps shifting. We're moving in the car or we're parked in the car. Time seems inverted. Movement, too. But isn't establishing a time frame one of a writer's obligations? With Schutt the refusal to be linear exacerbates her characters' stance, their fogginess. As the daughter says, "Just ask me how many times, I couldn't tell you." Schutt's story structure is characterological, not chronological. The dizzying, fucked-up, stoned, this and that of her female character is made painfully clear in the disjointed movement of the narrative. Form and content. And even more than that. The leaps and threading through the time frames keep forcing the reader to make links and assumptions without Schutt limiting her range by telling.

Schutt does this particularly well with dialogue. All the dialogue is disconnected. It is again the reader who is forced to figure out to what a character is referring. When the speaker says, "Just ask me how many times, I couldn't tell you," is she talking about her sexual escapades, her drug use, her hospital work? What is she talking about when she says, "Twice in a night it happened. I get confused." The ambiguous quality lets us connect the dialogue so that it seems larger than it might even be. The father says, "I can't get excited when I think about your mother"—a statement that could be read as flat-out refusal to deal with the ex-wife or a statement about his incapacity to be aroused by his daughter when he thinks about her mother. In ambiguity—supposedly deadly in the precise practice of prose fiction—can reside not a laziness but intention and enlargement.

As I have already suggested, by not specifying throughout the story what *it* refers to, the word becomes more and more ominously charged with meaning and wrongness. Looking at the dialogue is looking into negation, erasure.

I am not suggesting that not being specific is a good thing. In fact, Schutt is all about precision in the story. Remember hands. Remember feet. Throughout the story the body is detailed with gorgeous and frightening precision: "the skin on his face also seemed coarse to her—not boys' skin, her father's, not glossy, close-grained skin, but pitted and stubbled under all that color, rashed along his jaw and neck, her father's skin: rough." And a few pages later: "The wife has see-through skin and grainy eyelids bruised by nature." The exacting, under-the-microscope attention to physical textures informs the reader that the writer is conscious of what is being effaced. Names are effaced. *She, her father, T, it.* These are in contrast to the finely rendered physical world of "battered grasses" or "diving for soap chips in the boathouse."

Amy Hempel, in the opening sentence of her story "In the Cemetery Where Al Jolson Is Buried," declares, "Tell me things I won't mind forgetting. Make it useless stuff or skip it." With this declaration she establishes multiple tropes that thread through the story and ultimately inform the story's structure. For one, she sets in motion the ongoing trope of facts as delightful, quirky, the humorous, private engine of a friendship. But she also sets in motion the idea that it is not through facts that we are going to locate the essential—the deep love, anxiety, and panic in the face of mortality. What we need to learn in her story and in our lives, we are going to learn between the lines. After the fact.

Hempel's story is important in that it is entirely performed. There is no backstory, or what tiny fragments of the "past" that we learn are learned in sentences that pertain to the drama unfolding on the page. It is—to use the old phrase—entirely shown. What is told is declared up front as useless, forgettable stuff. Again, a refrain from that initial demand. In the third paragraph Hempel says, "The camera made me self-conscious …" We don't know what camera or where, though by the third sentence we understand they are in intensive care and the camera is a ceiling-mounted surveillance camera. But still who is being spoken about? Shouldn't we know? Are they both patients in the hospital? Hempel holds out on telling. We begin to answer these questions on page two when the speaker is introduced as the "Best Friend." Do we ever learn, for example, from what the young woman is dying? Another writer might feel it essential to say the friend has leukemia or AIDS. But in Hempel's omission there is an assertion being made. It doesn't matter from what her narrator's friend is dying—only that she is dying. Naming the disease would do nothing to further the emotional weight of the story. The specific illness, if named, would be clutter, would get in the way. So the literal "truth" of the illness's name is less important than the emotional truth of the story. The emotional truth resides in the speaker's relationship to death. Here we see how omission in the story is performative. The speaker would rather look away. The speaker would rather run away, not "be there" for her best friend, than risk the panic of looking at death head-on and seeing her own eventual mortality.

But omission also serves another function. It helps keeps the story out of the swamp of emotional bathos. Hempel is not just acting coy by not telling us things. She is a writer of every kind of cleverness. Here is a story that by virtue of its content—a friend visits her dying best friend—risks sentimentality. Hempel wants to get at the complex layers of that experience—the play, the panic, the friendship and abandonment. And to get at it all she goes about it sideways. She goes at it by underwriting.

Getting at things sideways.

Getting at things by not mentioning them at all.

For the most part, to say a thing directly in a piece of fiction, to say it directly from the get-go, diminishes tension. And the fictive enterprise is all about maximizing, creating a whirl of tension. So to say it right out, without the slant and swerve of human denial and apprehension, is to diminish the range and ambiguity of the human encounter. Hemingway, of course, understood this and gained extraordinary potency in his fictions from the not-said.

The not-said.

The mis-said.

Form is inextricable from content. Form informs content. Form becomes a choice, a way we have to manipulate the reader's experience of the text. One way Hempel achieves the intensity of the story is by keeping her young narrator purposefully, desperately light. We then become part of the narrator's experience of not-looking, of anxiety. We too are in flight, wanting to get out of there, despite our best intentions.

Another way Hempel keeps us in a state of anxiety not unlike her narrator's is through the use of section breaks. Both Schutt and Hempel make substantial use of section breaks in their stories. In Schutt's story, the section breaks set us into a world of fragmentation, a kind of jumbled jigsaw puzzle, where what and when things happen occur in a rotating dilation. Linear time is abandoned and even the simple question one might expect to have answered in a story—what is the story's time frame?—is unclear. Purposefully unclear and, more importantly, *effectively* unclear. We read the story in drug time, hazy with luminous moments. In the containment and claustrophobia of Hempel's hospital room, the section breaks keep us, like the narrator, from settling in for an overnight stay. She is skittish and so we too become skittish.

It is hard to resist, as a writer, the desire to show off a little on the page. To show our reader that we are smarty-pants who really do know what we are doing, that we understand our fictions. And while a bit of showing off can yield great effect, too much of being a smarty-pants only depletes the mystery of our prose. Because, of course, we are only *so* smart. And if our fictions have any power they have power not because we have understood the Big Themes, but because we have given weight and honor to the objects we have selected. If we honor the objects the prose must be smarter than we are. The layers that will be inextricably formed, sentence by sentence, will be vaster than any "story" or "theme" we could dream up. There is greater scope with fewer objects. And while this might shift our conversation too dramatically toward how we find our essential objects, it is worth at least discussing its immediate relevancy. Everything, and I think if you read through Hempel's story with a pen tracking images and phrases back to prior images and phrases, everything is yielded by what she has uttered in a prior sentence. The chimp returns and returns until the final heartbreaking time.

Hempel uses the witnessed world of "facts" to yield the world of emotions. Descriptions of the witnessed world are not important in fiction only to give the reader a feeling of where the characters are. The details of the witnessed world are essential because, properly selected, they become vehicles for understanding the human experience. The world looked at in this way becomes an essential metaphor to the story. As writers how do we pick the right things in the world around us? One answer would be "very carefully." But I also think that another equally valid and not altogether different answer might be "randomly." The random thing looked at long enough and from enough different angles will become essential and vital. As Hempel's story reveals, the more "useless stuff" is turned over and over, the more meaning will accumulate.

Shirley Jackson's "The Lottery" is another instructive story to examine in terms of what is and isn't said. The opening of this story is full of specific dates, times—the very kinds of details I've just been declaiming against.

> The morning of June 27th was clear and sunny, with the fresh warmth of a full-summer day; the flowers were blossoming profusely and the grass was richly green. The people of the village began to gather in the square, between the post office and the

bank, around ten o'clock; in some towns there were so many people that the lottery took two days and had to be started on June 26th, but in this village, where there were only about three hundred people, the whole lottery took less than two hours, so it could begin at ten o'clock in the morning and still be through in time to allow the villagers to get home for noon dinner.

The many specifics of date (June 27th), time (ten o'clock), place (the square between the post office and the bank), and the number of villagers (300) all help provide a tone of normalcy. The lottery is an event that is so established as to be held in all the villages. It has been, like any national event, routinized, as the specific details suggest. As the story proceeds the cozy specificity also proceeds. All the characters have names. Here we have the children: Bobby and Harry Jones, Dickie Delacroix (even the pronunciation is given), Bobby Martin, and the Hutchinson children—Bobby and little Dave. Here names matter. Everyone knows everyone in this tiny town. It is small-town America where, when Mr. Summers asks if someone can lend a hand, people step up and help. In this story, the names and such folksy details as the dishes left in the sink gain potency as the unsaid nature of the lottery begins unfolding. We don't know what the lottery is until the story's final sentence. But slowly the creepy nature of the ritualized event comes over us. And the child's play of choosing and piling up stones from the story's second paragraph becomes increasingly ominous.

Naming becomes a trope in the story. Naming, while seemingly innocent as a craft device, becomes a looming piece of the danger in "The Lottery." Here the victim is one of us. Here the perpetrators are us. Jackson's who, when, and where are as calculated and guileful as Schutt's erasure of proper names. Everyone is known. But why it happens is not known. Only that this is how it has been done, these are the old ways, the good old ways. We as readers are left with mystery. We never know why the stonings occur. Do the villagers? By naming but not explaining the action, Jackson opens the story to the larger questions of group behavior and the constitution of ritual in society.

Withholding the how and why and even the what of the lottery while seemingly rendering the quotidian with great precision is Jackson's primary method throughout the story. We could go through the story sentence by sentence and see this dichotomy in play. The lottery, an institution as reliable as the post office and the bank, is fully detailed but ultimately unexplained. Even the point of view has this same tension. By deploying anonymous narration, and by restricting omniscience to what is extraneous to the essential action of the story, Jackson heightens the emotional pitch of the fiction.

Beginning to think as carefully about leaving things out as putting things in will, I suspect, feel weird to those of us who worry and worry about how we can put more and more into our stories. I want to underline that I am not proposing a reduced fiction, a minimalism. I am proposing that there is bounty, often greater bounty, in the partial, the suggested, the entirely left out. Obviously, I might argue that muchness, a kind of swamp of stuff, could also provide glory on the page. And, by extension, a glut of objects is simply another potential strategy, another useful manipulation on the page. The pleasure for me in writing is how to make the words work. How to gain strength sentence by sentence. How each of these sentences begins to dictate the world I am making.

MULTI-CULTI LITERATI:

Or, Ways of Writing Fiction Beyond "PC"

By Xu Xi

Over a decade ago, I heard the term *multi-culti* uttered for the first time by a German arts promoter in China. She pronounced it, "moolti-koolti," in a playful language that was not quite English, to describe the Asian art, literature, and performances she wanted to showcase in Germany. World art, multi-culti, crossing borders of race, languages, perspectives, and forms. It was a term I would hear often after that around Asia and Europe. I found it liberating.

On the other hand, the term *multiculturalism*—so much a part of our literary landscape now—has proven startling, energizing but also daunting. There is such a *seriousness* attached to it that is not associated with multi-culti. Discussions around multicultural fiction are often more politically correct than revelatory. For example, we praise the replacement of old stereotypes of, say, the Charlie Chan Chinaman by more "enlightened" images of, say, the victims of Communist China, usually female, who are "liberated" by their "courage" to love democracy and the transformation of the cartoonish, turbaned, Indian snake charmer into the professional, a California doctor, say, and hence more "modern" member of our globalized society. We are increasingly multicultural, as the changing mix in the population shows; by 2000, Asians accounted for 3.6 percent of the total U.S. population, almost doubling the numbers of twenty years earlier. That figure is projected to rise to ten percent by 2050. Minorities continue to melt into our stewpot of humanity, and isn't America just so much better off for it? Don't we all simply *love* Vietnamese, Indian, Chinese, fill-in-the-blank food? *Aiyaa,* my Cantonese voice protests.

Mirror, mirror on the wall. Aren't we the fairest ones of all?

We need to examine our multicultural world because it exists, but more especially, we need to examine the world we fail to see because our view is misted by the rosy haze of our politically correct lens, multiculturalism.

As novelists and fiction writers, we reflect our existence by what we choose to write and not write, which is an extension of what we choose to know and not know. We don't write to be politically correct, but how sure can we be that we're not simply falling in line with the chorus of multiculturalism that assumes, at least on the surface, that this state of being is "desirable"? Since to write means to read, a closer look at a few excerpts of contemporary multicultural fiction might prove revelatory, if we do so with the following questions in mind: Is this our world as we know it, as we'd like to know it, as we don't know but need to know it? Or is this not our world at all?

Let us begin by asking "Who's Irish?"—the title of a story collection by Gish Jen, the Chinese-American writer who derives her pen name from Lillian Gish, a fact that in itself is multi-culti. The following excerpt from the title story is a monologue by an elderly Chinese woman in America.

> In China, people say mixed children are supposed to be smart, and definitely my granddaughter Sophie is smart. But Sophie is wild, Sophie is not like my daughter Natalie, or like me. I am work hard my whole life, and fierce besides.
>
> … My daughter is fierce too, she is vice president in the bank now. Her new house is big enough for everybody to have their own room, including me. But Sophie take after Natalie's husband's family, their name is Shea. Irish. I always thought Irish people are like Chinese people, work so hard on the railroad, but now I know why the Chinese beat the Irish. Of course, not all Irish are like the Shea family, of course not. My daughter tell me I should not say Irish this, Irish that.
>
> How do you like it when people say the Chinese this, the Chinese that, she say.
>
> You know, the British call the Irish heathen, just like they call the Chinese, she say.
>
> You think the Opium War was bad, how would you like to live next door to the British, she say.

> And that is that. My daughter has a funny habit when she
> win an argument, she take a sip of something and look away, so
> the other person is not embarrassed. So I am not embarrassed.
> I do not call anybody anything either. I just happen to mention
> about the Shea family, an interesting fact: four brothers in the
> family, and not one of them work.

In this story, the grandmother is at odds with three-year-old Sophie, who complains that Grandma hits her. Meanwhile, she's engulfed by the Irish family her daughter has married into, whose culture she compares unfavorably with her own. No one's on her side, but in her mind, it's because everyone else has it wrong. Will she find an ally or must she concede to this American culture she is now stuck in, a culture whose language she still can't and never will speak fluently? These are the kinds of questions that contemporary fiction can and does pose about our multicultural world. In much of her work, Jen sends up multiculturalism, depicting its rootedness in cultural stereotypes despite, or perhaps as a result of, its politically correct impetus. Just as Meathead will never completely conquer Archie Bunker's fundamentally racist and sexist worldview, Natalie may try to push her politically enlightened viewpoint, but clearly, her mother will remain unconvinced. The mother will concede to multiculturalism only when it flatters her Chinese heritage, deciding for instance that her granddaughter being mixed is acceptable since she's smart, as all Chinese must be. However, anything unacceptable about Sophie is due to the Irish blood in her veins.

By contrast, the Asian-Canadian author Madeleine Thien dramatizes the tragic side of multiculturalism through what appears to be the "inevitable" breakup of an interracial family. In her story, "Four Days from Oregon," a Vietnamese husband calls his unhappy, bad-tempered Canadian wife "crazy." One day while the husband is at work, the wife brings home Tom, a Caucasian friend, whom she introduces to her three young daughters. The protagonist, the youngest daughter, who was six at the time, narrates what happened when her father came home that evening:

> My sisters and I sat outside with him, our bare legs dangling
> between the porch steps. Our father pulled a photograph from
> his pocket. He'd come across it at the office, he explained, a pic-
> ture of Main Street from a hundred years ago. In the photograph,
> there were no cars, just wide streets but no concrete, dirt piled
> down, women in long dresses, their hems bringing up the dust.

I told my father I couldn't imagine streets without cars, trolleys and everything, horses idling on the corners. He said, "It's progress, you see, and it comes whether you welcome it or not."

Our father laid the photograph down. He said he could stand on the back steps and stare out until the yard fell away. He could see the house where he grew up, plain as day. It was in another country, and he remembered fields layered into the hillside. A person could grow anything there—tea, rice, coffee beans. I would always remember this because he had never talked about these things before. When he was young, he wanted to be a priest. But he came to Canada and fell in love with our mother.

The father's comment on progress proves prescient. His wife leaves him for Tom, taking their daughters with her, and disappears to North Bend. He never sees his family again. Years later, when the protagonist is an adult, she is still in North Bend, trying to make peace with the idea of progress as she guides Japanese tourists around her small town. The parents' multicultural marriage ultimately limits life for Thien's protagonist, while Jen's grandmother will never really see the point of her daughter's multicultural life since there will always be "interesting facts" to refute all arguments.

Do we read and write this multicultural fiction because it mirrors our world?
The 2000 U.S. Census tells us that of the 105,480,101 occupied households in the United States, 98.2 percent are single-race households. A mere 1.8 percent, or approximately 1.86 million households, comprise two or more races. These households are small; almost half are homes of two people or less. A racial snapshot of the entire population places Caucasians as the majority grouping at sixty-nine percent, or seventy-five percent if Hispanic Whites are included in the count.

If numbers tell us one kind of truth, what does literature tell us?
Multiculturalism is of course not just about race but also language, one of the roots of culture and the one which shapes our writing voice. Consider then this other statistical "reality": Of the total population, nearly eighteen percent speak a language other than English at home. A dozen languages are spoken by more than half a million people, and seven of them are spoken by more than a million. From lowest to highest these are Portuguese, Arabic, Polish, Korean,

Russian, Italian, Vietnamese, Tagalog (the language of the Philippines), German, French, Chinese, and by a huge margin the most widely spoken language is, as we would expect, Spanish. However, if we combine all the Asian Indian languages as one—these are broken down in the census into Gujarathi, Hindi, Urdu and Other Indic—that total figure ties for fifth place with Tagalog. The split of the top ten is, interestingly, fifty-fifty Asian and European languages.

Numbers, like plot, dialogue, or point of view, can be manipulated to tell the story we choose. The statistical truth is that Spanish is the only "foreign" language spoken at home by more than one percent of the total population (10.7 percent). Perhaps, then, we can be forgiven if we think that we're not really multicultural, that multiculturalism is something of a "fake book" since we still largely live in a racially segregated, English-speaking society.

So what kind of fiction can we think of as potentially multi-culti in our racially segregated, English-speaking United States?

Ha Jin, who won the National Book Award for his second novel *Waiting,* speaks English with a heavy Chinese accent. Like Nabokov, he mastered English as a second language to write fiction in this country. Unlike Nabokov, however, whose first English novel *Lolita* was set squarely in an American landscape, Ha Jin's published work to date has all been set in China.

In his first novel, *In The Pond,* he takes us to the "foreign" world of 1960s Cultural Revolutionary China. The protagonist Bin is trying to get an apartment from his work unit for himself and his wife Meilan, but is frustrated by what he perceives to be those in power who favor their friends. In retaliation, he publishes a satirical cartoon and is censured by the Party Committee, which threatens to withhold his bonus unless he writes a public self-criticism. Here is how Bin and Meilan respond:

> After hearing the Party Committee's decision, Meilan changed her mind and begged her husband to give up confronting the leaders, because there was 120 yuan involved. The loss really hurt. Without that money, they wouldn't be able to buy a TV the next year. They had saved almost 300 yuan for that and needed the bonus to make up the total amount. But Bin refused to give in, saying he wouldn't have to watch television and he would rather spend his time more meaningfully, studying and painting. Besides, how could he retreat now? People would think him spineless if he bowed to the leaders' wishes.

Clearly, this is not American work life or culture of the 1960s. Yet—or so the enlightened American literati would argue—Bin's frustration is surely that of any employee who has come up against an impasse with his or her boss, regardless of politics, culture, language, or race. Such arguments rein in messy life and allow us the easy comfort of placing whatever is disturbing and unfamiliar into the multiculturalist safe haven of "universality."

Similarly, the work by many South Asian and Indian writers in this country often invokes "foreign" urbanscapes. In *The Death of Vishnu*, Manil Suri takes us to present-day Mumbai, formerly Bombay. He encloses his novelistic world in an apartment block where Vishnu, an alcoholic handyman, sleeps on the staircase. Over the years, he has been tolerated by the residents. Now he is dying, slowly. Mrs. Pathak, who is hosting her first "kitty party" of bridge for a bunch of socialites she must impress, is devastated by Vishnu's presence.

> The kitty party had been a disaster from the start. The ambulance that Mr. Pathak said Mr. Asrani had called had not shown up. At one-thirty, only an hour before the guests were to arrive, Mrs. Pathak had sent frantically for the jamadarni, to have the mess around Vishnu cleaned up. The jamardani had demanded—Mrs. Pathak still couldn't believe it—thirty rupees! Thirty! The cheek of that woman, taking advantage of her when she was helpless! It had taken all Mrs. Pathak's bargaining power to bring it down to twenty, with the Russian-salad samosas thrown in. (Mrs. Pathak had tried impressing upon the jamadarni that the mayonnaise alone had cost five rupees, but unfortunately, the jamadarni had not known what mayonnaise was.) … Minutes before the first guests arrived, Mrs. Pathak had remembered Vishnu again, and pulled out an old sheet which she'd been saving to give the jamadarni at Divali (but certainly not *now*). She'd sent Mr. Pathak down to the landing with it to cover Vishnu up as best as he could. "Make it look natural!" she'd shouted after Mr. Pathak. "I want people to think he's asleep, not something else."
>
> But it hadn't worked. The first thing Mrs. Jaiswal had said upon walking in was, "If I'd known I'd see a dead man on your stairs, I would never have come! On a Saturday, no less! How inauspicious!"

These characters, who are speaking Hindi, echo some of Eudora Welty's folks in the South, or Dorothy Parker's in Manhattan. Isn't this the *why* of multiculturalism, to find the familiar in the new?

An Internet search under "multicultural" in *The New York Times* archives, dating back to 1996, yielded 991 articles, but this headline stood out in the media and advertising section: "Blacks prefer TV fare with Black casts, but tastes are converging, study says." Are tastes converging or is television spitting out what it *thinks* it's supposed to? We who write and read literary fiction are supposedly more intellectually enlightened than the producers and consumers of idiot-box fare. After all, there is all this "minority" and "immigrant" and "foreign" literature as proof.

But numbers don't *entirely* lie. Being American is a multicultural experience as long as diversity is categorized, tastes converge, and the walls of political correctness stand. Again, don't we simply *love* all that fill-in-the-blank food, since food is that safe *universal* need we can always count on?

Is universality really all it's cracked up to be?

Despite much media chatter to the contrary, it seems to me that globalism makes our world bigger, not smaller. The paths of diversity are myriad and confusing. As writers, we must read, so we cannot help but encounter all that messily diverse multicultural literature.

Reading literature is always, to some extent, a cross-cultural experience. Long before I stepped foot on these shores, I knew something of the American individualistic spirit, thanks to Huck Finn's shenanigans and Holden Caulfield's *angst*. My own M.F.A. studies led me to the novels of Ralph Ellison and Toni Morrison, which opened vistas on African America. Later, Oscar Hijuelos's *The Mambo Kings Play Songs of Love* proclaimed the power of globalism because *I Love Lucy*, which informs his novel, belonged to *my* television childhood and culture halfway round the globe in Hong Kong, just as it did to Americans in the 1960s. Don't we say in fiction workshops, "If it speaks to the universal, it's successful" regardless of culture or place?

Yet do we ever really read past "minority" or "immigrant" or "foreign"? Is our notion of "universal" that which we accept as long as we suspend disbelief of those minority, immigrant or foreign worlds? If China is Communist and freedom of speech is not a presumed right, or if India's caste system is still the norm in its civilized society, what perspectives or prejudices do we bring to bear when we read, and write, all this multicultural fiction? Is suspension of disbelief at work, or do we simply *ignore* that which does not fit our idea of what constitutes universal conflict, resolution, and the nature of humanity?

Consider this idea: Richard Nisbett, a cultural psychologist at the University of Michigan, concludes in his book *The Geography of Thought* that people in different cultures not only think about different things, they actually think *differently*. This particular study focuses on Asian versus Western modes of thought, but his scope of research has previously encompassed other cultures as well.

In experiments Nisbett and his associates conducted, Asian and American subjects were presented with mother-daughter conflicts and asked to analyze them. Americans quickly came down in favor of one side or another, whereas Asian subjects tended to see merit on both sides, with comments like "both the mothers and daughters have failed to understand each other." In another, subjects were asked to respond to this logical sequence: "All animals with fur hibernate. Rabbits have fur. Therefore rabbits hibernate." Americans tended to accept the validity of that argument, separating its formal structure, the syllogistic form, from its content. Asians, however, tended to judge the argument invalid based on its implausibility, since not all animals with fur do in fact hibernate.

Nisbett attributes these and other similarly divergent results of his studies to the origins of Western versus Eastern thought patterns. The former derives from formal rules of logic tracing back to ancient Greece while the latter is rooted in Taoist and Confucian modes of thought, in which the world is full of contradictions, constantly changing, and logic is relational rather than linear.

Since we're writers, not psychologists, let us apply this analysis to the classic Aristotelian dramatic arc of conflict, crisis, and denouement. This linear progression of causality still dominates the way we think about how we ought to write fiction in English. Chinese fiction, on the other hand, often evokes the worlds of society or nature to dramatize Confucian or Taoist principles, and those worlds are often as much the protagonists as are the individual characters who inhabit them. What happens to the characters can therefore be attributed to the philosophical and social order of these worlds, which by Western fiction standards might seem overly predetermined.

In one experiment with direct bearing on how we write and read the stories of contemporary existence, Nisbett details research comparing American and Asian perspectives on two similar incidents involving disgruntled employees as these were reported in *The New York Times* and the Chinese-language paper *The World Journal*, which is read in North America. In 1991, Gang Lu, a Chinese physics student at the University of Iowa, lost an award competition. He appealed, lost, and consequently did not get an academic job. He shot his adviser, the person handling the appeal, several bystanders, and himself. That same year, Thomas McIlvane, a postal worker in Royal Oak, Michigan, lost his job.

He appealed to the union, lost, and did not find a replacement job. He shot his supervisor, the one handling the appeal, several bystanders, and then himself.

In both cases, the stories in *The New York Times* focused almost entirely on the *individual characteristics* of these two men, such as existing psychological problems, a violent disposition, and few friends. *The World Journal*, on the other hand, emphasized *situational factors*, such as the relationship with their supervisors, the influence of other mass slayings, and the easy availability of guns in America. As a follow-up, the researchers played "what if?" games with Chinese and American subjects, asking them to judge whether the murders would have occurred if a number of situational factors were different, such as if the person had received a job or if each man had had more friends. The Americans generally thought the killings might still have happened, while the Chinese believed that they might well not have occurred.

Which story we read or tell has much to do with how we think about what we see and, if we really think differently, how *do* we get beyond "minority," "immigrant," or "foreign" to embody the *spirit*, and not just the letter, of multiculturalism?

What if we were to enter the funhouse and consider distortion *as our mirror to reflect, and perhaps even create, an* alternate *reality, a* multi-culti literati?

Let's return to the grandma in Jen's story. "In China," she says, "people say mixed children are supposed to be smart, and definitely my granddaughter Sophie is smart." Do we believe this character? This is *China*, remember, the country that built the Great Wall to keep out all those other bloodlines. What does it mean if we write a story that begins, "In America, people say mixed children are supposed to be smart"? America, where mixed-race marriages were once prohibited by law, but where today, adopted Chinese or Korean babies abound among couples of multiple ethnicities? Perhaps the real story underlying the voice of this opinionated, Bunker-ish, Chinese grandmother is that in America we do reinvent China, and by extension the rest of the world, with a certain impunity.

Now let's dip a toe in Ha Jin's pond. Can we choose to read his work as more than "writing about China," since he is after all an *American* writer? A Chinese writer he isn't; he's forsaken the language of that culture and we need not read him in translation. When Bin says, "People would think him spineless if he bowed to his leader's wishes," how do we read that? As frustration? Might it not be the case that, in China, people would think him absurd if he *opposed* his leader's wishes? Is the universality of frustration all we should take from this, or something more, a suggestion perhaps that we are not as alike as we think we are, that where we are located (physically and culturally) distorts our way of knowing? Should we not read Ha Jin, and Manil Suri, and other bi- or multilinguals, in a kind of "translation"?

How, for example, should we interpret the "universal" idea of love in Thien's story? To leave Vietnam because he fell in love is just about the worst decision the father makes. Love is not a redeeming force for his daughter either, the mixed-race narrator protagonist; instead, she seeks protection within the boundaries of North Bend, the town she, at thirty, is not sure she can ever leave, because only in this small North American haven, removed from her father's foreign origins, can she hold onto the past and her lost father, keeping them ever-present. "Some changes happen so slowly," she says towards the end of the story, "you can't know until it's done." Her voice echoes that of Ruth, the protagonist in Marilynne Robinson's *Housekeeping,* who ultimately forsakes the "normal" world and home to follow her aunt into an itinerant life and homelessness. Thien's mixed child is perhaps somewhat more mixed-up than smart like Sophie in "Who's Irish?" Perhaps multiculturalism sometimes contributes to creating survivor-victims who cross but cannot conquer borders, because conquest is neither necessary nor desired. Unlike census numbers that merely record numeric shifts in our racially segregated, English-speaking world, we can get more deeply into the meaning of things if we adjust or even *distort* our way of thinking.

Finally, in the "immigrant" or "foreign" literature that is *The Death of Vishnu,* the comic depiction of an irritated socialite may have universal resonance, but how might we read the appropriation of the Hindu god Vishnu? As a trope to replace the turbaned snake charmer with a beggar, dying on the stairwell of modernity in Mumbai? Or as *religious incorrectness* perhaps, only possible in America? Unlike Salman Rushdie, Suri offends a more forgiving god.

"Minority," "immigrant," "foreign"—such descriptions limit our reading of literature that can potentially broaden a multi-culti perspective. If, unlike the queen in Snow White, we are able to see our reflection for what it is, as opposed to what we'd like to believe it is, wouldn't we come a little closer to the truth we seek?

Let's try this: All happy families are *not* alike. Seven virgins in heaven is happiness for some, while the opportunity for the pursuit of happiness in life is necessary for others.

The mirrors of a funhouse distort our image almost beyond recognition, creating an alternate reality in the process. That reality still embodies ourselves and our humanity, as long as we do not reject the image. What if we were, unlike Tolstoy, able to see differences not only in unhappy families, but in *happy* ones? Perhaps the sad clinging to the past that is the epiphany of Thien's mixed-race protagonist *is* happiness, if we accept the Asian idea of a contradictory universe as the norm. Beyond happiness, there is the range of human emotions, which can be read against alternate realities. Despite the potential loss of income, the angry and rebellious protagonist in Ha Jin's novel decides to report the corrupt leaders to the commune. The letter he writes concludes with this question: "As a citizen of a great socialist country, do I still have the right to speak up for justice and democracy?" The answer is no, not if you want to be a Chinese citizen. Although the government embraces a concept of justice, it makes no pretense of being a democracy. Is Ha Jin really writing about China or about an American perspective of what China should and could be? Is the protagonist a Chinese man or a multi-culti one? In the China of this novel, Bin is destined to fail in his quest for an apartment, not because he is tragic, but because he is not "sufficiently" Chinese.

Can we hold up a distorting mirror and say that we need not necessarily bridge *all* the differences because, in fact, the reality of our existence dictates that we cannot and perhaps even *must* not cross those bridges? Could that be one way towards a multi-culti vision? To tilt our vision slightly askew to see and reflect those myriad humanities as ourselves?

Regardless of culture, it has always been acceptable to distort and play with literary forms. We lose ourselves in the funhouse as John Barth does, or leap down Lewis Carroll's rabbit hole. I suspect, however, that a multi-culti literati might point to a distortion of *perspective* rather than form. If we read and write for the universal, as we are used to doing, might we not miss the signals of differences, those tantalizing, tasty ways of thinking that deviate from our own? Do we reinvent Vietnam or India or South Dakota with impunity, or do we do so because it is our charge, our responsibility as writers, to create those alternate realities? Multi-culti realities that mirror the slow change, change that moves like the tortoise, but is moving nonetheless?

Perhaps we need to think beyond a willing suspension of disbelief and add a willing *distortion* of belief to inform our reading and writing of these myriad fictional universes. If we surrender to the spirit of multi-culti, that not-quite-English word, we will more likely read and write beyond the earnest, if well-meant, vision of that oh-so-politically-correct multiculturalism, one that might prevent us from understanding other worlds as a distortion of our own way of knowing and being, just as we are, as well, a distortion of theirs. I would rather acknowledge differences, and the discomfort they may create, than insist that "universality" rules, because, to borrow from Toni Morrison, I can never have that "bluest eye" unless I distort mine with a tinted contact lens.

In "The Anticreativity Letters: Advice From a Senior Tempter to a Junior Tempter," the same Nisbett cited earlier pays homage to C.S. Lewis's *The Screwtape Letters*, in which a senior devil advises a junior one how to win a soul for Satan. Nisbett's senior tempter is a psychologically astute devil working for the "Anti-Muse," and in these letters, he counsels a junior tempter on how to prevent a graduate psychology student, referred to as "the patient," from becoming a productive and original scientist. This excerpt is from the end of the third letter, which begins, like all the others, with the salutation "My dear Slump."

> Bertrand Russell wrote in his autobiography that many a time during the writing of *Principia Mathematica* he would start the day with a blank piece of paper in front of him and end the day with the same blank piece of paper in front of him. This is what you want to aim for. Don't let it occur to your patient to put a good book in front of him so that he can alternately think and read. Sitting down with a book has two effects you want to avoid. First, the book may facilitate his thinking, and second, even if it doesn't, he will at least have done some useful reading by the end of the day. Your affectionate uncle, Snidely.

Satire goes where fiction writers do not necessarily tread, but that doesn't mean we cannot learn perspective for the craft by browsing through the multi-culti bookshelves across disciplines, genres, cultures and forms. After all, we are still willing to believe in the devil, aren't we?

Reading "The Fisherman" by W.B. Yeats was what originally sent me scrambling down the path of this essay. The poem is a fitting conclusion and offers a challenge to all writers:

> Although I can see him still,
> The freckled man who goes
> To a grey place on a hill
> In grey Connemara clothes

At dawn to cast his flies,
It's long since I began
To call up to the eyes
This wise and simple man.
All day I'd looked in the face
What I had hoped 'twould be
To write for my own race
And the reality;
The living men that I hate,
The dead man that I loved,
The craven man in his seat,
The insolent unreproved
And no knave brought to book
Who has won a drunken cheer,
The witty man and his joke
Aimed at the commonest ear,
The clever man who cries
The catch-cries of the clown,
The beating down of the wise
And great Art beaten down.

Maybe a twelvemonth since
Suddenly I began,
In scorn of this audience,
Imagining a man,
And his sun-freckled face,
And grey Connemara cloth,
Climbing up to a place
Where stone is dark under froth
And the down-turn of his wrist
When the flies drop in the stream;
A man who does not exist,
A man who is but a dream;
And cried, 'Before I am old
I shall have written him one
Poem maybe as cold
And passionate as the dawn.'

THE TEXTURES OF FICTION:

An Inquiry

By François Camoin

I've just read a book, a novel. Malraux's *Man's Fate*, a cinematic look at the 1927 communist insurrection in Shanghai. It could just as well have been a collection of stories, or a memoir, but let's say for our purposes I've just finished reading a novel—this particular novel. Not a poem, or a collection of poems, because what I'm going to talk about probably doesn't apply to poems, and maybe not even to short stories. Just to those long Puritan narratives, those account books of the transactions of a life we call novels, or memoirs. Novels present life as a geology. Sedimentation. The slow sinking of minute particles which eventually reach a bottom and are in turn covered by new deposits. Crushed by the weight of time. Transformed into stones which, when we dig them up, or erosion uncovers them, are revealed to be layered like pages. It takes a long time to write a life. Longer than it takes to live it, as Sterne pointed out in *Tristram Shandy*.

I've just read a novel, and what has happened along the way, what made reading possible, is that I didn't pay attention all the time. Or I didn't pay the same attention at the same level, with the same intensity. I allowed the text to go out of focus for a paragraph, a page, a chapter. It's what makes life possible, too, I suspect, this ability to skip passages, to travel for a few miles with our eyes closed, to forget.

I've just finished reading (rereading, for maybe the fifth or tenth time) *Man's Fate*. I allow myself to dream of the author, fingering away on a portable typewriter in some picturesque prewar Paris apartment. Did Malraux, asking himself what word ought to come next, think I would pay attention to every syllable? Did he think that when I arrived at page 206 I would still be holding, fresh and brightly minted, page seven in my head? Did it occur to him that I would dream my way through pages seventy-eight and seventy-nine? And if it did, did he write the novel so that it would be read in that rather half-assed manner, by someone preoccupied with the failing foundations of his house, the failing foundations of his life? And did he take into consideration that, as Barthes explains, every time I read the book my attention would falter in different places?

Every reading of a book is different, and all readings are misreadings—inadequate readings, incomplete readings, incompetent readings. The categories overlap in unpredictable ways. The categories of reading/misreading are also not useful to organize our thoughts about readings; if all readings are misreadings, then misreading is a category that includes everything, and belongs in Borges's famous Chinese encyclopedia, along with animals that from a distance resemble flies and animals drawn with a fine camel's-hair brush. And "animals included in this classification." The question becomes how to misread, in what manner we wander through a narrative, and how to take such wandering into account when we write.

Forgetting and dreaming are not accidents that happen to reading; they make reading possible. We near the end of Malraux's narrative—Ferral has been rejected by his mistress, Tchen has blown himself up, trapped by the ecstasy of terrorist apocalypse, May is grieving the death of Kyo. We look back toward the beginning and see the early pages—the assassination of the courier, the rainy night streets of Shanghai, the phonograph shop—through a haze, blurred by the distance we have traveled, lacking detail, foggy and obscure.

If I press function key #5 on my little computer I am given a list which also reminds me of the Chinese encyclopedia.

> Pages
> Words
> Characters (no spaces)
> Characters (with spaces)

Paragraphs
Lines

All the ways in which my text can be broken into numbers. The list also reminds me of the digital nature of writing. Painting, sculpture, all the visual arts are analog—the original is always superior to any copy. It makes a serious difference whether you travel to the Louvre and see the Mona Lisa, or you look at a reproduction on a postcard, in a book, on the Internet. Something is inevitably lost. But read *Man's Fate*, or *Moby-Dick*, in a cheap paperback or in one of those Franklin Mint leather-bound editions—you're reading the same book. An infinite number of identical copies can be made. Whether a word comes out of the inkjet or the laser, it is the same word, just as the information is the same whether it's stored as an altered dye spot or a magnetic trace. Language is digital; it samples the world, stores tiny discrete slices that represent life, the universe, the self. Characters (no space). Characters (with spaces). A space packs as much meaning as a character, a one as much information as a zero.

This world which language samples is always more interesting than the imagination, because the only question we can ask of it (the only one it is capable of answering) is *how*, and never *why*, which is the question the imagination always tempts us to ask. It inquires *in what manner*, and never *to what end*. *Why* is a question which is not interesting, except to the technicians of the next world, the world that does not exist.

Tzvetan Todorov, in an essay on medieval narrative, spoke of the impossibility of a Christian fiction; he asserted that fiction is the text exclusively of the devil. There are those among us who would disagree, and I'm not certain that we are encouraged to read Todorov's assertion literally; I am also not certain that we are not. God and the devil are also of course rhetorical terms, weapons of discourse, markers and signs. Did Todorov mean that a rhetoric of fiction could not include God as a valid term? Maybe. Plato would have agreed.

What I want to talk about today, however, is that world that exists, makes itself known to our senses, even if the precise manner in which it makes itself known is rather problematic, and even if what it is, exactly, that makes itself known (*felt* might be a better word, or *apprehended*) is also problematic. Benjamin

Whorf said, "Reality is a convention shaped by language." When I discussed his assertion with a colleague who specializes in linguistics he informed me (it was for me a moment filled with charm) that there are in the discipline of linguistics *soft* Whorfeans and *hard* Whorfeans. The soft Whorfeans claim only that whatever reality lies beyond language is inaccessible to us except *through* language. The hard Whorfeans claim that there is no reality beyond language, that narrative, like the innumerable statues of Napoleon and Ulysses S. Grant and Joseph Smith, points a finger at nothing except that which the gesture itself conjures—a battlefield, a holy city, a universe that we only dream is tactile. But novelists and writers of memoirs cannot afford to be Whorfeans—hard or soft. We have to take the world into account, pretend that it's real, that it exists before language and more or less independent of words.

All fiction is realist fiction, or anti-realist fiction; that is to say, all fiction defines itself in terms of an implied contract to represent the apprehensible world— either it struggles to fulfill that contract, or it rebels against it. In either case it defines itself in relationship to a responsibility that fiction imposed on itself from the beginning as a condition of its existence. The naïve realists fulfill the contract by ignoring its existence, by assuming an uncomplicated, innocent relationship between the world and the word. The relationship between the two is in fact immensely complex, particularly since the word, whether it likes it or not, is always in the world.

While we have a moment: Borges's list.

Animals are divided into:

A : Belonging to the Emperor
B : Embalmed
C : Tame
D : Suckling pigs
E : Sirens
F : Fabulous
G : Stray dogs
H : Included in the present classification
I : Frenzied
J : Innumerable

K: Drawn with a very fine camel's-hair brush
L: *et cetera*
M: Having just broken the water pitcher
N: That from a long way off look like flies

To say that language samples the world and stores the samples is only to push back the question for a moment. At what rate does it sample? What information does it discard? Is the world frequency and volume? Brightness and color?

Imagination. No other word, not even, god help us, poetry, is universally spoken with such reverence. No handbook of creative writing is complete without innumerable respectful references to imagination. The only thing that can be said in defense of imagination is that its opposite thematic, observation, is almost as harmful when given as advice to impressionable writers. Take notes, they tell us, keep a journal. The attempt to quick-freeze reality in order to preserve it. It's like the nineteenth-century preoccupation with pressing flowers between the pages of books. Doesn't do much for the book, and it doesn't improve the flower. The patron saint of the art of the journal should be Audubon, who killed and stuffed small birds and then stuck the feathered corpses in living trees as subjects for his paintings.

I hope you're not taking notes, unless you're doing it as a defense mechanism, or to entertain yourself, or, at least, inaccurately.

Both imagination and observation live inside the old Socratic logic of language—we imagine something, or we observe it, and then we sit and ponder until we find the words to perfectly (or more probably imperfectly) express it. Language is reduced to expression (Oscar Wilde), or communication (Zola, Dreiser, Norman Mailer). The Socratic logic, in a paradoxical move, forces us to live outside the world, to observe it or to imagine it. It separates us from ourselves, from any possibility of ourselves. It leads to a Protestant writing, a Christian and capitalist literature with the writer as producer and the reader as consumer. We shouldn't feel too good too quickly, however, since what writers produce in such a system is the most marginal of commodities, and writing becomes a banal task, directed and corrected not by editors or agents or critics, but by focus groups and directors of marketing. Barthes refers to "these two desires, to change the economy of the relations of production and to change the economy of the subject …" (Note: Barthes here means "subject" in the sense of the speaking subject—you and me, in other words. Very confusing if you're thinking of the word as used in "The subject of the sentence …") Who produces us, and in what manner? We know all too well who uses us.

But this is a craft lecture. The deal is that I stand at the front of the room and get paid for telling you how to write. That too is an economy, the economy of teaching, and you and I take up our roles in it voluntarily. By which I may only be saying that we don't know who or what is forcing us to be here at this moment, you on the far side of the podium and me on the near.

Back to the business of the rubble of the world, then. Fiction is not communication. It is not the transmission of a body of knowledge and insight painfully gathered by the writer. Robbe-Grillet, a writer whose novels are boring in the best sense of the word, talks about the necessity of getting past the nineteenth-century concept of the writer as someone who dives deep into the heart of human nature only to re-emerge after his perilous journey bearing a precious insight which he holds out for our admiration. Robbe-Grillet wants to do away with the old myths of depth. We should listen.

Writing is best done by those of us who don't know precisely what we mean, certainly not before we write, but also, in the best-case scenario, after we've written. Which is not to argue for automatic writing, and is also not to come down on the side of Kerouac, disembodied poetics, the Naropa Institute, the philosophy of "first thought, best thought." Also not to dismiss it out of hand, either. I've seen stories ruined by revision, destroyed by the well-meaning advice of workshops. Mostly, though, the story, the novel, is born out of a dialogue between writer and text, a struggle for supremacy, a kind of ongoing coup d'état carried out on the page.

Fiction is not communication. I've sat in workshops in which someone expressed uncertainty about the central character's age, only to have the author triumphantly point out that in line six of page two the age is given as seventeen.

Or someone else said he didn't know where the story was taking place and the writer pointed to the word Ohio inscribed on page one. If writing were communication, that would be enough. But it isn't—it's an attempt to put the reader through an experience, to create a landscape for the reader to traverse. And a landscape is an ongoing enterprise—it's not a message, but a place. If I walk through Grand Wash, a narrow and beautiful canyon in Southern Utah, the walls go on and on; they are always there even when I'm not paying attention to them, when I'm walking head down thinking of the improbability of love, or the blister on my heel. I feel their weight at my back, their improbable scale; their shadow falls across me whether I'm thinking of them or not. And so it ought to be in a novel.

Texture is what we see out of the corner of the eye, even, or maybe especially, when we're not paying attention. Iteration is at the heart of the craft of fiction—this wall, then this wall again, different and still the same, and then once more, and yet again. Iteration invites a lapse in attention; it distracts at the same time that it convinces. It intrudes on the sequence of events that constitutes narrative—it delays the unfolding of the plot, makes us impatient to skip this paragraph, that page, so that we can get on with the action. But another way to look at fiction is to see the action, the plot, the drama, as unfolding itself not only in front of, but for the sake of, the relentless textured backdrop of the world. Little bits of action to keep us turning the page, to keep us moving through the landscape that is the point of the enterprise. The events and characters exist for the sake of the place; Madame Bovary is only there so Flaubert's rainy, muddy, depressing provincial town can come into existence. Her wild ride in the horse-drawn taxi with her lover is only the foreground for the desolate landscape of Rouen. Roquentin and his illustrious nausea exist only for the sake of Le Havre, so that Sartre can call it Bouville and place us inside its infinitely melancholy streets.

You could say that to read in this manner is perverse, that it performs an illegal operation on the text. But I'm in the mood for transgression. I love rules precisely because they make transgression possible. And transgression is one path to wisdom. I don't entirely side with that famous nineteenth-century Middle-European rabbi who told his congregation that in order to summon the messiah they each had to break all of the commandments every day, but I think I have a sense of where he was headed. If the road to hell is paved with good intentions, then the road to heaven must be paved with bad intentions. Excess, as Blake pointed out, leads to wisdom, and excess is, precisely, transgression, crossing the line that mustn't be crossed.

The careful reader who pores over every syllable of a novel with equal attention exists only in the dreams of academics. If we write for her, we write in bad faith—she's the one person who is absolutely certain not to read our book, since she doesn't exist. So we write for the misreader, the incompetent, the inattentive, the uninformed, the naïve. We write for ourselves. We build our landscape in such a way that most of it can best be viewed from a distance—diminished by memory, blurred by inattention. We write knowing that our narratives will be read by readers who come to them out of a sense of duty, driven by the economy of the academy, readers who are bored, whose concerns are elsewhere.

I have just finished reading Malraux's *Man's Fate*; I read it like an academic, making notes in the margin, rereading old notes I had made there which I no longer understand, which nobody any longer understands. I skipped some parts, read too fast, caught myself turning the pages without remembering what I had just read, turned back to read again, and again lost track. Sometimes I was bored. I'm the kind of reader you can hope for if you're lucky. Which is not a tragedy; it's how books exist in the world.

I am speaking to you this morning and many of you are not awake, are hungry, hot, tired, melancholy, agitated, bored, lustful, filled with inchoate desires. You look up for a moment, catch a phrase, glimpse an idea out of the corner of your eye, then you go back into yourself. I won't ask how many of you would rather be elsewhere, partly because it's a meaningless question. Given a Faustian choice—you pick, you can go anywhere, do anything—the answer is all of you. And me too. But you're here. And I have no one else to speak to.

SHOWING *AND* TELLING

By Laurie Alberts

For years I, like many of my colleagues, have exhorted students to write more scenes, dramatize, cut exposition, cut summary. Recently, a student responded that she liked books in which the author had a strong storytelling voice that commented on and explained the action. Wasn't summary where voice came through, she wondered. Her question was a good one. I began to ponder the uses of summary.

I'd just completed a creative nonfiction manuscript and throughout the writing I worried that I hadn't written enough scenes, and that my use of summary was flattening my story. I looked to nonfiction writers whose work I admired and considered fully dramatized. I was surprised to see how many of them use a great deal of summary. Tobias Wolff is a good example. I had read *This Boy's Life* and *In Pharaoh's Army* some time ago, and I remembered both books as vivid, scene-based works. Both books, it turns out, rely more on summary than on scene. Sue William Silverman's book *Because I Remember Terror, Father, I Remember You* struck me the same way. I thought of it as all scene. And certainly, in the early sections, when you are seeing the world through the eyes of a very young child lacking the perspective of time and the ability to interpret events, most is written in scene. But as the book goes on and Silverman enters her teen years, summary comes more and more into play.

How do these authors make their summary as alive as scenes? When is summary a distancing shortcut, and when is it an opportunity to deepen theme, reveal character, and express an author's distinctive voice? Where do scene and summary work best? How do good writers slide between these elements smoothly?

146

First, some definitions. I think of scene as the illusion of "real time" (all scenes require a time and a place) and summary as the connective tissue that holds those scenes together by providing background, exposition, or interpretation.

Janet Burroway, in *Writing Fiction*, says that

> Summary and scene are methods of treating time in fiction. A summary covers a relatively long period of time in a relatively short compass; a scene deals at length with a relatively short period of time. Summary gives information, fills in background, lets us understand a motive, alter pace, create a transition, leap moments or years.

Jerome Stern says, like a child in a tantrum, when you want everybody's full attention, you "make a scene, using the writer's full complement of dialogue, physical reactions, gestures, smells, sounds, and thoughts." According to Burroway, summary creates distance, scene create closeness.

Robie Macauley says:

> The traditional rule is that episodes meant to show important behavior in the characters, to make events dramatic as in theater, or to bring news that changes the situation should be dealt with in the scenic, or eyewitness, manner. Stretches of time or occurrences that are secondary to the story's development are handled by what is called a "narrative bridge."

Burroway distinguishes between two kinds of summary, sequential and circumstantial. She says that these two summary forms represent two methods of memory, which also condenses. In sequential summary, a writer tells you in compressed form what has happened in between the scenes or before the book has started. In circumstantial summary, the writer describes how things were or are, how they generally happen or happened, what was done repeatedly.

But, Burroway says, continuing with the memory model, for important things your mind provides a scene. Scene is always necessary to fiction—scene is the crucial means of allowing the reader to experience the story with the characters. Confrontation, turning point, or crisis cannot be summarized, Burroway believes. "If the author explains to us or interprets for us, we suspect that he or she doesn't think us bright enough to do it for ourselves. Writers should use significant details to convey ideas or judgments or both."

In an essay entitled "Show and Tell: There's a Reason It's Called Storytelling," Carol-Lynn Marrazzo disagrees.

> The wise writer is not afraid to tell … writers blend telling and show-ing … when the writer depends solely on showing and neglects the narrative that artfully shapes, characterizes, qualifies, or in some other way informs the character's actions, the reader is abandoned to extrapolate meaning based upon what is observed—for example, a character's sweating palms or nervous twitch—and the reader then, rather than the writer, creates the story.

In an example of the use of summary within scenes, Marrazzo demonstrates with Flannery O'Connor's story "Good Country People" what you would miss if you only looked at the showing. At a crucial moment in the story, O'Connor's interpretation of a character's interior life shows that this moment is transform-ing, while the actions would tell us little (the italics are Marrazzo's).

> She sat staring at him. *There was nothing about her face or her round freezing blue eyes to indicate that this had moved her; but she felt as if her heart had stopped and left her mind to pump her blood. She decided that for the first time in her life she was face to face with real innocence. This boy, with an instinct that came from beyond wisdom, had touched the truth about her.* When after a minute she said in a hoarse high voice, "All right," it was like surrendering to him completely. It was *like losing her own life and finding it again, miraculously, in his.* Very gently he began to roll the slack leg up.

If you were to read only the scene minus the summary, Marrazzo shows us, this is what you'd get: "She sat staring at him. When after a minute she said in a hoarse high voice, 'all right' … very gently he began to roll the slack leg up."

It's obvious that what is lost is all connection to the character's inner world. We see that she has agreed to his request but we don't know what it means to her. Of course, there is distance between the character's thoughts and the author's—O'Connor is being very ironic, since the Bible salesman then goes on to steal the woman's wooden leg.

Marrazzo, in contrast to Burroway, says that telling not only heightens the moment but reveals the transformation within the character. The interplay between both telling and showing is often crucial at transforming moments.

The good news is that we don't need to enter this argument. Good writing, whether fiction or creative nonfiction, puts both of these important elements to use to varying degrees, depending on the demands of the text and the temperament of the writer.

Let's look at a few examples from Wolff's *This Boy's Life:*

> Our car boiled over again just after my mother and I crossed the Continental Divide. While we were waiting for it to cool we heard, from somewhere above us, the bawling of an airhorn. The sound got louder and then a big truck came around the corner and shot past us into the next curve, its trailer shimmying wildly. We stared after it. "Oh, Toby," my mother said, "he's lost his brakes."
>
> The sound of the horn grew distant, then faded in the wind that sighed in the trees all around us.
>
> By the time we got there, quite a few people were standing along the cliff where the truck went over. It had smashed through the guardrails and fallen hundreds of feet through empty space to the river below, where it lay on its back among the boulders. It looked pitifully small. A stream of thick black smoke rose from the cab, feathering out in the wind. My mother asked whether anyone had gone to report the accident. Someone had. We stood with the others at the cliff's edge. Nobody spoke. My mother put her arm around my shoulder.
>
> For the rest of the day she kept looking over at me, touching me, brushing back my hair. I saw that the time was right to make a play for souvenirs. I knew she had no money for them, and I had tried not to ask, but now that her guard was down I couldn't help myself. When we pulled out of Grand Junction I owned a beaded Indian belt, beaded moccasins, and a bronze horse with a removable, tooled leather saddle.

The book begins with scene—although to be picky I might say that the first sentence is actually summary leading into the scene, and scene shifts in and out of summary in the last paragraph. The crash is vividly rendered, although the souvenirs that young Toby cadges are even more thoroughly described. What do we know from this scene? We've got the boy's character down cold—and his character (as well as his circumstances) is always central to this work. He's on the road with his mother, and the car has failed *again*, a very important word here. We see the mother's softness and her concern for her boy—which Wolff never questions in the book although we might question it, since she provides little stability and later puts him in harm's way.

The scene of the terrible crash sets up the mood of danger and precariousness that will be borne out throughout the memoir. Even more striking, though, is our response to young Toby. What an operator! This kid will try to use any situation to his advantage, and the adult Tobias Wolff is on to him. Wolff wants us to be on to him too, right from the start.

This short scene (with its brief flickers of summary) is followed by a very long summary, both sequential and circumstantial, that fills in background information:

> It was 1955 and we were driving from Florida to Utah, to get away from a man my mother was afraid of and to get rich on uranium. We were going to change our luck.
>
> We'd left Sarasota in the dead of summer, right after my tenth birthday, and headed West under low flickering skies that turned black and exploded and cleared just long enough to leave the air gauzy with steam. We drove through Georgia, Alabama, Tennessee, Kentucky, stopping to cool the engine in towns where people moved with arthritic slowness and spoke in thick, strangled tongues. Idlers with rotten teeth surrounded the car to press peanuts on the pretty Yankee lady and her little boy, arguing among themselves about shortcuts. Women looked up from their flower beds as we drove past, or watched us from their porches, sometimes impassively, sometimes giving us a nod and a flutter of their fans.
>
> Every couple of hours the Nash Rambler boiled over. My mother kept digging into her little grubstake but no mechanic could fix it. All we could do was wait for it to cool, the drive on until it boiled over again. (My mother came to hate this machine so much that not long after we got to Utah she gave it away to a woman she met in a cafeteria.) At night we slept in boggy rooms where headlight beams crawled up and down the walls and mosquitoes sang in our ears, incessant as the tires whining on the highway outside. But none of this bothered me. I was caught up in my mother's freedom, her delight in her freedom, her dream of transformation.
>
> Everything was going to change when we got out West ...

Notice that the summary contains sensory details as vivid as those found in any scene. People in the Southern towns where the car has broken down walk with "arthritic slowness" and "idlers with rotten teeth surrounded the car." At night, they slept in "boggy rooms where headlight beams crawled up and down the walls and mosquitoes sang in our ears, incessant as the tires whining on the highway outside."

No wonder my memory mistook summary for scene. Yet unlike a single scene, we realize, from this summary, that these idlers, these slow walkers, these crummy motel rooms are a repeated experience, a general condition of Toby and his mother's cross-country flight.

Wolff vacillates between various forms of narrative distance in his summaries. He uses the child's simple language in the assertion that "We were going to change our luck." Of course the adult Tobias Wolf knows (as does the reader) that their luck won't change for the better. Later he uses an adult language, asserting temporal distance, the wisdom of the adult self, when he says, "I was caught up in my mother's freedom, her delight in her freedom, her dream of transformation."

So we get, in this summary, the vividness of scene created by sensory detail, and we get the opportunity to view the world through the eyes of the ten-year-old boy that Wolff was, with all his hope and naiveté. We also see the world through the eyes of the adult Wolff, who will frequently comment on the action, interpret for us, and even jump forward in time to compare something happening to young Toby with something that will happen later to the adult Wolff (Vietnam, for instance). Scene alone would not offer up such layered information.

What other information do we get from this chunk of summary that occurs very early in the book? They don't have the money for a decent car, obviously. She has a "little grubstake." *Grubstake* is an interesting word—they are going to be uranium miners and there's the air of the gold rush, or pioneer about this term. We learn that she's impulsive enough to give a car away to a stranger, even if it is a lousy car. As the summary continues beyond the excerpt just quoted, we learn some of the mother's background—her life in California as the daughter of a millionaire before The Crash, her dream of a past in which she and her mother played at being sisters. Wolff doesn't comment further, but we learn that his mother won't be much of a mother, either. She had early days of glory and they were going to retrieve them. The child believes in her dreams and loves her entirely.

The major issue, when deciding on scene or summary, is to determine what it accomplishes. How does it further the movement of the piece, or help to carry the themes? When do you need to "get attention," as Stern said, or to fill in, set up? If Wolff had started off with all that background about traveling the west with his mother, I would not have been half as interested as I was after that quick glimpse, that shocking event in the scene that opens the book. I'm—to use a commercial word—hooked, and now I can step back to get the context. On the other hand, without the context provided by the summary, with just the scenes, I wouldn't have as great a sense of these characters, their hopes and expectations, their poverty, and as much doubt that their hopes will be fulfilled.

Before we leave Wolff, I want to offer another example of his effective use of summary:

> Dwight made a study of me. He thought about me during the day while he grunted over the engines of trucks and generators, and in the evening while he watched me eat, and late at night while he sat heavy-lidded at the kitchen table with a pint of Old Crow and package of Camels to support him in his deliberations. He shared his findings as they came to him. The trouble with me was, I thought I was going to get through life without doing any work. The trouble with me was, I thought I was smarter than everyone else. The trouble with me was, I thought other people couldn't tell what I was thinking. The trouble with me was, I didn't think.

Again we have the vividness of scene: Dwight's grunting over engines, heavy-lidded at the table with a pint of Old Crow and a package of Camels to support him in his "deliberations." (Here Wolff uses adult language to heighten the irony.) And we have repeated time, which we couldn't have in one scene. Through Dwight's "findings"—again, the adult wording heightens the irony that this dull-witted, mean man could ever *find* anything—and through the summarized dialogue, "The trouble with me" litany, we also get the contradictions in Dwight's observations that reveal his character. The repetitious summarized dialogue makes Dwight's complaints seem like a broken record. In scene alone we'd have to hear a character say (or think), "You always say that!" Wolff uses summary to give us, efficiently and subtly, the repeated action and his adult judgment of Dwight.

Tim O'Brien's brilliant story "The Things They Carried" is unusual in the extent to which it employs summary. In fact, the story depends on summary;

its intention is to load you down with the weight of what these soldiers had to carry, both literally and figuratively. It is about a particular platoon, but it strives for a universality of soldierly experience—or, rather, the experiences of American soldiers in Vietnam—that transcends the experiences of these individual men.

The movement within the story is the movement within Lieutenant Jimmy Cross, who, after the death of one of his men, Ted Lavender, blames himself. Cross hardens himself against his illusions about Martha, the girl "back in the world" who doesn't love him, as well as his illusions about being part of normal life. The movement of the story is also the movement within the reader as the summarized descriptions of what these men must carry accumulate and weigh us down as well.

> The things they carried were largely determined by necessity. Among the necessities or near necessities were P38 can openers, pocket knives, heat tabs, wrist watches, dog tags, mosquito repellent, chewing gum, candy, cigarettes, salt tablets, packets of Kool-Aid, lighters, matches, sewing kits, Military Payment Certificates, C rations, and two or three canteens of water. Together these items weighted between fifteen and twenty pounds, depending upon a man's habits or rate of metabolism. Henry Dobbins, who was a big man, carried extra rations; he was especially fond of canned peaches in heavy syrup over pound cake. Dave Jensen, who practiced field hygiene, carried a toothbrush, dental floss, and several hotel-size bars of soap he'd stolen on R&R in Sydney, Australia. Ted Lavender, who was scared, carried tranquilizers until he was shot in the head outside the village of Than Khe in mid-April. By necessity, and because it was SOP, they all carried steel helmets that weighted five pounds including the liner and camouflage cover. They carried the standard fatigue jackets and trousers. Very few carried underwear. On their feet they carried jungle boots—2.1 pounds—and Dave Jensen carried three pairs of socks and a can of Dr. Scholl's foot powder as a precaution against trench foot. Until he was shot, Ted Lavender carried six or seven ounces of premium dope, which for him was a necessity. Mitchell Sanders, the RTO, carried condoms. Norman Bowker carried a diary. Rat Kiley carried comic books. Kiowa, a devout Baptist, carried an illustrated New Testament that had been presented to

him by his father, who taught Sunday school in Oklahoma City Oklahoma. As a hedge against bad times, however ...

What's also unusual and striking in this story is that the platoon members are characterized via objects, and they are characterized almost wholly through summary rather than through action, gesture, or dialogue in scene. Yet they are individualized and humanized. We are told, outright, that what they carry is determined by necessity. The story alternates between summaries about the men and what they carried, moving from the exceedingly concrete—the 26-pound radio, and the 2.9-pound .45-caliber pistol—to the deeply abstract— the weight of the war, the weight of their fear, and Lieutenant Jimmy Cross's hopeless infatuation with Martha.

As with Wolff, there is nothing vague about O'Brien's summary sections. They are detailed, even more detailed, in fact, than the scenes. In a picture Jimmy Cross carries, we see the tautness of Martha's tongue while she's playing volleyball. We know she "respects Chaucer and has great affection for Virginia Woolf." We know the color of the pebble Martha sends Jimmy—oval, milky white with flecks of orange and violet; we know where she found the pebble and just what Jimmy wonders—who was with her that day at the shore. These summaries are not shortcuts. They are, like the objects the men carry, necessities.

Throughout the story we're reminded of Ted Lavender's death, and it is this event that removes us from the abstraction of general time, repeated events, the lulling boredom and exhaustion and purposelessness of the relentless "humping" up and down mountains, through jungles.

Lavender's death is central but it's interesting that we never get to know Lavender beyond mention of his fear, his dope, his need for tranquilizers. Yet his death—when it comes in a full, dramatized scene—shocks us with the reality of the threat these men live with. Every scene in this story is related to Lavender's death, including the following scene in which the soldiers draw numbers to determine who will investigate a tunnel.

> On April 16, when Lee Strunk drew the number seventeen, he laughed and muttered something and went down quickly. The morning was hot and very still. Not good, Kiowa said. He looked at the tunnel opening, then out across a dry paddy toward the village of Than Khe. Nothing moved. No clouds or birds or people. As they waited, the men smoked and drank Kool-Aid, not talking

much, feeling sympathy for Lee Strunk but also feeling the luck of the draw. You win some, you lose some, said Mitchell Sanders, and sometimes you settle for a rain check. It was a tired line and no one laughed.

Henry Dobbins ate a tropical chocolate bar. Ted Lavender popped a tranquilizer and went off to pee.

After five minutes, Lieutenant Jimmy Cross moved to the tunnel, leaned down, and examined the darkness. Trouble, he thought—a cave-in, maybe. And then suddenly, without willing it, he was thinking about Martha. The stresses and fractures, the quick collapse, the two of them buried alive under all that weight ...

In this scene, time slows down. We get the specifics of the tunnel, the atmosphere. Then we slide away with Jimmy Cross into his imaginings about Martha. The ruminations and fantasies about Martha that follow this excerpt take up more space than the actual death. But we are still in the scene, in the moment, there and not there, as Cross was. What does this scene accomplish? It's the "real" center around which the general life of these soldiers, their day-to-day existence, spins. It crystallizes all the vagueness. It is the underlying source of all terror. It is the cruel joke, the happenstance—killed while peeing. It is the primal scene, in essence, of the story, the one that must be returned to. It is the moment that determines Jimmy Cross's transformation.

Maddeningly, fittingly, O'Brien breaks away soon after to return to his litany of the things they carried. Yes, Ted's death is terrible, real, but just one of many they'll witness, those who live long enough. It's all part of business as usual, on some level. Back to the hump, back to the weight.

The most abstract "things" the men carry are mentioned after the detailed scene of Lavender's death. "They carried the weight of memory. ... They carried the land itself ... they carried gravity ... they carried their own lives ... the great American war chest." How does O'Brien get away with loading his men and his story with these big summarized abstractions? Through the specificity of the concrete details we've come to trust O'Brien. The particularized summary and the focused scene have set us up for the more abstract picture of these soldiers, and all the soldiers like them, who carried the burdens of the war.

Maxine Hong Kingston is another author who expertly alternates scene and summary. In a chapter from *The Woman Warrior*, Kingston focuses on her own silence, the silence of Chinese kids in American schools. She gives a long summary of her experiences in both American and Chinese schools and then uses summary to set up the crucial scene to follow, in which she attacks and torments another Chinese girl, who is even more silent than she, in an effort to "help" her talk. This attack would be much harder to understand without the context that the summary provides. We learn, via summary, about her embarrassment when her mother insists she ask for "reparation" candy from a pharmacist whose delivery boy mistakenly brought medicine to their house and so, her mother believed, cursed them with ill health. We learn that as a child Kingston believed that Americans find the Chinese language "Ching-Chong ugly." Through all this summary, we also find out that the Chinese kids who are so silent in their public schools are loud and rowdy in afternoon Chinese school. It isn't the fact of being Chinese, but the fact of being Chinese in the world of ghosts, that makes them so silent, and makes the scene of the attack so painful and powerful.

> I hated the younger sister, the quiet one. I hated her when she was the last chosen for her team and I, the last chosen for my team. I hated her for her China doll haircut. I hated her at music time for the wheeze that came out of her plastic flute ...
>
> One afternoon in the sixth grade (that year I was arrogant with talk, not knowing there were going to be high school dances and college seminars to set me back), I and my little sister and the quiet girl and her big sister stayed late after school for some reason. The cement was cooling and the tetherball poles made shadows across the gravel. The hooks at the rope ends were clinking against the poles.

When the scene begins with that tag, "One afternoon in sixth grade," time slows down. Kingston takes enormous care setting up the scene, the mood. She even uses summary within the scene to tell you the cost of staying late—the last time her mother called the police to say she'd been kidnapped. We hear about the sounds of the toilet pipes when they are flushed during school hours—the summarizing within scene here increases the tension.

When the attack begins, it is shocking:

> "You're going to talk," I said, my voice steady and normal, as it is when talking to the familiar, the weak, and the small. "I am going to make you talk, you sissy-girl."

> I thought I could put my thumb on her nose and push it bone-
> lessly in, indent her face. I could poke dimples into her cheeks. I
> could work her face around like dough ... I reached up and took
> the fatty part of her cheek, not dough, but meat, between my
> thumb and finger ...

It's one thing to know she hates this little girl because she hates the silence in herself. This girl has become representative of everything that makes Kingston feel unlike the other non-Chinese children—silence, weakness, inability to play sports, being well behaved. We get the point as she tells us all this. But we only understand the depth of her fury, her self-hatred and anger at the world, when we see how she attacks this little girl. It goes on and on and on until they are both crying.

Our response to this extended scene is visceral. We experience Kingston's emotions even as we have our own reactions to the events she dramatizes. The summarized parts that precede it evoke a more cerebral response. I admire how nicely Kingston sums up cultural differences when she says (a few pages before the excerpts here),

> Reading out loud was easier than speaking because we did
> not have to make up what to say, but I stopped often and the
> teacher would think I'd gone quiet again. I could not understand
> "I." The Chinese "I" has seven strokes, intricacies. How could the
> American "I," assuredly wearing a hat like the Chinese, have only
> three strokes, the middle so straight? Was it out of politeness
> that this writer left off strokes the way a Chinese has to write
> her own name small and crooked? No, it was not politeness; "I"
> is a capital and "you" is lower-case.

This is wonderful summary—we understand both the child's confusion and her intelligent attempt to sort out language differences, while we note the ways two cultures treat the idea of self through the word *I*. But if Kingston had only summarized, had she written merely that "In sixth grade I trapped a very quiet girl in the bathroom and demanded she speak," we would feel none of the depth of her emotion and how far it could drive her.

It's interesting to note that in the scene, when Kingston finally takes definitive action by attacking the quiet girl, she uses declarative subject verb sentences in which "I" is followed by action: "I reached up ... I shouted ... I squeezed ... I squeezed again ... I pulled ... I yanked ... I screamed ..." (Here

Kingston's voice is really heard.) In the summary sections, the verbs and the constructions in general are often more passive in relation to Kingston: "Once a year the teachers referred my sister and me to speech therapy."

The interplay, the balance and complementary effects, of scene and summary enhance the power of Wolff, O'Brien, and Kingston's writing. There are other writers, however, whose work is carried by voice to such a degree that it doesn't always matter if a particular passage is scene or summary. Sally Savic, in her novel *Elysian Fields,* demonstrates the graceful integration of these two elements. Witness these two passages:

> Lucy Nell slapped me when I said so. "You ain't the right girl," she said in her Arkansas twang. Her voice sounds like a guitar string when it busts, and sometimes it still zings through the room long after she's gone.
>
> I had never thought of him dead. I always tried to imagine other things ... Marshall catching trains and slow boats to sad, forgotten places, pinpointing destinations on maps no longer current, bumping through the darkness of a world that no longer goes by the same names. Siam. Atlantis. Babylon.

Savic's scenes are just as language-laden as her summaries:

> It's quiet tonight. From inside, through an open window, I can hear a radio talk show on the transistor in the kitchen. Mrs. Adele Corners from Happy Jack, Louisiana, is asking how to get a pork chop bone out of the porcelain canal of her toilet.
>
> "How did the pork chop bone get there, Mrs. Corners?" the talk show host wants to know. His voice is round and smooth and full of insinuation.
>
> "Somebody threw it down there," Mrs. Corners says breathlessly.

I love the oddity of the specifics: it's not just a plugged toilet but a toilet with a bone in it, and it's not just any bone, but a pork chop bone. It echoes a reference to the narrator being "bone tired" of being lied to earlier on the same page. The talk show host's voice isn't just oily; it's smooth and round and insinuating. There's a hint of blame (echoing Marshall's mother Lucy Nell's earlier accusation that the narrator is to blame for Marshall's disappearance), and of secrets; the woman with the plugged toilet is somehow guilty and breathless—all echoes of the narrator's fears about herself.

This is scene, but there are no great revelations or transformations. It's a scenic mood piece, a set-up for the background summary that follows in which the protagonist explains how she came to be in Louisiana, in that house, waiting for Marshall's return. It could just as well be done via summary, but in this novel, summary and scene blend so smoothly that you often don't notice the movement between them. This seems particularly fitting because the novel is about a passive situation—an abandoned woman waiting, wondering, searching ineffectually.

John Cheever often employed the sort of narration that my student was talking about when she said she liked a narrator who takes over the tale and is willing to interpret it for the reader. Many of Cheever's third-person narrators have total authority. In his story "Artemis, the Honest Well Digger," the narrator not only tells us what Artemis thinks and feels, but he is free to comment on related or even seemingly unrelated aspects of life. Yet he is never general. Look at the details:

> Artemis loved the healing sound of rain—the sound of all running water—brooks, gutters, spouts, falls, and taps. In the spring he would drive one hundred miles to hear the cataract at the Wakusha Reservoir. This was not so surprising because he was a well driller and water was his profession, his livelihood, as well as his passion. Water, he thought, was at the root of civilizations ...
>
> To get the facts out of the way: Artemis drilled with an old Smith & Mathewson chain-concussion rig that struck the planet sixty blows a minute ... Artemis rather liked the noise. He lived with his widowed mother at the edge of town in one of those little conclaves of white houses that are distinguished by their displays of the American flag ... This patriotic zeal cannot be traced back to the fact that these people have received than abundance of their country's riches. They haven't. These are hard-working people who lead frugal lives and worry about money. People who have profited splendidly from our economy seem to have no such passion for the Stars and Stripes. Artemis's

mother, for example—a hard-working woman—had a flagpole, five little flags stuck into a window box, and a seventh flag hanging from the porch.

Artemis's fascination with water is made explicit, as is his education, his house, etc. Whatever Cheever tells us works toward deepening themes or revealing character. For example, the narrator seemingly veers off on a tangent all his own about the displaying of flags on private property, who does it and who doesn't and why. He makes a judgment based on socioeconomics. But the fact that Artemis's mother displays flags isn't just some quirky detail to characterize Artemis's background or his home. The question of patriotism mentioned here is later echoed when Artemis becomes involved with a Russian woman while on vacation in Russia and is called in to report to the State Department. Each detail, even when summarized, contributes to the whole story.

Herein lies the distinction: We don't resent a bossy, judgmental narrator who is original in his or her observations and who draws us into the tale through vivid, significant detail. We *do* resent a summarizing narrator who either overgeneralizes or takes away the mystery, the act of discovery for us. Compare Cheever's passage to this pedestrian summary: *Artemis was a man in his thirties who wasn't married, owned his own well-digging business, and loved water.* Yes, we're informed, but we aren't engaged. The language is flat and the summary deadens the story.

Few of us can manage that sort of authority—few of us can walk that tricky line between knowing all and being a know-it-all. And few of us can manage to enthrall readers by virtue of what we have to tell instead of what we have to show. And contemporary readers are less willing to turn over authority to a narrator who will tell us, via summary, what is what—the Dickensian patriarchal narrator who announces "It was the best of times; it was the worst of times" has mostly gone out of favor. We have become suspicious of authorities. Yet when this form of authoritarian summary is successful—and Cheever succeeds perhaps because he possesses quirky charm, just as Lorrie Moore's quirky narrators succeed because of her humor—the story, essay, memoir, or novel is enriched. We feel that we are in good hands, and we relax into the joy of listening to a master storyteller.

PAINFUL HOWLS FROM PLACES THAT UNDOUBTEDLY EXIST:

A Primer of Deceit

By Robin Hemley

The heart is deceitful above all things, and
desperately wicked: who can know it?
—Jeremiah 17:9

There used to be a time, we believe, when
we could say who we were. Now we are
just performers speaking our parts. The
bottom has dropped out. We could think of
this as a tragic turn of events, were it not
that it is hard to have respect for whatever
was the bottom that dropped out—it looks
like an illusion now, one of those illusions
sustained only by the concentrated gaze of
everyone in the room. Remove your gaze
for but an instant, and the mirror falls to
the floor and shatters.
—J.M. Coetzee, *Elizabeth Costello*

1.

When Faulkner bought his house, he named it Rowan Oak, after two talis-
manic trees, one denoting strength, the other a shield against evil spirits, in

this case, reporters and visitors who were forever invading Faulkner's beloved privacy. By the time of my visit, nearly fifty years after his death, plastic barriers had been erected at the entrance of every room of Faulkner's house, but Bill Griffith, the curator, granted me special access to each room—occasionally, other tourists entered the house, and they watched with curiosity and, it seemed to me, envy, as I, and I alone (well, in the company of the curator and Anna Baker, one of the graduate writing students at Ole Miss), rummaged through Faulkner's belongings and listened to Bill Griffith's anecdotes and insights about the Great Man.

In Faulkner's study, there was a bed, a typewriter, and written on the wall, the outline to his novel, *A Fable*. A can of Scram powder sat on top of one of Faulkner's shelves—neighborhood dogs were constantly digging up the flowerbeds in Faulkner's day. He'd shoot them in the rump with his BB gun, but when this didn't work, he bought the Scram powder. Whether Scram worked or not (a sprinting dog was featured on the can) I have no record, but it was one of those details of Faulkner's life that I craved, that showed an ordinary existence, not one of greatness or perfidy, simply the getting-on-with-it that is the majority of our every days until we die. Whether he would approve or not was not the point. Faulkner had become more than his books, and we, I, marveled at this everydayness. By the phone in the hallway to the kitchen, Faulkner and his wife and his daughter Jill had written phone numbers on the walls. Plaster was worn away where Faulkner had tipped back his chair while talking. He hated the phone, but this is where he had received the call that he had won the Nobel Prize. Stockholm. Too far to travel for dinner, he thought. In the kitchen on a shelf of empties stood a bottle of Jack Daniels with a few thimbles of whiskey still inside. Bill Griffith fretted that it looked lower than it had before, that a prior student worker had sampled it. This was the bottle of whiskey Faulkner had sipped on the day he died. Bill let me sniff it. What was it there that remained?

That ineffable lingering of the body. That's where the trouble lies. We crave the literal. Even Faulkner, who wanted to be only his books, is finally reduced to blood and bones.

Faulkner never wanted his private life to interfere with his books. He wanted to be an erasure as a human. He said, "It is my aim, and every effort bent, that the sum and history of my life, which in the same sentence is my obit and epitaph too, shall be them both: He made the books and he died."

"J.T. LeRoy was born in 1980. He is the author of the novel *Sarah*. First published at the age of sixteen, he has also written articles and stories for *Spin*, *Nerve*, *NY Press*, *The Stranger*, and several anthologies, under the pseudonym Terminator. He lives in San Francisco."—Jacket copy of *The Heart Is Deceitful Above All Things*

"An eyewitness's imagination burns in [LeRoy's] language ... as vivid as a match held close to the face."—*The New York Times Book Review*

"Few writers can deliver LeRoy's sense of a child in the hands of angry adults—or handle it with such assurance."—*The Village Voice*

"Brilliant, gifted, and profound ... [J.T. Leroy] is the witness to all the tales that go on in the dark, and for all of us, long may he have the courage to remember."—*Vanity Fair*

Delightfully, from my point of view, J.T. LeRoy, this *"authentic wunderkind"* (*The Los Angeles Times*) never existed. LeRoy, or the woman who really wrote his "authentic" stories and "authoritative" novel, Laura Albert, apparently had no intention of ever revealing her true identity until her estranged husband decided to Take The High Road and write a tell-all book about the ruse. All this just proves we want the body, not the book. The book has become the body.

"LeRoy writes with honesty and authority ... [His stories] are desperate cries from the darkest corners of the American landscape, painful howls from places that undoubtedly exist but seem the product of a madman's imagination."—*Review of Contemporary Fiction*

Imagine this. A woman approaches the author Dennis Cooper with her stories but is afraid no one will be interested in stories by a thirty-something white woman. She enlists her husband in the con and others, including her husband's half sister, who played the excessively shy LeRoy in public, wearing a wig, letting Albert do most of the talking. Famous actors and authors become LeRoy's friends and supporters, chatting with him daily over the phone, hours at a time.

I wonder what the reviewers think of J.T. Leroy now that he has come out as a figment? Are there authentic figments?

Faulkner, too, was interested in deceit. In his Nobel Prize acceptance speech he spoke famously of the human heart in conflict with itself, that this is the wellspring of literature. Perhaps that's true of literature, but this isn't about literature. It is about the body and the heart. The author's heart of a sixteen year old in conflict with the author's thirty-something body. *If ONLY I were a sixteen-year-old homeless junkie hooker boy!* the author cries. The imagination has become something to view with suspicion by both author and a reality-sodden, literal-minded public, and so deception follows upon deception. Reviewers fall all over themselves to marvel at the Realness of the Author as if they had any notion what an "authentic" homeless junkie hooker boy sounds like, what a Native American thinks, what hell a Hiroshima survivor has lived through, or a Holocaust survivor. I revel, perhaps a little mean-spiritedly, in these little embarrassments, these hoaxes. I revel in them because, without fail, they topple the pious little constructions we've built around the Literature of Identity and Authenticity.

> "Though only 21, LeRoy writes with extraordinary maturity about harsh life … these ten stories will wring your soul and win your heart."—*Publishers Weekly*

> "Despite his age [J.T. LeRoy] has a genuinely authoritative voice … truly remarkable."—*Booklist*

Is it a lesser accomplishment or a greater accomplishment that these "frankly astonishing" (*Kirkus Reviews*), "flawlessly scribed" (*San Francisco Bay Guardian*), "genuinely authoritative" (*Booklist*), "powerful" (Abercrombie and Fitch) stories were invented by a forty-year-old woman named Laura Albert and not by a runaway hooker junkie boy, too shy to be seen in public, J.T. LeRoy, Terminator, a pseudonym with a pseudonym?

Let's ask Abercrombie and Fitch.

2.

From *An Historical and Geographical Description of Formosa: … Giving an Account of the Religion, Customs, Manners, &c., of the Inhabitants: together with a Relation of What Happen'd to the Author in His Travels, Particularly His Conferences with the Jesuits, and Others, in Several Parts of Europe: Also, the History and Reasons of His Conversion to Christianity, with His Objections against It (in Defence of Paganism) and Their Answers by George Psalmanazar:*

> Generally speaking all the Animals which breed here, are to be
> found in Formosa; but there are many others there which do not

breed here, as Elephants, Rhinocerots, Camels, Sea-Horses, all which are tame, and very useful for the service of Man. But they have other wild Beasts there which are not bred here, as Lyons, Boars, Wolves, Leopards, Apes, Tygers, Crocodiles; and there are also wild Bulls, which are more fierce than any Lyon or Boar, which the Natives believe to be the Souls of some Sinners undergoing a great Penance: But they know nothing of Dragons or Land-Unicorns, only they have a Fish that has one Horn: And they never saw any Griphons, which they believe to be rather fictions of the Brain than real Creatures.

George Psalmanazar was born in France in the 1680s, had blond hair, and apparently a better imagination than biography. He enlisted in a Dutch regiment and started telling tales of Japan—his native country, he said. In this way, he came to the attention of an army chaplain, the Reverend Alexander Innes, who asked Psalmanazar to translate some Japanese. Of course, Psalmanazar couldn't. Once Innes knew the truth, he decided to help his friend build a better deceit rather than expose the fraud. And so, Psalmanazar, whose name was not really Psalmanazar, but for purposes of authorship became Psalmanazar, shifted the geography of his birth several hundred miles and became a native of the island of Formosa. The two traveled through Europe, Psalmanazar entertaining throngs with stories of the rituals of his native island, of the rampant cannibalism, the polygamous natives, infanticide, human sacrifice, of the great revolutions that happened on the isle, of the laws enacted by the Emperor Meriaandanoo, of the postures of the body in adoring, of the marriage of Groutacho, of the priestly garments, of the ceremonies towards the dead, of the splendid Retinue that attends the "Vice-Roy" of Formosa, when he goes to wait upon the Emperor, of the money, of the musical instruments, of the diseases and their cures, the native animals and plants, of men, of women, of everything that lay beyond the experience of Europeans of the day, but not of George Psalmanazar's imagination. Thirty-seven chapters in all as well as an appendix formed his memoirs.

The book, written first in Latin, was soon translated into English, then French, German. Multiple editions appeared and he was, by all accounts, a literary sensation until eventually, inevitably it seems, the book was exposed us a fruud.

But Psalmanazar didn't disappear, not entirely. He became a middling scholar, a friend of Samuel Johnson, and towards the end of his life penned a follow-up memoir telling about his earlier fraud, his fantastic concoction, and then he died, without ever leaving the soil of Europe, without ever revealing his true name. But really, is his real name any more real than his pseudonym? The island of Formosa doesn't even exist anymore. Now, it's Taiwan, and it wishes it were China, and its small minority of indigenous people include the Atayal, Saisiyat, Bunun, Tsou, Thao, Paiwan, Rukai, Puyuma, Amis, Yami, and Kavalan. Psalmanazar's book is clearly not about them, but it remains a chronicle of something, at this remove at least, more intriguing than fact.

3.

At the opening of Joel and Ethan Coen's *Fargo*, the words "Based on a True Story" flash on the screen. A little jab, a tiny nod to our tawdry expectations. Maybe we'll lean in a little closer, our eyes a little bit wider while watching the wood chipper scene. The Coen brothers are displaying a bit of bravado with the tease. Film doesn't need the nudge of the Real to make it seem relevant. In fact, it's the rare documentary that grabs a wider audience than even the lowest-budget sequel to a sequel to a sequel. That's because we don't need to be convinced of anything when we're seeing it unfold right before our eyes. We don't even *mind* when films take supposedly true stories and shape them to the rigid and fantastic specifications of Hollywood. Put in a love interest where there was none. Make the father figure a villain. Kill off the little brother. It doesn't matter because we excuse Hollywood its exaggerations—it's the continuity of the story that counts, little else. Take, for example, Danny DeVito's character, Bobby Ciaro, in the biopic *Hoffa*, starring Jack Nicholson. Ciaro is Hoffa's ubiquitous sidekick, bumped off with Hoffa at the film's end. But did he exist? No. Does anyone care? No. Are there those who have seen the film who now believe Bobby Ciaro was a real person? Undoubtedly.

Words are leaden things really, little pellets that whiz by half the time and drop out of sight without forming any pictures in our minds. We need that extra nudge of Authenticity to make us pay attention. We need to know that it's worth the effort and it *seems* worth the effort only if what happened was both extraordinary to the point of being totally unbelievable while at the same time undeniably Real, as in Ripley's-Believe-It-Or-Not-Real. If we didn't want to believe, if we didn't need to believe in the miraculous, Ripley's wouldn't have had a business. We would *always* rather believe than not. When the weight of understanding tips too far to the "Not," rather than the "Believe It," we feel let down, if not betrayed.

What we want from literature is Redemption. We want Redemption stories and we want them to be Real. When Oprah first welcomed James Frey to her stage, she exclaimed that she couldn't believe that he had survived, that he had made it alive to her, and she was So Happy for him. The next time he appeared on her stage, she wasn't so happy.

Unbelievable, she said three times in a row when describing unbelievable events in the book that she had chosen to believe, and "*I COULDN'T believe it*," she almost screamed, awe-struck as though she had once believed Frey the Savior Himself, and *I can't believe it*, she said once, but her disbelief was not a negative thing when she was believing the unbelievable. It only became negative when pulled out of whatever dream James Frey had dreamed up for her and millions of others. The book couldn't have happened and yet it did because James Frey was Real and so Everything he said just *had* to be Real, too, didn't it? Nan Talese in defending the book countered that when *she* read it, the book had seemed So Authentic. Other books, she said, were bad books because they were not as Authentic as James Frey's book.

I'll say it again. What it comes down to is Redemption. We want to believe the unbelievable. We want to believe in miracles. A furniture salesman from Arcadia, Wisconsin, and I shared a laugh over this on the plane to Memphis on my trip to Mississippi. He asked me, like a number of other people upon hearing that I write nonfiction and even, *gasp*, memoir, what I thought of James Frey. I told him the headline of the *Chicago Tribune* should have read the day after Frey's Oprah appearance, "Millions Flee as Truth Bites Oprah in the Ass."

We talked about how all these stories of redemption are false, pablum, that the patron saint of the publishing world seems to be P.T. Barnum. This, the furniture salesman thought was incredibly funny and we both shared a laugh over it. "So you got no hope," he said, his face crinkling in laughter. "You're a junkie, you're going to stay a junkie. Basically, we're all screwed and we're going to die."

Yeah, basically. At thirty thousand feet, it seemed like a hoot.

4.

Thirty years ago, most memoirs were written by people of some fame or unusual accomplishment, but in the early- to mid-eighties, memoirs such as *This Boy's Life* by Tobias Wolff and *Blue Highways* by William Least Heat-Moon showed that anyone could write a memoir, that life itself was a kind of accomplishment, and this self-evident fact invited everyone to a kind of literary potluck that has not finished since—you no longer had to be Anne Morrow Lindbergh or George Burns or Dwight Eisenhower to tell a story about your life, undisguised as fiction, that might captivate readers. But before the advent of the memoir as we know it now, there was the *roman à clef*, a term we do not hear too often anymore, but one that served the purpose that the memoir serves today. The *roman à clef*, or thinly veiled, semiautobiographical novel, was, and still is to some degree, the bailiwick of first-time novelists, such as Thomas Wolfe, whose *Look Homeward, Angel* made residents of his hometown, Asheville, North Carolina, so incensed that he *couldn't* go home again for several years after its publication. The authors of *romans à clef* have often found that calling a book a work of fiction does not necessarily mean that everyone believes it is indeed is a work of fiction, as Truman Capote found out when many of his Hollywood friends deserted him after he published excerpts from his unfinished *roman à clef, Answered Prayers*. Now we have no need of *romans à clef*, but we have a need for an in-between category.

I propose a new literary subgenre, the *memoir à clef*, a thinly veiled novel disguised as a memoir. Obviously, the term *memoir* is insufficient by itself. Even after Lauren Slater titled her book *Lying* and subtitled it *A Metaphorical Memoir*, even after her first chapter read in its entirety, "I exaggerate," *still* many readers were upset that they didn't know whether she Really had epilepsy as a child or whether she was using the idea of her epilepsy metaphorically.

Okay, fine, but isn't that appropriation? What might Real and Authentic Epileptics feel about some literary psychologist pretending she had epilepsy simply to make some obscure literary point?

Well, first of all, it's not obscure and it's not simply a literary issue. It's one of the central questions of existence. How do we test what people tell us? And does lived experience trump the experience we experience in books and art?

"Nasdijj's critically acclaimed, award-winning memoir, *The Blood Runs Like a River Through My Dreams*, took the literary world by storm," reads the book jacket of *The Boy and the Dog Are Sleeping*. "'An authentic, important book,' raved *Esquire*. 'Unfailingly honest and very nearly perfect.' Now, this celebrated Native American writer has given readers a powerful, brave, and deeply moving memoir of the unconditional love between a father and a son."

Could we please please please take that word *authentic* and just rip its white little belly open, tear out its offal-stuffed guts, and float it down the river on a burning pyre, never to mention it again? Maybe stick its little helpmate *Honesty*'s head on a pike? These are two of the most meaningless words a reviewer could invoke, but they are invoked time and time again as though the reviewer holds the touchstones of Authenticity and Honesty in his hand. Of course, it's not about the Authenticity of the book really, but the Authenticity of the reviewer, the reviewer at least who wants to validate himself as much as he wants to validate the book he's reviewing or blurbing. *Look! I know a Native American when I see one. My positive, glowing, over-the moon review as much as binds me to the Navajo Nation, doesn't it?*

Yet, I resist blaming these authors. I blame the literalness of a culture that diminishes the role of the imagination in literature and demands that our authors should *be* their stories. Of course we're going to be shafted time and time again when we demand literalness of literature.

Nasdijj, born to a Navajo mother who died of alcoholism when he was seven and a white father who sexually abused him. When presented with a bio like that, what is it exactly we are reading—the book or the author? The praise surrounding his books is typically breathless:

> "A memoir of survival ... The flat-out best nonfiction writing of the year."—*Minneapolis Star-Tribune*

> "Mesmerizing ... A powerful American classic ... [that] doesn't just catch your breath, it stops your soul's progress in mid-stride."—*Rick Bass*

But what makes me breathless, what stops *my* soul mid-stride is the flat-footed irony of the author's Real Identity—the writer, Tim Barrus, before he became Nasdijj, was the author of such out-of-print gay porn titles as *The Mineshaft* and *My Brother, My Lover*. And Barrus is as Navajo as Psalmanazar was Formosan. Same story, more or less, with *The Education of Little Tree*, the story of a Native-American orphan growing up during the Depression. In the preface to my edition ("Over 1 million in print" reads its jacket), Rennard Strickland writes that this is "a book from which one never quite recovers," "an inspirational and autobiographical remembrance of a young Indian boy which might provide a fresh perspective for a mechanistic and materialistic modern world." A fresh perspective, indeed, and written actually by a white man, and not only that, but a member of the Ku Klux Klan.

Call me cynical but I'm not. I happen to still believe in the Imagination as something nearly sacred, and I'm not going back on my earlier confession that I take pleasure in these heavy-handed ironies, that I'm far from outraged. What's the use of railing against Carter and Barrus, wrapping ourselves in pieties about Truth in Nonfiction when we're begging really to be deceived by the next fake Indian, fake child prostitute, fake Hiroshima survivor? And I resist making this in retrospect a discussion of literary quality. While Nasdijj's prose truly seems awful to me, I can't say the same about Lillian Hellman's trilogy of *memoirs à clef*, for which she was famously taken to task by Mary McCarthy. "Every word she writes is a lie," said McCarthy, "including 'and' and 'the.'"

In Lionel Trilling's 1971 book, *Sincerity and Authenticity,* the famous critic tracked the rise and fall of Authenticity and Sincerity as components of the literary character. Who would ever wonder about the sincerity of the Patriarch Abraham or of Achilles? By the time we get to Polonius in *Hamlet* admonishing his son Laertes, "To thine own self be true," the advice seems to make a lot of sense. "With what a promise," Trilling writes, "the phrase sings in our ears! Each one of us is the subject of that imperative and we think of the many difficulties and doubts which would be settled if only we obeyed it. What a concord is proposed—between me and my own self: were ever two beings better suited to each other? Who would not wish to be true to his own self? True, which is to say, loyal, never wavering in constancy. True, which is to say honest: there are no subterfuges in dealing with him. True, which is to say, as carpenters and bricklayers use the word, precisely aligned with him. But it is not easy."

Truer words, I might add, were never written. It's not easy. Not only do we have to consider that Polonius, that old aphorism-spouting windbag, is the one giving this advice, but he's giving it in the play *Hamlet*, about perhaps the most conflicted, difficult-to-pin-down personality in the history of literature.

To praise a work for being "sincere" in Trilling's day was a kind of put-down, a way of saying that if it couldn't be admired aesthetically or intellectually, it could at least be praised for the innocence in which it was conceived. Now, to praise a work for its sincerity and authenticity is to bestow upon it the highest accolades and the highest readership our society can offer.

5.

But even the most sincere writer can deceive us.

> "An extraordinary memoir of a small boy who spent his childhood in the Nazi death camps."—Jacket copy of Binjamin Wilkomirski's *Fragments*

"This stunning and austerely written work is so profoundly moving, so morally important, and so free from literary artifice of any kind at all that I wonder if I even have the right to try to offer praise."—Jonathan Kozol, *The Nation*

"Beautifully written, with an indelible impact that makes this a book that is not read but experienced. *Fragments* is 'a masterpiece.'"—*Kirkus Reviews*

"Extraordinary. He writes with a poet's vision, a child's state of grace."—Julie Salamon, *The New York Times Book Review*

Binjamin Wilkomirski is no Tim Barrus, no Laura Albert. This is no charlatan trying to con a gullible public into believing he's someone he's clearly not. This Swiss-born instrument maker believes he was born in Riga, Latvia, and survived various concentration camps at an early age. The man, as Stefan Maechler's exhaustive investigation makes clear (*The Wilkomirski Affair: A Study in Biographical Truth*), is simply delusional. He did indeed have a hard childhood, but not that hard. Born at the outset of World War II in Switzerland to an unwed factory worker, he was shuttled between foster parents, though his mother wanted custody of him. Perhaps as a means of coping with the enormous pain of this separation, he reinvented himself—his father smiling a smile of reassurance at his son moments before a truck smashed him against a wall in front of his son's eyes. And this is only the opening of the book—in stark, flat prose, Wilkomirski ekes out a bare-boned story told in fragments (as its title suggests), horrifying dream-like images that conform to all our expectations of what a Holocaust memoir should contain.

But what of Holocaust deniers? I ask myself. Doesn't such a book as Wilkomirski's give them an opening? If we can imagine the Holocaust without having lived it, aren't we possibly leaving ourselves open to a world in which nothing is factual, in which everything can be questioned? The uncomfortable answer is yes, everything in the world can be questioned and always *is* being called into question. That's because the world changes and people change. I am less interested, finally, in the desire of someone to promote herself as a young homeless boy, a Native American, or a Holocaust survivor than I am in our desire to create fixed boundaries of experience. We cannot stop writers from fooling us, nor can we stop being fooled. Likewise, the connection between Fake Memoirs and the deceptions of the Bush Administration is absurdly overblown. We don't live in an age of "Truthiness" or "Deception" any more or less than any other age—the Past gives up only some of its deceptions. The rest are glossed as conventional wisdom and accepted fact.

Much of my favorite nonfiction, in any case, is fiction: W.G. Sebald's unclassifiable books, for example, and more recently, J.M. Coetzee's *Elizabeth Costello*, a book mainly of ideas as told by a fictional character with a completely believable biography. In fact, a number of Costello's experiences are Coetzee's own—no surprise there. But I would classify the book as nonfiction, or choose not to classify it at all, because it investigates its subject in the way nonfiction investigates, through a kind of sifting process of arguments and counterarguments about literature and morality. If you have difficulty conceiving of that, imagine that you discovered today that I, Robin Hemley, do not exist, that in fact, I'm just one of the innumerable figments of Joyce Carol Oates's imagination. Would you insist on classifying this essay as fiction or nonfiction, or simply allow it to inhabit two categories at once?

Imagine Plato being grilled by Oprah: "It was UNBELIEVABLE what you wrote about Atlantis! Just unbelievable. I couldn't believe it." Made up or not, the idea of Atlantis has been one of the most powerful and long-lived stories humankind has told itself. Was Plato sincere in telling the story? Was Herodotus, "The Father of History," sincere when he told of the Amazons? Did he write about them authentically? I guess we'll never know, will we?

6.

Now we enter the Land of Easier-Said-Than-Done, the Continent of Caveats. I can't hope to remove all the moral rough spots and rationalizations inherent in the *memoir à clef*. But what I can do is wish for us to get beyond simply making this a moral and ethical issue if only because harping on sincerity and authenticity is finally so boring. The *memoir à clef* is a subgenre that already exists—let's all be its devotees and fervent practitioners. Let's create fiction we call nonfiction and nonfiction we call fiction. Let's allow the soul of Rick Bass to continue its progress. Let's mix it up simply to be troublemakers and see what we can get away with. Let's get away with it all.

That's me as a writer. In my role as a reader, I, too, want the literal. I want the succor of proof, the comforts of the body.

I find myself back at Rowan Oak, being led now to the second floor of the house, to Faulkner's bedroom. We handle his grandfather's flintlock, fumble with his shotgun shells in our hands. Bill Griffith even shows me Faulkner's shoes. Removing a pair of wingtips from a box, he says, "This is my favorite pair of shoes. I wish I had a pair of shoes like that. If I did, I'd wear them every day." Griffith is full of illuminating anecdotes: Faulkner hated air conditioning and forbade it. On the day after he died, Mrs. Faulkner purchased an air conditioner. We have the receipts to prove it. Griffith tells me of taking Stephen King through Faulkner's house, and how appreciative and knowledgeable King was, and he tells of another author, a poet from New York, who lay down on Faulkner's bed in his study and stretched out her feet, then pounded on his typewriter. I was horrified by this information, as was Anna Baker, the grad student accompanying me. But really, what's so horrifying about that? Faulkner would probably be horrified to see his house turned into a museum, his objects treated as holy relics.

Faulkner forbade his daughter to have a radio and they fought over it. In the heat of their arguing he said coolly, "No one remembers Shakespeare's daughter."

She never forgave him for that and when she went away to college, she placed a radio by her bedside so he would always be reminded of his cruelty when he passed by her bedroom.

But when she was away at college, and his wife away on a visit, Faulkner remodeled the house, tearing out a beautiful garden and building a new writing room, building a new staircase, covering the old well. When his wife came back home, she offered him a divorce but he declined.

"Why would she want to divorce him for that?" Anna asked Bill.

"Because she had no say in the matter," I said. "It probably wasn't the only time he had done something without consulting her first."

"That's undoubtedly right," Bill said, and I swelled with a little pride that I saw through this little crack in the bubbling wallpaper into his family life.

The remodeling job took care of the radio, too. He fixed it so that he didn't have to pass by Jill's bedroom or see her radio ever again. And she never forgave him for that either, for refusing to face what she wanted him to face, for refusing to redeem himself.

THE FICTIONAL "I" IN NONFICTION

By Phyllis Barber

In Russia, there's a popular folk art known as matryoshka—*the art of carving and painting the nesting doll. I keep one of these dolls on my desk. She's painted in shades of green. She's wearing an elaborately detailed* babushka *that covers most of her red hair. She has large green eyes and a delicate face. A winter scene is painted across the front of her in lieu of a dress. Through the ages, people everywhere have been fascinated with the business of taking these dolls apart, splitting them open and open again to smaller and smaller versions until reaching the doll that no longer breaks apart. Maybe people see something of themselves in these dolls, something about removing layers or breaking one's self open to the mystery of their core, their essential "I."*

"The Fictional I." Over the thirty years of my writing life, the question of the first-person singular and just exactly what that is has been the single most perplexing issue I've dealt with as a writer. I'm currently wrestling with this issue in my seventh book. In fact, this admittedly self-indulgent wrestling match has slowed my progress considerably.

To state my conundrum simply: First, the book started out as a novel about the adventures of two women bicycling across the United States. A chick novel. I could make money! A year later, it veered toward being a novel about two women bicycling across the U.S. trying to unburden themselves of their guilt and personal failure. *But*, another year later, the text informed me in no uncertain terms that it was more memoir than novel and was about me taking an insane bicycle trip because my own life had seemed so inconsequential at the time and I'd lost track of my reasons for being. What was that all about?

Looking closer, I saw lurking beneath the surface of my get-rich, be-famous novelistic intentions, like a Loch Ness monster, this huge personal guilt that had been hanging around for years. It kept rising from dark waters to haunt me. It kept showing up in the pages of whatever I tried to write.

I wasn't sure what to do. Should I go for the jugular and tell the rawest truth I knew? Should I pull back the curtain and say, "It's me here. I'm the source." Or should I keep the curtain drawn and pretend I wasn't on the stage? Should I write a novel, a memoir, or some hybrid—a *memovel* or a *novoir*?

Some contradictory strands of advice were woven into the braid of this dilemma:

From parents, books on manners and political correctness:

> Don't talk about yourself too much. People don't want to hear
>   about you or your flaming ego.
> Don't open a letter with the word *I*.
> Avoid *I, I, I* and *me, me, me* at all costs.

From philosophical and spiritual teachers:

> Know thyself.
> Heal thyself.
> The truth shall set you free.
> The unexamined life is not worth living.

From classes on creative writing:

> Fiction is superior to nonfiction.
> Real artists write fiction.
> Transcend the self. Be more creative.
> Use your imagination. It's truer than the truth.

These notions and others like them had created such a stark duality that I felt as if I were being torn in two directions: toward a truth that needed to be told and away from a truth that shouldn't be told. And I felt I was two people: this person called "I" whom I'm not supposed to mention, and this person called "I" who must be examined. Others have solved this dilemma by turning to fiction, but for some reason, some of us are compelled to write in first person and tell it "like it is."

In my own case, I was taught to tell the exquisite truth at all times. That virtue was hammered into me as a child: I must be the honest, double square, full in integrity, Dudley Do-Right who always speaks all shades of the truth.

Therefore, I felt compelled to confront the truth, to face the guilt I'd been suppressing. I felt like Laurie Alberts, who says in her memoir *Fault Line*, "I have no right to fiction's veils and masks. They keep me too safe. In the fan dance that is fiction, I can play peekaboo with the truth, be coy, expose myself just so much, then deny everything." The truth, I decided, was more important than my safety.

What did I think I could gain by using memoir as my base of operation?

Possibly, no-holds-barred writing could touch closer to the truth, to the essence of what it means to be an individual human being here on this earth. Possibly, there was the chance to "tell it like it is" in my own voice that longed to be heard and understood. "This is me. I'm standing naked in front of you. What you see is what you get. The whole truth and nothing but the truth." Maybe I didn't want to wander through the labyrinth of illusion, fabricating stories, but wanted to give my unique self a time and place to be received as is. And maybe I thought this kind of writing was the only kind that mattered. It was the place to which I naturally gravitated.

I pause now to open the nesting doll in my hand. Inside is the second version of the painted woman with a golden babushka *covering all but one lock of her red hair. Another winter scene—a snow-packed road to a snowed-in house—is painted across the front of her body.*

Before I had much advanced education in writing, I wrote for several magazines and journals in Salt Lake City, Utah. My first submission to *Utah Holiday* was a personal essay entitled "Confessions of a Snowplow Queen," followed by "What Does a Nice Girl Like Me Get Out of Belly Dancing?" and "How to Plan Your Own Funeral" (written after the death of my three-year-old son). Among others, "How I Raised a Rock and Roll Band and Learned to Write" appeared in *Salt Lake Magazine*, and "The Walk Away from Mormonism, All the Time with a Stitch in My Side," appeared in *Dialogue: A Journal of Mormon Thought*. It seemed I wanted to write out my angst, put it on paper for me to better understand and, bonus-time, share it with readers. I did well with this approach. I found I could tell soulful stories and gather readers in my net.

I did, however, stretch myself, trying my hand at a broad range of nonfiction writing. I experimented with investigative journalism, feature articles, reportorial articles, impersonal essays, and book reviews. But just before publication of my most notable investigative reporting article, which was titled

"Culture Shock," and which was an award-winning piece later anthologized in *A World We Thought We Knew: Readings in Utah History*, the editor of *Utah Holiday* received a letter from a reader who said something to the effect of "I'm tired of reading about Phyllis Barber. Why don't you get her to write about something more than herself?" The tone of her letter was something like, "How dare she be so intimate with us about her life?" The editor thought the letter was mean-spirited and off the mark, and was also aware that the substantial investigative reporting article was coming out in the next issue. He chose not to publish the letter, but I did take note.

Why did I have this great fascination with myself? Isn't there something more in the universe than me and my issues? Isn't it totally indulgent to think other people want to hear about my life?

I pull the next doll apart to reveal the smaller version inside, still with the same golden babushka and red lock of hair in the middle of her forehead. She's getting smaller, possibly more intense. She's still painted beautifully in the same green paint and with the same lacy embellishments, but a different house on a different snowy road covers her chest.

I enrolled at the University of Utah to elevate myself and my writing, to aspire to the realm of *artiste*. After writing a year's worth of experimental fiction, I began a series of stories about growing up Mormon in Las Vegas. I fictional-ized the names, exaggerated the characters, invented things that would make for a better story, and proceeded to put together a book of short stories. But people who read them said, "These read like autobiography. This is a memoir." Even though I was bound and determined to rise to the elevated position of a writer of fiction, I realized that much of my fiction seemed convoluted, less direct, and more like impressionistic music than story, while my nonfiction had a directness that hit home with readers.

Finally, I decided to enter the Associated Writing Programs' annual writ-ing competition in the creative nonfiction category. Before submitting the manuscript, however, I called them to ask if I could submit the manuscript in its "fictional" form, though it was really a memoir. They said that wouldn't be a problem, but if I won the contest, I would have to change the names to the real ones. And when I did win, I did just that. I took refuge and solace in the word *creative* in "creative nonfiction" because I knew I had taken a substantial amount of creative license. I'd drawn these events from a cloudy, even fog-bound memory, put my own spin on it, and if you consulted with my sister, for instance, she would tell you a different story.

This was the point at which I began to be suspicious about the word *I*, about the possibility of telling the *truth* in personal essay or memoir. In my younger days, I believed if I dug deep enough into the self, I could find answers about who I was, but the authentic self is much more elusive and challenging to locate than one might imagine. Could I have possibly created a fiction about who I am in all of my nonfiction? Maybe I'd been building an aura around myself, creating my own legend, my own myth, my own explanation of myself to my self. I felt the need to ask the tough question, "How well do I see what I think I see and how much do I interpret what I see?" Was there someone known as "I" making up a lot of stories to entertain herself?

Again, I break open the matryoshka *in my hands. Tinier still, the fourth version of the doll appears the same, but the details of her face are slightly altered by the smaller scale, the diminished surface. Her winter scene is composed of snow-covered trees by a frozen stream. Has the doll changed by being opened up?*

I began to ask myself more and more tough questions, including:

1. Why do we choose to tell a particular story about ourselves? Maybe you think no one ever listens to you. Or maybe you think you're one tough cookie and want to tell this story to prove it. Do you tell a particular kind of story to get more attention (i.e., poor me, life mistreats me, I'm such a delicate creature I need to be handled with kid gloves, I am the Queen of Something Somewhere, so Give Me My Due)? Did you decide to tell a particular story to get the most for your time and money? Was it a decision based on real authenticity or based on the kind of stories people would listen to? We are survivors. Is literature, i.e., storytelling, necessary to survival? And whoever makes up the best, worst, or saddest story wins?

2. Do we tell stories to justify ourselves to ourselves? To clarify ourselves?

3. A story, by nature, pulls in bits and pieces of chaos and orders them into a narrative. Doesn't this very act of selecting fragments from the chaos imply the act of fiction?

4. Just how do we put together the story of ourselves? Are there objective, free-standing facts, or are all events seen through a subjective karmic lens?

How has the "I" arrived at *the* truth of its experience? How true does the truth have to be and how much of so-called "truth" is actually fiction because of individual perception?

5. Could it be that we, as both people and writers, are stuck in the notion of who and what the "I" is? Could this "I" that I so very much wanted to talk about be a subjective entity? Since subjectivity implies imagination, is it absolutely necessary to have this division between truth and fiction?

Carolyn Hengst, a therapist who worked with abuse survivors, says in *Mandala* magazine: "There's a power in the stories we tell ourselves about ourselves and the events of our lives. ... The step between an event arising and the words we use to explain the event to ourselves is the *critical event*, rather than the action itself or any arising circumstances."

Even as I think these things, I'm aware that the person I refer to as "I," me, this woman writing to you, is a complex entity. I've been many people. Once I was Phyllis Nelson, good Mormon girl with raven-black hair who desired to be a good mother and wife and concert pianist more than anything else. (But, as I stand back from this description to take notice of the words I've chosen to tell you my story—*raven-black hair, good mother, concert pianist*—I see I've chosen them for dramatic effect.) And there was a time when Phyllis Nelson wanted to be a Las Vegas showgirl, a high-fashion model, and an assistant to the Nevada Senator in DC. (I stand back again to confess these were only three of many options that occurred to me during the wild fervor of my youth, but I chose the jazzier selections for this essay.) Another time I was Phyllis Barber, a not-so-black-haired fiery rebel, community volunteer turned restless artist, belly dancer, a woman champing at the bit to be recognized in the world of the arts, wanting to make a significant contribution. And then there is this moment, now, when I am Phyllis Barber-Traeger, older woman with gray hair. But appearances may be deceiving. Maybe I'm a wise, distinguished older woman, or maybe I'm a frightened child in a woman's body. Maybe I'm a different "I" today from the one I was yesterday. Maybe I am everything I ever was.

So I ask, is there an essential "I" that is still me when all the trappings fall away? Maybe a skeleton? Maybe a spirit? Will I outlive my own flesh? Is the "I" inside of me an eternal entity? Is the "I" I feel so strongly something apart from my squirrel-cage mind and my body?

As I break open the matryoshka once again, I find the sixth doll is very small, but there's still a crack in the middle, which means there's at least one more inside. Her expression is less serene than that worn by her predecessors.

Here are five possible renditions of what might be the truth of the full-metal-jacket guilt I've been wearing for about thirty years now:

1. I had a hemophiliac son who died of a cerebral hemorrhage when he was three years old. The doctor, who had seen him two days before his death for a routine checkup, wasn't sure why, but a hemophiliac can step off a curb and start bleeding internally. My son had a bad cough, which could have been the cause.

2. I had a hemophiliac son who died. I may have snapped him on the forehead with my fingers when he was being impossibly unruly on a difficult morning. I can't remember for sure.

3. I had a hemophiliac son who died of a cerebral hemorrhage. The day before he died, I snapped him in the head, a snap of my fingers against his temple. I caused my son's death.

4. I had a hemophiliac son who died. I'm not sure what actually caused his death, but I've been racked with guilt ever since. I always felt guilty about having given birth to a handicapped child. It follows that I would feel guilty about his death.

5. I suspect myself of loving the tragedy of life. It is as true that I don't know what happened as it is true that I do know what happened.

The Zen master, Dogen, says on the back of a Brushdance greeting card:

> To study the way is to study the self.
> To study the self is to forget the self.
> To forget the self is to be awakened with all things.

Maybe the real meat of this essay has more to do with philosophy, or possibly Buddhism or the Biblical concept of the Great I Am than it does with writing. I do come to this page with a religious/spiritual background, I admit, and those beliefs continue to inform my sensibility. Maybe it has to do with a quote from Willa Cather: "Artistic growth is, more than it is anything else, a refining of the sense of truthfulness. The stupid believe that to be truthful is easy; only the artist, the great artist, knows how difficult it is." But what kept me going all those years when I continued to fall back into writing things I knew and felt guilty about it (as though I was insufficient because I couldn't create something greater than or apart from myself) was the conviction that if I dug deeply enough into myself and told of my barest, rawest, most difficult encounters with this business of rollercoastering up and down the days, I would be telling "everyone's story."

The irony is that the deeper I dug into my own self, my truth, the less I seemed to know my core. In fact, the more I tried to pin myself down, the more evasive the "I" became. On some days, "I" was impulsive, loving, generous, noble, while on other days, the "I" I call myself was greedy, biased, selfish, tender, caring, hopeless, etc. The self was much more slippery than I'd imagined. It was like mercury, if any of you were fortunate enough to play with it before it was deemed poisonous, highly toxic and lethal, how when you touch it, it moves away from the touch. Mercury is literally "nongatherable," for want of a more scientific word.

As Mallarmé says in *Crisis in Poetry*: "I say: a flower! And there rises the one that is absent from all bouquets."

At last, as I disassemble the doll, no further disassembling possible, I find the tiniest carving. She's a hard little thing, and yet she doesn't feel like a core, which I would imagine to be more like the molten center of the earth. She feels like the craftsperson had to stop because it was too difficult to break this small thing into two halves. She's inscrutable. A mystery.

There are some philosophers and esoteric teachers who believe that the "I" is only a construct of language. Maurice Nicoll, an English psychiatrist instrumental in explicating the ideas of G.I. Gurdjieff and P.D. Ouspensky, says in one of his books:

> [T]he idea ... is that just as we can change our position in the outer world by physical effort, so we can change our position in the inner world by psychological effort. ... Each of us has a psychology. ... At any moment you are somewhere physically and somewhere psychologically. Outer observation shews you where you are physically; inner observation—that is, self-observation—shews you where you are psychologically. To be in a bad state psychologically is as if you might be in a dark corner of a room, sitting there, morose and gloomy, when you might shift your position easily and stand in the light. ... Self-observation ... is to make us aware of where we are *psychologically* at any moment and eventually to shift our position. *Where we are psychologically at any moment is what we are at that moment, unless we are aware of it and separate internally from it.*

Every day, hour, even minute, the "I" goes through changes of psychological states. The individual is in a passenger car, riding through the changing landscape of boredom, stress, worry, anxiety, inferiority, and superiority.

When you say, "I am a loser," for instance, are you speaking of a permanent condition? I may be a loser for an hour; I may be something else in the next hour. "I am brilliant," same thing. "I am a great writer. I am a poor writer." The "I" can be all of these things at different times. But a psychological state is not the "I." It is a psychological state. Nothing more. Nothing less.

Nicoll says further that "if you cannot admit that you have a *psychology* at all and say 'I' to every state it leads you into you can get nowhere."

Could it be that there is not one unified I, but rather a collection of I's, as Gurdjieff suggests? So when we use the term *I*, to what are we referring? A particular psychological state—"I'm bored." "I'm angry." "I'm no good."—which is not consistent or permanent? Or are we referring to a particular physical state—"I'm tired." "I'm old." "I'm young"—which is also not consistent or permanent?

The Buddhists speak of the principle of the not-self as a means of opening the path to enlightenment. According to Thich Nhat Hanh, a Vietnamese Zen master and poet, "Not-self signifies absence of permanent identity. Not-self is impermanence itself. Everything is constantly changing. Therefore, nothing can be fixed in its identity. Everything is subject to not-self."

While thinking about this essay a few weeks ago, I went to the dentist's office, where she gave me a healthy dose of nitrous oxide. (You might be interested to know that I told this dentist that "Just Say NO" really means "Just Say Nitrous Oxide.") Under the influence, I had a vision. It was about how human beings are very much like blades of grass in a field. They like to distinguish themselves, try to be bigger or smaller than the next blade, richer or poorer, smarter or dumber, more sophisticated or less, but basically, human beings are all blades of grass, tied into the same natural order of things, the same nutrition, the same finite limitations.

There are other analogies that move closer to the mystical: Each individual is a drop of water in the Ocean of God, or, as the Hindus say, everyone is a cell on the body of God. Maybe we are all slivers or moods of the Great I Am. When we say, "I Am," might we be referring to Higher Power or the Divine Essence or to Something Beyond Our Understanding? Maybe "I Am" can never be contained in one human body.

Maybe, when we take a childhood memory—say, a memory of being criticized for being too thin-skinned—and commit it to paper, we also commit ourselves to one idea of who we once were. We have closed off other options about who the child we were might have been.

My contention, as should be clear by now, is that when you sit down to write a personal essay, memoir, autobiography, or even an intimate, thinly disguised novel, you are just as inventive with the creation of the "I" character as you are with any fictional character because you select fragments of yourself to support a thesis, much as a scientist uses various scraps of evidence to prove a particular theory.

A story is a creation. It is a pulling together from chaos. The life you live is intrinsically related to your perceptions about it. You may be so busy telling the story you've told a thousand times to yourself that you're unable to disentangle yourself from all the threads of the story you've invented to explain yourself to yourself. You've come to believe the story you invented in the first place. You've closed your mind.

Do you need a particular story of yourself in order to matter in the scheme of things? Do you need the reader's or listener's sympathy? How much easier is it to tell the story you're accustomed to telling? How willing are you to challenge your own stories about yourself? How much deeper do you want to look? And will you ever arrive?

Our personal history is inextricable from our writing life, however it manifests itself. You can't have one without the other, though I guess you could get rid of the writer. I've come to believe in allowing our oft-told tales about ourselves some breathing room. Only when you can see yourself differently and accept that the self is a mystery, not something that can be pinned down like a dead butterfly, is change possible. Maybe *novoir*, the term I coined in the middle of the night, is the best way to describe what I was doing.

I'll end by quoting Hafiz, a thirteenth-century Persian poet, slightly adapting one line:

> I have a thousand brilliant lies
> > For the question
> > [Who] are you?
> I have a thousand brilliant lies
> > For the question:
> > What is God?
> If you think that the Truth can be known
> > From words,
> If you think that the Sun and the Ocean
> Can pass through that tiny opening
> > Called the mouth,
> O someone should start laughing!
> Someone should start wildly Laughing—
> > Now!

THE MEANDERING RIVER:

An Overview of the Subgenres of Creative Nonfiction

By Sue William Silverman

The genre of creative nonfiction is a long river with many moods and currents. And even though it traverses waterscapes as diverse as the Mississippi, the Amazon, and the Nile, there are seven basic forms—or ports of call, if you will—which we might explore. At the head of the river lie the categories of biography and autobiography. From here, we flow on to immersion essays (or other forms of New Journalism) in which the author immerses him- or herself in an experience, before traveling on to memoir, to personal essay (including nature and travel writing), to the meditative essay, finally spilling into the lyric essay. In brief, then, the river flows from a relatively exterior focus to an intensely interior one, from a focus on actions and events to one on ideas and emotions. While we begin with a fairly straightforward narrative, we end with one that's subverted or fractured. Yet because this river is a continuum, we'll also find that the ports of call are sometimes so close together that it's difficult to tell where one ends and the other starts.

Let's begin the journey.

PORT OF CALL #1: BIOGRAPHY

A case could be made that biography and autobiography shouldn't be included in the genre of *creative* nonfiction, rather, that they are (or should be) strictly nonfiction, in the same tributary as academic and scholarly writing or journalism. However, given the inevitable subjectivity of the author toward his or her subject, as well as the fact that these two forms have such a long literary tradition, it would be difficult to begin our journey elsewhere.

Biography is a fairly consistent, factual rendering of someone's life, usually a chronological account of "first this happened and then this next thing happened." The author is *supposed* to be objective—although this isn't really possible. While being objective can be a worthy goal, it's a chimera, a necessary fiction. Lawrence Thompson's three-volume biography of Robert Frost is a good example of this subjectivity.

Thompson, Frost's authorized biographer, grew to dislike his subject and allowed his aversion to become part of the text. Especially in the final volume of the biography, Thompson paints Frost as a man who, among other foibles, sees himself as a poet whose gifts to the world aren't fully appreciated. "He wanted the consultantship [in poetry to the Library of Congress] to be treated as an office in which his views would be listened to by the men who were running the country, and in which he could achieve significant results for his 'cause': poetry, the arts—and (not inconsequentially) his own reputation." The quotation marks around *cause* and the parenthetical insertion of "not inconsequentially" reveal Thompson's real, subjective feelings toward Frost.

More recently, the poet and novelist Jay Parini released his own Frost biography, with its own subjective elements, albeit different from Thompson's. Indeed, according to reviewer Melanie Kirkpatrick, "Parini is a fan of Frost's, and seeks, in *Robert Frost: A Life,* to dispel the mythos created by Thompson." I doubt Parini would disagree with that characterization, even though it suggests he, too, has an agenda.

In an interview with Paul Holler on the online journal *Bookslut*, Parini talks about his own expansive view of biography:

> I make few distinctions between straight biographies and novels. They both are works of fiction. Fiction means "shaping" in Latin. I shape reality in both genres. There are demands that come from the genre itself: You can't really change points of view in a biography, and you can't make things up; but I think these are small considerations, and that in general they both involve creating narratives, and narrative is what I like: telling a story.

Although Parini doesn't go so far as to actually "make things up," other biographers do. The most famous example is Edmund Morris's *Dutch: A Memoir of Ronald Reagan*, in which Morris writes himself as a character into scenes where he was not present. Even though the reader knows Morris isn't physically present, nevertheless, wouldn't it be more honest for the author to admit up-front that objectivity is impossible to achieve? Have Morris, on the one hand (by reimagining events in order to make elements of Reagan's life more immediate), and Parini and Thompson on the other (by having a subjective point of view), subverted the whole notion of nonfiction?

What's real, what's fact—what, in effect, nonfiction *is*—is a question our metaphorical river runs into again and again.

PORT OF CALL #2: AUTOBIOGRAPHY

Autobiography is likewise, theoretically at least, a factual retelling of events. Like biography, autobiography is celebrity-driven (Elizabeth Taylor writes an autobiography; Ms. Ordinary Woman writes a memoir), based on one's "life of action," and thus told more historically than impressionistically—unlike a memoir. The "contract" with the reader, as such, is that the historical facts, at least, are true. For example, when President Clinton writes in his autobiography *My Life* that, after his re-election, the United States stopped enforcing the arms embargo in Bosnia, we believe him. Likewise, when he writes about his Middle-Class Bill of Rights, we believe the particulars of the bill. After all, we could check these facts in newspapers. Where facts might be debatable, however, is when Clinton, say, *subjectively* analyzes the success (or failure) of his policies in order to enhance his presidential legacy.

Unlike biography, autobiography allows some room for personal reflection. In fact, when the private, personal life intrudes upon the public persona, autobiography hovers closer to memoir—for example, when Clinton depicts, albeit in very general terms, his affair with Monica Lewinsky. Yet even as he allows the reader a glimpse of the personal man, the glimpse is just that: There's little reflection or psychological analysis. Instead, he uses generic terms such as *inappropriate encounter* and *selfish stupidity*. The deepest he explores a connection between the affair and a troubled childhood—which would be a gold mine for a memoirist—is to mention that, by keeping the affair secret, he once again lived parallel lives, much as he had as a teenager when his alcoholic stepfather abused his mother.

Since autobiography relies on a retelling of events as they happened, the Lewinsky affair is merely one stop along the way of the written life. In the paragraph following this relatively brief discussion about the affair, Clinton describes a meeting with Prime Minister Netanyahu. *I had an inappropriate encounter with Monica Lewinsky. I met with Netanyahu. I addressed Congress. I flew to Ireland.* Autobiography—unlike memoir, as we will see—tends toward both a certain documentary sensibility and a well-defined chronological structure. Also, since the goal of the celebrity autobiographer is usually to place him- or herself in a positive light, it's frequently not a search for moral or emotional truths or psychological insight.

PORT OF CALL #3: IMMERSION

In the immersion essay or book, the author, as the name implies, *immerses* him- or herself in an experience typically outside of his or her familiar milieu. Immersion essayists use the voice of an engaged participant, one who writes in first person, sets scenes, employs sensory description, structures the work with an arc—as opposed to the flatter, more linear voice of a journalist who "merely" covers a story.

There are two basic ways to approach the immersion book or essay.

In the first, the author is the protagonist, thus maintaining a strong, consistent "I" throughout, as in Barbara Ehrenreich's *Nickel and Dimed: On (Not) Getting By in America*. Ehrenreich investigates how the working class survives on the minimum wage, or worse. Rather than rely on interviews, research, labor reports, and statistics—as a journalist would—she herself works such low-paying jobs as waitress and cleaning woman. She is *in* the story; she's part of it. She writes of her experiences with direct and intimate knowledge.

In the second method, the author also writes in the first-person point of view but isn't as literally a participant in the story. Instead, the author deals with a broader context or more distant experience. For example, in *King Leopold's Ghost: A Story of Greed, Terror, and Heroism in Colonial Africa*, Adam Hochschild obviously couldn't participate in colonial events that subjugated the Belgian Congo. Nevertheless, through documents, research, interviews, and trips to the area, he immerses his emotional and psychic self into the events as much as possible. He writes with a clearly subjective belief about the events, as opposed to the dispassionate voice of an academic or journalist, or the less overtly subjective voice of a biographer. Hear his voice when he first learns of the Congo's "killing fields" in a book he just happened to be reading: "Why were these deaths not mentioned in the standard litany of . . . horrors? And why had I never heard of them? I had been writing about human rights for years." It was an "atrocious scandal," Hochschild continues, using language such as "blood spilled in anger" and "torn flesh." Just as Ehrenreich empathizes with those who struggle to survive on the minimum wage, so does Hochschild feel immersed in the terror of King Leopold's reign.

In the following short section from Hochschild's essay "Isle of Flowers, House of Slaves," we see how, through careful selection of detail as well as the first-person point of view, he manages to immerse both himself and the reader in the action.

> These days few spots are purely in the Third World or the First. In Dakar, Senegal, the sun-drenched, crumbling one-time colonial capital of French West Africa, bits of Europe are scattered ... like an archipelago. The First World islands are sleek [with] high-rise resort hotels. ... Virtually all the guests are white. In ... bars ... a liter bottle of Vittel mineral water costs the equivalent of several days' wages for a Senegalese laborer. ...
>
> Farther down [the] road, iron fences have gaps in them; coils of barbed wire on top have half rusted away. ... As I jog along the road early one morning, men are urinating in the street, getting up after sleeping the night in the ruins of buildings. ...

Even though this essay is more about Dakar than about Hochschild (he doesn't refer to himself until the second paragraph, more or less in passing, "[a]s I jog along ...") his presence, nevertheless, is felt throughout. He is the guide between these two worlds. His slant on the details reveals as much about *his* sensibilities as it does about Dakar. It's wrong for some to have so much while others have so little, he implies.

Therefore, compared to biography or autobiography, an immersion essay or book gives the reader access to a deeper, more emotionally authentic exploration of the author's subject. This isn't a straight, factual recounting as with a journalist's "who, what, when, where, and why" questions, either. The immersion writer guides the reader on an emotional as well as factual journey.

It is also worth noting the distinction between immersion and personal essay. In the latter, authors *don't* tend to stray far from their own habitats or familiar emotional landscapes. In immersion writing, as shown, the author usually immerses him- or herself in an environment quite distinct from his or her "normal" life: Ehrenreich is *not* a minimum-wage worker; Hochschild examines the Belgian Congo from the vantage point of another century. One of the early works of New Journalism is *Paper Lion: Confessions of a Last-String Quarterback* by George Plimpton, who "joined" the Detroit Lions football team to discover what it was like to be a professional football player—and then write about it. In short, unlike the personal essayist (whom we'll explore in a moment), the author immerses him- or herself in "events" *solely to write about them.*

PORT OF CALL #4: MEMOIR

Midpoint on our metaphorical river is the memoir, the subgenre most people associate with creative nonfiction, since it most obviously employs many of the same techniques we encounter in fiction: dialogue, setting, character development, plot, and metaphor. In the forms already explored, the text generally follows a relatively straightforward, chronological recounting of events; here, however, the story begins to find a more personal, emotional arc to follow. Unlike biography and autobiography, a memoir isn't about a whole life but, rather, one aspect of it. It's imperative that the author establish her or his clearly defined theme and focus.

What also distinguishes memoir from autobiography is the use of at least two "voices" to tell the story, to explore the depth of events: one I call an "innocent" voice, the other an "experienced" voice—to borrow from William Blake.

The innocent voice relates the facts of the story, the surface subject, the action—not altogether unlike autobiography. It conveys the experience of the relatively unaware persona the author was when the events actually happened. Whether the events are loosely connected by chronology or not, this voice gives the story a sense of "this happened, and then this happened, and then this next thing happened." It is the action, the external part of the story.

The experienced voice, on the other hand, plunges us deeper into the story by employing metaphor, irony, and reflection to reveal the author's progression of thought and emotion. It reveals what the facts *mean,* both intellectually and emotionally. Reflection is not just looking back, recollecting or remembering the past. It's a search to see past events or relationships in a new light. The experienced voice conveys a more complex viewpoint, one that interprets and reflects upon the surface subject.

Whether the memoir is essay- or book-length, both voices are crucial: One thrusts the story forward; the other plunges the reader into the real heart of the matter. As these voices intersect throughout the memoir, the author reveals the true nature of the journey.

Lisa D. Chavez's essay, "Independence Day, Manley Hot Springs, Alaska," begins with the innocent voice—the narrator describing how, in 1975, she and her mother depart southern California for Alaska seeking a new life. This voice describes the wonders of Manley Hot Springs as seen through the eyes of a twelve-year-old girl:

> Instantly I am occupied, walking our dog, wetting the toes of my
> canvas tennis shoes in the silty current, kicking sprays of gravel
> into the air. I narrate the scene to myself, add it to the elaborate
> and constant story I whisper of my adventures in Alaska.

Interspersed with the ongoing story is the experienced voice, the adult author-persona who *now* understands: "I do not see what is in front of me: a shabby small town where people stare openly at that frivolous car—bright orange and marked by its out-of-state plates—and the young woman in white, high-heeled sandals and her daughter that have emerged from it." In addition to the "experienced" voice that can describe the car as "frivolous," Chavez employs subtle metaphorical imagery here as well. By including the detail of the bright orange car, she implicitly compares it to the clothing hunters wear. However, as she goes on to show, *she* is the hunted, not the hunter. She is, as she so accurately says, "marked." She, like the car, is *other*.

This is clearly revealed when the narrator's young self experiences racial hatred. Late one evening, Lisa's mother asks her to walk the dog, and as she leaves their rented room above a bar, she is confronted by a man on the landing pointing a gun at her. "'I told all you goddamn Indians to get the fuck out of my bar,' he says."

In the following paragraphs, the two voices twine together, the innocent voice narrating how she escapes the man, and the experienced voice reflecting upon the event: "I thought [racism] was something else, people who called black people bad names, people who snickered when they heard my last name. Mexican, they'd sneer. ..." Chavez, the author-narrator, deepens the moment even more: "And now I have been shaken into a world I don't understand, a cold, foreign world, where men I don't know can hate me for the way I look." This voice of experience continues to explore her place in the world when she reflects how, in California, her darker skin was envied. There, she even secretly felt "superior." In Alaska, however, "brown skin did not mean beach and health, but it meant something ... shameful. ... Native. ... I would discover how that word could be spit out with as much disgust as any racial slur."

Because memoir is an examination of self, Chavez's persona at the end of the essay is different from her persona at the beginning. By the end, Chavez comes to understand fear; she sees herself and her world through less innocent eyes. "In just a few years … I would learn to put a name to what was happening to me, and learn to be angry. … Even later, I would learn to mold my anger into something I could use."

The lessons learned in memoir aren't as evident in autobiography. In autobiography the author may no longer be president of the United States or a box-office attraction, yet emotionally, he or she hasn't necessarily changed—at least on the page. With rare exceptions, autobiography isn't about exploring the subject's psyche. Memoir is. Autobiography isn't about turning a life into art. Memoir is. The autobiographer justifies "mistakes." The memoirist explores them. The autobiographer focuses on success while the memoirist tries to decipher how or why life events often go wrong. Memoir, therefore, is not a simple narcissistic examination of self—as some critics claim. By employing many of the same techniques as fiction, poetry, and *belle lettres*, memoir achieves universality.

Also unlike autobiography, memoir relies almost solely on memory. Memoirists may research old letters, conduct interviews with family members, examine family documents and photographs, but the reliance on one's subjective perceptions of the past is at the heart of memoir. Whereas autobiography tells the story of "what happened" based on historical facts, memoir examines *why* it happened, what the story means.

In terms of memoir, the reader understands and accepts this tacit contract that retrieving "facts" from memory is both a selective and subjective business. Yet, at the same time, a reader *doesn't* "allow" the memoirist to lie or make up facts willy-nilly. As Patricia Hampl says about critics' reactions to memoirs, "they're so assured that there is a thing called a 'fact' and that it can be found like a lost sock, and that once you've found it that's all you've got to do, state a fact. I think that misrepresents entirely the way the faculty of memory works." In short, subjective memory is acceptable, while pure invention isn't.

PORT OF CALL #5: PERSONAL ESSAY

Whereas memoir is a "slice of a life," the author of a personal essay examines an even slimmer piece of that life or, if you will, a single bend in the river. Personal essays encompass such topics as nature and travel, or social and political issues. Whereas memoir is an exploration of the past, personal essays can explore contemporary—even future—events. Instead of the memoirist's thorough examination of self, soul, or psyche, the personal essayist usually explores one facet of the self within a larger social context.

Memoirs and personal essays do have some things in common, however. In both genres, the author imbues his or her work with a strong personal point of view. In addition, personal essayists, like memoirists, usually don't stray far afield from their own habitats or ways of life. Unlike immersion essayists, who seek to immerse themselves in unfamiliar subject matter, personal essayists write about what they already know well. Annie Dillard, for example, writes about Tinker Creek, close to her home in Virginia, a habitat she knows intimately. Dillard, like many nature writers such as Edward Abbey, Farley Mowat, and Terry Tempest Williams, are already naturalists and environmentalists by inclination.

In her essay "The Molino," Melani Martinez explores her culture, her way of life, by focusing on the Molino—a machine that grinds corn for tamales—as the embodiment of her cultural world. We read three long paragraphs about this "grinder in the back of this old worn-down garage turned kitchen" before we directly "meet" the narrator herself. We smell and hear the machine and understand its impact on her particular world.

> It fills the room with its smell. A burning cloud. A grinding stone. It eats corn. … It gobbles it and changes it to something else. To money, to food, to questions and lifestyles. It prepares children for the rest of what will come. … It is a father. It is a dirty smelly father that works and works and pushes and shoves out the meat of little kernels of corn.

When the narrator finally appears, we learn it is *her* father who owns and operates the molino; this is her environment, in which others may live but cannot describe: "I watched it all," she writes. "The lime-covered caldron of boiling nixtamal and the oar he stirred it with were even older than him. … All the food and all the people and time that went by in that little garage kitchen." This kitchen is a neighborhood gathering place, where news and gossip are exchanged. In addition, most of the extended family works at the Molino, including the author, as a child. "My father subjected [me] to child labor before [I] knew how to spell it." By focusing on the molino, Martinez crafts it as a metaphor for the grind of eking out a living in the tamale business in a particular culture and time.

Of course, as Martinez explores the molino and what it represents, we have a strong sense of the author's personal sensibilities: "We [Martinez and her brother] paced the floor of that old garage dreaming of school days as the bottom of our tennis shoes stuck to the grime. Other than the corn, everything was black and filmed with … fat. … It was hot, it was humid, and for us there was no greater hell." As in a memoir, therefore, a personal essay reflects upon the author's experiences. Yet, instead of examining solely herself, Martinez allows the molino, as object and as metaphor, to reveal the secrets it holds for her family as well as for her culture.

PORT OF CALL #6: MEDITATIVE ESSAY

A meditative essay, as the name suggests, explores or meditates upon an emotion or idea by drawing upon a range of experience. It's a contemplation. Unlike the previous forms, the meditative essay is not necessarily triggered by a specific event. For example, Hochschild's essay begins when he visits Dakar; Chavez's essay starts with the move to Alaska. Such events aren't necessary in meditative essays. Instead, an image or an idea may propel it into being.

There are two ways to approach a meditative essay.

The first way is to examine an idea or emotion by embodying it, making it physical. Let's say someone you love has just died. The loss seems so big that you want to explore the whole notion of "loss"—not just one specific loss. In order to do so, you must discover objects that embody an otherwise abstract emotion. The abstractions must be rendered tangibly. You must discover images or metaphors to embody the ineffable.

The second way to approach a meditative essay is to begin at the opposite end of the spectrum, with the tangible thing itself. But to consider a physical object deeply one must uncover properties hidden *within* the object. Consider a jar of peanut butter. You might begin by describing the label. But then, as you continue writing, you will open the jar, tangibly and metaphorically, to discover what's inside. It's like unwrapping a present. What do you find inside? Peanut butter, of course! But to meditate upon an object, you must discover *more*, something suggested by the object, something that's not just personal experience, rather, some existential or cultural or social or political insight about peanut butter. John Updike does this in his essay "Beer Can," which is a funny, insightful meditation on the often maddeningly, impersonal onslaught of "progress."

Robert Vivian's essay "Light Calling to Other Light" provides another example. It begins with a physical candle, before journeying into the abstract notions of joy and belonging. He writes,

> Lately, I have started to push a wide, yellow candle into sunlight. …
> I move it … to capture the light and to hold it for a while. Then

> its entire fat body glows from within in a rich, mellow flame, like
> an improbable Buddha who is dining on the universe. Aglow on
> the table, it is an homage to light for light's sake.

By the end, he writes of the metaphorical warmth of a candle holding him "in a calm embrace in the duration of the sun passing from morning into darkness." The reader sees that the tangible quality of "light," within the "improbable Buddha," is, metaphorically, the discovery of joy within gloom, which is the theme of this meditation.

In short, the abstract idea needs a tangible body; the tangible object needs a soul. In the meditative essay, we see the ascendancy of the *narrative of image* over the *narrative of action*—a trend that has its roots in the personal essay (think of the imagistic metaphor of Martinez's molino). Here it is the image that drives the work, creating meaning and forming the narrative arc.

PORT OF CALL #7: LYRIC ESSAY

In the lyric essay, as in the meditative essay, the writer is not constrained by a narrative of action; the movement is from image to image, not from event to event. Here, the psyche works more in the mode of poets who "let what will stick to them like burrs where they walk in the fields," to quote Robert Frost. (Parini's good poet, not Thompson's bad one.)

In John D'Agata's "Hall of Fame of Us/Hall of Fame of Them," the very arrangement of words on the page suggests poetry:

> Ergo the town.
> Ergo, also, the fence.
> Most of Rachel, Nevada, lives near this fence.
> Come dusk, at the Little Ale'Inn, the town gets drunk
> on talk about the fence.

The images propel the essay forward, moving from the town, to the fence, to the people, to talk about the fence. The rhythm of this movement, a rhythm created by the short paragraphs and the elliptical storyline, makes the essay seem more like verse than prose. In fact, one reason writers use this form is to explore the boundary between essay and lyric poetry. As D'Agata himself writes in the *Seneca Review*, lyric essays, like poems, "require us to complete their meaning. ... The lyric essay doesn't care about figuring out why papa lost the farm, or why mama took to drink. It's more interested in replicating the feeling of that experience."

In this kind of elliptical writing, not all facts are neatly spelled out, understood, or resolved. The reader is required to fill in the blanks as much as possible while, at the same time, accepting that much will remain mysterious. As with poetry, the reader accepts the emotion of the piece itself as the essential "fact." The accumulation of images forms an emotional whole, if not a traditionally essayistic one.

TOWARD THE SEA

Creative nonfiction is all of the above, and more. Elements of two or more of the subgenres we've discussed can be combined to create "hybrid" genres as well. In many ways, for example, "The Molino," while at heart a personal essay, also includes elements of memoir in the way the author notes the impact of the molino on her life. At the same time, long passages about the molino itself are reminiscent of a meditative chant.

Myriad experimental structures exist in creative nonfiction as well. For the adventurous, anything goes. Memoirs and essays can be written as montages or mosaics. Harvey Pekar's *American Splendor* series of "graphic memoirs" helps redefine "comic books," while the film version of his life uses documentary to deconstruct the usual Hollywood clichés. In *Nola: A Memoir of Faith, Art, and Madness,* Robin Hemley incorporates short stories both by himself and his mother, as well as his sister's letters and artwork, into his own creative nonfiction text.

Pat Mora, in *House of Houses,* relies on poetic language and magical realism. Reading her work, we feel as if all of the members of her family, alive and dead, are present, talking together. Marjane Satrapi, in *Persepolis: The Story of a Childhood,* tells her story about growing up in Iran during the Islamic Revolution through a series of black-and-white illustrations, while Lawrence Sutin, in *A Postcard Memoir,* uses postcards, reproduced in the text, as portals into memory.

WATERS EBB AND FLOW

So, you're in the middle of writing *something,* but you don't know what. Is it memoir? A meditative piece? "How do I decide?" you ask.

Just as bodies of water all have a common element, so with creative nonfiction. As we have seen, the distinctions among these subgenres frequently blur.

Therefore, the differences are more in terms of degree than kind. For example, memoirs, personal essays, and meditations can all contain similar elements, such as employing one voice that relates the story, twined with another voice deepening it, metaphorically.

Yet, as with water—some being fresh, some salty—there are differences in creative nonfiction. In autobiography, immersion essays, memoirs, and personal narratives, an *action* drives the work. The arc is that of you, your persona, seeking to understand this action. This kind of essay falls more along an *axis of action*, a series of events you're following like a map of a river.

In a meditative or lyric essay, on the other hand, an *idea* or *emotion* drives the work. You seek to give shape to a thought or idea, making the intangible tangible. These essays fall more along an *axis of contemplation*, whereby images form a constellation. So while you may not be moving forward in time, you're moving deeper into the metaphorical river.

Whatever port of the river you decide to explore, I hope you'll enjoy the journey.

"I RECOGNIZE THY GLORY":

On the American Nature Essay and Lyric Poetry

By Sydney Lea

A premise: Nature, as commonly understood by the greatest writers in the genre under discussion, stands apart from all that is made or artificial, so that the "nature essay" is a contradiction in terms — and knows it.

I speak of the *American* nature essay, and more specifically of what I think its most interesting mode, whose practitioners derive from Thoreau and might include Aldo Leopold, say, or Edward Abbey, Gretel Ehrlich, Barry Lopez, James Kilgo, Rick Bass, or, in her one truly good book, *Pilgrim at Tinker Creek*, Annie Dillard. Though neat distinctions are always suspect, I ignore what seems the more European, and particularly British, tradition of rural writing, whose contemporary practitioners might include the likes of Noel Perrin or Wendell Berry, writers who shun the volatile city in order to witness more harmonious—and even, as in the writings on the harvest, more ritualized—human relations.

By contrast, Thoreauvian authors consider the development of human relations, ritual or otherwise, to be a perversion of their longed-for original relations to *nonhuman* nature. I quote the scholar Peter Fritzell, from whose brilliant and encyclopedic *Nature Writing and America* I have borrowed to the point of near plagiarism in what follows:

> … [T]he most conspicuous trait of American nature writing is its narrator, the prototypical "I" of so much American literature, an Ishmael-like figure ranging the gamut of philosophical stances and psychological states, constantly (and unpredictably) shifting

its point of view ... , continually changing its tenses, its vocabulary, and its stylistic techniques—in almost every way indicating both the basic instability of its positions or perspectives and its final reluctance to bring conventional, "civilized" order to an experience best lived and understood in a continual series of situational surprises or unanticipated discoveries ...

Fritzell implies that the nature essay is far closer to canonical American poetry and fiction than to anything else, and he elsewhere quotes for example a famous passage from Abbey's *Desert Solitaire*:

Standing there, gaping at this monstrous and inhuman spectacle of rock and cloud and sky and space, I feel a ridiculous greed and possessiveness come over me. I want to know it all, possess it all, embrace the entire scene intimately, deeply, totally, as a man desires a beautiful woman. An insane wish? Perhaps not—at least there's nothing else, no one human, to dispute possession with me.

... Near the first group of arches, looming over a bend in the road, is a balanced rock about fifty feet high, mounted on a pedestal of equal height; it looks like a head from Easter Island, a stone god or a petrified ogre.

Like a god, like an ogre? The personification of the natural is exactly the tendency I wish to suppress in myself, to eliminate for good. I am here not only to evade for a while the clamor and filth and confusion of the cultural apparatus but also to confront, immediately and directly if possible, the bare bones of existence, the elemental and fundamental, the bedrock which sustains us. I want to be able to look at and into a juniper tree, a pierce of quartz, a spider, a vulture, and see it as it is in itself, devoid of all humanly ascribed qualities, anti-Kantian, even the categories of scientific description. To meet God or Medusa face to face, even if it means risking everything human in myself. I dream of a hard and brutal mysticism in which the naked self merges with a nonhuman world and yet somehow survives still intact, individual, separate. Paradox and bedrock.

The voice here perfectly typifies that of Fritzell's "prototypical figure in American nature writing," who feels within himself the painful clash of nature and culture, his very craft being a manifestation of the "apparatus" he longs to escape. Language and writing themselves, especially "poetic" language and writing—these, just as much as science, are at variance with that abiding American desire to merge the self with something utterly other.

Which brings me back to the nature essay as oxymoron: its authors passionately want it to be about nature, but it turns out really, and often maddeningly, to be about their own perceptions of nature, and thus finally about their *self*-perceptions. In *Pilgrim at Tinker Creek* you now and then hear the narrator resort to hard-scientific terminology. In *Walden* the "I" here and there catalogues weather, weights, and measures. I could go on but mean mainly to say that in the nature essay, while the narrator occasionally seeks absolute clarity and factuality, he or she does so with immediate skepticism: Such civilized modes of responding to "nature in the original" can't be right, can they? And so the speaker falls into extreme self-consciousness and even self-irony.

And yet it is from that state that the best writing to be found in his or her work emerges.

I can put such matters personally, if crudely. Anyone who spends as much time as I do among woods (especially alone) must surmise the inutility of language. I cannot even here present the sort of experience to which words are inadequate, because I have to *use* words. *Tamarack. Raven. Doe. Granite. Spawning bed.*

The.

And.

Because.

And yet isn't the same dilemma encountered by anyone who spends a lot of time among deep feelings (especially alone) and who likewise wants to speak about that experience? As both essayist and poet, then, I think I share with an Edward Abbey a desire to witness the profoundest importances of my life in an unmediated way, to feel the dissolution of my separate, Whitmanian self … and a simultaneous desire to hang onto that self so I may *testify* to the profundities.

To put my argument tersely: The lyric poet's further dreams always involve some merger of words and fundamentals, of language and the unutterable—and in this respect they resemble the further dreams of the nature essayist. Whatever his or her context or subject, that poet's ambitions are founded on the very paradox that Abbey implies in the paragraphs I cited: Formulated language is an instant compromise of a subject's genuineness, an instant venture into the factitious.

It is therefore not news that the cry against "mere art" is more persistent in our poetics than in any other nation's. Always and everywhere, it seems, we hear the demand for our poems to be—what? Why, "natural," of course. Listen to poet-critic Jonathan Holden on this issue. After quoting a poem by Sandra McPherson, he likens it to "much contemporary poetry—particularly the kind being fostered in university creative-writing programs—a 'poetry of sensibility,' a cultivated attempt to imitate spontaneous vision, to produce through carefully muted craft the illusion of urgency."

What we have, then, is a poetry of what this commentator calls "affected naturalness." How's that for oxymoronic? And yet I do not mean, any more than Holden does, to condescend to anyone: The conflict between the literary and the natural is in some sense absolute, and perhaps we may be forgiven for our clumsier efforts at denying that actuality.

Such denial, you see, is what literary art is for—at least in the genres that lean least heavily on reason—and we undertake it in the clear knowledge that the best of our denials can never be more than half-successful. (This is another take on why Valéry spoke of poems' never being finished but only abandoned; it is why we write so *many* of the damned things.) And yet the only avenue I know to half-success begins with our temporarily throwing aside the very issues of "craft," of "cultivation," and, emphatically, of "meaning."

Though I scarcely believe good writing in any genre is necessarily, or ever, anti-rational, in the two I'm considering here—the lyric poem and the Thoreauvian essay—there is at least a great deal of nonrational energy. Or ought to be, I'd claim, if either is going to catch a reader's attention. Consider Rick Bass's *The Ninemile Wolves*. At the very start, in a page or so of marvelously evocative prose, the author imagines those Montana wolves pulling down a quarry; and then come some telling afterthoughts:

> They don't have thumbs. All they've got is teeth, long legs, and—I have to say this—great hearts.
>
> I can say what I want to say. I gave up my science badge a long time ago. I've interviewed maybe a hundred people for or against wolves. The ones who are "for" wolves, they have an agenda: wilderness, and freedom for predators, for prey, for everything. The ones who are "against" wolves have an agenda: they've got vested financial interests. It's about money—more and more money—for them. They perceive the wolves to be an obstacle to frictionless cash flow.

The story's so rich. I can begin anywhere.

I can start with prey, which is what controls wolf numbers (not the other way around), or with history, which is rich in sin, cruelty, sensationalism (poisonings, maimings, torture). You can start with biology, or politics, or you can start with family, with loyalty, and even with the mystic-tinged edges of fate, which is where I choose to begin. It's all going to come together anyway. It has to. We're all following the wolf. To pretend anything else—to pretend we are protecting the wolf, for instance, or managing him—is nonsense of the kind of immense proportions of which only our species is capable.

Bass, I would argue, is capable of prose that's as lyrical as any lyric in verse. And I'd argue that he is lyrical precisely in his willingness to abandon himself to his own materials, which are the primitive instincts of the raptor self and, in apparent contradiction, the primitive urge to speak. Neither of these urges conforms to an elaborate agenda, but only to its own hunger. Indeed, "agenda" is the very sort of notion it avoids like a trap. Both self and speech assume a coherence in the world, but neither assumes it will be discovered in a consecutive way. (A different sort of inquiry from this would consider the inevitably sinuous, heavily subordinated syntax of the nature essay.)

Like an animal on the scent, or like the most truly adept human hunter, the author follows signs that are at once cryptic and potentially eloquent. It is only the very act of pursuit that at length will lead to the connections among these signs.

I'm beginning to tend, almost perforce, toward some mystic-tinged edges myself, and toward abstraction. Let me once again try, therefore, to root my observations in personal experience. A typical nature essay will begin for me in the same manner as a typical lyric poem. I'm speaking here not only of aesthetics or technique but also of far more literal matters, such as my inclination to hike long distances in the woods by myself, seeking not to think up "subjects" but to let my mind float free until, over time, perhaps over a dozen hikes or even years, I find that certain things have lodged themselves in my consciousness and now demand meditation—that they have "subjected" *me*.

In my book *Hunting the Whole Way Home* is an essay called "On the Bubble." Here is how it starts:

Early June of 1992, below Stonehouse Mountain, Grafton County, New Hampshire—a place and time in which snowsqualls, routine enough just weeks ago, will at last deserve the name freakish. In freshet beds where waters flared and vanished, frail shoots of jewelweed declare themselves; grass bursts the voles' winter tunnels; geese trail the Connecticut northward; the buck deer's antlers are in velvet; the woodchuck's busy to double in weight; trout sip the ponds' ephemerids; everywhere, the love-sick insistence of birds.

Our family has lived ten years on this foothill's flank, but soon after down this morning—beckoned by the fully day ahead—I hiked down from its mild summit for perhaps the last time. The ramble, especially under such circumstances, brought back the many I'd made there, in company or alone, one recollection summoning another, and that one still another, till outward prospects opened onto vaster, more labyrinthine inward views.

Yet that last paragraph, in all honesty, is one I wrote late in the construction of this piece, *after* I happened on what the essay was "about"; for the way it began conceptually was in my somehow remembering a beautiful, brown-phase fisher that almost stepped across my toes one fall while I was deer-hunting; that, and the fact that, at the time I began feeling an itch to write this particular chapter, my family was on the point of moving from Stonehouse Mountain, which a developer had decided to ruin; that, and the memory of my son blowing bubbles one spring morning at the summit of the same mountain. Yes, these were the things that, although chronologically quite removed from one another, had lodged themselves in my consciousness. My essay therefore was, and is, about what they all had to do with one another. I began in the spirit of Rick Bass: "It's all going to come together anyway. It has to."

Or maybe I began in the spirit of Wallace Stevens, since my essay also was, also is, closely akin to what he called "the poem of the mind in the act of finding what will suffice," *finding* and *mind* being the words I'd stress, for total sufficiency will always escape us. As I said early on, the nature essay turns out to be about the essayist's perception of nature, and thus about his or her mind's perception of itself.

This cannot, however, be a static perception; it must be one that unfolds in the very process of writing either essay or poem—it is an act, or rather multiple acts, of finding. My aim as I sat down to indite "On the Bubble" was simply to see if I could write my way to a connection among a few things, however seemingly disconnected, that had stopped me in my tracks.

The appropriateness of the fragile bubbles my son blew, for example, to the theme of natural fragility that so exercised me when the bulldozers started to chew up the mountain I loved—that appropriateness was something that crept up on me, surprised me. To recall the words of Peter Fritzell to which I referred at the outset, the so-called "nature essay" seeks—however vainly and oxymoronically—to replicate "experience best lived and understood in a continual series of situational surprises or unanticipated discoveries."

In this the nature essay is like a poem, because in either case it turns out that even our own minds are things we must "find," and, at least in my experience, both the frustrations and the joys of poem or essay are intimately linked with that fact. When I say in the piece just quoted that "outward prospects opened onto vaster, more labyrinthine inward views," I am at once dismayed and exhilarated. Like an Edward Abbey, I too would like now and then to immerse myself entirely and exclusively in outward prospects, a desire doomed to failure, largely because, like him, I use language even when I'm silent. Hell, I'm a damned writer!

I'm a lyrical writer, too, which means one who takes profound pleasure in the discovery of his sensibility's capacity to forget associations in that nonrational, nonconsecutive fashion I earlier indicated. I had not known that a big brown weasel and my son's bubble-blowing had anything to do with one another, or with my reaction to the so-called "development" of Stonehouse Mountain. To learn that they did connect was revealing and oddly thrilling.

And yet I cannot end just here, for fear of seeming to advocate, in poetry or prose, the virtues of utter self-regard. Be sure that I too tire pretty easily of poems and essays founded on the belief that the least *frisson* of feeling on the author's part is unfailingly interesting to others. This is in part why I frequently resort to narrative strategies in poetry, and even to the willful "artificiality" of formal verse.

It is also why I am a passionate amateur naturalist. Yes, I may have opined that the ultimate subject of any American lyric or any American nature essay is the self's perception of the self, but at the risk of circular logic I'll also suggest that the lyric poet or essayist can be saved from mere narcissism by his or her immersion in subjects outside the self—especially ones that prove resistant to the individual human will, or at least the will's lust to heap meanings upon them. Such willful insistency, you see, is in my opinion the great enemy of what we call "creativity"; it is the faculty that works up an agenda for us to follow.

A virtue of the natural world is, precisely, that it forever resists rigid agenda of the mind or will. In this regard, it can serve as a model. As such a model, the natural world has some further virtues as well, one of them being that an essay about it, a "nature essay," demands accuracy. Fakery will wreck it. Indeed, one of the prime foibles I have noticed, for example, in undergraduates who want to write "on nature" is that they like the idea of being green, but are green in quite another way. They are as apt to put Osage oranges in northern Vermont as hop hornbeam, anhingas on Lake Ontario as goldeneyes, and so on.

Yes, "the mind in the act of finding what will suffice" may be as much the final subject of a nature essay as of a poem, but the essay can't just say any old thing that occurs to it. As Puritans like me are fond of claiming, it must "earn" its right to speak. It must establish its authority. The connections among its things and thoughts and emotions may and should be nonrational, but that's a long way from saying that its facts are finally irrelevant.

The factual fascinations of a Thoreau or a Dillard or a Barry Lopez represent some measure of self-defense, but they also provide appropriate ballast to essays that might otherwise be so self-conscious as to become utterly private … and unpersuasive. If we speak only of our emotional workings, we exclude the reader. Likewise, if we don't know one tree, one bird, one rock, one fish, one animal from another, how seriously can our "love" for all these be taken?

In this regard, too, the demands of the nature essay seem models for the lyric poem. If I hear even so fine a poet as Donald Hall, for instance, describe how "quail scream in the fisher's jaw" in his adoptive New Hampshire, I'm a little disinclined to listen to him on less factual subjects, there being no wild quail in that state at all. Brendan Galvin, in his excellent essay "The Contemporary Poet and the Natural World," makes a similar point after reading Gerald Stern's claim to have once been awakened by "two or three daws" in West Virginia, or Larry Levis's report on some Missouri linnets.

Galvin aptly quotes Robert Graves in this connection: "Fact is not truth, but a poet who willfully defies fact cannot achieve truth." The same, I would claim, for the poet who is ignorant of the facts on which she or he purports to found insight.

To every student I've ever had, then, I've stressed the importance of a sort of homework, though in the case of the nature essay the term is at best inexact. But whatever the genre, say I, let it involve something Out There. I'll even venture that for us to concentrate, to the distressingly small extent we possibly can, on the Out-There may be the very discipline to deliver us, unexpectedly, into the realm of the imagination in its least solipsistic typology.

I'll say that that sort of imagination is glorious, an adjective which intentionally echoes a favorite of the great "nature poet" William Wordsworth at a sublime turn of *The Prelude*. So rapt in his observations of the French Alps had he once been as a young man that he did not even know he had crossed them. He describes his feelings after inquiring and being informed that the Simplon Pass was behind him:

> Imagination! Here the power so called
> Through sad incompetence of human speech,
> That awful power rose from the mind's abyss
> Like an unfathered vapour that enwraps,
> At once, some lonely traveler. I was lost;
> Halted without an effort to break through.

Years later, however, he understands something:

> But to my conscious soul I now can say,
> "I recognize thy glory ..."

No, nature doesn't "do" essays or poems. It exists in a way that quite specifically frustrates essays and poems, dramatizing as it does the "sad incompetence of human speech"; but in that very frustration, it may free up "awful powers" within us, ones that have lain undiscovered until the very moment we find them. To speak of them may, in some philosophic sense, be a come-down, a recognition of relative incompetence.

But we have to keep trying. It's what, as writers, we do.

POETIC TECHNIQUE IN NONFICTION WRITING

By Cynthia Huntington

Much has been written, justly, about the importance of fictional technique in nonfiction writing. Something, at least, remains to be said for the abundant use of poetic structures and logic in the genre, particularly in short nonfiction, most particularly in the personal essay. In this brief essay, I want to try to shift the conversation ever so slightly, to acknowledge and explore some of these poetic techniques in nonfiction. I will offer some comments about the use of image and metaphor as structural elements in nonfiction, as well as some thoughts on voice, authenticity, the presentation of the self, and the reflexive nature of lyric. I will make a case, albeit a modest case, that in many ways the poet and the essayist appear to be of one mind.

The importance of fictional techniques is obvious. In these techniques I include: narrative development, plot, character, scene construction, dialogue, point of view, and especially the *movement through time*, which characterizes the novel.

I don't need to enumerate the ways in which these are employed. Nor do I take issue with their importance. But when I read, in one very well-known and otherwise excellent text (*Creative Nonfiction*, by Philip Gerard), that "Creative nonfiction *is* narrative, it *always* tells a good story" (emphasis mine), I feel that something has been elided. Perhaps we constrict our possibilities in this genre, even as we are trying to open them, if we give in to a temptation to narrowly construe nonfiction as some sort of shadow partner to fiction, the novel with different rules of evidence, perhaps.

I would qualify Gerard's pronouncement, which I repeat here because it seems to echo prevailing approaches to both teaching and critiquing nonfiction. I'd rather say: "*Much* creative nonfiction is narrative; it *often* tells a good story." And even then, the *story*, in any imaginative work, is far from the whole story. And so my intention in this essay is not to construct an opposition, but to call attention to other possibilities already in existence.

If fiction takes for its main tools those listed above—narrative, conflict, characterization, scene, dialogue, movement through time—how might we describe the elements of poetry? The central difference between prose and verse—the turning of the line, with its accompanying possibilities and complications of white space, doubling meanings, directing emphasis, etc.—clearly does not obtain. I am not making a claim that an essay actually *imitates* a poem, or could ever be mistaken for one. (Leaving aside for the moment the ever-vexed question of the prose poem.)

The list for poetry might begin with metaphor, image, compression and intensification of language, and extend to emphasis on voice and a temptation to identify the voice of the essay with the writer. Some of these are formal properties of poetry; some (especially the illusion of personal voice) are mostly circumstantial and limited to a particular time in social and literary history (the late twentieth and early twenty-first centuries).

I want to stop and acknowledge that these elements I'm calling "poetic" are used in fiction freely. Just as poems use narrative and dialogue and so forth, of course novels and short stories employ metaphor, voice, and image (which fiction writers like to call "significant detail," which is certainly one way of looking at it).

It's a question of the relative importance of any of these elements in propelling and structuring a piece of writing. So before I get caught in an entirely circular argument, let's take a look at how this works. For my first example, I'll examine the following essay by Tim O'Brien.

The Vietnam in Me

LZ Gator, Vietnam, February 1994—I'm home, but the house is gone. Not a sandbag, not a nail or a scrap of wire.

On Gator, we used to say, the wind doesn't blow, it sucks. Maybe that's what happened—the wind sucked it all away. My life, my virtue.

In February 1969, 25 years ago, I arrived as a young, terrified pfc. on this lonely little hill in Quang Ngai Province. Back then, the place seemed huge and imposing and permanent. A forward firebase for the Fifth Battalion of the 46th Infantry, 198th Infantry Brigade, LZ Gator was home to 700 or 800 American soldiers, mostly grunts. I remember a tar helipad, a mess hall, a medical station, mortar and artillery emplacements, two volleyball courts, numerous barracks and offices and supply depots and machine shops and entertainment clubs. Gator was our castle. Not safe, exactly, but far preferable to the bush. No land mines here. No paddies bubbling with machine-gun fire.

Maybe once a month, for three or four days at a time, Alpha Company would return to Gator for stand-down, where we took our comforts behind a perimeter of bunkers and concertina wire. There were hot showers and hot meals, ice chests packed with beer, glossy pinup girls, big, black Sony tape decks booming "We gotta get out of this place" at decibels for the deaf. Thirty or 40 acres of almost-America. With a little weed and a lot of beer, we would spend the days of stand-down in flat-out celebration, purely alive, taking pleasure in our own biology, kidneys and livers and lungs and legs, all in their proper alignments. We could breathe here. We could feel our fists uncurl, the pressures approaching normal. The real war, it seemed, was in another solar system. By day, we'd fill sandbags or pull bunker guard. In the evenings, there were outdoor movies and sometimes live floor shows—pretty Korean girls breaking our hearts in their spangled miniskirts and high leather boots—then afterward we'd troop back to the Alpha barracks for some letter writing or boozing or just a good night's sleep.

So much to remember. The time we filled a nasty lieutenant's canteen with mosquito repellent; the sounds of choppers and artillery fire; the slow dread that began building as word spread that in a day or two we'd be heading back to the bush. Pinkville, maybe. The Batangan Peninsula. Spooky, evil places where the land itself could kill you.

Now I stand in this patch of weeds, looking down on what used to be the old Alpha barracks. Amazing, really, what time can do. You'd think there'd be something left, some faint imprint, but LZ (landing zone) Gator has been utterly and forever erased from the earth. Nothing here but ghosts and wind.

The narrative is attenuated, though real. O'Brien has returned to LZ Gator and now stands there thinking. Then the ghost of a narrative appears in memory—but not a narrative in which one thing gives way to another. Nothing will happen. The movement here is the movement of thought, and still, nothing will happen.

Scene is a strong element—a single scene folding into memory. With little snips of remembered scenes.

There's no *plot*, no place where conflict leads to change. What drives this essay is the movement of thought over two scenes superimposed, past and present. What drives and informs this thought is the elaboration of a central metaphor, stated right up front: the idea of *home*. What *home* is in this essay becomes a question that is worried, considered, and reconsidered, to yield layers of meaning. Follow me through some recurring phrases (emphases mine):

"I'm *home*, but the *house* is gone." House/home. A house is not a home—dispossession, return. The underlying question of *safety* in relation to home.

"Sucked away." The house gone, O'Brien finds his life, and his virtue compromised. What is home?

In the third paragraph we read again that "LZ Gator was *home*" and, a little later, "Gator was our castle," echoing the old cliché "a man's home is his castle" and evoking again the question of safety, security, and permanence in relation to home.

"LZ Gator was our castle. Not safe exactly, but far preferable to the bush." Then we go into the comforts of home, juxtaposed with the irony of "behind bunkers and concertina wire": "hot showers, hot meals ... beer, sex, music." Here "home" begins to refer not just to a literal home (better than the bush) or to the America he's left behind for this "home" but to a metaphorical home, his youth. Once he's evoked the true home of nostalgia for his lost youth, O'Brien's memory begins to wander. He unearths bits and pieces of old memory, and home is gradually identified as something lost, faint and irrecoverable. Doubling of time: O'Brien standing there in 1994 sees the old LZ Gator as gone, sucked away, but *inside* the memory of 1969 the idea of home is already lost. Loss folds into loss, until at the end he's left to say: "Amazing, really, what time can do." The "nothing left" of LZ Gator is at one with what was sucked away from the young man.

LZ is finally defined, after great delay, as standing for *landing zone*. Another definition of home appears at this point, a definition much more ironic and tentative than "house" or "castle" or "America." But they're *all* gone—nothing but ghost and wind, and we end where we began, having imagined ourselves full circle, back to the wind that doesn't blow, but sucks.

I want to say more about this essay, but first I want to consider a different non-narrative structure in the following essay by Ian Frazier.

Crazy Horse

Personally, I love Crazy Horse because even the most basic outline of his life shows how great he was; because he remained himself from the moment of his birth to the moment he died; because he knew exactly where he wanted to live, and never left; because he may have surrendered but he was never defeated in battle; because, although he was killed, even the Army admitted he was never captured; because he was so free that he didn't know what a jail looked like; because at the most desperate moment of his life he only cut Little Big Man on the hand; because, unlike many people all over the world, when he met white men he was not diminished by the encounter; because his dislike of the oncoming civilization was prophetic; because the idea of becoming a farmer apparently never crossed his mind; because he didn't end up in the Dry Tortugas; because he never met the President; because he never rode on a train, slept in a boardinghouse, ate at a table; because he never wore a medal or a top hat or any other thing that white men gave him; because he made sure that his wife was safe before going to where he expected to die; because although Indian agents, among themselves, sometimes referred to Red Cloud as "Red" and Spotted Tail as "Spot," they never used a diminutive for him; because, deprived of freedom, power, occupation, culture, trapped in a situation where bravery was invisible, he was still brave; because he fought in self-defense, and took no one with him when he died; because, like the rings of Saturn, the carbon atom, and the underwater reef, he belonged to a category of phenomena which our technology had not then advanced far enough to photograph; because no photograph or painting or even sketch of him exists; because he is not the Indian on the nickel, the tobacco pouch, or the apple crate. Crazy Horse was a slim man of medium height with brown hair hanging below his

waist and a scar above his lip. Now, in the mind of each person
who imagines him, he looks different.

Here we have no narrative to speak of. The facts of Crazy Horse's life
and the narrative of history in which he appears are held in the background
and treated as a kind of grab bag the writer can reach into over and over for
evidence. In fact, the *absence* of narrative here works to enhance the writer's
argument, which is that Crazy Horse is noble and great. By reaching in, apparently at random, and emerging with sequentially unrelated information, all of
which confirms this greatness, Frazier builds the implication that *any* evidence
will yield the same result, and that the author's conclusion is inevitable. It's a
formal structure of repetition/variation, one that "ignites pleasure centers in
the brain," as Tom Lux once said. The repetition of "because" is obvious and
highly stressed. It's a syntactical structure, actually a very specific device called
anaphora, the device of organizing lines or sentences by repeating the same
word or phrase at the beginning of each. (Think of the King James Bible, and
Whitman's "When I Heard the Learn'd Astronomer.") Used here, it does almost offer a feeling of lineation and enjambment in what is, of course, prose.

The cumulative force of any repeating figure draws upon the constantly
resonating shifts of meaning and rhythm that are generated. Repetition here
functions further by a pattern of *negation* and *fine distinctions*. Look at the
structure of some of these phrases (emphases mine):

"*Even* the most basic outline of his life"—a qualification if not an outright
negation—builds quickly to "surrendered … *never* defeated," and "killed …
never captured. He "*didn't know* what a jail looked like," "he *only* cut Little
Big Man on the hand." Further examples accrue: "*unlike* many people," "*not*
diminished," "*never* crossed his mind," "*didn't* end up," "*never* met," "*never*
rode," "*never* wore," "*never* used," "took *no one* with him," and "he is *not* the
Indian on the nickel."

And, after all these negatives, Frazier gives us a single statement—what
can be said, and so resonates more strongly: "Crazy Horse was a slim man of
medium height with brown hair hanging below his waist and a scar above
his lip."

Speaking of fine distinctions, all of these negations can be seen to isolate
and distinguish Crazy Horse. We are told what he would do versus what he
would refuse or manage to avoid. His greatness is to elude description, definition, and confinement within the terms of a society that can't comprehend
him. He is *never captured*. In this, we read an implied negation of, resistance

to, "our" technology, and "our" culture. We arrive at the conclusion, implied throughout, that Crazy Horse is more advanced, refined, and subtle than "we" are. Which leads to a shocking reversal: all this talk of civilization, and it turns out that *we* are the ones not advanced enough to photograph him— which means, in the context of Frazier's essay, to understand, comprehend, or really *see* him.

And, what's more, Crazy Horse retains control over these distinctions. *He was never captured.* This establishes his singularity, his integrity. No one can use a diminutive, make him not himself, his full self. He *eludes* knowledge by negating and passing between categories and assumptions, until he resides wholly in the sympathetic imagination.

Again, I will return to this essay after a look at a very different piece of writing, this one by Richard Shelton.

Nostalgia

Whatever happened to the crepuscular? It's never mentioned anymore. Years since I heard any reference to the crepuscular. I wonder if anybody notices it now as we once did, creeping in and out with silent majesty, leaving some of us with lumps in our throats. It would be a relief from the carnage and mayhem. I remember sometimes at that time of day in the autumn when there was a chill in the air and somebody was burning leaves somewhere, I could nearly die of happiness. But I am older now and it's illegal to burn leaves. So I guess nobody notices the crepuscular anymore. Or the bucolic. Nobody ever says, "Let's go spend a bucolic weekend in the country." And nobody calls anything idyllic. Whatever became of idyllic afternoons beside the river? And grand passions? Passions don't seem to be grand anymore, just sort of everyday affairs. I guess it's hard to have a grand passion without idyllic afternoons and crepuscular evenings, and we are just too busy to take the time for such things. And nightingales? I never heard one myself, but I certainly read about them, and they seemed to be almost everywhere at one time. Perhaps they were no longer needed and they died out or somebody shot them. Might be a few left in a zoo somewhere, I wouldn't know about that. But surely gentility has survived. You mean gentility is gone too? Lord!

> But whatever happened to peace and quiet? Somewhere there
> still must be some peace and quiet. And whatever happened
> to kindness … ?

What governs this essay? A process of association—voice, tone, word association. A querulous tone informs this piece, a tone which characterizes the speaker as nostalgic, if a little ironic in his complaint. To whom is he complaining? To whom are all these questions addressed? I'd venture to say it appears that these questions are put out to the universe, in a kind of "How long O Lord" plaint—a tongue-in-cheek meditation on loss and decline.

So much depends here on our willingness to pretend along with the speaker that a word falling out of use indicates a passing of the phenomenon it represents. Here, the word is taken so literally that its existence is declared necessary to uphold the speaker's world. This extended indirect argument leads to what poets call a "conceit," a dominating metaphor. We suspend our disbelief in the literal accuracy of the metaphor in order to enjoy its imaginative elaboration as the work unfolds.

The other strong factor in this piece is the persona of the speaker. This is not something that belongs to poetry alone, of course. But in this case, the voice, with its irony and querulousness, extends the theme—it asks rhetorical questions, recalls the old days fondly, appears alternately afraid of or disapproving of the present. It points not so much to any real, or even potentially real, speaker, but to the exaggeration of an attitude—for effect.

Shelton's expressions are notable as much for their tone as their content here. Consider the cumulative effect of phrases such as: "what happened to," "years since," "as we once did," "I remember," "die of happiness," "nobody notices." And the jarring glumness contained in "It would be a relief from the carnage and mayhem."

The voice enacts the abstract promise of the title—this *is* nostalgia speaking—muttering, even whining a bit, in love with its own regrets, its vague resentments and longings, its sentimental blurrings of definition, as well as its valorization of the past and fear of engagement with the present. (All these "nostalgic" words are gentle ones; not sharply defined, they smooth the edges to preserve illusion.)

The nightingales referred to were never seen by the speaker: "Somebody shot them." That's today for you, a world where "they" shoot imaginary nightingales. The piece ends by trailing off, because nostalgia can't be satisfied, can't quite succeed or ever give up its illusions.

Doubling back now, I want to say a few things about voice in these essays, and here I might be on shaky ground. Let me venture a few observations, more circumstantial than formal.

The narrator in fiction is a fictional mask that prevents us from readily identifying the speaker with the author. Only the most naïve reader believes that Nabokov endorses sleeping with twelve-year-olds, or that J. D.Salinger *is* Holden Caulfield, in every detail, in spite of myriad temptations to conflate the two. The attempt to impress this single distinction on any beginning writer can occupy much of any writing teacher's energies for a semester at least.

Poetry may employ fictional masks as well, but in the late, dearly departed, twentieth century, there was an increasing tendency in *much* poetry for the voice of the poem to become identified with the voice of the poet. Even in our new century, the confessional mode is alive and well. Sincerity, authority of witness, the presentation of *self*, all offer the reader an implied biography behind the poem. At this point in history, the reader must consciously resist the assumption that the speaker *is* the poet. In the personal essay, there is, similarly, no fictional mask. We believe the speaker speaks for him- or herself and much of our response to the essay rides on how much we like, believe, or trust the speaker. Authenticity and authority rest heavily on this identification. (Part of the unsettling humor of Shelton's essay rests on the way he plays with that assumption and risks a persona who may not be taken entirely at face value.)

"The Vietnam in Me" is a work of personal testimony. Were we to "discover" that O'Brien had never been to Vietnam after all, our confidence, and even our interest, in the essay would be less. Not so in a piece of fiction. And Frazier inserts himself into a story that is not his own by using *his* love for Crazy Horse as the occasion for and the basic point of the essay. "Personally, I love Crazy Horse," the essay opens. He tries to earn his right to make claims at the end for "each person who imagines him" by a return to the personal, now extended to include the sympathetic reader.

Another characteristic that subtly and deeply distinguishes lyric from narrative technique is *the reflexive nature of lyric*. In a sense, a lyric poem occupies no time; for every move forward, line to line, image to image, even when narrative movement is contained within the poem, something calls us back—repetition, the turning of the line, images speaking to one another. As we are pulled through a poem we are constantly being called back to whatever came before.

Often nothing has changed by the end, in real-world terms. A lyric poem may occupy a single moment in depth, may skip around in time without apparent narrative progression, or may end where it started. Fiction, however, especially the novel, advances by change in time. Conflict sparks crisis and something changes and you can't go back.

Nonfiction may be linear in this sense, but, particularly in shorter forms, it needn't be. "The Vietnam in Me" accomplishes a movement of the mind within what may be a single instant of thought. We end where we began: "I'm home, but the house is gone. ... Nothing here but ghosts and wind."

Frazier takes us through his argument, from "Personally, I love Crazy Horse because ..." to "Now, in the mind of each person who imagines him ..." He wants us to accept his vision of Crazy Horse so that through a kind of alchemy he becomes equally present in each person's mind. There is movement here, but it is not linear, or time-bound. It is more exponential, as I said—or perhaps alchemical.

We wander with Shelton's speaker through the dusty alcoves of his mind until we are released with as little urgency as summoned us. "Whatever happened to the crepuscular," it begins, and it ends, "and whatever happened to kindness ..." That ellipsis signals a circling back, the sigh that subsides, a little bit of energy spent on the air. Nothing has *happened*. We stay in one place.

For the poet, writing nonfiction may require less of a leap than a move to fiction might entail (not that many of us do not *like* to leap). Many of the poet's habits of mind and strengths of imagination translate naturally into this form. If we are truly entertaining the idea that nonfiction is a fourth literary genre, it's helpful to remain aware that all these borrowings exist in order to open possibilities, to make more possibilities available and to make something new out of everything we've taken, invented, even misrepresented or imperfectly understood.

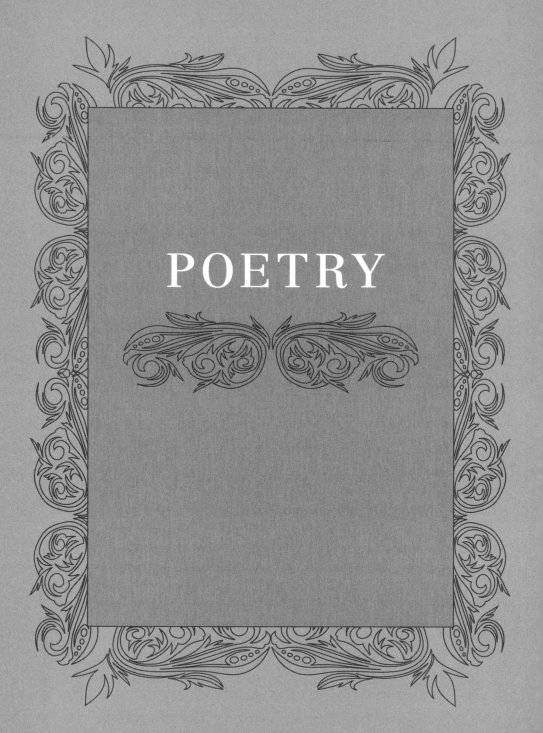

POETRY

COLLABORATING WITH CHAOS:

Not Knowing and the Creative Process

By Jack Myers

CHAOS THEORY

The nineteenth and twentieth centuries traded in static and relatively predictable Newtonian worldviews in favor of a more unknowable, constantly shifting *Weltanshauung* based on process, uncertainty, and the element of chance. Therefore the metaphor of gambling seems an appropriate model to look at in terms of illustrating a simple example of chaos theory. In the Pachinko game, a small ball trickles through a number of nail-like obstacles and, as in roulette, randomly lands in one of the many available slots at the bottom. An initial impulse in the form of a plunger propels the ball up a chute to the top of the machine where with the help of gravity and inertia it will fall down between rows of pins. Suppose we put bumpers along the path at mathematically precise points, but a few of the bumpers have several micrometers less elasticity than some of the others; then we put in a few holes into which the ball could drop and then reappear at one of several other places. If it reappears at a special place, the reward is that you can shoot it again.

We could go on and on adding new uniform and irregular elements to this very simple example of controlled chaos—including how the player might try to affect the roll of the ball by banging on the machine—and add to our consideration causal factors outside the rules, such as dust particles or grease on the board, or malfunctioning parts, or city blackouts and earthquakes.

Now, in the infinitely more complex, self-correcting, and unpredictable creative process, it seems absurd to think that we can or should try to control its limitless variations, such as:

- our own free will;

- creativity's leaping associational paths;

- the permutating, connotative, and denotative levels of meanings in words;

- the subtle logical interaction among linear and nonlinear groups of words;

- the universal and particularized mix of images;

- advanced formal training in our art and medium;

- our matrix of cultural preferences, biases, and ignorances, and personal and cultural myths;

- the universal and archetypal characteristics of gender, age, and psychology;

- our degree of awareness of the levels of consciousness operating within us;

- the context of the styles of the age we live in;

- the locale in which we were born;

- the place in which we now choose to live, down to whether or not the phone rings while we're writing.

If all of the known micro- and macro-universe—from the behavior of atoms to the works of nature to the formation of galaxies—works according to this principle of order coming from chaos, how naïve it is for us to think that we know more about what we are doing in the creative process than what we don't know. As Richard Hugo casually remarked, "Knowing can be a limiting thing."

CHAOS IS NATURE'S MEDIUM FOR CREATIVITY

The secret of artists and other creative people throughout the millennia—whether they are conscious of it or not—is that they know how to collaborate with chaos. Yet, oftentimes it is the very presence of chaos and confusion that leads to fear of failure and instills resistance in us at the very beginning of the creative process. The most oft-cited characteristic of creative people (aside from popularly being thought of as slightly crazy) is their ability to remain open during the rain of uncertainty, to embrace the difficult states of paradox, opposition, and ambiguity that are the gateways of opportunity.

There are as many entrances into chaos as there are kinds of people entering it. But there is only one way out, and that is the "con-fusion" of disparities. That's why every time we make a new poem or story it seems as difficult to do as it did the first time. Mass production of the same thing is easy because it's endlessly reproducible. Once we open ourselves to chaos, immerse ourselves in it, a strange and exhilarating thing occurs: We lose our self-consciousness of what we are doing, of the time and place we are in, and we become one with the flow. It feels as if things are streaming, as if we ourselves are streaming, and all our being is flowing. Then a new development occurs: We have a growing sense that something is beginning to be shaped. We sense that what we are doing is shaping itself as we partner with it in shaping it. We have gone so far into the particular that we emerge onto the level of the universal, and we are empowered to say an old thing in a new way.

If artists had one wish that could be granted, they'd wish to be able to summon up the creative process, the magical "zone," at will, to have a dependable closed system guaranteed by some particular ritual or time or place or access to some trigger to that special consciousness. But that is not the nature of creativity. If we were told to write a poem or story in the next fifteen minutes, we'd feel a natural resistance to doing it. On the other hand, if we were asked to compete in the next fifteen minutes at something we can already do well, that wouldn't be hard to do. This is because competition is based upon the known, upon repetition, consistency, and systemization, which are anathema to the quirky creative spirit whose only repetition is to throw itself into what it doesn't know and what it hasn't yet done. In his now-infamous essay "Poetry and Ambition," the poet Donald Hall criticized creative writing students in workshops across America as all producing the "McPoem," the one-page, publishable, predictable "Workshop Poem." I think he was saying that if you think writing poetry is like making a hamburger, that there's some specific method to be learned and repeated over and over again, you're in the wrong business. Like everything else in creation, we, too, have been thrown into and live in uncertainty and indeterminacy. There is no one, safe answer or secret to writing. Searching for such an answer would be like the bee, the flower, or the apple asking the gardener what the secret to truth and beauty is. The gardener is the last one to know these mysteries. All he knows is that he loves what he's doing.

A good teacher can tell you with practical, technical precision what is and what isn't going on in a poem you've written—what it is, and how it might be made better. But he or she can no more explain the creative process than a gynecologist can explain love.

INSIDE CHAOS

Within systems of chaos, such as rushing water, wind, and the geological formations of irregular terrain, there is something called "the strange attractor effect." It is akin to that vaguely sensed stage in the creative process where we feel something is beginning to shape itself. Chaotic background is the feeding ground for the emergence of regular, self-forming, coherent patterning. The firing of neurons in our brain provides a rich and high level of neural chaos that is the birthplace of self-organized thoughts and perceptions. In terms of who we are, if we could trace the conditions under which the last thousand couples of our ancestors met, and the difference in who they were, which eventually resulted in us, we would have to conclude that the complex and exponential combinations of happenstance simply amount to chaos. Well, at least we know who *we* are. Or do we? When I say "I," I think I have a solid, unquestioning, simple sense of the entity called "I." But I am, in fact, not a thing but a process that is in flux in any direction and on any level of existence that I care to look. And it is exactly because of this diversity and nature's method of chance operation that things evolve into new and strengthened formations.

COMPLEXITY AND SIMPLICITY

Every organic and inorganic process couples the inverse operations of building simplicity-within-complexity-within-simplicity, and the opposite structure of complexity-within-simplicity-within-complexity. Small simple units called fractals aggregate and build into natural, infinitely complex structures that mirror the macro-level of nature. I remember visiting a friend in Pasadena, California, and noticing an irregular crack in his wall, which he explained had been caused by a recent earthquake. Upon flying out of L.A., I looked down and saw that the local mountain range had the same shape as the crack in my friend's wall. The complex can become simple, and the simple can become complex. Within the neural chaos of our brain, which I.A. Richards aptly described as "a connecting organ," we form an abstract gestalt of our experience and personality and thereby implant in ourselves an internal sense of order. And by that imposition of an abstract "self," we reconfirm that gestalt by attracting whatever is in and around us to conform to what and who we think we are, as if a flame thought itself a moth.

This seems to be how the creative process works, too. After an initial period of confusion and chaos and being immersed in what we do not know, a vague gestalt within the creative act of composing forms and acts in effect as the composition's brain, if you will, developing, ordering, and transcending the very materials that brought it into being. This interaction of order and irrationality, of dispersion and coalescence, produces infinite combinations of possibilities. In other words, complexity and simplicity are not things, but ephemeral results of an interaction of these processes within other larger and smaller processes, within other larger and smaller processes, etc.

It has not gone unnoticed that, ironically, art aims to fix this flux into the stasis of perfection. But how we as artists interact with our creativity—whether we try to control it, resist its depths, or simply go with it—is the definition of our attitude toward it, which in turn determines the nature of its results, the poem you make or the story you tell.

STAKING THE CLAIM TO THE TITLE

By Nance Van Winckel

I can't recall a day I *wasn't* on the hunt for a title. When *don't* I have a poem in need of one? My title antennae remain in a permanent up position. That's how it seems I often find titles; they drift in on the airwaves, and I like to stay on alert, ready to receive. I recall a case in point from twenty years ago. My husband Rik and I were having a "discussion" that quickly escalated. Voices rose. "Well, you said X," and "No, I didn't; I said Y." And then, amid the nasty smirks, Rik let go with, "But, Nance, in the larger context of the evening, you know you've been implying Z." Suddenly I smiled and threw my arms around him. "Thank you, Sweetie," I said. "I've been looking for that title all week." "In the Larger Context of the Evening" was the perfect title, which the poem in question had been nagging me to find. Maybe, in the larger context of our marriage, it was even worth the argument. But poor Rik, I remember how he just stood there, suffering himself to be hugged and muttering, "@!***#! writers."

Titles are crucial. Titles can give a poem a context, a mystery, or a spark. Titles can infuse a poem with power and authority, or with seductiveness or simple charm. Bad titles can be lead weights; clever ones can kill or poison. If Eliot had kept his original title, *The Waste Land* would be called *He Do the Police in Different Voices* and "The Love Song of J. Alfred Prufrock" would be "Prufrock's Pervigilium." And if Whitman had kept his, our beloved *Leaves of Grass* would be called *I Am the World, We Are the People*. Yikes!

A title is usually the first piece of information the reader takes in—often absorbing it more than reading it. We can't exactly "read" the title at the outset—i.e., get a sense of its meaning or relevance—because it doesn't yet have enough context to allow for that. So we glance at the title, perhaps muse a split second, then store it away. I like this storage aspect, and many titles work well simply because of how they hover in our mental periphery—looming, accumulating the force they will eventually deliver. Consider how the title functions for this poem by Inara Cedrins:

Inward

The driver works the wheel all night, toward Dharamashala,
past the blue-faced gods in their shrines among the trees,
between banks so steep it is like being in a cave
with mounds of prehistoric pottery at intervals.
Your hands, your lips. The soft white wool of my shawl
wound over us both in that tantalizing journey
toward each other. We enter a still space
as if the Himalayas were gauze and had parted
to let us in, as from the bus station
the silent streets we follow steeply up
lead under the lightening sky to a hotel, where they tinker
with the hot water heater but finally leave us alone.
You spit on your hand before entering me, saying
this first time will be fast, it will not be slow. I know this.
Afterward, the monkeys thumping over the tin roof,
the calm in your eyes that are the color of tender ferns
that grow beside streams flowing icy
from the highest mountains.

Here several things activate the poem: the narrative of the journey, the lush exotic detail of place, and the tension and anticipation as the lovers move toward each other. The simple voice of "I know this" leaps out at us, strikingly, through these various fields of action and description. Nearing the poem's end, I recall the title. And when I do, that word seems to illuminate the poem from within. It's a multicolored light. There's the inwardness of this journey, a bus trip to the country's interior. And of course, there's the literal, physical "inward" movement implicit in the lovemaking. But equally as luminous is the inward psychic thrust: the vertical moment. The poem replicates a moment of *ekstasis*, a punching through and beyond the temporal, spatial world into a spacelessness and timelessness that feel primal and primeval. And, I would assert, it's the title that has helped make possible this shared inwardness between the reader and the poem. Though the poem may have created the passageway, the title has illuminated the way.

A title can be so much more than a label for the work. A label is the name under which you save a poem on your disk while you're waiting for the real title to get within radar range. If Plath had saved a poem under the label "Death Wish" for a while, she knew enough later to call it "Lady Lazarus."

I recently spoke with title maestro Thomas Lux, who told me that a poet's job is "to write poems that are hard *not* to read." A title, he said, is the first way a poet sets up that inevitability. The title stakes a claim. It immediately reaches out and grasps the reader's imagination. Then it's up to the poem to maintain its spell over the reader. A good title, like every component of a poem, must be at once both a surprise and an inevitability. Here's one of Lux's titles that works hard for the poem:

A Man Gets Off Work Early

and decides to snorkel in a cool mountain lake.
Not as much to see
as in the ocean, but it's a tranquil (no sharks) floating
face down into that other world.
The pines' serrated shadows reach
across the waters,
and just now, just below him, to his left,
a pickerel, long and sharp and … *whuppa whuppa whuppa*, loud,
louder, behind him, above him, the water, louder,
whuppa whuppa whuppa … Two weeks later,
twenty miles away, he's found,
a cinder, his wetsuit
melted on him, in a crablike position
on the still warm ash
of the forest floor
through which fire tore unchecked,
despite the chemicals,
the men with axes and shovels,
despite the huge scoops of lake water
dropped on it
from his friend the sky,
on whom he turned his back.

If we notice the lowercase first word of the poem *as* we take in the title (thus realizing the title reads into the poem), the title has worked to catapult us into the poem. We're disinclined to turn away and *not* follow the sentence's syntax through to its natural end. Here Lux has given us a fine first line, but it's even more compelling as the title since, by the end of the poem, it resonates with so much else: the poor worker who tried to take in a little of the natural world, when *whuppa whuppa whuppa*, it took *him* in. This title underscores a rather ordinary irony of daily life that the poem as a whole reveals in its extraordinariness.

Stephen Dobyns, in his book *Best Words, Best Order,* says, "A poem has emotion, idea, physical setting, language, image, rhythm, and tension. The degree that the poem is successful is the degree to which all these elements are made important to the reader, and at least one must be made important as soon as possible, either in the title or in the first line or two. Even the most gentle poem must be aggressive."

A reading habit of mine illustrates the truth of Dobyns's advice. Often when I travel, I bring along five or six literary journals. I flip through them as I wait for planes, sometimes dropping them behind like breadcrumbs in airports and rental cars. As I thumb through them, I'm taking in the title first, usually with a split-second expectation and response. If the title captures me, I'll read the first few lines. Then it's up to the poem itself to keep me reading.

James Wright was adventurous with titles. They frequently imbue his rather somber poems with a tongue-in-cheek tone, which sets up an immediate tension. Consider "As I Step Over a Puddle at the End of Winter, I Think of An Ancient Chinese Governor" or "Depressed by a Book of Bad Poetry, I Walk Toward an Unused Pasture and Invite the Insects to Join Me." Emily Dickinson, on the other hand, favored a kind of mysterious, headless-horseman effect. In her case—and probably for all those who opt for "Untitled"—it should be remembered that anthology editors may blithely proceed to retitle any "Untitled" with the first line of the poem.

Poems acquire their titles in this manner more frequently than we may know. Dickinson's famous "I Will Not Stop for Death" was initially called "Eternity" by her first editor, her sister-in-law. Several of W.C. Williams's most famous poems, including "Spring and All," "To Elsie," and even the famous "The Red Wheelbarrow," bear titles created not by Williams himself but by editors. Each of these poems, surrounded by prose, was a small part of the book-length work *Spring and All.* None of these titles is particularly riveting *as* a title, but perhaps if Williams had created his own titles, they might have been more arresting.

Through the Romantic and Victorian periods, poem titles frequently cued us to the poem's intention, the poet's state of mind, or the poem's inspirational genesis. Consider, for instance, Tennyson's "The Vision of Sin," Coleridge's "Fears in Solitude," or Shelley's "To a Skylark." Modernist poets were inclined towards titles that resonated with large metaphorical overtones, e.g., Eliot's *The Waste Land* and Crane's *The Bridge*. This movement toward metaphoric titling is surely connected to the high modernist aesthetic which, among other things, argues that art is autotelic in nature—or, put more simply, that art makes its own world.

As postmodernists have continued to interrogate what and how language means, titles have become less tied to "guiding" the reader, and consequently their potentials have expanded, and the relationship between poem and title has intensified. Take, for example, C.K. Williams's collection *Dream of Mind*, or these titles of two recent books of poems: *It Is Hard to Look at What We Came to Think We'd Come to See* (by Michele Glazer) and *At the Site of Inside Out* (by Anna Rabinowitz).

Wallace Stevens is, of course, the uncontested master of titles. Helen Vendler, in reviewing a book about Stevens, discusses his technique of titling poems after what she terms first-, second-, or third-order experiences. Citing Stevens's "No Possum, No Sop, No Taters," Vendler explains that his characteristic way of writing was "to take his worst first-order experiences, find an impersonal second-order vehicle for them ('The field is frozen'), write in the second order as though it (and not his experience) were the governing subject, and then sum up the whole with an ironic, deprecatory, and oblique title (here the rural phrase 'possum, sop and taters'). …"

No Possum, No Sop, No Taters

He is not here, the old sun,
As absent as if we were asleep.

The field is frozen. The leaves are dry.
Bad is final in this light.

In this bleak air the broken stalks
Have arms without hands. They have trunks

Without legs or, for that, without heads.
They have heads in which a captive cry

Is merely the moving of a tongue.

Snow sparkles like eyesight falling to earth,

Like seeing fallen brightly away.
The leaves hop, scraping on the ground.

It is deep January. The sky is hard.
The stalks are firmly rooted in ice.

It is in this solitude, a syllable,
Out of these gawky flitterings,

Intones its single emptiness,
The savagest hollow of winter-sound.

It is here, in this bad, that we reach
The last purity of the knowledge of good.

The crow looks rusty as he rises up.
Bright is the malice in his eye ...

One joins him there for company.
But at a distance, in another tree.

I find Vendler's distinctions and terminology useful in thinking about titles. For this particular poem, then, a first-order title might have been "Winter Doldrums," a phrase providing a kind of "label" for the metaphorical tenor of the poem. A second-order title would refer to the vehicle itself of the metaphor—here, as she mentions, "A Frozen Field." But Stevens veers towards something not directly linked to either tenor or vehicle. We must forge our own connections to this title, which is only tangentially associated with the text of the poem. Moreover, the tonal contradiction between the colloquial diction of the title and the austere diction of the poem's body sets up an immediate and enduring tension. I also like how in the title Stevens seems so present, and in the poem itself so absent. Only by sitting awhile with the poem do we infer its broader meanings. But how much more deeply they then resound: because we *discover* them, or at least believe we do.

As Supreme Emperor of Titles, Stevens collected them like exotic bugs. His notebooks contained over 300 titles. Here are just a few that, sadly, never invoked the poems to go with them:

Commands to Genii
The Cow in the Clouds

The Alp at the End of the Street

The Rain was Meant to Fall in Salamanca

The Halo That Would Not Light

A Jackass in His Own Clothes

Pretty Hot Weather for Dead Horses

The Last Private Opinion

Lunch Without Frank

Black Gloves for This Bishop

Still Life With Aspirin

Although few creative writing textbooks offer aspiring writers much advice on titles, one I perused suggested that a poet try to find a title that would sum up what the poem was about. Please consider that a series of dark black X's has been drawn through this last sentence. I would rather aspiring writers get no advice at all on titles than this advice! This was how, as a young newspaper reporter, I was told to think about writing headlines for news stories. I think there's no surer way to sap a good poem's energy than to laden it with a phrase that "sums it all up."

Consider how flat this lovely Linda Gregg poem would be with only a second-order title (a.k.a. "label"). But here it is with its real title, which forges a meaning a poem called simply "Meadow" could not:

Twelve Years After the Marriage
She Tries To Explain How She Loves Him Now

Beyond the mountain is a meadow with iris.
The shade of the firs determines the measure
of their color. Violet so pure the purple
is almost not there. The difference
between air and the sky's blue.
The irises hold color because they are a thing,
but mysteriously, making both the substance
and the invisible more clear.

During the time I'm on the hunt for the perfect title, I know certain operations are taking place. I am mulling over—and often on a subconscious rather than conscious level—what the poem is about. This seems to be part of directing those antennae. This is another reason I like the hunt itself. I am wading through layers of meaning, discovering interconnections. Often then, as I lay claim to a title, I am laying claim more completely to the poem's larger ramifications.

Still, it's etymology, not accident, that puts *title* and *titillate* in such close proximity in the dictionary. Some titles I love because of the pizzazz they give to their books or poems. From a recent catalog of poetry books, these titles seemed especially titillating: *Antebellum Dream Book* (by Elizabeth Alexander), *The Throats of Narcissus* (by Bruce Bond), *Why the Ships Are She* (by Terri Ford), and *The Next Ancient World* (by Jennifer Michael Hecht). But titles, I believe, like every other part of a poem or book, ought to be interesting at the level of language itself. Good titles also usually accomplish some actual *work* for the piece. Here are a few possible jobs: a) establish tone, b) provide information the piece needs early, c) locate us, d) lift to the surface some important feature that might be missed, e) create context, f) clarify focus, and g) establish tension and develop expectation.

The connection between the title and the body of a poem can truly *make* the poem. This little exercise may serve to illustrate. A group of my students selected these four lines from a student poem and we wrote them on the board:

> Two Gypsy women put their palms on the loaf
> as if it's a feverish forehead. Since dawn
> it has taken in the mountain air
> and must now heave itself up.

I then asked the students to think of title possibilities for these lines. Notice how each title transforms the poem:

> *Spring Morning: Elk, Washington*
> *You Were Gone When I Awoke*
> *Slow Day at the Satellite Café*
> *Lingering Hangover*
> *Entering the Carpathian Village, 1987*
> *Their Silver Bracelets Make Silver Music*

Consider the work these titles do for their poems:

> **A Message Hidden in an Empty Wine Bottle That I Threw**
> **Into a Gully of Maple Trees One Night at an Indecent Hour**

> Women are dancing around a fire
> By a pond of creosote and waste water from the river

In the dank fog of Ohio.
They are dead.
I am alone here,
And I reach for the moon that dangles
Cold on a dark vine.
The unwashed shadows
Of blast furnaces from Moundsville, West Virginia,
Are sneaking across the pits of strip mines
To steal grapes
In heaven.
Nobody else knows I am here.
All right.
Come out, come out, I am dying.
I am growing old.
An owl rises
From the cutter bar
Of a hayrake.

>   —James Wright

A Tattered Bible Stuffed With Memos

I stood at the southwest window for
a long time just staring out at the field
and empty road. A hawk on the telephone
line studied the field for any sign of movement, then eventually he swooped down and
had his snack. A tractor pulling a wagon-
load of hay has crept over the hill. Five teenagers in a green convertible passed him at
a great speed and disappeared behind a cloud
of dust. A storm was rolling in, I could
feel the barometer dropping. This is where
the chicken catches the ax.

>   —James Tate

Out Over the Bay The Rattle of Firecrackers

and in the adjacent waters, calm.

>   —John Ashbery

Surprised Girl of the North

The sun sinks,
a blue plum in brine.
Tiny birds flicker in the heads of trees.
Two rodents come out.
The birds eat out the eyes
of a long-since-dead and gnarled
sunflower head.
The rodents enter my house.
As cartographers used to cram monsters
in the void of their maps
and call it terra incognita,
I don't know anything anymore.
The astonishment of astronauts
must be like this,
when at the height of dawn,
in Damascus,
a lamb is sacrificed
in front of the television
as scenes of the blastoff are shown.
       —Mary Ruefle

The Forties

And in the desert cold men invented the star
       —Franz Wright

  Sometimes I'll approach a title for a poem in the way I believe a painter might think about titling a painting. He or she is looking for ways the title might speak back to the painting. There's a painting by Susan Bennerstrom that is mysterious to me: In a room of softened primary colors that are so full and explosive is the stark emptiness of a cleared table. But how much more I linger on this work when I discover its title is *Waiter*. But wait, I think, there's no waiter here. Or at least not yet. Or perhaps the table *is* the waiter, the thing in wait. Or *we* are the waiter and the world is a table to which we must attend. There's a kind of narrative disconnect between the text and the image, which takes me aback and makes me reconsider the image again, and again. The richness of the world looms in what *isn't* here, in what's waiting to be set before us.

René Magritte's painting *The Key of Dreams* presses even harder on this disconnect between the words of the title and the image(s) of the painting. In it, the words *the door* appear beneath a horse, *the bird* beneath a pitcher, *the wind* beneath a clock, and *the valise* beneath a valise. Words alone, this piece suggests, can't fully express what's seen. The same is true for the title of a literary work. A title can only help us reach toward the fullness. I sit before *The Key of Dreams*. Hmm … maybe time *is* the wind? Yes, since the valise seems to be a valise. And how is the horse a door? Certainly while riding, one can have the sense of an "opening." The pitcher—now I'm positing its birdness in my imagination. There's a linkage the four small titles within the larger title expect me to make. Our dreams are codes. Who's got the key?

When we find the right title for our poem, the valise opens and a bird rides out on the wind through a door.

ON BEGINNINGS

By Mary Ruefle

In life, the number of beginnings is exactly equal to the number of endings:
No one has yet to begin a life who does not end it.

In poetry, the number of beginnings so far exceeds the number of endings
that we cannot even conceive of it. Not every poem is finished, many poems
are abandoned, some catch fire and are carried away by the wind. That may
be an ending, but it is the ending of a poem without an end.

Paul Valéry, the French poet and thinker, once said that no poem is ever ended,
that every poem is merely abandoned. This saying is also attributed to Sté-
phane Mallarmé, for where quotations begin is in a cloud.

Valéry also described his perception of first lines so vividly, and to my mind
so accurately, that I have never forgotten it: The opening line of a poem, he
said, is like finding a fruit on the ground, a piece of fallen fruit you have never
seen before, and the poet's task is to create the tree from which such a fruit
would fall.

In the beginning was the Word. Western civilization rests upon those words.
And yet there is a lively group of thinkers who believe that in the beginning was

the Act. That nothing can precede action—no breath before act, no thought before act, no pervasive love before some kind of act.

I believe the poem is an act of the mind. I think it is easier to talk about the end of a poem than it is to talk about its beginning. Because the poem ends on the page, but it begins off the page, it begins in the mind, the mind acts, the mind wills a poem, often against our own will; somehow, this happens, somehow a poem gets written in the middle of a chaotic holiday party that has just run out of ice, and it's your house.

An act of the mind. To move, to make happen, to make manifest. By an act of Congress. A state of real existence rather than possibility. And poets love possibility! They love to wonder and explore. Hard lot! But the poem, no matter how full of possibility, has to *exist*! To conduct oneself, to behave. How a poem acts marks its individual character. A poem by Glandolyn Blue does not sound like a poem by Timothy Sure. To pretend, feign, impersonate. That, too, yes and always, because self-consciousness is its own pretension, and has been from its beginning; the human mind is capable of a great elastic theatre. As the poet Ralph Angel puts it, "the poem is an interpretation of weird theatrical shit." The weird theatrical shit is what goes on around us every day of our lives; an animal of only instinct, Johnny Ferret, has in his actions drama, but no theatre; theatre requires that you draw a circle around the action and observe it from outside the circle; in other words, self-consciousness *is* theatre.

Everyone knows that if you query poets about how their poems begin, the answer is always the same: a phrase, a line, a scrap of language, an image, something seen, witnessed or imagined. And the lesson is always the same, and young poets recognize this to be one of the most important lessons they can learn: If you have any idea for a poem, an exact grid of intent, you are on the wrong path, a dead-end alley, at the top of a cliff you haven't even climbed. This is a lesson that can only be learned by trial and error.

I believe many fine poems begin with ideas, but if you tell too many faces this, or tell it too loudly, they will get the wrong idea.

Now here is something really interesting (to me), something you can use at a standing-up-only party when everyone is tired of hearing there are 1,000,003,295 words used by the Eskimo for snow. This is what Ernest Fenollosa said to Ezra Pound: You know, some languages are so constructed—English among them—that we each only really speak one sentence in our lifetime. That sentence begins with your first words, toddling around the kitchen, and ends with your last words, right before you step into the limousine, or in a nursing home, the night-duty attendant vaguely on hand. Or, if you are blessed, they are heard by someone who knows you and loves you and will be sorry to hear the sentence end.

When I told Mr. Angel about the lifelong sentence, he said: "That's a lot of semicolons!" He is absolutely right, the sentence would be unwieldy and awkward and resemble the novel of a savant, but the next time you use a semicolon (which, by the way, is the least-used mark of punctuation in all of poetry) you should stop and be thankful that there exists this little thing, invented by a human being—an Italian as a matter of fact—that allows us to go on and keep on connecting speech that for all apparent purposes is unrelated.

You might say a poem *is* a semicolon, a living semicolon, what connects the first line to the last, the act of keeping together that whose nature is to fly apart. Between the first and last lines there exists—a poem—and if it were not for the poem that intervenes, the first and last lines of a poem would not speak to each other.

Would not speak to each other. Because the lines of a poem are speaking to each other; not you to them or they to you.

I will tell you what I miss: I miss watching a movie and at the end, huge scrolled words come on the screen and say: *The End*. I miss finishing a novel and there on the last page, at a discreet distance from the last words of the last sentence, are the dark letters spelling *The End*.

It was its own thrill. I didn't ignore them, I read them, even if only silently, with a deep sense of feeling: both the feeling of being replete, a feeling of satisfaction, and the feeling of loss, the sadness of having finished the book. As Barbara Herrnstein Smith said, "The idea of termination suggests both dread and satisfaction."

I have never, in my life, read a poem that ended with the words *The End*. Why is that, I wonder? I think perhaps the brevity of poems compared to novels makes one feel that there has been no great sustention of energy, no marathon worthy of pulling tape across the finishing line. And then I found a poem of mine that I had carefully written by hand in the sixth grade, and at the bottom of the page, in India ink, beautifully apart from the rest of the text, were the words *The End*. And I realized children very often denote the end because it is indeed a great achievement for them to have written anything, and they are completely unaware of the number of stories and poems that have already been written; they know *some*, of course, but have not yet found out the extent to which they are not the only persons residing on the planet. And so they sign their poems and stories like kings. Which is a wonderful thing.

Roland Barthes suggests there are three ways to finish any piece of writing: the ending will have the last word or the ending will be silent or the ending will execute a pirouette, do something unexpectedly incongruent.

Gaston Bachelard says the single most succinct and astonishing thing: We begin in admiration and we end by organizing our disappointment. The moment of admiration is the experience of something unfiltered, vital and fresh—it could also be horror—and the moment of organization is both the onset of disappointment and its dignification; the least we can do is dignify our knowingness, the loss of some vitality through familiarization, by admiring not the thing itself, but how we can organize it, think about it.

I am afraid there is no way around this. It is the one true inevitable thing. And if you believe that, then you are conceding that in the beginning was the act, not the word.

The painter Cy Twombly, on a scrap of paper: "The image cannot be dispossessed of a primordial freshness which ideas can never claim."

Easy and appropriate thing for a painter to say. Cy Twombly uses text in some of his drawings and paintings, usually poetry, usually Dante. Many men and women have written long essays and lectures on the ideas they see expressed in Twombly's work.

Bachelard's sentence simply says this: that origins (beginnings) have consequences (endings).

The poem is the consequence of its origins. Give me the fruit and I will take from it a seed and plant it and watch grow the tree from which it fell.

Barbara Herrnstein Smith has said, "Perhaps all we can say, and even this may be too much, is that varying degrees or states of tension seem to be involved in all our experiences, and that the most gratifying ones are those in which whatever tensions are created are also released. Or, to use another familiar set of terms, an experience is gratifying to the extent that those expectations that are aroused are also fulfilled."

But there is no book I know of on the subject of how poems begin. How can the origin be *traced* when there is no form or shape that precedes it to trace? It is exactly like tracing the moment of the Big Bang—we can go back to a nanosecond before the beginning, before the universe burst into being, but we can't go back to the precise beginning because that would precede knowledge and we can't "know" anything before "knowing" itself was born.

I have flipped through books, reading hundreds of opening and closing lines, across ages, across cultures, across aesthetic schools, and I have discovered that first lines are remarkably similar, even repeated, and that last lines are remarkably similar, even repeated. Of course in all cases they remain remarkably distinct, because the words belong to completely different poems. And I began to realize, reading these first and last lines, that not only are there the first and last lines of the lifelong sentence we each speak, there are the first and last lines of the long piece of language delivered to us by others, by those we listen to. And in the best of all possible lives, that beginning and that end are the same: In poem after poem I encountered words that mark the first something made out of language that we hear as children repeated night after night, like a refrain: *I love you. I am here with you. Don't be afraid. Go to sleep now.* And I encountered words that mark the last something made out of language that we hope to hear on earth: *I love you. You are not alone. Don't be afraid. Go to sleep now.*

But it is growing damp and I must go in. Memory's fog is rising. Among Emily Dickinson's last words (in a letter). A woman whom everyone thought of as shut-in, homebound, cloistered, spoke as if she had been *out*, exploring the earth, her whole life, and it was finally time to go in. And it was.

SOULS ON ICE

By Mark Doty

In the Stop 'n Shop in Orleans, Massachusetts, I was struck by the elegance of the mackerel in the fresh-fish display. They were rowed and stacked, brilliant against the white of the crushed ice; I loved how black and glistening the bands of dark scales were, and the prismed sheen of the patches between, and their shining flat eyes. I stood and looked at them for a while, just paying attention while I leaned on my cart—before I remembered where I was and realized that I was standing in someone's way.

Our metaphors go on ahead of us; they know before we do. And thank goodness for that, for if I were dependent on other ways of coming to knowledge I think I'd be a very slow study. I need something to serve as a container for emotion and idea, a vessel that can hold what's too slippery or charged or difficult to touch. Will doesn't have much to do with this; I can't choose what's going to serve as a compelling image for me. But I've learned to trust that part of my imagination that gropes forward, feeling its way toward what it needs; to watch for the signs of fascination, the sense of compelled attention (*Look at me*, something seems to say, *closely*) that indicates that there's something I need to attend to. Sometimes it seems to me as if metaphor were the advance guard of the mind; something in us reaches out, into the landscape in front of us, looking for the right vessel, the right vehicle, for whatever will serve.

Driving home from the grocery, I found myself thinking again about the fish, and even scribbled some phrases on an envelope in the car, something about stained glass, soapbubbles, while I was driving. It wasn't long—that same day? the next?—before I was at my desk, trying simply to describe what I had seen. I almost always begin with description, as a way of focusing on that compelling image, the poem's "given." I know that what I can see is just the proverbial tip of the iceberg; if I do my work of study and examination, and if I am lucky, the image I've been intrigued by will become a metaphor, will yield depth and meaning, will lead me to insight. The goal here is inquiry, the attempt to get at what it is that's so interesting about what's struck me. Because it isn't just beauty; the world is full of lovely things and that in itself wouldn't compel me to write. There's something else, some gravity or charge to this image that makes me need to investigate it.

Exploratory description, then; I'm a scientist trying to measure and record what's seen. The first two sentences of the poem attempt sheer observation, but by the second's list of tropes (abalone, soapbubble skin, oil on a puddle) it's clear to me that these descriptive terms aren't merely there to chronicle the physical reality of the object. Like all descriptions, they reflect the psychic state of the observer; they aren't "neutral," though they might pretend to be, but instead suggest a point of view, a stance toward what is being seen. In this case one of the things suggested by these tropes is interchangeability; if you've seen one abalone shell or prismy soapbubble or psychedelic puddle, you've seen them all.

And thus my image began to unfold for me, in the evidence these terms provided, and I had a clue toward the focus my poem would take. Another day, another time in my life, the mackerel might have been metaphor for something else; they might have served as the crux for an entirely different examination. But now I began to see why they mattered for this poem; and the sentence that follows commences the poem's investigative process:

> Splendor, and splendor,
> and not a one in any way
>
> distinguished from the other
> —nothing about them
> of individuality.

There's a terrific kind of exhilaration for me at this point in the unfolding of a poem, when a line of questioning has been launched, and the work has moved from evocation to meditation. A direction is coming clear, and it bears within it the energy the image contained for me in the first place. Now, I think, we're getting down to it. This élan carried me along through two more sentences, one that considers the fish as replications of the ideal, Platonic Mackerel, and one that likewise imagines them as the intricate creations of an obsessively repetitive jeweler.

Of course my process of unfolding the poem wasn't quite this neat. There were false starts, wrong turnings that I wound up throwing out when they didn't seem to lead anywhere. I can't remember now, because the poem has worked the charm of its craft on my memory; it convinces me that it is an artifact of a process of inquiry. The drama of the poem is its action of thinking through a question. Mimicking a sequence of perceptions and meditation, it tries to make us think that this feeling and thinking and knowing is taking place even as the poem is being written. Which, in a way, it is—just not this neatly or seamlessly! A poem is always a made version of experience.

Also, needless to say, my poem was full of repetitions, weak lines, unfinished phrases and extra descriptions, later trimmed. I like to work on a computer, because I can type quickly, put everything in, and still read the results later on, which isn't always true of my handwriting. I did feel early on that the poem seemed to want to be a short-lined one; I liked breaking the movement of these extended sentences over the clipped line, and the spotlight-bright focus the short line puts on individual terms felt right. "Iridescent, watery," for instance, pleased me as a line-unit, as did this stanza:

> prismatics: think abalone,
> the wildly rainbowed
> mirror of a soapbubble sphere,

Short lines underline sonic textures, heightening tension. The short *a*'s of *prismatics* and *abalone* ring more firmly, as do the long *o*'s of *abalone, rainbowed* and *soapbubble*. The rhyme of *mirror* and *sphere* at the beginning and end of the line engages me, and I'm also pleased by the way these short lines slow the poem down, parceling it out as it were to the reader, with the frequent pauses introduced by the stanza breaks between tercets adding lots of white space, a meditative pacing.

And there, on the jeweler's bench, my poem seemed to come to rest, though it was clear there was more to be done. Some further pressure needed to be placed on the poem's material to force it to yield its depths. I waited a while, I read it over. Again, in what I had already written, the clues contained in the image pushed the poem forward.

Soul, heaven ... The poem had already moved into the realm of theology, but the question that arose ("Suppose we could iridesce ...") startled me nonetheless, because the notion of losing oneself "entirely in the universe / of shimmer" referred both to these fish and to something quite other, something overwhelmingly close to home. The poem was written some six months after my partner of a dozen years had died of AIDS, and of course everything I wrote—everything I saw—was informed by that loss, by the overpowering emotional force of it. Epidemic was the central fact of the community in which I lived. Naively, I hadn't realized that my mackerel were already of a piece with the work I'd been writing for the previous couple of years—poems that wrestled, in one way or another, with the notion of limit, with the line between being someone and no one. What did it mean to be a self, when that self would be lost? To praise the collectivity of the fish, their common identity as "flashing participants," is to make a sort of anti-elegy, to suggest that what matters is perhaps not our individual selves but our brief soldiering in the broad streaming school of humanity—which is composed of us, yes, but also goes on without us.

The one of a kind, the singular, like my dear lover, cannot last.

And yet the collective life, which is also us, shimmers on.

Once I realized the poem's subject-beneath-the-subject, the final stanzas of the poem opened swiftly out from there. The collective momentum of the fish is such that even death doesn't seem to still its forward movement; the singularity of each fish more or less doesn't really exist: it's "all for all," like the Three Musketeers. I could not have considered these ideas "nakedly," without the vehicle of mackerel to help me think about human identity. Nor, I think, could I have addressed these things without a certain playfulness of tone, which appeared first in the archness of "oily fabulation" and the neologism of "iridesce." It's the blessed permission distance gives that allows me to speak of such things at all; a little comedy can also help to hold terrific anxiety at bay. Thus the "rainbowed school / and its acres of brilliant classrooms" is a joke, but one that's already collapsing on itself, since what is taught there—the limits of "me"—is our hardest lesson. No verb is singular because it is the school that acts, or the tribe, the group, the species; or every verb is singular because the only *I* there is a *we*.

The poem held one more surprise for me, which was the final statement—it came as a bit of a shock, actually, and when I'd written it I knew I was done. It's a formulation of the theory that the poem has been moving toward all along: that our glory is not our individuality (much as we long for the Romantic self and its private golden heights) but our commonness. I do not like this idea. I would rather be one fish, sparkling in my own pond, but experience does not bear this out. And so I have tried to convince myself, here, that beauty lies in the whole and that therefore death, the loss of the part, is not so bad—is in, fact, almost nothing. What does our individual disappearance mean—or our love, or our desire—when, as the Marvelettes put it, "There's too many fish in the sea …"?

I find this consoling, strangely, and maybe that's the best way to think of this poem—an attempt at cheering oneself up about the mystery of being both an individual and part of a group, an attempt on the part of the speaker in the poem (me) to convince himself that losing individuality, slipping into the life of the world, could be a good thing. All attempts to console ourselves, I believe, are doomed, because the world is more complicated than we are. Our explanations will fail, but it is our human work to make them. And my beautiful fish, limited though they may be as parable, do help me; they are an image I return to in order to remember, in the face of individual erasures, the burgeoning, good, common life. Even after my work of inquiry, my metaphor may still know more than I do; the bright eyes of those fish gleam on, in memory, brighter than what I've made of them.

A Display of Mackerel

They lie in parallel rows,
on ice, head to tail,
each a foot of luminosity

barred with black bands,
which divide the scales'
radiant sections

like seams of lead
in a Tiffany window.
Iridescent, watery

prismatics: think abalone,
the wildly rainbowed
mirror of a soapbubble sphere,

think sun on gasoline.
Splendor, and splendor,
and not a one in any way

distinguished from the other
—nothing about them
of individuality. Instead

they're all exact expressions
of one soul,
each a perfect fulfillment

of heaven's template,
mackerel essence. As if,
after a lifetime arriving

at this enameling, the jeweler's
made uncountable examples,
each as intricate

in its oily fabulation
as the one before.
Suppose we could iridesce,

like these, and lose ourselves
entirely in the universe
of shimmer—would you want

to be yourself only,
unduplicatable, doomed
to be lost? They'd prefer,

plainly, to be flashing participants,
multitudinous. Even now
they seem to be bolting

forward, heedless of stasis.
They don't care they're dead
and nearly frozen,

just as, presumably,
they didn't care that they were living:
all, all for all,

the rainbowed school
and its acres of brilliant classrooms,
in which no verb is singular,

or every one is. How happy they seem,
even on ice, to be together, selfless,
which is the price of gleaming.

ROOTS IN OUR THROATS:

A Case for Using Etymology

By Natasha Sajé

Every piece of writing depends on two language tools—syntax and diction—tools so basic that writers don't pay enough attention to them. Of course, a story can employ very simple syntax and diction—like the folktale—and still be a wonderful story. But if we want to become better writers, we have to refine our skills in every way possible. My focus here is diction: English comes primarily from the Anglo-Saxon and from Latin or Greek, and a writer can often choose between these "families" to achieve a particular effect. Moreover, understanding the etymology (origins) of words can help a writer imbue her writing with greater power: buried or historical meanings of words carry amplifying images with them. And finally, accessing etymology is a way to access history and understand ideological change.

Language changes more slowly than culture, which prompts important questions about the disparity between the two. For example, the word *malaria* comes from "bad air" in Italian, which tells us that when the word was coined, the disease was thought to be caused by the air around Roman swamps, rather than mosquitoes carrying protozoa, which we know to be the case now. Another example is how the word *pride* has changed, from being a sin in Milton's era—indeed the first sin—to being a badge of honor today. The change in context is due to a change in thinking about individual power. A contemporary American contemplating "man's first disobedience" would most likely praise him for his initiative. Etymology is a tool that helps writers understand their cultures.

My understanding of etymology and the ideological nature of language has been shaped by philosophy, specifically the work of Friedrich Nietzsche,

Martin Heidegger, Ludwig Wittgenstein, and Jacques Derrida. In his essay "Building, Thinking, Dwelling," Heidegger states: "It is language that tells us about the nature of a thing, provided that we respect language's own nature. In the meantime, to be sure, there rages round the earth an unbridled yet clever talking, writing, and broadcasting of spoken words. Man acts as though he were the shaper and master of language, while in fact language remains the master of man." Language represents ideology, a web of assumptions about how the world is, a web too large and powerful for any one person to change. Language supports the status quo, which is, in the case of English, patriarchal. Understanding etymology, however, gives us a way to access ideology and thus a way to understand the ramifications of particular problems.

FAMILIES OF WORDS

The English language is lexically rich because of its history. When the Norman French invaded England in 1066, French became the language of the court and the ruling class, and Germanic-based Old English was relegated to "the common people." For a period of four hundred years, English responded to the French influx via variance in spelling and by using different letters to make the same sound (as in, for instance, "doe" and "dough"), but most obviously by expanding its vocabulary. By Shakespeare's time, English had absorbed many Latin and Greek words. When Samuel Johnson wrote his dictionary in 1755, he was attempting to standardize what had already become an unruly—or gloriously rich—language, infused with new words prompted by colonization, exploration, and technology. When English came to the New World, it was further enriched by Native American words like *canoe* and *moccasin*. Although English, like French, German, and Italian, has Indo-European roots, its diction is less pure and more interesting because synonyms have roots in both the Anglo-Saxon and the Latinate/Greek, and because it has absorbed New World words.

Until our era, most writers learned Latin and Greek and had training in the history and structure of English, and in etymology. Even William Blake, who was not trained in classical languages, taught himself enough about Latin and Greek to use etymology in his poems. Times have changed, however. While 41 percent of high school students study a foreign language, only 1.5 percent of that group studies Latin, much less Greek. This means that most contemporary readers and writers must make a conscious effort to learn etymology by looking up words in a dictionary that lists word roots.

The writer who chooses words with an eye (and ear) to their history is able to make his writing more effective. Consider the word *inculcate*, which is sometimes used as a synonym for "teach." The root of *inculcate* is the Latin word for heel, *calx,* so the word carries with it the image of a heel pressing something into the ground; when used as a synonym for *teach,* the metaphorical meaning is colored by this violent image. The first listing for *inculcate* in the Oxford English Dictionary is a 1550 use by Coverdale: "This practyse dyd the holy elect of god in the olde time not onli inculcate and teach with words but also expresse and performe in dede." Like Coverdale, contemporary writers can choose words from one or both families of our language. For example, the Anglo-Saxon word *woods* suggests something different from the Latinate *forest,* even though the two are equivalents. Imagine the Latinate version of Frost's poem, "Stopping by [the Forest] on a Snowy Evening": "Whose [forest] this is I think I know" ... The Anglo-Saxon branch of our language is a boon to poets in particular because of its many monosyllabic words, which are easier to work with in metrical verse.

Below is a list of some Anglo-Saxon words and their Latinate or Greek "equivalents":

fear / phobia
truth / veracity
mad / insane
lazy / indolent
fat / obese
woods / forest
shit / excrement
worry / uneasiness, anxiety
speak / discourse
dark / obscure
greedy / rapacious
short / insufficient
light / illumination
fire / conflagration
eat / consume
weird / idiosyncratic
sorrow / anguish, melancholy
green / verdant
skin / epidermis

chew / masticate
heart / cardio …
water / aqua …
first / primary
horse / equine
thrill / ecstasy
fair / equitable
will / testament

Lawyers, as you might notice from the last two items on the list, tend to play it safe and use one from each column to convey a single idea. Football coaches tend toward the Anglo-Saxon and bureaucrats load up on Latinate diction because—pun intended—it obfuscates. Writers have a choice between Anglo-Saxon "gut" and "body" words and Latinate or Greek "head" words that sound, at least to an American ear, more intellectual. When I gave this paper to an audience that included a native speaker of Italian, she pointed out that to her, the Latinate words sounded more natural and body-centered. Even within cultures, people may hear words idiosyncratically, based on regional, family, and bodily differences. But these differences are subtle. English is a dance between the Anglo-Saxon and the Latinate/Greek, although some writers tend more to one than the other.

Look, for example, at these two sentences from stories by Henry James and Raymond Carver: (1) "The pair of mourners, sufficiently stricken, were in the garden of the vicarage together, before luncheon, waiting to be summoned to that meal, and Arthur Prime had still in his face the intention, she was moved to call it the expression, of feeling something or other." (2) "The four of us were sitting around his kitchen table drinking gin." James and Carver set up their stories in an identical journalistic fashion, laying out who's doing what, when, and how. But the difference in their choice of diction signals James as a primarily Latinate/Greek writer and Carver as a primarily Anglo-Saxon writer. This makes sense in light of James's concern with consciousness and his distaste for the body's grossness in contrast to Carver's pride in his working-class roots. Most writers tend not to be so clearly one or the other—in fact art depends on balancing the two, using an Anglo-Saxon word when it might carry more weight or fit the meter and the Latinate when it might surprise or suggest a shift of thought.

Look at what happens when the poet Josephine Jacobsen restricts herself to Anglo-Saxon diction:

The Monosyllable

One day
she fell
in love with its
heft and speed.
Tough, lean,

fast as light
slow
as a cloud.
It took care
of rain, short

noon, long dark.
It had rough kin;
did not stall.
With it, she said,
I may,

if I can,
sleep; since I must
die.
Some say,
rise.

I often teach this poem when I teach diction, and I ask students to "mess up" Jacobsen's poem by substituting Latinate or Greek words for her monosyllables. The results are hilarious and instructive. The word *die* has a different connotation and sound than the word *terminate* or *expire*, and *rise* is very different from *ascend*, to mention just two of the possible substitutions. Anglo-Saxon diction, as Jacobsen points out, has "heft and speed." Using it exclusively in a poem like this also dictates the short line lengths. Imagine the poem with pentameter lines: "One day she fell in love with its heft and speed." Because the monosyllables are more concentrated, or pack in more meaning in a shorter space, the reader needs white space surrounding them in order to have time to absorb the poem. If the monosyllable were not Jacobsen's point, a Latinate word or two would provide merciful relief. Interestingly, 60 percent of English words have Latin roots, but 90 percent of English words containing more than two syllables come from Latin.

EMBEDDED MEANINGS

The etymology of a word can deepen the meaning of a poem by carrying an image, as in the poem below by Madeleine Mysko. See if you can guess which word carries an important image here.

Out of Blue

It wasn't wind or thunder; color foretold
A summer storm. The orange tiger lily,
The yellow black-eyed Susan, the pink phlox
Were too much themselves in the charged light.
The trees to the west sharpened against the sky.
The sky was exaggerated, a purple hue.

I set out to gather toys from the yard
And towels from the line, but at the hedge was struck
By hydrangea blue. I felt it travel,
Through me, toward the ground of a day
I couldn't quite remember, and I was left
Bewildered, bereft of I didn't know what.

I had to lean into the broad leaves, to reach
Deep, to snap stems until my arms
Were filled with blooms as big as baby bonnets.
The broken-green odor blessed the air
As I carried that crucial blue across the lawn,
And the maples blanched at the first gust of wind.

Mysko's poem tells the story of a woman who goes into her yard to gather toys before a summer storm. She is sad, "bewildered, bereft of I didn't know what." She snaps some hydrangea blossoms to carry back into the house and is consoled. The poet refers to the color of the flowers as "crucial blue," and *crucial* comes from *crux*, Latin for "cross." Of course the reader who doesn't know the etymology of *crucial* can still understand the poem, but the reader who does know sees the image of the woman carrying the blossoms as a suggestion of Christ carrying the cross, and the poem more clearly becomes a poem of faith and redemption. The word *blessed* is another hint that the woman is bereft without faith, and that faith consoles her.

Another embedded etymological meaning is contained in Paisley Rekdal's poem, "Stupid," which refers to the Darwin Awards, "commemorat[ing] those who improve our gene pool by removing themselves from it in really stupid ways." Rekdal relates stories, such as that of a man who drowned in two feet of water or another who was stabbed to death by a friend while trying to prove a knife couldn't penetrate a flak vest. Braided together with these instances of human stupidity in Rekdal's poem is the story of Job, "that book of the pious man / who suffered because the devil wanted to teach God / faith kills through illusion." Toward the end of the poem Rekdal addresses Job directly, "Job, you are stupid for your faith as we are stupid for our lack of it, / snickering at the stockbroker jogging off the cliff, though / shouldn't we wonder at all a man can endure / to believe …" The etymology of the word *stupid*, although not mentioned in the poem, deepens its meaning. *Stupid* comes from Latin, *stupere*, to be astonished, which comes from the Greek, *typein*, to beat. It is the root of our words *stupefy* and *stupendous*. Rekdal's poem considers the borders between faith and insanity, joy and despair, life and death. When the reader keeps in mind the image of a person being astonished as the origin of *stupid*, this image changes the evaluation of the behavior discussed, and consequently the Darwin Award winners, like Job, seem to be acting on faith rather than merely exercising poor judgment.

Examples of embedded etymological meanings are abundant in the work of earlier poets such as Chaucer, Shakespeare, and Milton. Milton, thanks to his knowledge of roots, prefixes, and suffixes, coined many words, including *pandemonium, disfigurement*, and *displode. Dis,* Neil Forsyth tells us, is related to the Greek *dis*, "but picks up the flavor of the Greek prefix *dys*, meaning unlucky or ill." *Dis* is also the name of the inner city and principal inhabitant of Dante's Hell. This understanding gives the first line of *Paradise Lost*, "Of man's first disobedience and the fruit," deeper significance. The writer who uses etymology draws upon deep resources. The reader who understands this web of etymological connections has a richer experience than one who does not.

Ralph Waldo Emerson's much quoted "language is fossil poetry," from his essay "The Poet," speaks to his understanding of the primacy of etymology. The essay argues that the poet's power comes from his ability to use the archetypal symbols that are words. Emerson calls the poet "the Namer, or Language-maker" and writes, "The etymologist finds the deadest word to have been once a brilliant picture." Walt Whitman also championed the use of etymology: "the scope of [English] etymologies is the scope not only of man and civilization, but the history of Nature in all departments, and of the organic Universe, brought up to date; for all are comprehended in words, and their backgrounds." Joseph Kronick goes as far as to argue that "Whitman's project will be to refashion the language through an etymological uncovering of origins. This presumptive historical task will, however, be conducted on common speech, American slang to be precise, rather than within the Indo-European family of languages."

Gerard Manley Hopkins is another poet whose interest in etymology is well documented in his diaries. For instance, the entry for September 24, 1863, is an etymological riff on the word *horn*:

> The various lights under which a horn may be looked at have given rise to a vast number of words in language. It may be regarded as a projection, a climax, a badge of strength, power or vigour, a tapering body, a spiral, a wavy object, a bow, a vessel to hold withal or to drink from, a smooth hard material not brittle, stony, metallic or wooden, something sprouting up, something to thrust or push with, a sign of honour or pride, an instrument of music, etc. From the shape, *kernel* and *granum, grain, corn*. From the curve of the horn, *κορώύς, corona, crown*. From the spiral *crinis*, meaning ringlets, locks. From its being the highest point comes our crown perhaps, in the sense of the top of the head, and the Greek *κερας* , horn, and *κάρα* , head, were evidently identical; then for its sprouting up and growing, compare keren, cornu, *κέρας*, horn with grow, *cresco, grandis, grass, great, groot* ...

This is only half of the entry! In it, one can see Hopkins's mind ranging over the word and its histories, even inventing etymology as a way of combining images with history.

In the hands of a skilled etymologist, such riffs become ways to think about cultural and historical change, as when Martin Heidegger follows the etymologies of the German word for "build," *bauen*, which originally meant "dwell."

> The real meaning of the verb *bauen*, namely, to dwell, has been lost to us. But a covert trace of it has been preserved in the German word, *Nachbar*, neighbor. The neighbor is in Old English the *neahgebur; neah*, near, and *gebur*, dweller. The *Nachbar* is the *Nachgebur*, the *Nachgebauer*, the near-dweller, he who dwells nearby. ... The way in which you are and I am, the manner in which we humans are on the earth, is *Buan*, dwelling. To be a human

> being means to be on the earth as a mortal. It means to dwell.
> The old word *bauen*, which says that man *is* insofar as he *dwells*,
> this word *bauen* however also means at the same time to cherish
> and protect, specifically to till the soil, to cultivate the vine.

At a time when building usually means ruining the earth by imposing our will on it, Heidegger reminds us how we have drifted from the notion of "cherish and protect."

A contemporary American novelist passionate about etymology is Paul West, whose book *The Secret Lives of Words* is a personal and entertaining etymological dictionary. West admits that he began a novel about astronomy with the word *consider*, which means "set alongside the stars" (from the prefix *cum* meaning "with" and *sidus* meaning "star"). West writes, "Ancient astrologers such as Roman practitioners of divination coined this word, but more recent astrologers fix on planets. Tracking the courses of stars soon weakened into observing them, and that into observing in general, and in no time observing has become 'remarking,' not in the sense of 'notice' but in that of 'saying,' in which case it joins the abominable modern 'I was' and 'I went,' both referring to speech." West's book, like Hopkins's diary entries, testifies to the addictive nature of learning etymologies. Every unknown word is a mystery waiting to be solved.

FALSE ETYMOLOGIES

An etymological dictionary that begins to unravel these mysteries and that specifically chronicles the American influence on the English language is Allen Metcalf and David Barnhart's *America in So Many Words: Words That Shaped America*. Their entry on the word *turkey* offers another model of an etymological journey:

> Whoever named the bird *turkey*—a word that English speakers began mentioning as long ago as 1541—made a big mistake. Although that bird came from Guinea in Africa, the English apparently first imported it from Turkish merchants. So, naturally, they called it a *turkey*. When English speakers established their first colony in Jamestown, Virginia, in 1607, they thought they saw turkeys there too. "We found an ilet, on which were many Turkeys," wrote one. These birds were not from Turkey and were not related to the guinea fowl of Africa. But *turkeys* they were

called, and *turkeys* they remain. Much of what we know about the Jamestown colony was written by Captain John Smith, whose efforts preserved the colony from collapse and who in turn was preserved by the Indian "princess" Pocahontas. Smith's accounts of the colony frequently mention turkeys as food, gifts, and objects of trade. In 1607, Smith writes, to celebrate the first peace after the first armed clash, the Indians brought "Venison, Turkies, wild foule, bread, and what they had, singing and dauncing in signe of friendship till they departed." Elsewhere Smith noted that the Indians made warm and beautiful cloaks from turkey feathers. Further north, as the Plymouth colony neared the end of its first year in 1621, Governor William Bradford likewise observed "great store of wild Turkies, of which they tooke many." Undoubtedly turkeys were among the "fowl" served at the first THANKSGIVING (1621) dinner …

The entry also gives a sense of how "false" ideas take hold and then go on to have a life of their own.

So does Susan Mitchell's poem, "The False Etymologies of Isidore of Seville." Isidore (560–636 A.C.E.), a Christian bishop and scholar, produced *Etymologiae,* or *Origines,* as it is sometimes called. Enormously popular throughout the Middle Ages, this work attempted to compile all knowledge in an encyclopedic fashion. Isidore's quest points to a recurrent theme in etymology, that of the search for origins and universal truth. Mitchell writes that Isidore of Seville believed, "This one / from that, eyrie from air, so ear from airy, the ear / a nest that hears in air its own name" but then admits that she's "translating," that she's "making this up." However, if Mitchell invents the particulars, the gist remains: Isidore's desire to understand origins led him to make erroneous connections on his religious journey.

He wants to follow the initial S for Salvation,
pursue the long curve of the swan's
song back up to the winding
throat and dab the first fruit with his own saliva.

He'll do it on hands and knees, the pilgrimage
of each word to its source, first sound
from which the others
bubbled up, original gurgling innocent of sense.

Mitchell's poem suggests that the poet's interest in language is rooted (pun intended) in a different religion, that of pleasure: "I haven't his patience. I haven't got / all eternity. I skip to the parts I love best, the vowels / steeped like peaches in brandy ..." The poem ends by stating that the language of pleasure is childish but also that pleasure is as powerful a motivation as scholarship:

> The language of pleasure is makeshift, leaves and branches
> hastily thrown. Of mud and dribble.
> Of huff and puff and higgledy-piggledy.
> Of rampage, ruckus. Of blow your house down.

If "true etymology" reveals history, then "false etymology" reveals wishful thinking, the connections we make in our effort to order the world. Often the "essential truth" of etymology reaches to Christianity. Gjertrud Schnakenberg's poem "Supernatural Love" gives us another vision of the "dictionary mystic" and the search for truth, focusing on the etymology of the word *carnation*, whose root is Latin, *carne*, meaning flesh. The speaker's father "bends to pore / over the Latin blossom" of words, while his four-year-old daughter is trying to needlepoint. The little girl refers to carnations as "Christ's flowers," which prompts the father to look up the word *clove* (the scent of the flower) and he finds, "from French, for *clou*, meaning a nail." Thus in Schnackenberg's poem the child makes an etymological link that produces a mystical (but false, as the carnation takes its name from the color that the flower shares with blood) truth:

> The incarnation blossoms, flesh and nail,
> I twist my threads like stems into a knot
> And smooth "Beloved," but my needle caught
> Within the threads, *Thy blood so dearly bought*,
> The needle strikes my finger to the bone.

Other examples of poets who create "false" etymologies to think through problems include poets as disparate as Elizabeth Alexander and Allen Grossman. In Elizabeth Alexander's poem "Affirmative Action Blues," the speaker implores her boss not to use the word *niggardly* even though its etymology, she admits, is "probably / derived from French Norman, and that Chaucer and Milton and / Shakespeare used it. It means 'stingy,' and the root is not the same as 'nigger,' / which derives from 'negar,' meaning black, but they are, perhaps, / perhaps, etymologically related. The two 'g's' are two teeth gnawing, / rodent is from the Latin 'rodere' which means 'to gnaw.'" The poet is replicating the kind of leap common in a false etymology—a leap that makes sense even if it isn't accurate.

Similarly, Allen Grossman's poem "Sentinel Yellowwoods" is a kind of ode to the yellowwood tree—*cladrastis lutea*. The root *lutea* comes from the Latin word for yellow, while the word for the instrument lute comes from German and Arab roots that contain no reference to color. Grossman riffs on "odorous silent adorning lutes," synesthetically combining the sight, scent, and sound of the trees into an intimation of his own mortality: "I am going to die soon, and their shadow foretells it / enlarging the world." That Grossman knows he is creating a "false" link is apparent from his reference to "flowers Arabian, and blazing with gladdening metals / Mysterious flies . . ." True or false, etymology in poems becomes a way to access ideology—that is, assumptions about what is normal in our culture. Word histories are traces of evolution (or devolution) in our thinking.

HISTORICAL IMPACT

The word *etymology* itself comes from the Greek root, *eteos*, for true. Understanding word origins is a way of understanding history, and more specifically understanding that context changes meaning. For much of the twentieth century, Formalism (Structuralism or New Criticism are other terms for essentially the same thing) reigned supreme, and literary critics examined literary texts divorced from their context. Gradually literary criticism has once again begun to appreciate—even rely on—contexts. Poststructuralist criticism often focuses on such contextual issues as history, gender, race, and sexual orientation. Even when a poststructuralist critic focuses solely on the text, it is to look for slippages, gray areas, and the non-sense of the thing—what is sometimes termed a Derridean reading, or deconstruction. Poststructuralists insist that etymology is important not as a search for fixed origins, but rather as a search for determinations.

Because narrative especially lends itself to contextual study, more exciting theoretical work is being done on narrative than on lyric poetry. For example, a New Historicist might ask us to look at colonial American medical records in order to understand the high rate of premarital pregnancy in eighteenth-century America, and this understanding changes one's reading of the novels of that time. Lyric poetry does not lend itself as easily to New Historical criticism because it draws from human universality. Sappho's poems, for example, speak to us 2000 years after their writing because of the primacy of desire—a speaker who wants her love object to see her:

He's a god, that man who sits with you, who listens to you talk
and laugh. Seeing you with him makes my heart pound, and because you are lost to me, I can't speak, my tongue breaks into
pieces, and fire runs under my skin. I'm blinded, my ears ring,
sweat pours down, and my body trembles. Paler than summer
wheat, I might as well be dead ... (*my translation*)

No wonder that Sappho is more popular today than a poet like Dryden, whose
poems require so much understanding of context. History is interested in the
unique, in things that happen once and only once, or the relationship of the
singular to the cyclical, while lyric poetry focuses on the repeated feeling, on
a timeless evocation of the human condition, particularly human emotion.
Etymology, however, is a way for the lyric poet to access history and a way for
the reader of lyric poetry to read more contextually.

While Isidore of Seville saw etymology as a path to concrete origins and
lasting truth, since then philosophers have been chipping away at these ideas.
Nietzsche writes, "Woman (truth) will not be pinned down." Derrida elabo-
rates on the analogy, pointing to the positive aspects of truth that is not fixed.
Derrida argues that Nietzsche understood that women (like Jews) are artists
and masters of style, and that style (the superficial) is a more useful way to
think about truth than permanent core or centrality. Truth is transient, contextual, shifting; it is not behind a veil, it *is* the veil, according to Derrida—not
something to be uncovered, but rather contained only in movement. Derrida
is one of the more recent philosophers who, over the last two hundred years,
have gradually moved to this understanding of truth. They have abandoned
the notion of Descartes, for example, that truth could be arrived at through
reason, and that once arrived at, would remain fixed. The Enlightenment confidence in rationality and definitive science has been challenged on this and
many other fronts as when, for example, philosopher Ludwig Wittgenstein
stressed language as truth's unstable "carrier." Language then—and by extension etymology, the unfolding meanings of a word—is not a vehicle for
direct and final meaning (logocentrism) but is instead the medium through
which constellations of power shape the true and the false. As such, etymology becomes a means to analyze these wrestling discourses. Truth changes
according to context.

Quite a few contemporary poets make etymology their explicit subject
for poems, offering occasions for thinking about contexts, history, and shifting truth. Etymology is also a resource I counsel students to use when they

are stuck; I tell them to open the dictionary to a word or word history they don't know and put it in a poem. The key to this exercise is the initial state of inquiry that sends the poet on a journey of discovery. The poet doesn't know what the poem, finally, will be "about" when he uses the word's etymology as a starting point before he knows the twists and turns of its history. For example, when I decided to write about vanilla as part of a series of poems about food, and started researching its etymology, I discovered that it comes from the Spanish *vainilla,* diminutive of *vagina,* the Latin term for "sheath." Thus, the pod-shaped bean was named after a human vagina, and the vagina itself was named for the function it provides for a penis. This seems to me to be the quintessential demonstration of patriarchal language, a demonstration that might seem shocking, as when one magazine editor to whom I submitted the resulting poem asked if the ending—"no matter that some words glide over the tongue, / entice us with sweet stories, / we're still stuck / with their roots in our throats"—were a reference to *Deep Throat.* If we had continued our dialogue, I would have said yes, in the sense that women are dominated by the patriarchal nature of language in the same way that Linda Lovelace was dominated.

I can't imagine that Heather McHugh knew that her poem would take the shape of a "dirge" when she started looking up the string of words in the poem below. This element of surprise is important in writing poems that feel fresh to the reader: If it feels fresh to the writer, it will feel fresh to the reader.

Etymological Dirge

'Twas grace that taught my heart to fear …

Calm comes from burning.
Tall comes from fast.
Comely doesn't come from come.
Person comes from mask.

The kin of charity is whore,
the root of charity is dear.
Incentive has its source in song
and winning in the sufferer.

Afford yourself what you can carry out.
A coward and a coda share a word.
We get our ugliness from fear.
We get our danger from the lord.

The etymology of plants is the subject of a poem by Gary Snyder where etymology broadens the scope and shows human relations to the natural world. Snyder's poem "Earrings Dangling and Miles of Desert" is an extended definition of sagebrush, *Artemisia*, the plant that grows over vast stretches of the American west, a plant rapidly being choked out by nonindigenous and faster-growing annuals such as cheatgrass. Combining prose and poetry, Snyder tells us the growing habits and uses of sagebrush, as well as its variations around the world: for example, "mugwort and moxa in China" as well as its Paiute names. He ends the poem with a lyric ode:

Artem in Greek meant "to dangle" or "earring"
(Well-connected, "articulate," art. ...)
Her blue-gray-green
stretching out there
sagebrush flats reach to the edge
bend away—
emptiness far as the mind can see—
Raincloud maidens come walking
        lightning-streak silver,
gray skirts sweeping and trailing—

Hail, Artemisia,
    aromatic in the rain,
        I will think of you in my other poems.

Snyder uses etymology to create the image of the earrings, the title for his poem, and as a way of "humanizing" a plant whose destiny concerns him. Etymology becomes a way of thinking about what is—and, more importantly, what is possible. Through etymology, writers have the power to understand how ideology works and, perhaps, even to tug its tail. Understanding what is and why it is permits us slowly, incrementally, to change. The writer who uses etymology, implicitly or explicitly, accesses not only the history of words, but of ideas.

MIND THE GAP

By Betsy Sholl

It only takes one little stammer, one little break in the flow, to become aware of how speech negotiates between our private consciousness and social engagement. Our speech patterns—diction, tone, rhythms—form a kind of runway between the inner life and the outer life. Often, that inner/outer negotiation occurs seamlessly, accomplishing complex patterns of approach and avoidance, ambiguity and improvisation. When disruption occurs for us stutterers, the negotiation is not subtle; it is blocked or broken, a small crisis for the speaker and a discomfort for the listener. It reveals something vulnerable, fragile in what we consider a most normal form of social intercourse and self-expression. Our means of being a self in the world encounters an obstacle, and arouses angst.

While surely there are more stutterers who are not writers, it is interesting to note some of the stutterers who are. Benson Bobrick in his book, *The Knotted Tongue*, includes in the list: Demosthenes, Virgil, Aesop, Cotton Mather, Charles Lamb, Leigh Hunt, Erasmus and Charles Darwin, Lewis Carroll, W. Somerset Maugham, Henry James, Winston Churchill, Harold Brodkey, Robert Heinlein, Philip Larkin, Edward Hoagland, John Updike, Alfred Kazin, Margaret Drabble, and John Montague.

One of the earliest figures associated with stuttering is Moses, who, before the burning bush, when charged with a mission from God, made excuse after excuse, all coming down to his inability to speak. "They will not believe me," he says to God, "or listen to my voice. I have never been eloquent, neither in the past, nor even now that you have spoken to your servant; but I am slow of speech and slow of tongue" (Exod. 4:10). This doesn't seem to bother God. Maybe God is sick of smooth talkers, rhetorical wizards, preachers, and senators. Anyway, it's interesting to think of his hesitation, his halting speech, as reflecting the duality of Moses's life—pampered child and outcast, rescued Jew in the Egyptian court, man both favored and found guilty of murder. Such a gap, a bifurcation in his life, expressed in a bifurcation between speech and thought.

Lately I've been looking at ways various bifurcations, hesitations, blocks, and gaps appear in poetry. Just a casual reading can turn up a small stream of references to stuttering, as if disfluency is both a fear and an acknowledged aspect of language for those who shape it. Fluency is what the stutterer longs for, craves like food and water. Stuttering is considered a handicap, an impediment. To hesitate is to be slow to act, speak or decide, to pause in uncertainty, waver, to be reluctant, speak haltingly, falter. But if the stoppered-up silence of utter blockage is on one end of the speech spectrum, then at the opposite extreme, heading toward white noise, must be glibness. And as James Wright says, glibness is one of the biggest temptations a poet has to resist. So perhaps a little halting, a little reluctance can be a good thing.

"B-b-b-bad to the bone," "B-b-b-back in the U.S.S.R.," "Ch-ch-ch-changes," "Ba-ba-ba-ba-ba-bra Ann," "Talkin' 'bout my g-g-generation"—I confess I don't understand the phenomenon of stuttering in popular music. Is it mostly about rhythm, the beat of the music, and not really an intentional stutter at all? Does it suggest emotional excitation pushing the speaker to the edge of language? Do these fractured sounds come from an underlying anti-heroic sensibility, cultural angst like a verbal fright wig, half terror, half humor? Are they sounds that in an earlier time would have been crooned as long continuous notes? Often enough these days we feel wary of straight narrative and pure lyricism. We tend to view fragmentation, mixed media, elements of obscurity as closer to our natural states of mind, perhaps less manipulative, or more hip, less in danger of romanticizing experience. Hence, the notion of stuttering has become a sort of buzzword in some critical circles, glamorized into a concept of style that draws on fragmentation, interruption, incompleteness. But another element of stuttering is how it slows down the process of speech, so for a moment at least words become physical, like a dry biscuit in the mouth or a square block too big for the mouth's round opening. Language suddenly comes in a series of still shots rather than moving film. Stutterers don't exactly mistrust language; it's too hard to come by. But because we know our own tendency to quick-switch a word when we see a block forming up ahead, we do mistrust the very fluency we long for.

It seems to me that poetry has a similar attitude, involving a constant interplay between fluency and resistance. Line breaks, caesuras, and white spaces are all forms of resisting or redirecting the flow. Poetry, and art in general, resists by shaping the constant barrage of sensual information, stopping some things, letting others in. Our experience of mind at work includes patterns of flow and fragmentation, riffs and rifts, focus and distraction. Then there's the world—our experience of everything out there, not us—how stubbornly it resists our endeavors to fully know it, to master, name, define, contain. If language acts as a gatekeeper, articulating some perceptions and consigning others to the background, the unconscious of the unnamed, that process can go on almost unnoticed, until the gate becomes rusty or jammed or otherwise apparent. I think of Brenda Hillman's experiments with leftover words, those concurrent perceptions given in small print at the bottom of the page, like droppings or refuse not swept away and tidied up, as if she wants the gate to swing wide open to include a view of what got edited out of the poem, those by-products of composition.

I don't know if Jean-Luc Godard is a stammerer or not, but Gilles Deleuze speaks of the filmmaker in those terms:

> In a certain sense, it's always about being a stammerer. Not a stammerer in his speech but a stammerer in language itself. Generally, you can only be a foreigner in another language, but here, it's rather a matter of being a foreigner in your own language. Proust said that the great books are necessarily written in a sort of foreign language. It's the same with Godard's program. ... It's this creative stammering, this solitude that gives Godard his force.

Though I'm wary of romanticizing the reality of stuttering, nevertheless this is a good reminder that as much as we must try to master our mother tongue, we must also resist that mastery. To be a foreigner in a language is to hear with fresh ears, to wrestle with it, to be aware of its recalcitrance, to recognize its physicality, the implications of its grammatical patterns, and to use it in ways that are perhaps outside convention, releasing new, if awkward possibilities. Charles Wright approaches a similar concern when he says, "if one of the primary urges of a work of art is to become circular and come to a completion, then one of the real jobs of the artist is to keep this closure from happening, so he [sic] can work in the synapse, the spark before the end." When our aim isn't to flow smoothly toward unobstructed resolution, it becomes possible to linger within the tensions, to consider the value of digression, the electricity generated by interruption, and to acknowledge the limits of our language. If we assume fluency is a major aspect of poetic composition, perhaps we can also notice the other side, or underside, the places in poems where the continuity is disrupted, and consider what effect that creates. As Tomas Tranströmer says in "The Scattered Congregation":

> We got ready and showed our home.
> The visitor thought: you live well.
> The slum must be inside you.

We don't have to look to extremes or wildly innovative poets to see how hesitation and fluency co-exist. We can find many examples of poets resisting their own eloquence by creating hesitations, gaps, that express a tension between the desire to speak and a reluctance to reveal, or the longing to express and the intransigence of experience, its refusal to be converted into language.

Let's look at Whitman's "After the Supper and Talk," a poem which is quite literally about hesitation.

> After the supper and talk—after the day is done,
> As a friend from friends his final withdrawal prolonging,
> Good-bye and Good-bye with emotional lips repeating,
> (So hard for his hand to release those hands—no more will they
> meet,
> No more for communion of sorrow and joy, of old and young,
> A far-stretching journey awaits him, to return no more,)
> Shunning, postponing severance—seeking to ward off the last
> word ever so little,
> E'en at the exit-door turning—charges superfluous calling back—
> e'en as he descends the steps,
> Something to eke out a minute additional—shadows of nightfall
> deepening
> Farewells, messages lessening—dimmer the forthgoer's visage
> and form,
> Soon to be lost for aye in the darkness—loth, O so loth to
> depart!
> Garrulous to the very last.

In the first line's little stutter-step of parallel phrasing, the poem resists a forward motion. Then there are the ongoing participles that continue to slow down the action: *prolonging, repeating, postponing,* etc. There are the parenthetical lines, the gestures enclosed in dashes, the anaphora, the slow fadeout, also the long *o*'s of the penultimate phrase—and the last touching self-portrait, "Garrulous to the very last," which creates a kind of open closure, maintaining the scene in our minds. There's a tremendous effort, as all of Whitman's often-progressive cataloging techniques serve here as ways to linger on this one gesture, to hesitate, to create a dramatic scene wavering on the point of departure.

Another interesting aspect of this poem is its perspective. Early on, we could read the poem as a third-person account of the traveler's emotions: "So hard for his hand to release those hands—no more will they meet ... seeking to ward off the last word ever so little." Toward the end, it seems we are watching from the doorstep as the traveler leaves, growing dimmer, then is finally lost in darkness. If the narrator is observing the forthgoer, he is also empathetically identified with him. It reminds me of the sort of electric field that stammering creates, when sp-sp-speaker and li-li-listener are locked in the static tension of broken language, listener often knowing what speaker intends but cannot say.

As Whitman's poem reveals, careful use of syntax, fragmentation, self-correction, digression, blank space, and open closure are some ways poets work against their own glibness. Of course, for each poetic style glibness may have a different manifestation, so the glib in Stevens would be different from the glib in Williams or Creeley. And insofar as these patterns of resistance involve craft and skill, it is possible for them to become facile or glib in turn. Thus, the ever-constant need to press on, be vigilant.

Perhaps for Elizabeth Bishop the glib would consist of pure description, moving seamlessly from beginning to end, in unquestioned acts of observation with a slightly fussy or superior tone. Instead, her poems are full of self-correction, small elaborations that complicate, re-speak, rethink, take back and start again. Bishop uses her eye and her language like a blind person feeling her way through a scene. In "Brazil, January 1, 1502," she works with qualifiers, with questions, parentheses, and corrections, building toward an acute awareness of the actual world, as well as a metaphorical entrance into the past:

> Januaries, Nature greets our eyes
> exactly as she must have greeted theirs:
> every square inch filling in with foliage—
> big leaves, little leaves, and giant leaves,

blue, blue-green, and olive,
with occasional lighter veins and edges,
or a satin underleaf turned over;
monster ferns
in silver-gray relief,
and flowers, too, like giant water lilies
up in the air—up, rather, in the leaves—
purple, yellow, two yellows, pink,
rust red and greenish white;
solid but airy; fresh as if just finished
and taken off the frame.

She lingers, repeats—big leaves, little leaves, giant leaves; corrects—"up, rather, in the leaves"; refuses to rush or be rushed through this experience—"purple, yellow, two yellows, pink, rust red and greenish white …" The language here is generative, creating not only the lush world before her, but also preparing us for the tapestry, and for the world of the sixteenth-century conquistadors. At the end of the poem, Bishop again uses her exact observation, eyeing and re-eyeing the Spaniards:

Just so the Christians, hard as nails,
tiny as nails, and glinting,
in creaking armor, came and found it all,
not unfamiliar:
no lovers' walks, no bowers,
no cherries to be picked, no lute music,
but corresponding, nevertheless,
to an old dream of wealth and luxury
already out of style when they left home—
wealth, plus a brand-new pleasure.

Notice how she interrupts the main clause, making the men almost comic briefly, before they come and take over. Then there's a series of negative definitions, which slows things down and also suggests our entry into the men's consciousness, preparing us for the frustrated violence of the final lines:

Directly after Mass, humming perhaps
l'Homme armé or some such tune,
they ripped away into the hanging fabric,
each out to catch an Indian for himself—
those maddening little women who kept calling,

calling to each other (or had the birds waked up?)
and retreating, always retreating, behind it.

What complicates the poem here is how the poet has entered into the minds of those conquistadors, at least enough to represent the scene from their perspective. As readers we become implicated through our recognition of that old dream and of the men's frustration. That stutter-step of apposition—"those maddening little women who kept calling"—and the brief self-doubt—"or had the birds waked up?"—define an emotional state that is not foreign to us, even if the brutal response is. Bishop takes her time, insists on the physicality of the scene—both landscape and tapestry—and resists what could have been facile judgment, thus making the scene more complex and searing. We are entangled in the morality play of this tapestry, and what tore it to shreds.

Another thing to note here is how Bishop has at her command a full range of syntax and punctuation: periodic sentences, appositives, negative definitions, analogies, and extended descriptions. She uses all these tools to contextualize and complicate the poem.

William Carlos Williams is another poet who creates stutter steps in his poems. In Williams the effect is often one of disruption or distraction, as if the poem's vessel isn't strong enough or willing to resist the meteor crash of experience, or even the poet's own second thoughts. There's the lurching, tilting radical enjambment of the first section of "Spring and All":

By the road to the contagious hospital
under the surge of the blue
mottled clouds driven from the
northeast—a cold wind. Beyond, the
waste of broad, muddy fields
brown with dried weeds, standing and fallen ...

There's a poem like "A Unison," addressed to a friend, and filled with conversational asides:

The grass is very green, my friend,
and tousled, like the head of—
your grandson, yes? And the mountain,
the mountain we climbed
twenty years since for the last
time (I write this thinking
of you) is saw-horned as then

upon the sky's edge—an old barn
is peaked there also, fatefully,
against the sky. And there it is
and we can't shift it or change
it or parse it or alter it
in any way. Listen!

Here the poet interrupts, hesitates, starts again—and certainly the last comment implies its shadow desire to do precisely what he says can't be done: shift, change, parse, alter experience. If the speaker is bent on not falsifying— "we'd better acknowledge it ..."—and "Not twist the words to mean what we should have said ..."—he is also aware of how easily writing does in fact twist and alter experience. In a sense this is a poem about resisting the facile, the falsification of experience by desire. The two companions have been on this hill before and have been moved by the experience enough to call the grove sacred, idyllic, a shrine "cinctured there by the trees, a certainty of music! / a unison and a dance, joined / at this death's festival ..." "Hear! Hear them! / the Undying," Williams says. Clearly the poet's work here is to evoke this place, these voices—but to do so in a manner that does not impose the speaker's desire for transcendence on the literal. The figure of the Undying suggests elements in the natural world, but also something else less material that the speaker struggles to acknowledge against his own reluctance—some "certainty of music! / a unison and a dance ..." The syntax struggles, the referents are almost lost in dashes, dashed-off interruptions, lost antecedents:

Something
of a shed snake's skin, the beginning
goldenrod. Or, best, a white stone,
you have seen it: *Mathilda Maria
Fox*—and near the ground's lip,
all but undecipherable, *Aet Suae,
Anno 9*—still there, the grass
dripping of last night's rain—and
welcome! The thin air, the near,
clear brook water!—and could not,
and died, unable; to escape
what the air and the wet grass—
through which, tomorrow, bejeweled,
the great sun will rise—the

unchanging mountains, forced on them—
and they received, willingly!

Interjections, cut-off trains of thought, clipped phrases—all seem to be attempts to resist what the poet/speaker must fear could be sentimentalized. As a reader I can't fully put these telegraphic lines together, which may be the point: "Stones, stones of a difference / joining the others at pace ..." Difference and joining at once, both aspects preserved through the discontinuities we have to be urged to hear: "Hear! / Hear the unison of their voices ..." In a sense, it's the struggle to arrive that is moving here, as if this voice is speaking with the strained breath of a climber, whose thoughts take in the natural world and the human world in jagged pieces. Everything's about to appear, emphatically. But something could not, was unable. All around the voices of the Undying—perhaps the brook, the birds, the trees, but also the carefully placed stones, and the dead who were unable to—what? escape what the entire natural world forced on them, and which in the end they received willingly? It's jumbled together, life, death, beauty, fate—and the lingering unison of their voices, a chorus slightly frenetic and haunting.

Thelonious Monk at times plays the piano like a stutterer; striking the so-called "wrong" note in a familiar melody is like the stammerer substituting a different word for the one that is threatening a block. And Monk's percussive striking of keys is like a stutterer giving a little extra plosive push to get the word out. It's a way of deliberately emphasizing the offbeat, changing the timing. In Monk's art, hesitations, delays, and surprising emphases defamiliarize the tune for the listener, making it new.

Creeley operates in a similar way. There's rarely a word we don't know. But the timing's off, or on a different track, the words repeat, interjected phrases break up the flow of thought, the radically enjambed lines create unexpected hesitations, so the most familiar experience takes on new and fraught significance. Here's a poem we probably all know:

I Know a Man

As I sd to my
friend, because I am
always talking, —John, I

```
sd, which was not his
name, the darkness sur-
rounds us, what

can we do against
it, or else, shall we &
why not, buy a goddamn big car,

drive, he sd, for
christ's sake, look
out where yr going.
```

I can't help wondering if this poem picks up on a line of Williams's, the end of part eighteen of "Spring and All," "no one to drive the car." Creeley's speaker is driving in his own reckless and halting manner. He's approaching then jumping away from his angst; he interrupts his own thought, and is interrupted in turn by his friend. Creeley breaks up the possible fluency with conjunctions, interjections, a self-answered question. The line breaks force us into a lurching rhythm and emphasis, creating a sense of breathless speed and blockage at the same time—which of course is one thing people often say, probably mistakenly, of stutterers, that they block because they speak too fast.

A completely different kind of resistance occurs when the blockages or gaps are not consciously chosen by the poet, but rather by some other force—that of time, censorship, human or natural catastrophe. In Anne Carson's translations of Sappho she attempts to create the experience of reading those damaged papyri. The fragments remain fragments, rather than being translated into the illusion of seamless poems. Leaving the gaps in place—or at least attempting to recreate the drama of those gaps—creates not just an experience of absence but also a different kind of presence. There's the absence of the language, the missing lines, but there is also the presence of time, the almost dizzying sense of centuries, destruction, cataclysm. Here is one example, number twenty-three in Carson's listing:

```
]of desire
]
]for when I look at you
]such a Hermione
]and to yellowhaired Helen I liken you
]
```

]among mortal women, know this
]from every care
]you could release me
]

   ]dewy riverbanks
   ]to last all night long
   ] [

It's a fragment, which at the same time holds together, at least in terms of mood and feeling, the longing for intimacy, the speaker's imagining an idyllic place and night. Here's a translation that appears to fill in details and make the poem's meaning fluent. A title is also provided:

I Am Awed by Your Beauty

For when I look upon you face-to-face
It seems Hermione even never was
One such as you:
               more like pale-haired Helen
I must say you are than any maid that dies.
And your tender beauty—O I shall confess—
I'd give all my thoughts in holocaust to it
And every sense for you in homage.

I can't account for the difference in imagery—why one translation says "dewy riverbanks" and the other "thoughts in holocaust"—unless the second version has merged two fragments. Many of us are so used to Sappho's voice being treated more like the second version, we wouldn't want to throw those translations out. Still, there's something evocative, and incredibly moving, about the Carson version, the fragility we're forced to recognize, the way we can't avoid the tear, the vulnerability of the physical artifacts that contained Sappho's work. A living writer whose works have not been destroyed by marauding guardians of public morality and forces of censorship needs to use fragments carefully, being wary of cleverness or affectation. But Carson's fragments raise the possibility of a different approach to narrative, one that is more aware of the gaps, the memory holes, the multiple versions, the disjunctions, and doesn't try to cover them up.

Just mentioning guardians of public morality and censors brings to mind Czeslaw Milosz and his discussion of the post-World War II writers in Poland. Suffering from the betrayal of culture, finding the poetic traditions around them corrupt and inadequate to express their experiences, personal and communal, many poets resisted glibness initially by not writing at all. When they began again, their poems were often minimalist, stripped-down collections of details without ornamentation, commentary, or any attempt at generalized insight. Clearly, one way to resist glibness is to resist ornament. Milosz gives this example from Miron Bialoszewski, a poet mistrustful of culture, and of language, "for language is the fabric from which the garments of all philosophies and ideologies are cut." While he calls Bialoszewski untranslatable because of his penchant for fragments and stenographic notation, he does give us this poem, which clearly resists any kind of glib resolution:

A Ballad of Going Down to the Store

First I went down to the store
by means of the stairs,
just imagine it,
by means of the stairs.

Then people known to people unknown
passed by me and I passed by them.
Regret
that you did not see
how people walk,
regret!

I entered a complete store:
lamps of glass were glowing.
I saw somebody—he sat down—
and what did I hear? What did I hear?
rustling of bags and human talk.

And indeed,
indeed
I returned.

Paul Muldoon displays an almost opposite sensibility. Voluble, overflowing with verbal wizardry, a kind of manic or mongrel savant, Muldoon can be as naturally facile as any living poet. His ways of resisting that, when he does, include working with elaborate formal patterns—innovative sonnets, haiku sequences, insanely complex rhyme schemes, among other things. He also plays with a sophisticated kind of verbal nonsense. "Incantata" is a long elegy for a former lover who died of cancer, a poem with a complex stanza pattern, plus a rich texture of historical and literary allusion. Midway through the poem, the speaker breaks down into nonsense syllables. Well, they are also allusions to Samuel Beckett's *Waiting for Godot*, so not quite nonsense or breakdown. But the effect is of a kind of verbal howl at his lover's resigned fatalism, and the meaninglessness of the speaker/poet's attempt to salvage something from this loss:

> The fact that you were determined to cut yourself off in your
>   prime
> because it was *pre-determined* has my eyes abrim:
> I crouch with Belacqua
> and Lucky and Pozzo in the Acacacac-
> ademy of Anthropopopometry, trying to make sense of the
>   'quaquaqu'
> of that potato-mouth; that mouth as prim
> and proper as it's full of self-opprobrium,
> with its *'quaquaqua,'* with its *'Quoiquoiquoiquoiquoiquoi*
>   *quoiq.'*

This approaches certain jazz performances in which the musicians let all order and balance break into chaos, let misrule reign for a while and blow itself out. It's interesting to note that where he breaks his words—the *c* on the end of "*Acacacac*" and the *q* on the end of "*quioq*" increase the cacophony and chaos.

If one danger in narrative poetry is the way the forward momentum of the story can tempt us to cover over the gaps in our knowledge of events, there are many ways of responding to this. There is the way Larry Levis uses digression, accumulation of subplots, asides, all to complicate the narrative and keep it from too easily coming to its closure. There is the way Susan Mitchell, in a poem like "Self Portrait With Young Eros," explores the edge of verbal representation, or explores the experience of self and otherness beyond language, introducing lines that are either from another language or from a made-up one—I'm not entirely sure which. But the effect is the same: of language that becomes physical in the mouth, utterly foreign and meaningful only as the sounds, like musical notes, move the lips that reproduce them. For the average reader at least, no other meaning comes from them, just their sounds, their physical presence and the feelings that arise from certain consonantal clusters.

The poem's speaker has returned home with groceries and seen a heron, which creates a kind of ontological shock and leads into a long meditation. Eros, the invisible lover, flickers through various sections of the poem. Several times the poem breaks into this physical, ancient-sounding language:

> the heron with its own stylus writing
> the lake's margins
> materials impermanent flowing
> mucosa of the shore and current reflections
> defalcations seed drift laufs fiscs
> flashings akrs
> Sawel swen sunthaz, penu poi? Poi
> frijaz? Frathjan?
> Can the other
> ever be other enough?

I hate my ignorance here, not knowing what, if any, language this is drawn from. But surely the poet knows most readers will be in the same bind, and has written to that bind, the longing for the other, for everything that slips through the cracks of facile speech, those abstractions that blot out the plethora of sensual experiences nudging and brushing us all day long. A little later in the poem, the speaker seems to imply a question:

> To fabricate more real, or less. To fabricate
> widespread beating air. To make sounds
> out loud: at either end
> disconnected, not yet placed,
>
> language like a circle of light floating in the floating
>
> To fabricate budding from the other feelings
> unknown in the self (earnest, fierce, unsparing)—
> is this possible, just the stutter
> of them, as if a hand gripped
> your hand too hard, and the other's face—

It's as if Mitchell is trying to find a way to approach experiences that fall through the sieve of language. "Just the stutter"—not the word itself, but one component stopped and repeated, as if to go on would be to shut down other possibilities, would be to leave the electric shock of otherness and enter into the facile assumptions of the familiar? "Just the stutter"—because that is the moment of discomfort when language becomes a deer in headlights, stopped, seen eerily strange and beautiful? "Just the stutter"—because the budding is only beginning: a start, not the blossom, but the promise of the not-yet placed? Is it more real to make sounds not yet placed, unconnected—language sunk down into physical experience, rather than abstracted and outside observing? Interestingly, the most recent theory of what causes stuttering is that it's neither organic nor psychological, but a misfiring, a misconnection between different speech centers in the brain, a sound not yet placed in its syllable slot, so the timing between conception and vocalization is thrown off.

In an essay subtitled "A Step Toward a Crippled Poetics," Jim Ferris speaks of his own physical asymmetry leading to an interest in asymmetrical patterns in poetry. He quotes Louis Pasteur saying that the universe is asymmetrical, that "living species ... primordially, in their structure and in their external forms, [are] a function of cosmic asymmetry." Ferris says he's come to think that most interesting poems limp in one way of another. I take this to suggest the possibility of using language not to compensate for our shortcomings, losses, our faltering, but rather to enact the rhythm or shape of those experiences, or at least to explore the limits and possible insights they may hold. The stutterer feels an unease in the world of public speech. John Updike says his stammer comes from a sense of doubt regarding his authenticity. The self panics at its own assertion, fears being found inauthentic, disingenuous, bogus—which, of course, on some levels, it is.

To a stutterer, spoken language feels both precious and mercurial, a kind of trickster at any moment capable of throwing up a roadblock, or otherwise turning a mocking eye on the speaker. Written language can be a safe recourse, an opportunity for fluency. But perhaps it shouldn't be too safe, or too enamored of its own fluency. Perhaps it's important to remain a foreigner in our mother tongue, to acknowledge in our writing the twin sides of language as gift and trickster. Perhaps we need ways to admit we can't talk ourselves into or out of every state of being. Perhaps our hesitations, interruptions, blockages and gaps can provide a way to honor the mystery, the density and resistance of experience. Who knows what might flow into the gap, how new and strange the world might become in the moment of hesitation. Who knows what depths of experience we don't have words for might be reached by letting our words fail. As César Vallejo says, "There are blows in life so violent—I can't answer!"

TOWARDS A POETICS OF
PULL-AND-RELEASE:

Some Thoughts on Silence in Poems

By Leslie Ullman

As artists, most of us have had to struggle first to make, then keep, a commitment to our originality and our quirky freedom, aspects of ourselves we cannot easily explain to loved ones or sell in the marketplace. We live in a culture that is dismissive and often hostile towards idiosyncrasy—at least more so now, at the start of a new millennium, than in the early 1970s, when many of us who teach allowed ourselves to become serious about writing. In those days, as a former magazine editor newly arrived at the University of Iowa Writers' Workshop, I thought myself especially fortunate to be embarking on my journey at a time when, thanks to the innovations that had surfaced in the late 1950s and throughout the 1960s, many kinds of expression seemed promising and viable, and the dynamics of experiential reading were explored with real passion.

In the past thirty years, I have watched the pendulum of taste swing to narrative poetry, to New Formalism, to Language poetry, to the many ramifications of political correctness, to several resurgences of irony, and to different forms of self-consciousness or lack thereof. And without my quite being aware of it, the joy I originally experienced as a reader and writer of poetry has felt incidental at times, edged aside by new values and voices; as a result, I sometimes have found myself increasingly hesitant to share it with others. I would not deny that ongoing attention to craft and technique, innovation that pushes us beyond our comfort level, and sensitivity to diverse cultures are vital to the discipline we have chosen. Nevertheless, I wish to recall us to the aesthetic of openness of the early 1960s, an aesthetic which I regard not as laziness on the reader's part or self-indulgence on the writer's part, but an actual discipline that requires a fair degree of athleticism of thought and feeling.

All of us, at times, bring ingrained habits to poems without meaning to. These habits can stem from a need to control, which arises by reflex in any situation where we feel threatened or uncertain or tired or distracted. Without warning we can feel imposed upon, then willful, and as a result we can become publicly or privately imposing. Many of my undergraduates were introduced to poetry by teachers who treated poems as codes to be unlocked rather than as mysteries to be solved at best partially, and often by indirection. Most of us who attended and now teach in writing programs have been in at least one workshop in which the criticism seemed querulous, constricting. But as artists, too, we know that when we impose and constrict in such ways, we put ourselves in opposition to otherness, hence to the flow of energy that can startle us into stepping beyond ourselves. We judge, and the judgment eventually works against our own freedom. Whether we are readers, teachers, poets, or, as is often the case, all three, our alertness and a sense of adventure can be dampened by a preoccupation with performance or acceptance, or with proscribed kinds of clarity, in such a way as to pull a poem and its audience into an unconscious contest of wills.

I have in mind an alternative paradigm of control, one I've learned by becoming, well into my adulthood, a serious student of horsemanship. When a horse begins to lose his concentration and accelerate his stride, the rider's tugging at the reins will only make the horse tug against the rider, whom he outweighs by more than a thousand pounds. But if the rider pulls briefly on the reins and releases them, pulls again and releases, she's engaging the horse in a different dynamic; she's getting his attention and then giving him a moment to respond. She's applying some degree of pressure and then backing off so he can make himself more comfortable by settling down. This method usually works if the rider stays patient and quiet and waits the moment out, and if the horse isn't too distracted by something else to yield his attention. He doesn't slow dramatically so much as steady himself, relax his stride, lower his head, and get on with the work at hand. In this paradigm, "control" becomes guidance by suggestion, and its impetus stems from intention tempered with restraint, as opposed to reflex and thoughtless will.

Pull and release. Pull again and release. It's more of a dance than a contest. It gives both parties a role. It gives the horse, who is not at the initiating end of intention, a chance to make some decisions of his own.

Silence, either within a poem itself or within the consciousness of a reader as she navigates a poem, is analogous to the invitation of a "release" as it facilitates a give-and-take relationship between reader and text. While silence is conventionally understood as restraint, it is also an aspect of rhythm, the down-swell that follows a decisive gesture made by language. It is like an intake of breath, without which the rhythm of breath's action and the force of breath itself would not be possible. Silence is often but not always white space. It is a moment created by the poem itself. Silence is easier to experience while reading a poem at one's own pace than while listening to one read aloud at someone else's pace. It is usually least detectable in a first reading and then richer, more conducive to real savoring, with subsequent readings.

While well-contexted silences contain and communicate what is indescribable, unparaphrasable, and ultimately most meaningful about a poem, I wish nevertheless to be as specific as I can in identifying and illustrating the kinds of work silence can do. Here is a short poem which contains a central, pivotal silence that offers space for the reader to enter the poem. Such space is alive. It shimmers. It demands and then rewards the reader who is willing to enter it.

In Dispraise of Poetry

When the king of Siam disliked a courier,
he gave him a beautiful white elephant.
The miracle beast deserved such ritual,
that to care for it properly meant ruin.
Yet to care for it improperly was worse.
It appears the gift could not be refused.
          —*Jack Gilbert*

The silence in this poem dwells physically in the space between the title and the body of the poem, and it dwells tangibly in the friction between the abstractness of the title and the concreteness of the anecdote—between the fullness of the word *poetry* and the more astringent, ironic bit of reportage which brings the title down to earth—to its senses, in a way, like a dose of smelling salts. The gap between title and text is the place where crucial implications flower, where the poet steps back, or "releases" the "pull" of the poem's two decisive gestures. The reader may not feel this dynamic very much or even at all during a first reading, but once she has the end of the poem to hold in mind, the title and space immediately following become electric. In Gilbert's piece, the title may well be the first half of the poem, and the text the second half. The reader can best feel the brunt of the poem's wit and implication when balanced right between the two, literally in the space that contains no words.

Here is another short poem that uses silence even more subtly, certainly less physically than Gilbert's.

From Memory

The old poet riding on horseback in winter
came face to face with a thief who had
beaten his horse to a pulp. Once and for
all, they recognized each other without
speaking; one held a bright knife to the
other's throat while the other offered the
bleeding velvet of his animal to show that
he, too, had smuggled his life through
every conceivable hour.

—*Mary Ruefle*

For me, the central silence in this poem is the phrase, "Once and for / all, they recognized each other without / speaking ..." Or perhaps more accurately, the central silence falls on either side of this statement, this moment, which arrives so smoothly in the flow of narrative yet forces the reader to pause, startled at the implication that the two startled figures have met before. This moment touches upon what the poem doesn't say, what the poem may have subtracted from itself in order to reach its provocatively pared-down state. And because the reader is never told what the poet and the thief "recognize" in each other, she is forced more deeply into the utterances the poem does make; in other words, she is forced not so much to "understand" the context of this phrase as to enter it and take it in like the air she breathes. Something very complex is being said here, and with disarming restraint. The astonishing moment of recognition equalizes these two archetypal figures, one the supposedly gentle poet and one the supposedly reprehensible thief. It brings them into an ambiance of metaphor without actually finishing the metaphor into an image, and without doing anything else to clarify or persuade. The two simply are held up as parallel concepts, and in that moment the reader is invited to make some effort, to push these archetypes even farther through an implicit sense of their differences, into some recognition of their similarities. True, the poem offers some help in its last two lines, but even this seemingly direct statement of how the two are similar is itself full of silence, and therefore of *implication,* which is a vital component of all good poems, whether or not they work by means of such compressed, active silences. To "smuggle [one's] life through every conceivable hour"—this is exhausting and thrilling to contemplate. "Every conceivable hour"—an "hour" becomes physical, like a mail slot or a tunnel or an international boundary. This brief passage offers a great deal to think about.

Like Gilbert's poem, this one taps something profound and indescribable about the nature of poetry and does so without exertion, without explanation. It is the reader who does the work of insight, having entered the space the poem clears within itself by raising a question, an opening in which a felt or implicit answer bubbles up from the text as well as from the reading/dreaming self who has come to the poem.

It is difficult for a poem to get away with making such demands on a reader, and with giving a reader so much freedom to roam, without falling apart. Ruefle's poem pulls it off because each utterance it does make carries great weight and is instantly graspable, not to mention elegant. The two images it offers are lovely and surprising—"bright knife" and "bleeding velvet of his animal." They serve to ground the poem in a visualizable world that provides balance to the more philosophical dimensions the poem reaches for and attains. In addition, this poem is spoken line by line with quiet confidence. It allows the reader to feel guided even as he is provoked. In my own reading, I find myself inclined to trust it enough to settle in and do the work it asks, like the skittish horse whose rider keeps her own body quiet and makes intermittent, decisive gestures.

Now I offer a longer poem whose silences, though aided by the use of tercets and fairly short lines, nevertheless are not built into the poem itself as clearly as they are in Gilbert's and Ruefle's poems. Instead, Sandra McPherson's "On a Picture of My Parents Together in Second Grade" invites the attentive reader to create silences in her own mind—to pause voluntarily and often in order to savor the provocations offered by each of the poem's moments. Its speaker is ungroomed and unselfconscious, someone apparently not concerned with a need to elaborate upon, or craft transitions between, utterances that seem to come from the spontaneous formation of thought as it gropes its way through memory. The scene she depicts is rendered impressionistically so that the reader gets only a partial sketch of the literal elements that lead to the rich interiority of the experience even though it is occasioned by both a photograph and the occurrence of a minor accident. The poem's texture is quite different from the more cohesive, often more self-examining texture of a poem whose impetus comes from narrative or reflection. It contains holes but is not threadbare.

On a Picture of My Parents Together in Second Grade

Dust as beige pongee,
'cot blossoms inside the margins,
the palms with thin tigerstripes of blood and gravel ...

But today, without a license, as I drive
a car black as the blind mules
in the old McPherson cinnabar mine,

it's for some foolish emergency
that I crash into the schoolyard,
into the fence that worried over everyone

both our generations knew.
This is the last time for me.
I will never go anywhere so quickly as into the past.

I wait but no one comes to help or accuse.
The square is full of devils
winding all free dust up into themselves. The accident

has spared each brick, electric bell, cursive letter, girl
in hula skirt and principal behind
the bricks, daydream

of lilac scent, violet
of iodine.
Anyone I might have hit,

their intelligence ordered here from madness of their parents'
bed to sit by surname and stand by height,
still belongs to tomorrow,

to the very green soap, salamander tank, and
zither which have always kept them wise
and curious.

A little mixing on the fingertips and my blood forms brothers,
the dust spins over the crosswalk,
I slam the door and follow the cloud home.

They will be glad I too am still together.

This poem acts upon me as a string of stunning single moments, arrivals, which make me want to pause over each one even as they generate energy that helps the poem move forward and occasionally, surprisingly, circle back on itself by means of its gathering echoes. I pause often in this poem, each pause a voluntary moment of silence, and I experience each of them a little differently. The first pause is one of astonishment and pleasure at the image of the "car black as the blind mules / in the old McPherson cinnabar mine." "Black" and "blind" create an intense sense of blackness, especially in implicit relation to the underground world of the mine. Yet "cinnabar" warms this blackness, if one knows the deep coral color of this substance; if not, then the music of the word itself, like a single note from an exotic Middle Eastern instrument, may send a glowing thread through the blackness.

I pause again at the line, "into the fence that worried over everyone" because I feel the poem suddenly gathering itself towards a new dimension, away from the literal scene—now I can sense the *something more* that is at stake in the poem. And then, I inhabit a pleasurable sense of suspension over the stanza break to the arrival in the next line, "both our generations knew," where I suddenly feel the quiet force of the poem's confidence, its ease with dwelling in two realms at once. Now I have entered the poem's second realm, perhaps the realm that fueled the poem in the first place, the ambiance of family history.

I pause again soon after, at the line, "I will never go anywhere so quickly as into the past." This sentence, which takes on an arresting, unspoken physicality as a metaphor for the literal crash, pushes me even deeper into my felt sense of the poem's real subject, and then leaves me to my own devices while the next stanza returns to the literal scene and begins a section marked by lower intensity.

A few lines later, I experience several small pauses, like the syncopated bursts of light and color made by some fireworks, in the specific list of images behind the school's brick wall—the "single cursive letter, girl / in hula skirt" (why a hula skirt? What exuberance might have led to its being worn?), the appealingly mixed sensations I get from the phrase "violet of iodine," and so on. Each item in this list startles me, moves me beyond my expectations, reminds me that even in this linear section grounded in the literal scene, McPherson's poem wants to work fundamentally through the more holographic landscape of imagination and memory. In addition, it is boldly subjective in what it chooses to observe among the things it could have observed—names carved into desks, for instance, or chewing gum stuck to chair bottoms—and it draws the reader in to share in its boldness, its oddness.

I pause for different reasons in the middle of this list, in the entire stanza beginning with "their intelligence ordered here from madness of their parents' / bed to sit by surname and stand by height, / still belongs to tomorrow." Here, I savor the elegance of the syntax, the tremendous amount of ground covered in all three lines, the pleasing rhythms and alliterations in the phrase "sit by surname and stand by height." I love the flow of my attention—a physical sensation, a kind of dance—ordered by the line breaks in that stanza.

And finally I pause at the notion that the objects in the schoolroom "have always kept" the children not just amused or informed, as one would expect, but "wise / and curious." The children are not just witnesses; these objects have given them a greater energy of curiosity, which they bring back to the objects in a continual dynamic of reciprocity. And they have been kept "wise" as well, kept in a state of alertness and transformation. Their relation to the schoolroom's objects feels similar to mine with this entire poem.

Thus, it is as a satisfied and well-exercised reader that I slip through the rest of the poem, whose energy diminishes towards the end but does so in such a way as to let me savor the layerings of nuance I've been given. By the time I reach the last line, I've caught up with the poem and am poised to share in the final little leap it makes. I do not feel the same breathlessness at the end of this poem that I've felt several times along the way; rather, I experience a welcome sense of comprehension that seems graceful and appropriate; my circuits have been charged but not overloaded.

Having identified as best I can my own experience as a reader of this poem, I am now in a position, as I shift from reader to teacher, to help an undergraduate literature class understand what it means as well as what it does, or to further examine it in a graduate-level workshop; in other words, I can now articulate its themes and subthemes and the role played by sections I respond to less viscerally than the ones I've mentioned. Or I can question it.

These issues apply to a less immediate, more cerebral, and perhaps to some readers or students a more useful level of response. But I maintain that our interaction with the silences in a well-made poem engage us in a preliminary intuitive connection with the impulses of the text and thus supply a crucial foundation for subsequent layers of response.

Clearly, as the poems I've discussed reveal, silence in a poem often follows an image which resonates in the reader's consciousness, or a moment caught and frozen like a tableau. Silence often surrounds a moment in which the juxtaposition of two almost-but-not-quite-dissimilar images is experienced, the kind of leap Robert Bly talks about in his book *Leaping Poetry*, a dynamic common in poems that draw energy from Surrealism.

I used to think only the image could generate energy, by itself and in conjunction with other images, like a stone thrown in a pond to create concentric rings; that is, I used to think the crucial point of energy was concreteness, the appeal to the senses and to our sense of being part of matter ourselves. But lately I've come to see that skillfully contexted *statements* can carve out space for themselves too, in the form of a reflective leap the mind makes, a slanted observation, a comment that goes a step or two ahead of the expected arrival, or an odd twist of thought. Statements work this way in poems by Louise Glück, William Stafford, Linda Gregg, and Jack Gilbert. A statement, like an image, can create a moment of paradox, or a place where two elements are seamlessly juxtaposed and reconciled.

And in the silence that follows, which is also a gesture in its implicit recognition of the importance of what has just been said, the reader becomes the active agent by invitation. The reader actually *does* something in a space or a silence; his or her thought moves beyond the stimulus to finish the thought, the moment, the gesture, and perhaps to recognize a starburst of implications. In a successful poem, the reader advances the thought of the poet like a relay runner accepting the baton. There's a rush of comprehension that can be felt instantly at many levels though not easily articulated. And it can occur several times along the way, not just at the end of a poem.

What I have just described is nothing new, either in critical theory or in terms of most readers' experience if they have read and enjoyed a fair amount of poetry. I would guess that most of us who write started doing so after we had experienced others' poems as though we had written them ourselves; we got to experience the high, the endorphins generated by someone else's exercise, and we were hooked. But I continue to be amazed at how easy it is for us to breathe bad faith into poems, our own and others', and how it often leads us to want to control them in accordance with some outside agenda. A reasonable amount of good faith may well be the opposite of control—good faith as acquiescence and the willingness to wait, even work, for gratification. Yet I'm also amazed at how little critical vocabulary there is for describing specific poems in terms of how the reader might acquiesce to them. Writers like William Stafford and Paul Carroll explored this area in the 1960s and 1970s, but their voices have faded from the classroom and lecture hall. Robert Bly did too, in his essay, "What the Image Can Do," where he described in detail the image as a conduit between the conscious and unconscious realms.

But the writer who has come closest to enacting the dynamics of participatory reading consistently in book after book, although he never would have called himself a literary critic, is the French philosopher of science Gaston Bachelard, who embraced a phenomenological approach to literary works and articulately lost himself to the sensual and associative impact of not so much whole works as their individual moments. Colette Gaudin, one of his translators, describes him in the introduction to a compilation of selections from his many books, *On Poetic Imagination and Reverie,* as he might have described himself: "an avid reader, an advocate of leisurely and repeated reading." Ecstatic yet precise, his responses to poetic passages bloom with references, images, and speculations that occur to him as he reads. His analytical writing is incandescent and admiring, enlivened by his trust in what he feels to be the poet's original "reverie" and in the reverie the poem consequently sparks in him, the reader.

Gaudin defines phenomenology, as Bachelard used it in his appreciation of literature, as "a description of the immediate relationship of phenomena with a particular consciousness …" In my discussion of McPherson's poem, I tried to follow this approach, using my reactions as a way to make objective observations about the poem as the initiator of those reactions. For Bachelard, Gaudin says, "the best way to study images is to explore their power of trans-subjectivity. They *reverberate* in the reader's consciousness and lead him to create anew while communicating with the poet."

Susan Sontag stresses in her essay "On Style" the dependence of a work of art "upon the cooperation of the person having the experience, for one may see what is 'said' but remain unmoved, either through dullness or distraction." She continues, "Art is seduction, not rape … art cannot seduce without the complicity of the experiencing subject."

Complicity, then, is the key to how a reader and a poem might engage and finally transform one another. This alchemy is possible when will is absent (or nearly so) on both sides, and willingness, or faith, is aroused instead. Still, some poems invite this openness more than others. Many fine poems do not contain much silence, or space for a reader to step in and act. For obvious reasons, a more discursive or narrative poem will contain few or none of the jolts, leaps, and idiosyncrasies of the kind of poem I've been talking about.

In a workshop setting the kind of poem I've been talking about, when it works, can provoke students and teachers alike to stretch their critical vocabulary as well as exercise their trust in their own instincts. Sontag suggests a whole new realm of terminology when she maintains that the ultimate aim and justification for a work of art is the "act of comprehension accompanied by voluptuousness." Bachelard uses words like *élan, excess,* and *exaltation* to describe responses certain images generate in him. It is difficult to find words for the deeply engaged, visionary states of mind, or the visceral sensations, which a poem may evoke. But we can be poets in the classroom as well as on the page; we can keep trying to approach with words what words fail to describe. And in the process we can learn to question ourselves briefly before we jump—here I borrow a phrase from a lecture by my Vermont College colleague Betsy Sholl—to "refine the surprises" from others' poems as well as our own. For me, it has helped to use terms like *felt logic, felt connections,* and *choreography,* which make at least modest room for idiosyncrasies in a poem, and for intuitive work on the part of the reader. In addition, some poems have *charisma, chutzpah,* a crazy sort of authority that can win us over.

Still, the kind of poem I've been talking about is exceptionally vulnerable, not only to being dismantled for wrong reasons but also to not working even on its own terms. There is only so much a willing reader can and should do. What techniques, then, and what kinds of attentiveness might we cultivate in order to write a poem that invites a reader into its explicit or implicit gaps and then rewards the effort? Here are a few concrete suggestions about how we can write poems that skillfully use silence.

Contexting of elements is of paramount importance; a writer can get away with putting anything in a poem if she sets up a context for it. Contexting has to do with the selection and ordering of images and observations, which I mentioned earlier, and it requires considerable patience. In this case the writer has to engage in complicity with her own poem. She must be willing to hear the "reverberations" of her own material independently of her intentions for that material and then be willing to arrange and re-arrange and re-arrange again, until the piece achieves a flow that feels provocative and right; i.e., oddly logical, perhaps inexplicably so. And in the process she often must sacrifice passages that just don't carry their weight despite the role they may have had in making her believe in the poem in the first place. Conversely, she may find that a statement that at first seemed flat or rhetorical may become electric, compelling, in a context where it works in friction with another element or advances the poem beyond the expectations it seems to have set up, as we saw in Ruefle's and McPherson's poems.

I still see the *image* as essential to establishing immediacy and grounding a poem in a sense of place or motif or occasion, in addition to engaging the reader's senses in complex and pleasurable ways. Even a few well-envisioned and well-placed images can give a poem the kind of authority that allows it also to make statements or use abstractions without disintegrating into low-energy language. In other words, images can do much to set up a context that allows other moments in the poem to work successfully.

Recurrence, re-evocation of a central motif, is also a helpful device, especially because it gives cohesion to a poem that wants to move by means other than that of a mediating voice. The McPherson poem contains several references to generations, to ancestry, to the simultaneous existence of past and present, which repeatedly pull the reader not so much into a comprehension as into a *sensation* of her family history as it centers around the schoolyard. It is my participation in this motif that makes me ultimately appreciate the resonance of her title. Then the references to dust devils, dust and blood on the hand, and dust on the crosswalk provide another pattern of repetition, so that the poem establishes a kind of material dialogue with itself, a pattern supple and open as a spider web. Recurrence can also take the form of repeated words, phrases, or lines—think of the unpolished and emotionally intense cohesion of some sestinas, pantoums, and villanelles.

And finally, *consulting others.* Especially with the kind of poem I'm talking about, it is important to consult readers whose judgment can be trusted, because it is important to hear one's poem through others' ears. If a poem is to invite complicity from the reader, its writer has to know where and how that invitation may be giving mixed signals.

I have used the word *intention* several times in this discussion, and I would like to conclude by focusing on it, especially as it accomplishes what will would accomplish but in a different way. To return to my paradigm of horse and rider, I picture a rider taking a horse over a pattern of jumps that requires a tight turn after each jump to set up the approach to the next. Novice riders are taught to look straight ahead while going over a jump, but on a more advanced course, the straight aim of the rider's gaze will cause her to make the turn too late and too wide for an effective approach. Most of that turn will be spent in pulling on the reins, overcorrecting, and confusing the horse. However, if the rider goes over a jump with her head turned and her eyes focused on the next jump, the horse will land already canted into the turn, keeping his forward momentum and making a smooth track to his destination. To feel this difference on horseback is amazing; the first method requires a tremendous exertion of energy, is scary, and often doesn't work, while the second works so immediately it seems to bypass the muscles altogether in a kind of telepathic exchange. In the literal sense, the rider's turning her head engages balance rather than strength. The horse follows the direction of the rider's gaze because a chain reaction has been set up through the rider's body and consequently through his own.

Intention, for a poet's purposes, is like that of the rider visualizing the overall course well enough to anticipate mentally, hence physically, each next step. Intention, in other words, is an unarticulated but felt sense of direction that can ease us writers into acquiring a measure of the calmness, the grace under pressure that makes athletes perform well. It has to do with the visceral sense we bring to a poem, our intuitive link to its fledgling impulses, and our faith in the trajectory we feel as its potential even as we negotiate the demands of craft.

THE WORD OVERFLOWN BY STARS:

Saying the Unsayable

By Richard Jackson

We live in secret cities
And we travel unmapped roads.

We speak words between us that
we recognize
But which cannot be looked up.
—Alberto Ríos

I. SOME VERSIONS OF THE UNSAYABLE

We might begin by imagining, as Kierkegaard did in *Fear and Trembling,* how Abraham, accompanied by two servants and bearing the burden of an un-speakable command, sets out with his son, a knife, the cup of fire, and a bundle of wood before anyone wakes. He wants to encounter no one, for what would he say? As Kierkegaard points out, he is "able to utter everything, but one thing he cannot say, i.e., say it in such a way that another understands it." When he tells Isaac "God will provide," the words themselves are a metaphor for what is beyond understanding. As Paul Celan wrote in his poem "Solve," scriptural texts are those we "flee" *towards*: "nameable un- / utterable / names." One name for God in Hebrew, in fact, is untranslatable—by law unsayable except by a high priest at which time any listener must fall prostrate—but suggests something like past, present, and future all existing as one and at once. A more positive sense of this presence unfolds in the medieval *Cloud of Unknowing*, in which the writer warns "that great caution is necessary in interpreting words used in a spiritual sense" and further suggests that words like *in* and *up* are metaphors that don't say what they seem to say. As he says, "to hide something purposefully is to cast it deep into your soul" beyond simple interpretation.

The sense of God as the unsayable Eternity is something that Robert Penn Warren has in mind in "Tell Me a Story," the seventh poem of his sequence, *Audubon: A Vision*:

[A]

Long ago, in Kentucky, I, a boy, stood
By a dirt road, in first dark, and heard
The great geese hoot northward.

I could not see them, there being no moon
And the stars sparse. I heard them.

I did not know what was happening in my heart.

It was the season before the elderberry blooms,
Therefore they were going north.

The sound was passing northward.

[B]

Tell me a story.

In this century, and moment, of mania,
Tell me a story.

Make it a story of great distances, and starlight.

The name of the story will be Time,
But you must not pronounce its name.

Tell me a story of deep delight.

Part A begins with a sense of time (the poet's past) and space (a dirt road in Kentucky) that is bound, but as soon as the geese enter, the perceptions start to radiate outward into the moonless darkness lit only by stars, as the time becomes seasonal and therefore cyclic, and the place marked by otherness, by direction. In the second part, time (now both a century and the moment of utterance) reflects the "mania" of the age, a story, a narrative so huge it can only be of the "distances and starlight" that were projected in part A. It is a metaphysical sense of time, Time with a capital *T*, a Time that is so internalized, so "deep" within the self's experience, that it cannot be pronounced, or, if so, pronounced only as a lie. Time is the name of the story but not the story: Time is our experience of the story in the language of Warren's poem that also tries to say what it can't say. It is a story of emptiness and vastness, but also of the way the imagination can fill them, a kind of religious, transcendental experience, playing on the origins of the word *delight*, that harkens back to the Biblical sense I described above. It's language, after all, that allows us to make the absent present. For Gaston Bachelard, everything is at stake in this sort of situation, in every word. It creates an effect he calls "intimate immensity," a sense of everything in every little thing, Blake's "infinity in a grain of sand" or "eternity in an hour."

The Canadian poet Gwendolyn MacEwen provides an even more direct statement about this intimate immensity. Her poem, "The Red Bird You Wait For," addresses an Other or Others about an unnamed presence that they and the speaker have in common: It is given in a series of metaphors and similes that gather around the image of the bird. But it is a bird that is "buried in your blood" as well as "moving above me." MacEwen takes on the voice of a prophet in order to utter what cannot be uttered:

> You are waiting for someone to confirm it.
> You are waiting for someone to say it plain,
> now we are here and because we are short of time
> I will say it: I might even speak its name.
>
> It is moving above me, it is burning my heart out,
> I have felt it crash through my flesh,
> I have spoken to it in a foreign tongue,
> I have stroked its neck in the night like a wish.
>
> Its name is the name you have buried in your blood,
> its shape is a gorgeous cast-off velvet cape,
> its eyes are the eyes of your most forbidden lover
> and its claws, I can tell you its claws are gloved in fire.

> You are waiting to hear its name spoken,
> you have asked me a thousand times to speak it,
> you who have hidden it, cast it off, killed it,
> loved it to death and sung your songs over it.
>
> The red bird you wait for falls with giant wings—
> a velvet cape whose royal colour calls us kings
> is the form it takes as, uninvited, it descends,
> it is the Power and the Glory forever, Amen.

The vague shape of the "Bird"—the shape of a cast-off cape—suggests more of the ineffable, undefinable nature of the Unspoken. Curiously the speaker keeps deferring, though it is also the Others' hiding, casting off and killing the "word" that has also caused the deferral: The passive role of the Others is revealed as more active, at least in the past. Even the last line, playing off The Lord's Prayer, doesn't help, finally, for it alludes not to God but to His kingdom. In the end, it is possible that the kingdom is the "here" of line three, which is in a sense not a place but a way of life that involves the feeling, speaking, stroking, casting off all the verbs of the poem. It is, then, a "no-place." In "Poems in Braille," MacEwen says, "all your hands are verbs" and goes on to describe how

> I name all things in my room
> and they rehearse their names,
> gather in groups, form tesseracts,
> discussing their names among themselves.

There is, in this view, a whole world that is inaccessible except by the words that themselves can only suggest the immense worlds they fail to name, worlds we seem doomed to be excluded from.

In some ways the precedent for MacEwen lies in the story of Ezekiel, who hears the voice of God as the sound of mighty waters and/or the roaring of four sets of huge wings on a mystic chariot. It is important that the voice is described as being beyond words, and yet he also must use words to describe how the unsayable is said to him. In the second chapter of this incredible poem he is given a scroll of "lamentation, and wailing and woe" that he is commanded to eat. This is explained when the Voice says, "take into your heart all that I speak to you," suggesting again that the unsayable can be said but in a way that is beyond simple language (Ezek. 2:10, 3:10).

In "De Profundis," the great Austrian poet Georg Trakl wrote, "I drank the silence of God / From a spring in the woods / ... there is a light that dies in my mouth." Indeed, Ezekiel is technically (though perhaps only figuratively) dumb from chapters three to twenty-four yet communicates his prophecies, the use of parables and allegories suggesting how language must be used to do so. In this, Ezekiel prefigures Paul, who describes in Second Corinthians (12:4) how he "heard ineffable things, which no one may utter," and yet all his writings bear witness, in different words, to what he heard. Some truths, in other words, are unsayable and yet get said. In his *Tractatus*, Wittgenstein describes this sort of truth as one of those things "that cannot be put into words. They make themselves manifest. They are what is mystical." Echoing Ezekiel, Denise Levertov, in her "Tree Telling of Orpheus," has the tree say: "I listened, and the language / came into my roots / out of the earth / into my bark." Words seem to "leap and dance" over Orpheus's shoulders because, in a sense, they have become words incarnate, and yet they create a "silence" "at the heart of my wood."

I can't think of a better definition for what gives resonance and depth to poetry than this "unsayable" dimension. What Genesis, MacEwen, Warren, Ezekiel, and Paul are struggling with are what appear to be ultimate truths, an ultimate reality. Meister Eckhart called this a "subversive" kind of knowledge, the "unspeakability of universal knowledge." In his *Ecrits*, the French psychoanalyst Jacques Lacan describes this sense of the "Real" as the "impossible to say." It is like Penelope, who in Book 19 of *The Odyssey* cannot even utter the name of Troy, the hidden reality that has governed her life. In *The Bow and the Lyre,* the Mexican poet, Octavio Paz, writes that "Language, turned in on itself, says that which by nature seemed to elude it. ... Poetic expression expresses the inexpressible." On one level, this is partly the sort of language game that Wittgenstein plays in *The Blue and Brown Books* and which Wislawa Szymborska also toys with in her little poem, "The Three Oddest Words":

> When I pronounce the word Future,
> the first syllable already belongs to the past.
>
> When I pronounce the word Silence,
> I destroy it.
>
> When I pronounce the word Nothing,
> I make something no non-being can hold.

These sorts of paradoxes are at the heart of the unsayable: Words turn out to be lies in the sense that they can't ever duplicate the experiences they refer to since those experiences remain beyond the realm of language.

One of the most moving poems that expresses the inexpressible is Tomas Tranströmer's "April and Silence." In some ways my own experience of the poem contains this unsayable element. In 1998 I was at a writers' conference centered in Lake Bled, Slovenia. It was here that I met Tomas, who could understand everything but communicated with great difficulty following multiple strokes several years before. We began by tracing birth dates of writers we knew on the dusty table of an outdoor café in nearby Skofia Loka, then a word or two of a poem, often assisted by his wife Monika. It seemed the other writers didn't know how to or were afraid to communicate with someone not using a more visible language, but for us, and Bridgette Bates, a student of mine, at that little table, the unsayable was all we had. A few days later Monika and Tomas asked me to read the poems for him in English while she read in Swedish. The reading was about to begin, and so I had no time to prepare. The last of the four poems we read was "April and Silence," with Tomas literally an arm's length away from a tiny stage in Ljubljana. What the poem said to me, given those last few spring days, welled up into something behind or beyond the words, and I nearly broke as I approached the last few lines:

> Spring lies desolate.
> The velvet-dark ditch
> Crawls by my side
> Without reflections.
>
> The only thing that shines
> Is yellow flowers.
>
> I am carried in my shadow
> Like a violin
> In its black box.
>
> The only thing I want to say
> Glitters out of reach
> Like the silver
> In a pawnbroker's.

There's an incredible tension here set up by the play between light (shining flowers, glittering words) and dark (the ditch, the shadow); by the play between the openness around the spring scene, however desolate, on the one hand and the confinements of the box, the ditch, and behind the pawnbro-ker's window on the other hand; by the inability to speak and the silence of the violin; by the potential desolation and the beauty of the flowers. All the while the poem's arc of development is suggested by how first the spring lies as if still, which is then followed by the feeble, metaphoric "crawling" of the ditch, then the flowers' "shining," which suggests a hint of movement, then the way the speaker is "carried"—slight or passive movements that culmi-nate in the Tantalus-evoking image of the words themselves that are out of reach. And yet, some words are indeed spoken, and despite all that, and even if one did not know the situation of Tranströmer the man, the speaker in the poem has communicated something far beyond the words themselves. They say simply more than they say; they say the unsayable, which conveys, by using images and metaphors that spread out geographically from coun-try to city, a whole world that is the reality of the speaker's condition. And more, the first word, *spring*, even though it describes a scene of desolation, also describes a beginning, a paradox enforced by the tension of opposites I described above.

For me, the poem exemplifies how Kierkegaard in his *Either/Or* defined the poet: "a man who in his heart harbors a deep anguish, but whose lips are so fashioned that the man's cries which pass over them are transformed into ravishing music." The words he says are only an "outward appearance" and they do not simply communicate some inward expression, but rather act as "a telegraphic communication which tells us that there is something hidden deep within," a mystery that can only be hinted at. It's what the Italian poet Giuseppe Ungaretti calls "this poetry: / the merest nothing / of an inexpress-ible secret." This is given a more tactile sense in his poem "Envoi":

> Dear
> Ettore Serra
> Poetry
> Is the world's humanity
> One's own life
> Blossomed from the word
> The limpid marvel
> Of a wild ferment
>
> When I find
> In this my silence

A word
It is dug into my life
Like an abyss
(my translation)

Here the word itself is the emptiness, the hole, the abyss within the self, but it is an emptiness that contains all humanity, all life, the marvel of poetry's art that gives birth to the word and its wilder originating experience. In "Variations on Nothing" he describes the way time is both fleeting and held in memory, both ineffable and felt as physical passage, a sense of a moment and of a greater passage. A tiny grain of sand serves as the main image as it slips though an hourglass: "And is silent, is the only thing now heard, / And, being heard, doesn't vanish in the dark." In an opposite move, as in "Envoi," it is as if the silent grain could fill all time.

But the "hole" is, then, also an emptiness that is "something." This is what Wallace Stevens is trying to express in "The Snow Man":

One must have a mind of winter
To regard the frost and the boughs
Of the pine-trees crusted with snow;

And have been cold a long time
To behold the junipers shagged with ice,
The spruces rough in the distant glitter

Of the January sun; and not to think
Of any misery in the sound of the wind,
In the sound of a few leaves,

Which is the sound of the land
Full of the same wind
That is blowing in the same bare place

For the listener, who listens in the snow,
And, nothing himself, beholds
Nothing that is not there and the nothing that is.

The poem enacts its inability to say exactly what the "Nothing that is not there and the nothing that is" really are; it does so by starting off with two positive clauses that are what Emerson would call "optative," and then, in the middle of the sixth line, introduces a turn towards the negative statement. What began as being about something begins to be about what it is not. That is, the poem is not about the externals, the simple coincidence between a cold mind and cold weather, but rather between a cold mind and a cold heart, one that cannot understand the landscape as revealing a "misery." But now the poem makes another turn, for the misery is not simply something one can feel or not, but is within the soul of the speaker who is both speaker and listener, and so the poem projects this back outward. That is, for the speaker, "misery in the sound of the wind" is revealed by the movement of a "few leaves," which projects the sound of "misery" now given by a whole "landscape" that is a "bare" or empty place. What is revealed is an utter blankness in which speaker, landscape, and the unsayable are all "Nothing" and yet are all made present, but only in a sort of negative way, by the very act of mentioning their absence. In a sense, the whole poem becomes a metaphor for what is unsayably behind every visible landscape. "We are unable to circumscribe concepts we use," writes Wittgenstein in *The Blue and Brown Books*, "not because we don't know their real definition, but because there is no real 'definition' to them." And further, in terms of poetry, Schopenhauer notes that "We are entirely satisfied by the impression of a work of art only when it leaves behind something that, in spite of our reflection on it, we cannot bring down to the distinctness of a concept." What Stevens is getting at seems to be some sort of reciprocal movement between inner self and landscape that we don't really have words for: it is a new relationship, a discovery. As Kierkegaard says in "Shadowgraphs," the "outward appearance has significance, it is true, but not as an expression of the inward, but rather as a telegraphic communication which tells us that there is something hidden deep within." In "Connoisseur of Chaos" Stevens goes on to say:

> The squirming facts exceed the squamous mind,
> If one may say so. And yet relation appears,
> A small relation expanding like the shade
> Of a cloud, a shape on the side of a hill.

It is language itself that generates the something that is nothing and that arises out of nothing: It is the creative act of poetry itself. This act is the "path of saying" that Heidegger describes in *Poetry Language Thought* and other late texts, a movement of language that comes to and reveals a "clearing" of Being, by which he has in mind something like an opening or meadow in a forest of everyday, one-dimensional words that only relate what is, what Stevens's simple snowy landscape would be with no misery or reciprocal action. Heidegger's complex, often twisted metaphors suggest precisely how difficult yet how important this "clearing" is. For him the word *language*, used in a poetic sense, is more of a verb than a noun: It acts, it projects, it throws itself into the unknown, it says the unsayable.

In "A Common Ground," the opening poem of her book *The Jacob's Ladder*, Levertov describes how she wants to move beyond "vegetable words" or at least to have them grow into something unexpected. In the last section she says that the poem's language should

> follow 'the path
> between reality and the soul,'
> a language
> excelling itself to be itself,
>
> a speech akin to the light
> with which at day's end and day's
> renewal mountains
> sing to each other across the cold valleys.

For Levertov, poetry is made, as she says in "I learned that her name was Proverb," of "the secret names / of all we meet who lead us deeper / into our labyrinth / of valleys and mountains," a labyrinth that resembles Stevens's landscape, but these names are words that bring back entire landscapes of memory to a point of arrival, a boundary, a clearing of being, an unknown place, so unsayable.

II. THE SWELL OF WANDERING WORDS

If poetry, as I have suggested, is made of "secret names" and "unsayable" notions that create nonetheless a "path of saying" where "relation occurs," then we need to look now at some ways various poets have created resonance in their work through this seemingly paradoxical vision. When Wittgenstein says, in *The Blue and Brown Books*, "the object of our thought is not the fact it is the shadow of the fact," he is suggesting the shadowy nature of language itself. As Paul Celan says in "Speak You To":

> ... don't split off No from Yes.
> Give your say this meaning too:
> give it the shadow.

As he says later in the poem, "Speaks true who speaks shadow." And where does one find the shadow? One finds it in the "thread / the star wants to descend on / ... in the swell / of wandering words." And where does one find these words? What sort of language do they comprise? For Celan the word is always an "ensilenced Word," as he says in "Argumentum e Silentio"; it is a word that "testifies." It testifies "to each the word that sang to him and froze." It is a "Word" that is "star-overflown," that is, filled, paradoxically, with the empty spaciousness of the sky, but also, as we have seen in other poets, with the self:

> Then where's
> the Word dawning, tell me, if not with Night
> in its riverbed of tears,
> Night that shows plunging suns the sown seed
> over and over again?

It is a word that links seed and sun, beginning and process of nourishment, in a cyclic movement that is always trying to regenerate, always discovering something new. Poetry is a way to discover, not report; perceive, not represent. It is a conversation with the silent world "from smokemouth to smokemouth," Celan says in "Landscape with urn beings," a poetry of silences unspoken. Or as Levertov says in *The Poet in The World*, citing Heidegger, language is always a "conversation," a reciprocal movement, as we saw with Stevens. Celan's smoke, Wittgenstein's (and Freud's) shadow, Kierkegaard's "shadowgraphs" all refer to the metaphoric value of language that, for Celan, takes us away from the world's devalued language that can only say what was, not what might be, what we might be able to imagine:

> A RUMBLING: it is
> Truth itself
> walked among
> men,
> amidst the
> metaphor squall.

This is an incredibly sophisticated and complex idea. While language, metaphors, might not actually reveal Truth for all the shadowy storm around them, it is among metaphors that one must search to find any truth. His poem "Where the word" suggests his poetics of metaphor:

> WHERE THE WORD, that was undying, fell:
> into heaven's ravine behind my brow,

> led by spittle and dreck, there goes
> the sevenbranch starflower that lives with me.
>
> Rhymes in the night house, breath in the muck,
> the eye a thrall to images—
> And yet: an upright silence, a stone
> evading the devil's staircase.

Language, rhyme (here, traditional poetry), and metaphor do not so much reveal certainty as evade despair, a limited victory perhaps, but one that Celan, haunted by the Holocaust, finds solace in. And he is also suggesting something that is crucial for us in a more general sense: As a firsthand witness to one of the most horrible realities ever, he suggests that the metaphoric value of language, its ability to metamorphose and transform, to create rather than report, to think of the future rather than the simple past, is of utmost importance.

In our own time Larry Levis, writing about the horrifying events in the former Yugoslavia in his posthumous book *Elegy*, relates, as often happens in this book, how stories intertwine in ways that are not so much explained but left to, as Levertov noted, "converse" with each other, for what they could say, if they could be summarized, is beyond saying. "I can't imagine it enough," he says in "Elegy Ending in the Sound of a Skipping Rope":

> I can't imagine how to get back to it, with something
> In your eye, something always in your eye,
>
> And everything becoming a scrap of paper ...

Until in the end the "annoying, unvarying flick of the rope" replaces speech, replaces words, because the horrors he refers to are beyond the power of words to describe with any real accuracy, just as they were for Celan. For Levis, each strand of a story acts as a metaphor not for some central meaning, but for other stories in an endless process of relationship building.

This sort of progression is also what motivates a poem like Stevens's "Prologues to What Is Possible," the first part of which begins by describing an "ease of mind," then through a series of similes and metaphors associates that ease with being on a boat on a calm sea, then describes the boat, the oarsmen, even a helmsman who belongs to the "far foreign departure" of the vessel and is

> lured on by a syllable without any meaning,
> A syllable of which he felt, with an appointed sureness,

> That it contained the meaning into which he wanted to enter,
> A meaning which, as he entered it, would shatter the boat and
> > leave the oarsman quiet
> As at a point of central arrival, an instant moment. ...

At that point the poem pauses and begins a second part in which now the helmsman is not only in the poem as a metaphor but outside it as a reader: "The object stirred his fear. The object with which he was compared / was beyond his recognizing" because the poem has moved "beyond resemblance" towards the inner self of the man who was the inner metaphor of the poem, whose whole being increases with each spark of language, each "name and privilege over the ordinary of his commonplace." That is, a language that brings the man, the reader, all of us, out of our everyday lives, a language that goes beyond the utter reality of the everyday. This everyday is what Heidegger calls "earth," the simple physical reality that we move through each day; it is opposed to "world," which is what we create through our imaginations out of mere earth. That imaginative leap, a "transport," as Longinus called it centuries ago, is the function of metaphor. It is, as Stevens says,

> A flick that added to the real and its vocabulary,
> The way some first thing coming into Northern trees
> Adds to them the whole vocabulary of the South,
> The way the earliest single light in the evening sky, in spring,
> Creates a fresh universe out of nothingness by adding itself,
> The way a look or a touch reveals its unexpected magnitudes.

It is the unexpected magnitudes that constitute the unsayable here, a "fresh universe" that demands a new language that is not yet invented. One has the sense here of an imagined world, a "supreme fiction," as Stevens calls it in "A High-Toned Old Christian Woman," that cannot be put into words. The technique is taken up in our own age by Kenneth Koch in his "One Train May Hide Another." He begins:

> In a poem, one line may hide another line,
> As at a crossing, one train may hide another train.
> That is, if you are waiting to cross
> The tracks, wait to do it for one moment at
> Least after the first train is gone. And so when you read
> Wait until you have read the next line—
> Then it is safe to go on reading.

And then continues to let one line reveal or lead to the next in an associative process that leads him to understand his own vision:

> One idea may hide another: Life is simple
> Hide Life is incredibly complex, as in the prose of Gertrude
>   Stein
> One sentence hides another and is another as well.

As Stevens says in "An Ordinary Evening in New Haven," there is always unsaid something underneath what we do say, "an and yet, and yet, and yet—" The unsayable opens up "the never-ending meditation" that is the resonance and richness of poetry. In a good poem the ordinary is never ordinary. The poem doesn't simply report or witness as a reporter or journalist might but continually explores possibilities. It suggests the richness of experience as something beyond a newspaper sort of account that attempts to relate all the "facts" of an experience: Poetry says the unsayable because it is metamorphic— it transforms the world it sees.

Linda Gregg's "The Unknowing" enacts such a transformation. It begins with an unnamed "it" which, if anything, must be the "unknowing." Gregg then goes on, as Stevens, Levertov, and Ungaretti did, to give a kind of substance to this nonbeing:

> I lie in the palm of its hand. I wake in the quiet,
> separate from the air that's moving the trees outside.
> I walk on its path, fall asleep in its darkness.
> Loud sounds produce this silence. One of the markers
> of the unknown, a thing in itself.

Language then begins to generate its own world: the expression "*When I was in love* gives birth to something else." That leads to a memory, the girl she was "riding her horse" in a place where "the unknown was hovering" among "the shade and the moving shadows." It is that place, like Shelley's hidden peak in "Mont Blanc," that is

>   a birthplace
> of the unknown, the quick, the invisible.
> I would get off my horse and lie down there,
> Let the wind from the ocean blow the high grass over
> My body, be hidden with it, be one of its secrets.

What Gregg has masterfully done is start with nothing and create a memory, create in the sense that the memory emerges out of the language's gradually assigning of a reality to the pronoun *it*. The poem transforms experience, memory, time, and place to reveal not just the memory but the fact of a secret, still unspoken, still hidden at the end of the poem, but whose power still drives the poem. The poet has it both ways, a kind of metaphysical irony. She enters the world of the poem she has created much like Stevens's helmsman. As Lacan says in relation to imagination: "I have only to plant my tree in a locution; climb the tree, even project on to it the cunning illumination a descriptive context gives to a word; raise it so as not to let myself be imprisoned in some sort of communiqué of the facts," to create a rich and resonant world.

"Language goes beyond the circle of relative meanings," Paz says, "the *this* and the *that,* and says the unsayable: stones are feathers, this is that." In "Notes on Poetry and Philosophy," Charles Simic says that the "poet is at the mercy of his metaphors." The language of the poem takes the poet on a journey, he says, for every poem is "an invitation to a voyage" made of words that don't so much tell us where we are or where we are going, but the myriad possibilities for each. "The poem I want to write is impossible. A stone that floats," he writes in *The Uncertain Certainty.* Or as the Spanish poet and philosopher Miguel de Unamuno says, "the really real, is irrational." It is beyond words.

While Gregg can build such worlds, and generally does in her poems, she also recognizes the transitoriness of the experience, of language itself, which is part of the unsayable, as that little poem by Szymborska I quoted earlier comically suggests. Robert Frost suggests a more metaphysical approach in "For Once, Then, Something." Looking down into a well, Narcissus-like, Frost also sees the world above him reflected there, and the two worlds coalesce for a moment and are linked by the thing, whatever it is, that he sees. Then, suddenly

> Water came to rebuke the too clear water.
> One drop fell from a fern, and lo, a ripple
> Shook whatever it was lay there at bottom,
> Blurred it, blotted it out. What was that whiteness?
> Truth? A pebble of quartz? For once, then, something.

To be honest, he can't answer except with the vague "something," which is not much different than Stevens's "nothing that is." The mystery lies in its transitoriness and may exist on a physical level (quartz), a sensory level (whiteness), or a metaphysical level (truth). It is also a world that has its own language in which water can "rebuke" water, and in a sense rebuke his own inflated vision of himself as a sort of Narcissus, "godlike," as he calls himself. And yet he too, in being unable to name what he saw, paradoxically creates a world, the whole experience of kneeling, as if in reverence, at the well.

This paradoxical sense of the transitory is related to another technique, counterpointing, in which each term exists in a set of shifting relationships with other terms. When Sylvia Plath says at the end of "The Moon and the Yew Tree" that "the message of the yew tree is blackness—blackness and silence," it is the synthesis of two perspectives represented by the two objects, one bright and yet "drags the sea after it like a dark crime" and one black ("The trees of the mind are black") and yet has a prayerful, "Gothic shape" that lifts itself towards the moon it sees as mere brightness. Both perspectives fail because the truth lies in the unspoken that is more than the sum of their parts: The earthly perspective of the yew tree can only yield, in the end, that "silence." One has to have, as she says through the title of another poem, "The Courage of Shutting-Up":

> No, the tongue, too, has been put by
> Hung up in the library with the engravings of Rangoon
> And the fox heads, the otter heads, the heads of dead rabbits.

Here no one speaks except the mirrors that "kill and talk" as they hold the vanished image of a dead man the way words can hold the unsayable beyond the life of speech. On a more positive note, even when she describes the voice of an infant, as she does in "Morning Song," she says more than the infant's utterances could possibly say:

> All night your moth-breath
> Flickers among the flat pink roses. I wake to listen:
> A far sea moves in my ear.

The words start to include a distance, start to create their own world that seems, like Tranströmer's pawnbroker's, just out of reach, and yet somehow spoken:

> Your mouth opens clean as a cat's. The window square
>
> Whitens and swallows its dull stars. And now you try
> Your handful of notes;
> The clear vowels rise like balloons.

"The function of language," as Lacan would have it, "is not to inform but to evoke" and what is evoked here is done so by the counterpointing of distant stars and tactile balloons, the mouth's words and the window's stars, in a way in which the two worlds somehow start to synthesize in the singular experience of the poem itself, the traditional "Morning Song," which is a love song of joy and union.

One of the great examples of proceeding by opposites is Dante's *Paradiso*. It is here, rather than in *Inferno* or *Purgatorio,* that he tries to go beyond physical representation for what he experiences: "How much my words miss my conception," he complains in the last canto. When he tries to describe how quickly he has risen with his guide, Beatrice, and how natural it is, he has her describe it by referring to an opposite motion:

> You should not, as I see it, marvel more
> At your ascent than at a river's fall
> From a high mountain to a valley floor.

By using an opposite motion, falling for rising, Dante signals to us how much our language of experience cannot describe what happens to him. Falling becomes a metaphor for rising, just as it does at the end of Rilke's *Duino Elegies,* where "happiness" is described not as the expected "rising" but as "the emotion that almost overwhelms us / whenever a happy thing falls." And as Beatrice explains to Dante later, she must use a language he understands to reveal what cannot be spoken, just as later Milton's Gabriel will describe the war in heaven to Adam in *Paradise Lost* as a process of language "accommodation." Language does not suffice: Dante uses a variety of metaphors that are always as inadequate as one's trying to see "a pearl upon a milk white brow." And yet, as we have seen, the metaphor does at least hint at what the experience *would* be like. Heather McHugh says in "A Stranger's Way of Looking,"

> The unsaid shapes itself in our imagination only at its boundary,
> where the said reaches its limits. To us the unsaid seems to
> surround the said and to extend endlessly out from it. ... Any
> poem, any work of art, negotiates this dubious relation. For part
> of the unsaid is the world of non-words related to by the said, a
> corresponding world, a matching world.

Counterpointing also emerges in catalogs, like the one that allows Trakl to find some momentary hope in the midst of the unspeakable horrors that surrounded him during World War I. Trakl, in "On The Way," tries to fill the void of the unsayable, his own sense of death, with a long catalog of images, to populate it, as it were, with perception upon perception. The poem begins with a funeral procession where a "stranger is carried to the morgue," but there is quickly a mention of more pleasant "red sycamores" and loud "jackdaws" yet also a sun that has "set in black linen." The worlds of death and life, his sister playing Schubert but her "smile" sinking "into a crumbling fountain," constantly contend, but gradually, as the poem shifts place to remember less confining, though still deathly, images ("dark gold of rotting sunflowers"), the poem begins to lift itself. Addressed to an unknown other ("the mysterious red stillness of your mouth"), the poem ends with a kind of Brahmsian wind-up catalog and final, desperate acknowledgment that suggests that if the idea of death is unsayable, so too is the hope for something that counters death:

> A guitar-song rings out from a strange tavern,
> The wild elderbrushes, a long gone November day,
> Familiar steps on the dark staircase, a vision of rafter turned
>   brown,
> An open window on which a sweet hope remained—
> It is so unsayable, O God, that you fall to your knees.

That final gesture, falling to his knees, suggests the kind of reverence he has for the unknown, the unsayable: The poem ends with an acknowledgment that, despite all the evocative images and metaphors, there is always something beyond what is said on the surface.

Of course, the immense difficulty of the unsayable is that if we don't find some language to deal with it, it becomes a kind of Tantalus-like vision beyond us. Trakl's use of images of song, nature, a staircase, and an open window at the end create a language of suggestion that, in sum, hints at something beyond, and allows him to find solace in the "unsayable." Levertov, in one of her last poems, "Immersion," wonders about God's silence, the unsayable of the sort we discussed at the beginning, and then concludes he is "trying to immerse us in a different language," which is precisely what great poetry is trying to do. "Our own words," she says, "are for us to speak, a way to ask and to answer." What Levertov understands is that all language is metaphoric, as all our attempts at "saying" are metaphors, in this sense, for the unsayable. Emily Dickinson, too, has numerous poems in which language proves inadequate to get at the heart of an experience, and yet somehow manages to suggest what is unsaid. In "I Heard a Fly Buzz," for example, the speaker experiences a "Stillness in the Air," the silence, perhaps of the deathbed mourners, but also something beyond that silence, but one that is spoken only by the "Blue—uncertain stumbling Buzz" of a fly that almost comically substitutes for God ("the King") before the poem ends mysteriously with her lack of understanding— "I could not see to see." But the image of the fly, often associated with death, and also with the devil, suggests a possibility for her life after death that is in itself almost unspeakable, the possibility of damnation. The poem utters it without uttering it by using the symbolic metaphor of the fly. "Truth," wrote Nietzsche in "On Truth and Lies in an Extra-Moral Sense," is "a mobile army of metaphors, metonymies, anthropomorphisms ... truths are illusions that we have forgotten are illusions."

In his Ninth Duino Elegy, Rilke perhaps summarizes this quest for a human language that transcends the everyday:

> And, above all, the heaviness,
> and the long experience of love,—just what is wholly
> unsayable. But later, among the stars
> what good is it—*they* are *better* as they are: unsayable.
> For when the traveler returns from the mountain slopes into
>   the valley,
> he brings not a handful of earth, unsayable to others, but
>   instead
> some words he has gained, some pure word, the yellow
>   and blue
> gentian. Perhaps we are *here* in order to say: house,
> bridge, fountain, gate, pitcher, fruit-tree, window—
> at most: column, tower. ... But to *say* them, you must
>   understand,
> oh to say them *more* intensely than the Things themselves
> ever dreamed of existing.

This involves nothing other than changing the very nature of language by using it as a base rather than an end for communication: The intensity comes not from trying to describe the mountains, the world, but from attempting to gives them a meaning and existence beyond what they normally communicate. It involves, as Heidegger describes it, a "fourfold"—relating the objects of physical "earth" to a larger, Heraclitean sense of time and change ("sky") and human history and usage ("mortals"), to a metaphysical sense of what it means to exist, of Being, how all these things are connected to the cosmos ("gods"). For Rilke, the stakes are enormous: At the end of the elegy he describes how our experience of the earth arises as "invisible" within us as world. But there is still no simple language for what that might be, except to exclaim in the last two lines, "Superabundant being / wells up in my heart."

Ángel González, in his "Useless Words," describes the "hunt" for "the furtive word / ... that means exactly what you are." Addressing a lover, he continues a "hunt for words that don't exist" and tries expressions for how he might touch the beloved, how he might gaze into the Other's eyes, and uses several direct expressions. But at the end he realizes that perhaps the best way is to describe not the physical lover and his actions, but something else, in words that do not say what he wants to say but which provide an intense metaphoric experience:

> —perhaps
> it would be better to say: evening smoke,
> faint music that the autumn rains down,
> fog, that falls slowly upon a valley—
> advancing toward me,
> spinning
> penetrating me
> until it floods my chest and lifts
> my redeemed heart, unharmed, suspended
> above the faint foam of happiness.

What he finds is a language of nature that corresponds in some way to what he cannot say in words because the beloved is more than the body, earth, more than their own relationship: The beloved represents a whole worldview that the self expresses and, in a sense, has become. A similar language informs Mona Van Duyn's "Earth Tremors Felt in Missouri," which uses an earthquake as a metaphor for the language of the earth that speaks its otherwise unsayable secrets to her husband: "the earth said last night that what I feel, / ... you feel; what secretly moves you."

Finding that metaphoric language, then, is a way of finding the self, diving into the self, or as Adrienne Rich would have it, "Diving Into the Wreck." In that famous poem she says: "I came to explore the wreck. / The words are purposes. / The words are maps." The whole poem counterpoints the physical wreck and the speaker's progress towards it as she imagines herself, for example, as one of its victims and also as a mermaid. And yet what she finds is not her old self, which is now as mythical as the wreck, but, in returning to the wreck in the process of writing the poem, a new self beyond myths:

> We are, I am, you are
> by cowardice or courage
> the ones who find our way
> back to this scene,
> carrying a knife, a camera
> a book of myths
> in which
> our names do not appear.

The great Romanian philosopher Ernst Cassirer describes myth as the original way we looked at the world. It is not created by the self as much as it creates a new self, that is, a new relationship to the world. For Cassirer this is also the source of language's metaphoric essence: "before man thinks in terms of logical concepts, he holds his experiences by means of clear, separate, mythical images." The "unsayable," in this context, is the ultimate myth, the ultimate, primordial truth.

III. CALL IT MUSIC

What I have been arguing against is the sort of poem one reads all too often. It is confessional. It tells us something has happened to the speaker, often something tragic like an abusive situation or the death of someone, and it usually reports it in plain language. It tells us we should care simply because the experience happened to the speaker. We are supposed to feel what the speaker feels because we are human, and the truth is, if we knew the speaker personally, we certainly would sympathize. But this sort of poem gives us a reality we already know or understand, and it relies on our relating our own experiences to the experience of the poem, because the poem itself doesn't give us an experience. It provides nothing new, no mystery, no sense of a complexity beyond the words on the page, no sense of the unsayable that is at the heart of our deepest feelings.

A good poem is an art object, a made thing, in words, and words cannot duplicate an experience. But the experience we have with the language, how it engages us, is an experience that leads our imaginations further into the world of the poem: The language of poem becomes a metaphor for the experience, and we feel the experience by feeling the power of the language. Jacques Derrida was fond of saying "metaphor is never innocent" because it orients our view of the world. As George Lakoff and Mark Johnson write in *Philosophy in the Flesh*, metaphors are "conceptual" in that they provide modes of thought, patterns of thinking. Stevens writes in his *Adagia*: "Reality is a cliché from which we escape by metaphor." And later: "Reality is not what it is. It consists of the many realities which it can be made into." That is, it is beyond words; it is unsayable. In a good poem we have a sense of so much that could not be known or uttered, of the unnamable beyond the words of the poem. Cesare Pavese describes this experience in his poem, "Poetical." It begins with a boy who believes a myth about trees, how they must, like him, suffer, and indeed how all plants suffer in an unspoken "silence." This "magical background" is what he wants to give words to. What he experiences as he returns to the city is a remote silence of the city that is also a remote memory of the forest. In a way the houses and trees, the two landscapes, merge, become metaphors for each other. To talk about and experience one is to talk about and experience the other:

> A remote silence
> That catches the breath of all who pass by is flowering
> In their sudden light. They are the ancient trees
> Of the boy. And their light has sung to him ever since.
>
> And so he begins, in this transparent scene, a poem
> To pass the silence. In the street nobody
> Ever reveals the pain that rots away a life.
>
> *(my translation)*

For Pavese, the creative process involved in writing the poem is something that absorbs the silence of words: The words of his poems show us not the everyday world of their surface, but always suggest, as the end of this poem does, what is not revealed by the words. While a poet like Trakl piles up image after image to suggest the depth of a void to be filled, Pavese weaves an intimate narrative in which we sense that the everyday surface relationships are more mysterious than can be admitted, or described.

One poet influenced by Pavese is Philip Levine. In the last poem of *Breath* he interweaves his sitting at home in Brooklyn and a story about the trumpeter Howard McGhee and Charlie Parker. When Parker sees something beyond words, something entirely "foreign he clenched his eyes, / shook his head, and barked like a dog," McGhee takes his arm and brings him home. McGhee sees the mythical Bird as also the very human Charlie Parker, sleeping, breathing. Levine, at home too, begins to

> listen to my breath
> come and go and try to catch its curious taste,
> part milk, part iron, part blood, as it passes
> from me into the world. This is not me,
> this is automatic, this entering and exiting,
> my body's essential occupation without which
> I am a thing. The whole process has a name,
> a word I don't know, an elegant word not
> in English or Yiddish or Spanish, a word
> that means nothing to me.

What links the two worlds are the silences—"the silent music / of Charlie Parker," the "silent miles" of our lives, the silence of sleep, of breath, of that unspoken word that would describe what unites us all. In the end Levine can only "Call it Music," as the title of the poem goes:

> To him Bird
> was truly Charlie Parker, a man, a silent note
> going out forever on the breath of genius
> which now I hear soaring above my own breath
> as this bright morning fades into afternoon.
> Music, I'll call it music. It's what we need
> as the sun staggers behind the low gray clouds
> blowing relentlessly in from that nameless ocean,
> the calm and endless one I've still to cross.

Levine's "nameless ocean," which is related to the unknown word earlier in the poem, leads us to the ultimate unsayable, the experience of our own death, something that Heidegger, for instance, says is the unspeakable essence of ourselves. The simple story reveals, in what isn't really spoken, something essentially human and yet also, in Heidegger's words, "unapproachable" in its "nearness." Breath is the body's music here, the language that joins Parker, Levine, McGhee, and us *in* and *through* the language of the poem, metaphorically, that is, and yet that metaphoric experience is as real as an actual handshake. It is the mystery and the triumph of the art of poetry.

Robert Hass's "Meditation at Lagunitas" provides us with a theoretical summary and also an experience of this triumph:

> All the new thinking is about loss.
> In this it resembles all the old thinking.
> The idea, for example, that each particular erases
> the luminous clarity of a general idea. That the clown-
> faced woodpecker probing the dead sculpted trunk
> of that black birch is, by his presence,
> some tragic falling off from a first world
> of undivided light. Or the other notion that,
> because there is in this world no one thing
> to which the bramble of blackberry corresponds,
> a word is elegy to what it signifies.
> We talked about it late last night and in the voice
> of my friend, there was a thin wire of grief, a tone
> almost querulous. After a while I understood that,
> talking this way, everything dissolves: justice,
> pine, hair, woman, you and I. There was a woman
> I made love to and I remembered how, holding
> her small shoulders in my hands sometimes,
> I felt a violent wonder at her presence
> like a thirst for salt, for my childhood river
> with its island willows, silly music from the pleasure boat,
> muddy places where we caught the little orange-silver fish
> called *pumpkinseed.* It hardly had to do with her.
> Longing, we say, because desire is full
> of endless distances. I must have been the same to her.
> But I remember so much, the way her hands dismantled bread,
> the thing her father said that hurt her, what
> she dreamed. There are moments when the body is as numinous
> as words, days that are the good flesh continuing.
> Such tenderness, those afternoons and evenings,
> saying *blackberry, blackberry, blackberry.*

The opening hypothesis, that thinking is always thinking about loss, has a corollary that is also worked out in the poem: Thinking involves words that are "elegy to what they signify," that is, words themselves are always about loss. The poem as a whole deconstructs the neat logical bit of balanced, parallel language that is its opening couplet. Those lines can't describe the "endless distances" that are referred to later in the poem. This is why words like "justice, / pine, hair, woman, you and I" seem to "dissolve." These words reveal something that is "unsayable." But there is another corollary: All loss is always about thinking. And to think is to use language, to listen to what the language says, and also, as Heidegger says in *On the Way to Language,* a way of "listening to the unspoken." That is precisely why the poem continues speaking and why his friend's voice "was a thin wire of grief" and "tremulous" as they try to find a way out of what would otherwise be an absolute muteness. So the speaker explores memory associations, relationships: the woman who herself is an unfathomable mystery that creates a sense of "wonder" and leads him to remember his own childhood culminating in the "spoken" word *pumpkinseed.* Indeed, the whole train of associations "hardly had to do with her," for she is simply the triggering subject originating in the word *woman* in the catalog of words that dissolve. In the end, the whole body is what thinks, "as numinous / as words," as spiritual, as transcendent. The repetition of the word *blackberry,* going back to one of the original senses of loss, transforms the word and the world: The repetition creates a kind of presence for the unspoken tenderness that imbues the whole scene, the unsayable depth of emotion that evokes all the mysteries of the poem from "the thing her father said that hurt her" to whatever feeling it is that the sense of loss has led him to "summon," as Heidegger would say, "whatever is present to appear and to fade."

I suppose in some ways I am arguing here that all poems should have an enormous amount at stake in them: That is not to say that poems should be about life and death crises, but that in what is described in a poem we should get a sense that the speaker acknowledges that there is always more, whether it is the invisible, the unspoken, the unsayable—something that gives resonance to the work. It's what makes a poem by Ashbery, for example, seemingly detached on the surface, contain a kind of mystery—"Something I'm / not big enough to see over," as he says in "My Philosophy of Life," a poem whose philosophy lies in the strategy of its evasions, its inability to name a philosophy of life, and so places the burden on the reader at the end. And yet, in many ways, that *is* the philosophy: It cannot be said because it is always on the verge of coming into being. It is always, as Heidegger says, at a threshold, always in a state of "betweenness." For Ashbery this is not a cause for alarm, but rather, as he says, "there's a lot of fun to be had in the gaps between ideas. / That's what they're made for!" For Ashbery, the quiet detachment, its evasions, even the joking around as in that last line about a "Philosophy"—"Look out! There's a big one …"—are meant to cover up a profound sadness that is not spoken: A philosophy always about to come into being is also a situation in which the speaker is isolated and alone (a fact suggested also in the way one might "attend a wedding of two people you don't know" a few lines earlier). This sort of unsayable sadness permeates Ashbery's work in much the same way as it does the work of a poet like James Tate, though in Tate's case the surface is generally more comic.

For example, his "Constant Defender" runs through a number of comic scenes that, on second reading, are all related to death and loss: He is in "a rush to meet my angel," is "talking to my mule about glue futures," his furniture is all used furniture, and words like *withered* and *burial* emerge from the comic surface. Even the idea of the kleptomaniacs suggests, in its odd way, another loss. The speaker portrays himself as a "wind-up toy / unwound." And so when the poem ends with a surreal giant clam falling "from the stars" to enter "our midst," the poem ends, but so then does the pretense as he reveals in the last lines: "I say 'ours' out of some need— / I was alone when it hit me." Those lines reveal what the poem is unable to say, a profound sense of loss of all that is around him or potentially around him, an emptiness almost beyond words.

Charles Simic takes this idea a step further when he says in "Evening Talk," "Everything you didn't understand / Made you what you are." What we don't understand, he says, are "the mysteries," how, for instance, one should have

> Followed that obviously demented woman
> With the long streak of blood-red hair
> Which the sky took up like a distant cry.

The woman at the end emerges, as it were, from the crowd at the beginning, mystery becomes the distant sky, the evening light modulates into her red hair, as the images start to metamorphose, as they so often do in Simic's work, to suggest something larger than the sum of their parts. For Simic, the unsayable is what any one image can only reveal in relation to the other images.

I think, finally, of Heather McHugh's great poem "What He Thought," which describes a dinner of poets in Rome who try to define poetry. As it turns out, the most conservative and unpoetic-looking of the participants arrives at the essential definition by referring to a statue in the nearby Campo dei Fiori—poetry, he says, is in essence a language of the unsayable.

The statue represents Giordano Bruno,
brought to be burned in the public square
because of his offense against
authority, which is to say
the Church. His crime was his belief
the universe does not revolve around
the human being: God is no
fixed point or central government, but rather is
poured in waves through all things. All things
move. "If God is not the soul itself, He is
the soul of the soul of the world." Such was
his heresy. The day they brought him
forth to die, they feared he might
incite the crowd (the man was famous
for his eloquence). And so his captors
placed upon his face
an iron mask, in which

he could not speak. That's
how they burned him. That is how
he died: without a word, in front
of everyone.
                And poetry—

                                (we'd all
put down our forks by now, to listen to
the man in gray; he went on
softly)—
        poetry is what

he thought, but did not say.

THE POEM, AS AND OF ADDRESS

By Ralph Angel

In my family, and in the history of my people, names have special power.

As a sign of respect, my sisters and I were given the names of our living grandparents.

I was given two names, the name on my birth certificate, my civil or secular name, and the Hebrew name by which I am addressed within the family.

My father, too, has two names, his secular name, and the Hebrew name by which he is addressed within the family.

My mother was not given a Hebrew name, but she was given a Ladino name along with her secular name. In fact, she was given two Ladino names for an extra measure of protection, as so many stillborns and brothers and sisters who did not survive adolescence had preceded her.

Other members of the community were named only after grandparents who had died, for it was thought that naming a child after a living person might shorten the life of one of them.

The names we are "called by."

And our sacred names.

Sacred names are used in the family, or when one is called to the Sefer, or when someone prays for your health or grieves over your death.

So much is our fear of the Angel of Death that, historically, naming is our way of confusing him. In the Middle Ages, some of us had secret names. Some refused to marry a person who had the same name as one's mother or father. Some would not live in the same village as other persons who bore their names. How could the Angel of Death be counted on to tell them apart?

In Poland, if one was born into a household where many children had died, one was given a name that signified long life, like "Old" or "Grandmother." In Yemen, in households where children had met premature deaths, one was protected by receiving one's mother's or father's name. To this day, throughout the Jewish world, it is common to change the name of a person on his or her deathbed—that the Angel of Death might bounce forever, forever disoriented, upon his trampoline.

In primitive times, names harbored power. A name could be used like a talisman, as a remedy for illness or to ward off evil spirits. It was not unusual to conceal the name of a child, to call it instead by its magic name—that the magic name might confound Lilith and her wrecking crew. At times the child was not named at all, or the name was kept entirely secret, or by using a special name the true given name would never have to be pronounced by anyone.

Even in recent times, a boy's name is often kept secret until his eighth day of life, until the day of his *bris*, and a girl's name is often kept secret until the first time the Torah is read after her birth, because up to that time the child is especially vulnerable.

Names identify and protect us. How many superstitions make them possible. How many rituals attend to them. Such fear. Such willfulness.

In the beginning was the word.

To expand on Charles Simic, in the beginning was the myth and the epic and the allegory and the fable and the folk tale.

We trace lyric poetry to the seventh century B.C.E., to Sappho or Archilochos, mostly because their fragments and poems were written down.

They wrote down the pronoun *I* and wondered about what they had done, as have lyric poets to this very day.

Emile Benveniste said the pronoun *I* "refers to the act of individual discourse in which it is pronounced, and by this it designates the speaker … the speaker proclaims him [or her]self as the 'subject.'"

I is the name we give to ourselves, as in *I exist*—oh so consciously so.

I is he or she who speaks the word *I*.

Something in poetry changed forever in the seventh century B.C.E. Gods and heroes and battles gave way to the absolute presence of the self, to being, to being present—solitary, and aware of one's solitude.

"The moon and Pleiades are set," wrote Sappho,

> the night is half gone
> and time speeds by.
> I lie in bed, alone.

We are born alone and without choice, and so, too, shall we die alone, and without choice.

The lyric poem speaks. It speaks on its own behalf. But of what does one's own behalf consist if not complexity—the contradictory, illogical, ineffable fact of one's reality? The look and feel of the grain of an oaken table, a silken tie, or the dream bird fluttering above the dream hearth in your living room as it breaks into ashes, into powder, into shadow. The imagined embrace. The remembered smell of moss-covered flagstone, without the memory's story.

Or the tiger cages of the Vietnam war, or Kafka's elaborate killing machine inscribing the accused's crime on his back.

Or starving to death a child shackled for months to a bedpost, or gassing and burning six million human beings in the *shoah*. Or taking one's clothes off. Or tasting sweetened tea.

Being is complex, at times overwhelming, always strange.

I is the name we give to our strangeness.

Poems are just words.

Paul Celan said that "Poetry … is the turning of our breath … the poem … [i]s one person's language becom[ing] shape and, essentially, a presence in the present."

Like turning toward the other, turning away from one's strangeness toward another's strangeness. Like the give-and-take of speaking, like things made of language and, therefore, *en route*.

Thought does not shape language. Language shapes thought.

It's in its nature. As in the nature of the pronoun *I*, for example.

Benveniste maintained that "in and through language ... man constitutes himself as a *subject*, because language alone establishes the concept of [self] in reality, in *its* reality, which is that of being." And "consciousness of self is only possible if it is experienced by contrast."

I speak the word *I* because I am not anyone or anything else. I am my strangeness, my presence. And by acknowledging it thus, by naming it, I am intending, hoping, I am going elsewhere, toward what I am not.

Emily Dickinson gazed upon a sunset and wrote it down. And by writing it down, by speaking, she acknowledged her difference.

> Bloom upon the Mountain—stated—
> Blameless of a Name—
> Efflorescence of a Sunset—
> Reproduced—the same—
>
> Seed, had I, my Purple Sowing
> Should endow the Day—
> Not a Tropic of a Twilight—
> Show itself away—
>
> Who for tilling—to the Mountain
> Come, and disappear—
> Whose be Her Renown, or fading,
> Witness, is not here—
>
> While I state—the Solemn Petals,
> Far as North—and East,
> Far as South and West—expanding—
> Culminate—in Rest—
>
> And the Mountain to the Evening
> Fit His Countenance—
> Indicating, by no Muscle—
> The Experience—

Dickinson spoke, and in speaking named a moment in time, and as time passed she became more and more estranged from that moment. Estranged from the natural world in which we live and of which we are wholly other—to be conscious is to be separate. What does nature know from time? or naming? or intention? or hope? What does nature know from conversation?

And what does nature know from Emily Dickinson—a person who perceived, who turned toward and addressed and questioned the ongoing phenomena of its unfolding?

We say *I* only when we are speaking to someone or something else, to some kind of *you*. "*I* posits another person," wrote Benveniste, "the one who, being, as he is, completely exterior to 'me,' becomes my echo to whom I say *you* and who says *you* to me."

Celan said, "I am you, when I am I."

"Take art with you into your innermost narrowness," he said. "And set yourself free … [B]y dint of attention to things and beings, we c[o]me close …"

Eugenio Montale. "In Sleep":

> The cries of the owls, or the intermittent heartbeats
> of dying butterflies,
> or the moans and sighs
> of the young, or the error that tightens
> like a garrote around the temples, or the vague horror
> of cedars uprooted by the onrush of night—all this
> can come back to me, overflowing from ditches,
> bursting from waterpipes, and awaken me
> to your voice. The music of a slow, demented dance
> cuts through; the enemy clangs down
> his visor, hiding his face. The amaranth moon
> enters behind the closed eyelids, becomes a swelling
> cloud; and when sleep takes it
> deeper in, it is still blood beyond any death.

There is no intimacy without attention. The lyric poem is lonely.

"Attention is the exercise of Reverence," wrote Denise Levertov, "for the 'other forms of life that want to live.' ... from Reverence for Life to Attention to Life, from Attention to Life to a highly developed Seeing and Hearing, from Seeing and Hearing to the Discovery and Revelation of Form, from Form to Song ... [Making] poetry is a process of discovery, revealing *inherent* music, the music of correspondences, the music of inscape."

By attending to things and beings, one forgets about oneself, and travels some distance.

Language becomes voice in that open space. As Celan said, the poem, "at its very inception," is already present there, "in the *'mystery of encounter.'*" Attention establishes that which is addressed, gathers it into "a *you* around the naming and speaking *I*. [And] this *you*, come about by dint of being named and addressed, brings its otherness into the present"—its "immediacy and nearness."

"All things are in conflict," wrote Martin Heidegger. "That which keeps things apart in opposition and thus at the same time binds them together ... is called 'intimacy.'"

The poem is lonely. Poets project their voices toward otherness, for they are in search of themselves. They sing to a *you* who just might be listening.

Celan:

> With all my thoughts I
> went out of the world: and there you were,
> you my quiet, my open one, and—
> you received us.
>
> Who
> says that everything died for us
> when our eyes broke?
> Everything awakened, everything began.

Great, a sun came drifting, bright
a soul and a soul confronted it, clear,
masterfully their silence mapped out
an orbit for the sun.

Easily
your lap opened, tranquilly
a breath rose up to the ether
and that which made clouds, was it not,
was it not a shape come from us,
was it not
as good as a name?

The Poem of Address, in particular, and by its very nature, depicts a degree of intimacy, or the lack thereof. No matter what else it might be doing, or what else it might be about, it enacts the fact of its intimacy.

All through Guillaume Apollinaire's "Zone," in every wide-open space there, even distance is kept near.

You in Marseilles among the watermelons

You in Coblenze at the Hotel Gigantic

You in Rome beneath a Japanese tree …

You are in a cavernous restaurant at night …

You're alone when morning comes …

You walk to Auteuil …

The *I* and the *you*, the most personal pronouns, "are linguistic forms indicating 'person.' They exist in every language," Benveniste said, "no matter what its type, epoch, or region may be. A language without the expression of person cannot be imagined."

And the *I* and the *you*, the most personal pronouns, are unique.

The *I* stands firm. *I* holds its ground, even as *I* turns toward the other, turning toward oneself, ultimately—*I* exists by contrast.

But the *you*, too, is uniquely *person*, for it is the name we give to the being who is addressed directly.

He is not *person*, really, nor is *she*. The third person is an object, forgive me, outside of direct address.

"While *I swear* (or *I promise*) is a pledge," wrote Benveniste, "*he swears* is simply a description, on the same plane as *he runs,* [or] *he smokes*."

Even *we* "is a sheltered, childish world in which no individuality has yet emerged," wrote Martin Buber. *Us* and *them*. "There are many ways to live in a world without *you*."

No matter what or who the *you* is, it is made present in the same space the *I* moves through.

It's in the nature of the pronoun. *You* exist because *you* are addressed directly. There is no *you* without an *I*.

God does not exist, some would say. But God exists in César Vallejo's "The Weary Circles." In intimacy, in torment, God is wholly present.

> There are desires to return, to love, not to go away,
> and there are desires to die, fought by two
> opposite waters that will never become isthmus.
>
> There are desires for a kiss that would shroud life,
> that withers in Africa of a fiery agony,
> suicide!

There are desires to … not have desires. Lord,
at you I point my god-murdering finger.
There are desires not to have had a heart at all.

Spring returns; it returns and will go away. And God
curved in time repeats himself, and passes, passes
with the backbone of the universe on his shoulder.

When my temples beat their mournful drum,
when that sleep etched on a knife hurts me,
there are desires not to move an inch from this poem!

Attention takes a lot of work. It's where the poem is. It's where language takes
shape, becomes voice. It's where reverence and devotion become song.

Intimacy is dangerous. *I* turned wholly toward the other, who is, also, perfectly here. And what might one discover in the "mystery of encounter"? That
a sunset, as it spreads and fades, is the face of one's own estrangement? That
one's God neither consoles nor speaks? That even a bed of flowers is more
alive than oneself?

Sylvia Plath. "Poppies in July":

Little poppies, little hell flames,
Do you do no harm?

You flicker. I cannot touch you.
I put my hands among the flames. Nothing burns.

And it exhausts me to watch you
Flickering like that, wrinkly and clear red, like the skin of a mouth.

A mouth just bloodied.
Little bloody skirts!

There are fumes that I cannot touch.
Where are your opiates, your nauseous capsules?

If I could bleed, or sleep!—
If my mouth could marry a hurt like that!

Or your liquors seep to me, in this glass capsule,
Dulling and stilling.

But colorless. Colorless.

The poem is lonely because people are alone, strangely conscious, consciously so.

"You do not always know what I am feeling," exclaims the speaker of Frank O'Hara's "For Grace, After a Party,"

Last night in the warm spring air while I was
blazing my tirade against someone who doesn't
interest
     me, it was love for you that set me
afire,
     and isn't it odd? for in rooms full of
strangers my most tender feelings
         writhe and
bear the fruit of screaming. Put out your hand,
isn't there
     an ashtray, suddenly, there? beside
the bed? And someone you love enters the room
and says wouldn't
     you like the eggs a little
different today?
     And when they arrive they are
just plain scrambled eggs and the warm weather
is holding.

The Poem of Address, by its very nature, by addressing the *you* directly, risks intimacy. It is its burden, the exhilarating weight of its revelation, of its immediacy and presence—*you* and *I* in the moment of our indivisibility.

The Poem of Address resides in our separateness, in the ultimate isolation of the *I*. Its heart beats in the secrecy of naming and in the *I*'s deliverance.

The Poem of Address is lonely, and it calls forth the *you*, and the *you*, in particular, universally, is a way out, a way out of its kernel of containment, its encapsulation.

The way Michelangelo, too, was a lyric poet. The way Michelangelo painted the Poem of Address on the ceiling of the Sistine Chapel. And God's long, gorgeously tapered finger, saying *you*, and Adam's long, gorgeously tapered finger, saying *you*, touch there.

And so I leave you, even as the poem keeps us here, with "Watching You," by James Schuyler:

> Watching you sleep
> a thing you do so well
> no shove no push
> on the sliding face
> of sleep as on
> the deep a sea bird
> of a grand wingspread
> trusts what it knows
> and I who rumple crumple
> and mash (snore) amble
> and ankle about wide
> awake, wanting to fold,
> loving to watch sleep
> embodied in you my
> warm machine that draws
> me back to bed
> and you who turn
> all toward me
> to love and seduce
> me back to sleep "You
> said 9:30, now it's
> 10": you just

don't seem to care
cold coffee (sugar,
no milk) about time:
you never do, never
get roiled the way
I do "Should I nag
you or shut up? If
you say, I will"
always be
glad to return to
that warm turning
to me in that
tenderest moment
of my nights,
and more, my days.

THE CHANGING OTHER

By William Olsen

To whom then does the poet speak? To
this day, the question still plagues us.
—Osip Mandelstam

There are two voices, and the first voice
says, "Write!" and the second voice says,
"For whom?"
—John Berryman

In this essay I am going to turn my indeterminate self to an even more indeterminate subject, audience. I am currently more interested in the latter because the indeterminacy of self has been talked to death, whereas indeterminacy of audience is and always has been a stickier subject. Most talk on audience turns on cultural questions, retreating back to questions of self—or the poet, and his or her role as such. As role is a social form of responsibility, such talk by default restricts itself to the social realm. Even the terminology I have so far used marginalizes all but social concerns. *Audience* implies more than one, or many more than one in those hopes expressed in many essays sounding out frantic alarms over whether American poetry has lost some truck with the populace that it never had; and our term for an audience of one, the *addressee*, has built into it public and formal properties. You address an envelope with the consensus reality of your home address (I have nothing against the mail). You address a superior (I have many superiors). You address, if you are George W. Bush or Bono, coliseums and congresses and multitudes of television viewers.

To think of audience in other than social terms is not to make a brief for elitism. It's just that in the realm of discourse called poetry, audience is less fixed. You don't always, if ever, completely determine whom you are talking to, and that uncertainty extends *beyond* Keats's idea of negative capability because it is an uncertainty that will not allow one to rest in it without some irritable reaching. Yeats's glorious mythic masks, one for each day of the month; the apt if sometimes wishful postmodern notions of a polyphonic voice—isn't the other, aren't the others, as given to mask-wearing; isn't the other as polyphonic? If there are chameleon poets, perhaps there are chameleon others.

Listener, a better term, is still inadequate. At the least it reminds us that poetry is a human activity. But other forces—nature, creation, death, the whole business of the sun and the moon and the stars—speak through human activities, and a poetry that discounts these forces saps poetry of vital powers. And if to count on a listener implies a higher authority, it also implies being *listened to.* Now we may want to be listened to, but by whom? Our parents? Our neighbors? Our leaders? Our government? Uncomfortable yet?

Good listener, allow me to introduce my scared self to yours. Eavesdroppers or wiretappers notwithstanding, for my own part I want my poetry to be listened to. At the heart of that want, I think I place a shaky faith in some sort of benevolence, whether that of a reader who I must take it on faith has some interest in and love for poetry, or that of something far other. The assumption of benevolence is the first condition of poetry. The poet who confronts a reader in poetry does so out of a longing to connect with the reader, to gain the reader's attention and respect, as the whole enterprise of confronting a reader hinges upon the precondition of attraction. We may address the body politic or the ruling ideology ("Moloch! Solitude! Filth! Ugliness! Ashcans and unobtainable dollars!"), but we do this with the assumption that over and above any target of our jeremiad is a reader who might be simpatico. An instructional poetry assumes in the reader the benevolent willingness to be instructed. The assumption of benevolence is a blessing, and it is a given that must be summoned. But not through a summons or by any legislated critical design. We never agree to a contract with the reader nor the reader with us: There is no dotted line to sign.

Audience, listener, reader—all shorthand for the mysterious hope Martin Buber says must have existed in the first act of communication between humans, "the possibility of being heard." This one identifiable source of poetry can never go by a single name any more than the emotional life of a poem can. The necessity of the poem *creating an audience for itself* is a half-truth, for you don't have to be Bishop Berkeley for it to occur to you that any audience for your poem has another comfortable existence independent of it. It is interest, not audience, that a poem must create, and it does this in part through summoning, imploring, chastising, revealing, beckoning, seducing, pleading—all agencies of the human voice.

Voice is perhaps the quality least conspicuous in that school of at-one-time experimental poetry most recognized as such, Language poetry. The best of it, like the best poetry from any school, has something resoundingly to do with being human. The worst of it settles for a kind of collectivized narcissism. It has the guise of objectivity, but it is actually a sentimental project, assuming poet and reader can meet without discord and free of any doubt as to whether any two humans ever do meet, in some cleansed arena called the text. Stevens says sentimentality is a failure of feeling. A lesser poetry never chances that failure. With respect to audience, Language poetry is currently our most idealistic school of poetry. It risks dehumanizing the writer into a text and therefore, as one text endlessly reads another, unto *infinity*, an illimitable resource of historical and ideological forces, a meta-egotistical sublime. It overidealizes audience into Eliot's "one perfectly intelligent reader who does not exist."

I feel my limitations more acutely than I do the illimitable. And one text may read another, but I have yet to witness a book reading another book or paging through itself. Voice in poetry is unprivileged and unideal, its freedoms operating under tremendous pressures. The reader may have a hand in forming the poem, and may in some abstract sense even have a hand in forming the poet behind the poem, but the poet and the reader always operate at a literal distance from each other. That distance informs tone. By *tone* I mean, more or less, attitude, though attitude is something you are usually aware of having, and tone also has less conscious sources. To say a poem has tone is to say its speaker has attitude *consciously or unconsciously*, and for attitude to exist something outside the speaker must exist. I see a lot of current poetry as toneless, or tone deaf, or tonally mute. Here is the last stanza of the title poem, "There Are Three," from a 1998 book by Donald Revell, an original and often powerful poet who shares with Language poets some of the same frustrations over conventional narrative and fixed lyric approaches:

> My life disordered itself
> amply in chronology
> and voices of wolves.
> No more voices!
> This is a tune.

Perhaps you could say that the voicy exclamation mark after "voices" belies the imperative. And "my life," I trust, indicates human presence. But that presence seems to wish only to erase itself. Someone sufficiently well read in contemporary poetry may recognize coded into this poem an admission of, and a desire to be free of, such presumed falsities as personal history and chronological or linear understandings of history. The theoretical subtext is that any poetry giving voice to these forces alone gives in to prevailing ideologies, and is as wolfish as any Stalin ever was. The stanza may begin in personality, but it ends in the transcendence of personality. Only the phrasing of that transcendence ("this is a tune") is curiously atonal. Tune requires melody. This poem renounces the very quality it desires, or feigns to desire—song—for the sake of the meta-egotistical sublime. It seems to have in mind for its audience not just readers of poetry but those readers of poetry who share the same convictions about poetry that the poem intimates. Is it too obvious to say that its sense of audience is far more fixed than its de-centered self?

On the other end of the spectrum are spokespersons for poetry who take it to task for having abandoned a general readership altogether. Perhaps they should. The urgent need of readership and the nature of the threat to it and what might be done to win some readership back are the concerns of Michael Ryan's essay "Poetry and Audience," the most level-headed recent essay on the subject, in part because it eschews the usual apologias and refuses to attack contemporary poetry in general. The drift of it is that somehow poetry has become increasingly untied from some original tribal sense of audience, first with the Renaissance poet and his courtly audience encouraging difficulties that take poetry well beyond the more folkish sense of audience of, say, the popular ballad; then with the highflying Romantic poet "[who] in isolation, and with a self-projected, imagined audience ... acquires enormous potential for solipsism and self-aggrandizement"; then with the modernist poet and such elitist aspirations as led Pound to say poetry is a "communication between Intelligent Men" who "manage the rest," created in Pound a "cultural version of right-wing economics" and brought most of the rest of Pound's generation to "an insular, genteel poetry in which the linguistic surfaces become glittery, privileged, subjects agreeable, and emotions tepid"; then more recent poets who feel and accept the "material worthlessness of his product" as a means of reaching absolute freedom from readerly expectations generated by a market driven economy, resulting in "a dizzying proliferation of poetic styles and almost no commonality of taste." In every case what is surrendered, besides the contact and the corrective of a real audience, is "the poet's role as citizen."

The sacred, the argument goes, lies in commonality, "collective emotions," or, to quote Eudora Welty, "the bloom of shared pleasure." In lieu of a tribe to belong to, the twentieth- and twenty-first-century poet opts for the community of the polis.

I won't gainsay any of this. But an aesthetics that assigns a role to the poet also unwittingly assigns a role to the reader. Ryan's advocacy for the poet as citizen can be traced back to Auden. A Horatian himself, and one fed no doubt by a time not so long ago in our history equally tyrannized by a "cult of personality," Auden says that "insofar as there can be said to be any ulterior purpose to poetry, that purpose is to disenchant and disintoxicate." True, but only partly: Was there ever a poet in the past century more intoxicated with the full range of the music of poetry than Auden? The proscriptive stances in Auden's prose help to ground the aery pleasures he took from poetry. But if a poet conceives of himself as a citizen, does this mean he conceives of his reader as a citizen, too? Isn't there more to both? There is something tyrannical to this conception. I don't read only as a citizen or only to be a citizen, I refuse to put my straight shoulder to the wheel. The poet who addresses a reader strictly as citizen may be likened to a cheerful old street-crossing guard shepherding schoolchildren across busy lanes of traffic oblivious to questions of citizenship altogether. When Wordsworth in his "Preface to *Lyrical Ballads*" argues that the poet is "a man speaking to men," he aptly characterizes the voice of Wordsworth the essayist, but not the far more complex voice of Wordsworth the poet. His *Prelude* never settles for one range of voice; it invokes oratory, rhapsody, overheard self-confrontation, addresses to friends that broaden out to the voice of a public "we," even odal apostrophes—to Coleridge, to Dorothy by the end, sometimes to nature itself. Its speaker can never quite settle on who or what he is talking to.

I do not always exist to myself as an "I": I also exist to myself as a "you," a "he," a "we." Sometimes I do not exist as a pronoun at all, but among the elements or in the vast interiority of body. If a poem seeks my full attention, it has to evoke as many of these shades of being as it can. Mandelstam, acutely aware of the abstruse, audience-indifferent poetry of the Symbolists, tried to renew in poetry its connections to its reader and reinvest lyric poetry with "the mutuality which attends the act of speaking." Taking the subject of audience beyond questions of social roles, Mandelstam claims that a pseudo-civic poetry flatters its audience by designating it a "proper audience." Its fundamental appeal is crass: It works on everyone's desire to feel included. Mandelstam isn't arguing for eschewing audience: Only a madman, he says, would argue for that, as "the madman never takes you into account, nor even recognizes your existence." He argues instead for a poetry that bears the fullness of the individual reader and the full mystery of writing a poem and finally of the poem itself. If poetry "is always directed toward a more or less distanced, unknown addressee, in whose existence the poet does not doubt, not doubting himself," then the unknowability of the listener creates a need for an inner authority, or "some sort of certainty in the face of it all." The fact of an audience is never doubted, but who or what that audience is the poet determines only at the peril of his poetry, for "in addressing someone known, we can speak only of what is already known." If we wholly understand our addressee and can wholly count on the addressee's attention, we will feel no great need to interest him. No anxiety about readership at all is assumed in works of "prose," or in essays. The prose writer "is compelled to stand 'higher' than, to be 'superior' to, society," whereas "François Villon stood far below the median moral and intellectual level of the culture of the fifteenth century." The only way the poet has to avoid boring the reader is to avoid boring himself, and the only way to do that is to write with the "desire to be astonished by [his] own words." Mandelstam is advocating an audible *distance* between poet and reader, bridged only by the poet's full engagement in the freshness of his language: "Whispering to a neighbor is boring. But it is downright maddening to bore one's own soul."

While I am actually reading I may not be conscious of the troubled mutuality that Mandelstam argues informs all lyric poetry, but even so it seems to me that at least some of the best poetry actively encounters an anxiety about audience. A poetry cured entirely of this anxiety may hold little human interest. Sheerly sincerist stances toward audience are sheerly presumptuous. Sheerly ironic stances towards audience, common in postmodern poetics but not confined to them, often succumb to the banal intrigues of a drama that goes like this—*if I need to TELL you I don't care if you are listening, I am lying to myself.* Poetry is gutted when it idealizes its other or otherness. As Ryan says of the Romantics, "in the absence of a living, breathing audience, in the presence of a grandiose, imagined one, the poet's self-aggrandizement is a natural trap." The prose of the Romantics may well bear this out. But a poet's prose and his or her poetry can be as alternate universes.

In the venue of the workshop most talk about audience orbits around technique, strategy, conventions and the breaking of conventions—that is, around the assumption that if the poet is good enough at his art and confident enough in his abilities, his work will find a readership. The poet, then, is free to create his audience. The idea of a speaker creating his own audience finds its first and ultimate expression in the book of *Genesis*. The Old Testament God—a response, many Biblical scholars say, to the need for the Israeli people to dissociate themselves from a world characterized by natural religion, fertility rites, cyclic thinking, and the idea of creation as the product of divine intercourse—solves the problem of audience by starting creation from scratch. When God announced, "Let there be light," to whom was he talking? God to God? God to chaos? In *Genesis* the desire for an audience, and the presumption of one, precedes *and* enables creation. God brings on the light that sponsors creation and makes it apprehensible, and that medium of apprehension in turn becomes a creative force, herb yielding seed, and seed yielding fruit, bringing form up from an earth without form. To accomplish all that, God must prophesy his own audience, which the very act of prophecy creates. He is the god of Vallejo's *Trilce*, a "God in alien peace." A flawless if not necessarily sympathetic listener—there is no mutuality in God's verbal creation of his own audience.

Whitman: "A few first class poets … *creating* the atmosphere out of which they have arisen." Whitman's temptation, which in his prose he cannot resist, was to become God, if not Vallejo's god of alien peace or Pushkin's bird-eyed god of remove and if not a god of ends, a creation-centered god. A great "I" that creates an equally great "you," a great poetry that creates a great audience. This is the Whitman of the preface to the 1855 edition of *Leaves of Grass* and the opening of "Song of Myself."

But in his dearest poetry he resists this temptation. "Song of Myself," for instance, is in quick fashion more haunted by its "you" than by its "I." That "you" is less stable—it may seem to be created, as the world in *Genesis* is created by God, at the outset of the poem, but ultimately the "you" eludes Whitman for the entire poem. No god of alien peace would be capable of some of the anxious tonalities of the poem. Whitman becomes *human* in "Song of Myself." That and nothing else is this poem's great ambition—a reverse apotheosis, permitting the poet not just to celebrate but also at times simply to speak, to come down from divine equipoise to the human: "I am the man, I suffer'd, I was there." After twenty-six songs of celebration, Whitman says, "Now I will listen." With this turn at the poem's midpoint, Whitman relinquishes the hyper-creative role of the poet for a role that is role-less, or which has no exact identity. And listen he does, to voices too disparate to fall under one name, and in the process he becomes a channeler who has, as Keats said of the poet, no identity:

Through me many long dumb voices,
Voices of the interminable generations of prisoners and slaves,
Voices of the diseas'd and despairing and of thieves and
　　dwarfs,
Voices of cycles of preparation and accretion,
And of the threads that connect the stars, and of wombs and
　　of the father-stuff,
And of the rights of them the others are down upon,
Of the deform'd, trivial, flat, foolish, despised,
Fog in the air, beetles rolling balls of dung.

This catalog, all equanimity, gets harder and harder to take: the listener-poet and the listener-reader become, so to speak, less self-prepossessed. The image of the beetles rolling their balls of dung stings because it has some analogous bearing on the great swelling catalogs of the poem itself. Whitman no longer poses as an industrious God who can create his very audience, he simply hears that audience out. He becomes its outlet. In "Death's outlet song of life"—as he calls it in "When Lilacs Last in the Dooryard Bloom'd"—he is too content to become, and he knows it, the death aspect. It is up to the rest of the poem to offer him means to resume and suffer identity, if not personality. All the recommendations in his prose for a transparent style aside, it is not precisely transparency that Whitman is after. The last line of "Song of Myself"—"I stop somewhere waiting for you"—is the most displaced expression of hopefulness in Western poetry. The last line begins with "I" and ends with "you," mimicking the structure of the entire poem, and a whole cosmos runs interference between the two.

But the mystery of the poem resides in the microstructures of the songs themselves, in their minute phrasings, in the tonal shifts and varying gestures. Its speaker's identity reveals itself, as identity always does, most fiercely in specific gestures—this categorical truth is the raison d'être for "close" reading. In short, you don't read a poem closely to reveal some inhuman perfection; you read a poem closely to get at the human. "Close" in both senses: A "close" reading is an intimate reading.

Let me try to illustrate this by looking closely at a few passages from two long poems. First, song six of "Song of Myself," a section that improvises its own epistemology by lampooning the scientific method and in turn throwing the speaker upon his own designs:

A child said What is the grass? fetching it to me with full hands;
How could I answer the child? I do not know what it is any more
　　than he.

I guess it must be the flag of my disposition, out of hopeful
green stuff woven.

Or I guess it is the handkerchief of the Lord,
A scented gift and remembrancer designedly dropt,
Bearing the owner's name someway in the corners, that we may
see and remark, and say *Whose?*

Or I guess the grass is itself a child, the produced babe of the
vegetation.

Or I guess it is a uniform hieroglyphic,
And it means, Sprouting alike in broad zones and narrow zones,
Growing among black folks as among white,
Kanuck, Tuckahoe, Congressmen, Cuff, I give them the same, I
receive them the same.

And now it seems to me the beautiful uncut hair of graves.

Tenderly will I use you curling grass,
It may be you transpire from the breasts of young men,
It may be if I had known them I would have loved them,
It may be you are from old people, or from offspring taken soon
out of their mothers' laps,
And here you are the mothers' laps.

This grass is very dark to be from the white heads of old
mothers,
Darker than the colorless beards of old men,
Dark to come from under the faint red roofs of mouths.

O I perceive after all so many uttering tongues,
And I perceive they do not come from the roofs of mouths for
nothing.

I wish I could translate the hints about the dead young men and
women,
And the hints about old men and mothers, and the offspring
taken soon out of their laps.

What do you think has become of the young and old men?

And what do you think has become of the women and children?

They are alive and well somewhere,
The smallest sprout shows there is really no death,
And if ever there was it led life forward, and does not wait at the
    end to arrest it,
And ceas'd the moment life appear'd.

All goes onward and outward, nothing collapses,
And to die is different from what any one supposed, and
    luckier.

The tonalities of this passage—at turns comic, vatic, self-revelatory, pleading, despairing, resolute—have everything to do with the speaker's shifting sense of whom or what he is addressing. In the first stanza, the child introduces himself to the speaker by way of a question, the child speaking his query through Whitman, and for him. This concrete listener, in a sense, initiates the poem, tying the epistemological to the sensory. There is a stealthy irony in that first line: The child's full hands are already rewarded with the bounty of grass, its material presence—the being of its existence—providing the answer to this or any such question. The act has more meaning than any answer the speaker could provide: The speaker in the first line is transparent: he reports the line. This question prompts a question of his own—"How could I answer the child?"—and for one instant Whitman finds himself in the child's position of not knowing, thereby placing the reader in the superior position the speaker found himself in just a line ago. The second stanza modulates to a more seemingly tentative voice, though tonally Whitman is a poet of mischief: the self-effacing quality of "I guess" is belied, for a moment, with the prideful "flag of my disposition," a shrewd image—a flag is public, a disposition is personal—that parodies the very egotism it advertises. Whitman never underestimates his reader: We are expected to get such subtle jokes. With the intentionally gawky phrase "hopeful green stuff" the tone shifts from the tentative to the wishful. The reader is now someone before whom the speaker, no longer a braggadocio, can admit with less than perfect eloquence to his own wishfulness. By the third stanza we begin to see that what is unwinding is an improvisation, both hopeful and playful. This tonally far-flung stanza begins with self-revelation, evokes the ultimate listener, God, and aligns the speaker with his readers by shifts into a public "we"—but just as quickly the stanza nosedives with speaker and reader back into the realm of the questioning child, "that we may see

and remark, and say *Whose?*" In the very next stanza this temporary alignment of speaker, reader, and child renders the image of the grass as a child
an inevitability. With the fifth stanza the metaphor changes yet again, with
a more public, democratic voice comically micro-cataloging the melting pot
of America—to wit, the preposterous oxymoron "uniform hieroglyphic" and
the presence among its retinue of races of "Congressmen"—and finishing with
a grandly oracular gesture. By the next delicate one-line stanza—"And now
it seems to me the beautiful uncut hair of graves"—the speaker feels enough
confidence to speak not just for but "to" himself.

With the following stanza the speaker shifts into odal address with some
of the abandon of Neruda's *Elemental Odes*, frustrating the serious tone of the
traditional ode by refusing to use the ode as a form of strictly public utterance.
Just as Neruda's odes focus on homely objects like watermelons or socks, Whitman focuses on nothing more, or nothing less, than grass. Neruda's metaphors
destabilize the object: To quote Jane Hirshfield's essay "Thoreau's Hound: On
Hiddenness," they "throw off the boundaries of the literal" and recognize that
even the simplest fragment of existence can carry multiple uses, possibilities,
connections. Whitman's odal address to the natural world takes us squarely
back to the human, and the bodily human at that, and the "you" that begins
the stanza begins to seem less and less identifiable, and more and more a
pronominal vortex. We are included in that "you" sufficiently enough that we
couldn't understand any more directly our interconnectedness with something
larger than poetry. In the next stanza any certitude of address comes undone,
and interconnectedness gives way to separation—the "you" becomes "this
grass." The voice no longer sounds so certain, and darker images take hold.
The speaker now is a little troubled by the strangeness of creation, or the grass
growing from the faint red roofs of mouths, so he contradicts his own deft
transformations. Though it is never just himself Whitman contradicts: He
finds his way into a contradictory otherness. And contradiction may contain
multitudes, but any containment here seems troublesome. "O I perceive after
all so many uttering tongues"—an image of grass and of humankind, the
tongues belonging to the "red roofs of mouths"—has a faint sadness to its
mouth-feel, particularly in the slow vowels and stresses of "all so many uttering tongues." It recovers some species of optimism, but almost as immediately,
in the next stanza, the speaker's improvisational hedging announces itself as
"wish" and ends, in the same stanza, in an image of "offspring" that emphasizes
separation more than possibility.

The questions of the ensuing stanza extend farther than ever into uncertainty even as the poem now directly addresses the reader—who has been

one element of otherness all along. The literal answer to the stanza's two questions—that the children grow up and perish—transforms reader and poet alike into something transient. You can almost feel yourself losing your human form if you try to respond to these questions. The questions, if ever so slightly chiding in tone, are ultimately earnest. Between question and answer, in the white space between this stanza and the next, reader and Whitman plunge into a crisis-like moment of alignment: That stanza break couldn't provoke a more active silence. The speaker doesn't and can't wait for an answer; he is thrown back on his own devices. There is no rest in the phrase "if ever there was," only restlessness, ongoingness. The reader isn't finished, nor is the poem: As the 1855 preface says, "the great poem is no finish to a man but only a beginning." With death "ceasing," it paradoxically takes on mortality, thereby becoming a strangely intimate force that contributes to a sense of continuity. Perhaps continuity requires the belief in some greater contradiction, something beyond mere self-contradiction. How else could the poem allow cessation and reappearance to occur as a source of solace in the same line, the same breath?

Whom do these last two stanzas answer? And who is doing the answering? I do not know any more than I know the name for my own soul. The soul—a sourcing *novismus*—the newest thing there is. The ushering forward. "All goes onward and outward, nothing collapses." The last line, more evidence of Whitman's no-holds-barred, wholly disclosed optimism, is also a gesture of withholding. Of the speaker's withholding. Of a human withholding. Whatever else death is, it is a riddle that answers only to itself, and the "luck" of it, if a source of regeneration, still eludes "anyone," including, presumably, this poet, who is perhaps as surprised by the equanimity of the line as the reader is. The two very audible adjectives of this last line, *different* and *luckier*, yoke good fortune not with cosmic unity but with some disjunction between self and world. Both the poet "I" and the reader have become "anyone," but elemental differences abide among us, and between us and the world. I don't think I sense Whitman's personality here. I sense something else, not just personality, not just identity, but the smallness of both. That last line comes full circle to answer the child's question with a categorical truth about the out-of-reach.

Whitman's "epic" poem is intent on a lyric project that locates the unknowable in the internal as well as the external. This is to say that poetry is a matter of life and death, as neither of these characters is very good about keeping to borders. As the songwriter Doc Pomus wrote in his journals, if you look in the mirror, all you can say in total honesty is "hello stranger, hello stranger." There is no other place but that strangeness from which a loving poetry can reach. *O darling*, whoever you are, whatever you are, *save the last dance for me.*

In a certain kind of poetry hyped largely by its own energies, language itself, as Jorie Graham has astutely observed, becomes an Other. Such poetry becomes a record of the exile from a paradisiacal language. James Wright's lovely language that "we once had" and "did not listen" to. Creeley's sense that a poetic language is "the utterance of our becoming." A sentence, as Creeley says, that is unending, that we could spend our entire lives within, "a single locution which is coterminous with our own bodies." That seems true in Graham's own ambitious poetry, a poetry of sentences that extend with the faith that there is a single sentence that never ends, a sentence all-inclusive, a sentence that reaches all *over creation*. The faith in a prelapsarian language may explain why sometimes in a Jorie Graham poem the "you" figures as an invasive presence, the presence of the Absentee At High that is responsible for the fall from a paradisiacal language in the first place: the presence of an interpreter. But if language alone is Other, where is a reader in all this? Heidegger: "Poetry calls the world into being by naming it." Heidegger could be exactly right in theory, which is to say that in any locale outside theory, he could be exactly wrong. "Being" *knows* better—even my own. If poetry flies on two wings, one of them is otherness:

> And if in this way we bang head-on
> into the absurd,
> we'll cover ourselves with the gold of having nothing,
> and will hatch the yet unborn wing
> of night, the sister
> of this orphan wing of day,
> that by dint of being one wing is no longer a wing.

The one wing of day, in the context of Vallejo's *Trilce*, a poem that somehow directs its focus both on and beneath creation, is the wing of the prosaic. A poetry that doesn't even have an other ends up nothing but orphaned prose. A poetry that fixes its sense of other is mere taxidermy.

My own generation's thinking about audience sometimes seems every bit as stiff as that of the modernists, and perhaps even more so than that of the middle generation. John Berryman's poetry, the whole of it, provides an increasingly useful example of responsiveness to the complex issues of audience. He was the only member of that generation who in his prose troubled to debunk Eliotic notions of a poetry of impersonality and tried to work out a conscious and explicit counterpoetics. His poetry has been derided too quickly as one that transforms personality into cultdom, and his poetics have been ignored altogether. It is not, by his own account, a poetics of confessionalism: When asked by Peter Stitt in 1970 how he would react to this label, he responded: "With rage and contempt! ... I understand the confessional to be a place where you go and talk with a priest." A confessional poetics construes audience or listener as a higher authority, the sort of ur-listener of whom Buber says, "we can only address, never express." Berryman's poetics are too rebellious, too tied up with failures and foibles of humanness, and too concerned with the complexities of human relationship as these complexities exist inside the human voice to pitch themselves—with the possible exception of "Eleven Addresses to the Lord"—to a higher authority. The difference between the self as it exists inside the poem and outside the poem is one of contingency and circumstance: Berryman says that the Henry of *The Dream Songs* "both is and is not me ... but I am an actual human being; he is nothing but a series of conceptions—my conceptions. I brush my teeth ... He doesn't brush his teeth. He only does what I make him do." The fictive self that exists in a poem is for Berryman that part of self which, when we express it, expresses our freedom to create a fiction of ourselves. But it also expresses something of our submissiveness because it can only do the bidding of the author. At times poetic voice becomes prismatic, or as Berryman quotes John Crowe Ransom on Theodore Roethke, "A true self or soul or mind of the highly compounded authorial." As Berryman says, "For Whitman the poet is a voice. Not solely his own—let us settle this problem quickly: a poet's first personal pronoun is nearly always ambiguous. ... A voice, then, for himself and others; for others as himself."

Yet the resolute faith-keeping of the art with the singular embattled existence of its artist is something Berryman insists upon again and again. "The impression is unavoidable that he *enjoyed* writing these scenes, and *was* excruciated," he says of Christopher Marlowe. Of Shakespeare, "When Shakespeare wrote, 'Two loves I have,' reader, he was not kidding." *The Colour of the Soul*, he called his first version of his work on Stephen Crane, a study which, like his studies of Shakespeare and Marlowe, insists upon proving "that poetry is composed by actual human beings, and tracts of it are very closely about them." Berryman's own poems have a dramatist's focus on voice as the place best suited for an understanding of how social forces work out. They view person both as a static and isolated state of affairs and as a profound interaction, a drama always going on, of acknowledgment and response. Whitman's accomplishment, Berryman says, is that after a lot of cosmic sympathy he can "resume the overstaid fraction," and for the sake of the poem that requires a human voice, die back into "the Body ... which is also part of his subject, a fraction of Man."

Berryman's insistence on the continuity of life and art finds equivalences between the needs of the poet and those of audience. A voice burdened by personality: beginning to sound close to home? It doesn't matter whether Berryman's personality is speaking in *The Dream Songs*, or whether a persona or a mask is speaking, or whether this sequence constitutes some perpetual fan dance of revelation: It is still a poem about *having a personality*. And a personality at its fullest, in all its registers, all its ways of being in the world and apart from the world, all its ruses and moments of insights, posturings, and honesties. Artistic self-consciousness in *The Dream Songs* lays bare how much of our personhood is artifice and evasion. Berryman's conviction was that only a full self-portrait can speak with the full range of a human voice, and that this portrait must include all our capacities for deflection, evasion, dishonesty, irony, ruse, and *love*—a force which, as Berryman said of Frost's "The Draft Horse," "can render evil impotent."

And how different Berryman's claims for poetry sound from those of the modernists. Here is one of Berryman's contentions with the notion of the impersonality of the poet, this time from his brilliant essay on Pound:

> This perverse and valuable doctrine, associated in our time with Eliot's name, was toyed with by Goethe and gets expression in Keats' insistence that the poet "has no identity—he is continually in, for, and filling some other body." For poetry of a certain mode (the dramatic), this is a piercing notion; for most other poetry, including Pound's, it is somewhat paradoxical, and may disfigure more than it enlightens. It hides motive, which persists.

We do not ever expunge ourselves of motive, Berryman's poems say again and again: Our one hope is in our future selves, and that future self figures as much into audience as anything else. Even when we imagine our deaths, we are imagining not our own deaths but the death of a future self: "the death a man considers is his own *now*, not his own *then*, when it will actually take place, to himself another man." Berryman's poems, by his own account, "regard the individual soul under stress. The soul is not oneself, for the personal 'I,' one with a social security number and a bank account, never gets into the poem;

they are all about a third person. I'm a follower of Pascal in the sense that I don't know what the issue is—the issue of our common human life, yours, mine, your lady's, everybody's, but I do think that one way in which we can approach it, by the means of art ... is by investigating the individual human soul, or human mind, whichever you prefer—I couldn't care less." Whatever we choose to call the soul, Berryman means always to honor its possibilities, and in the process to rebel against some aboriginal hopelessness.

This intention could find no truer embodiment than in Berryman's first and arguably greatest long poem, *Homage to Mistress Bradstreet*. Berryman's prose tends towards defiance; *Homage* is a tender poem that means to express human hope as truly and justly as possible, even if at the cost of never realizing it. Its many concerns and needs and personal and social experiences are positioned inside the human voice. It is a poem that in its very process was a "vivid waiting"—to be precise, five years of waiting after the first two strange stanzas came. It must have involved additional waiting for Berryman to have placed a pane of glass over first drafts in order not to revise initial strangenesses out of the poem. This artistic process is paralleled by Bradstreet's own long waitings—to finally get pregnant, for her husband to come home, for her child Simon to return from overseas, for her fits of fever to pass—eliciting, as opposed to how "God awaits us" with the utmost in patience, this self-characterization, "Sacred & unutterable Mind / flashing through the universe one thought, / I do wait without peace." Waiting becomes a kind of homing, as Bradstreet puts it in a letter to her children: "God that never suffered me long to sit loose from Him, but by one affliction or other hath made me look home ..." *Homage* honors the Whitmanic tradition by trying, as Berryman said of Whitman's poetry, to put "a Person, a human being ... freely, fully and truly on record," and it balances precariously between what Berryman himself saw as the two tendencies of the long poem, "the *mere* putting-on-record [the ironic italics are Berryman's] and the well-nigh universal current notion of creation, or making things up." It was Whitman's candor and his transparency of style that stirred Berryman: "The poet as creator plays no part in Whitman's scheme at all." *Homage* keeps a more austere record of a person's life, by flensing Bradstreet's personal history of almost all but the most emotionally telling details, obstinately literal details that summon her to record them and that turn her attention literally and figuratively home. In a sense, the poem is a history of a human voice.

Of two human voices. It is difficult to know what to make of Berryman's accounts of the poem and just as difficult not to make too much of these accounts. Berryman avers that he "did not choose [Bradstreet]—somehow she chose me—one point of connection, at any rate being the almost insuperable difficulty of writing high verse at all in a land th·t cared and cares so little for it." Berryman's wife Eileen Simpson in her memoir *Poets in Their Youth* claims that Mistress Bradstreet was "vividly present in the apartment at all hours of the day and night (John's working schedule). Her life was so intertwined with ours it was sometimes difficult for him to distinguish between her and himself, between her and me." In other words, Bradstreet, the addressee of the poem, is *herself* a compounded "I." Bradstreet must finally prompt Berryman out of addressing her into listening to her: In effect, the creator of the poem must become "mere" recorder of its primary source. And Berryman must come down from the notion that the poet calls the world into being by naming it. In the end the poem's method of ventriloquism and of maintaining the loopy dialogue between Berryman and Bradstreet goes transparent enough to catch something of the human voice at its most pressured and its most complex, in mutual longing and mutual despair. By the end of the poem we don't know if Berryman is the ventriloquist or the dummy, and we don't exactly care: The overt illusion-making of it reminds us of the struggle of the artist against the artifice of poetry itself—though Bradstreet is very willing to serve up remind-ers of artifice to Berryman, such as this: "Be kind, you who leaguer / my image in the mist." Intimacy constantly destabilizes, and voice is constantly being summoned beyond literal reference points of address.

Toward the tradition, for one thing. Poetry as Berryman sees it is at least this Eliotic in intent and method. *Homage* evidences Berryman's belief that "a staggering quantity" of an "original" poem "has direct sources, even verbal sources, in other poetry, history, philosophy, theology, prose of all kinds. … Poetry is a palimpsest." Its "long stranger," Berryman himself, is no stranger to learning or to the facts of Bradstreet's life. The poem looks forward to the future of poetry and offers its own "sourcing"—by pitching itself to the dead Bradstreet, it re-confers a future on her poetry and on all poetry. And to ad-dress the dead is an attempt at life as well as art: You could say, as Whitman says of poetry, that *Homage* "refuses to separate the dead from the living," that it "raises corpses from their coffins." In this sense the poem shares in its purposes the "great objective" Stevens talks about, "the truth not only of the poem but of poetry." It yields an unswerving generosity to its own art, evinc-ing Berryman's notion that "one works partly to open fresh avenues for other writers (though one would not dream of admitting it)."

Yet there is little in it of the flinty voicings you find in Eliot's "The Waste Land." Berryman's poem, summoned by and to human voice, speaks only indirectly to literary history. Voice at its liveliest, always sheering off, its hold breaking again and again, its sense of its audience shifting, shimmering, and disappearing, voice at its most nerve-rackingly intimate, less guarded about its facts and its desires—the dramatized desire, say, of the seduction of Bradstreet by Berryman's speaker after her account of her first birth—than we are with our closest friends. The poem can do this in just measures because underlying its speaker's doubts is Berryman's unaccountable faith that it was Bradstreet herself he was speaking to. For that reason the distance between her and him creates great urgency. From its very opening the poem insists on getting to the human presence that underlies the social and the titular:

1

> The Governor your husband lived so long
> moved you not, restless, waiting for him? Still,
> you were a patient woman—
> I seem to see you pause here still:
> Sylvester, Quarles in moments odd you pored
> before a fire at, bright eyes on the Lord,
> all the children still.
> 'Simon …' Simon will listen while you read a Song.

Immediately we have Berryman's characteristic syntax in rebellion against the straightforward. This syntax facilitates thought, reflection, connection, relation, and emotional diffraction. If you were to diagram this first sentence, you would need more than several transparencies to draw the diagram on, but at least one sense here is "the fact that your husband lived so long in his title as Governor of the colony and as your husband in name seems in itself not to have moved you?" Both these social senses of him, "husband" and "governor," are destabilized. In his essay on the euphrastic prose of Thomas Nashe, Berryman laments "what has been lost in our prose by the uniform adoption of a straight-on, mechanical word order (reflecting our thought-less speech)," and goes on to wonder "whether our prose has not become puritanical: straightforward, pompous." Bradstreet's own poems, charming and emotionally authentic as some are, were often shackled by their use of heroic end-stopped couplets, and the poetry of her influences, Sylvester and Quarles, were no less "puritanical" for their straightforward syntax than hers was. The syntax is the principal agent, then, of rebellion, and in the process and against all the verifiable facts marshaled into this first stanza it proposes the counter-fact of an inner language, a language that fathoms its connections from within. With "Still" suggesting the stiffness of a corpse and signifying "dead" or "even now" as well as "nonetheless," in that first address Berryman seems called upon to defend Bradstreet against self-criticism: Thinking of her missing husband as she pauses before her father's grave—he's named Simon, too—she is implicitly preoccupied not with the divine but with the dead and the missing. Just as Berryman is. Which is why the "seem" should connote something less than perfectly real and why in its halting rhythms the address itself should seem to founder, only—as with the dash after line two—to recoup. The "here" of line four, as it references the poets who follow that colon, suggests both the scene of Bradstreet's father's grave and poetry itself, or the tradition that Berryman would belong to in life and that Bradstreet belongs to in death and that even Sylvester and Quarles belong to if only as nearly forgotten figures. Their names seem to exist to be registered and nothing more. This stanza is about how easily we forget each other. The literal "pause" of Bradstreet before her father's grave is acted out by that colon—and in this halting rhythm we hear the speaker pause, too, in a hesitation of belief that a poem can reincarnate the dead. In that pause Bradstreet "lingers," reading poetry—as the reader is reading this poem—"in moments odd," or in whatever moments Bradstreet could have found for the contemplative activity of reading. Bradstreet doesn't pore "over" these two dull poets, she pores "at" them, eyes on some true Author, who in another syntactic rebellion finds Himself in uncanny appositional relation to "all the children" who are still. "Simon" would refer most directly to Bradstreet's first child, but it resonates with the absence of her husband and her father as well. Somehow, in a nonetheless charmed-seeming circle, Bradstreet has found a natural and familial audience composed of the present and the unaccounted for.

Almost as if in response, the poem offers up a vision of the harsh nature of transience and penitence. Berryman counters that cruel and random nature—it's "this blast, that sea" that buffets the scene—by insisting on the validity of the human voice, even, or especially, when the quality of its address morphs again and again:

2

Outside the New World winters in grand dark
white air lashing high thro' the virgin stands
foxes down foxholes sigh,
surely the English heart quails, stunned.

I doubt if Simon than this blast, that sea
spares from his rigour for your poetry
more. We are on each other's hands
who care. Both of our worlds unhanded us. I ie stark,

3

thy eyes look to me mild. Out of maize & air
your body's made, and moves. I summon, see,
from the centuries it.
I think you won't stay. How do we
linger, diminished, in our lovers' air,
implausibly visible, to whom, a year,
years, over interims; or not;
to a long stranger; or not; shimmer and disappear.

These two stanzas could scarcely be more indeterministic in their apprehension of who is listening. Even the foxes seem bereft in their "sighing" *down* foxholes, as if even they, too, were sourcing the grave in some sense. "We are on each other's hands" seems at once intimate in gesture and public in its claims for a radical sympathy that never ends in a single locatable concern, and the line break is perfect, exempting just in time Bradstreet and Berryman, and whoever else might be listening, from Berryman's abiding sense that human nature is too often murderous. The phrase is *encrypted*—Berryman invented this postmodernist strategy. Underneath it lie two phrases: "Our own blood is on each other's hands" and "We are on each other's minds." The oddness of the preposition *on*, along with the bending of grammar, creates a latitude of sympathy and at the same time tests that sympathy with hard reality. When "who care" comes, it comes with a feel of rescue, but at the cost of inflecting the public and intimate "we" into a less identifiable, more ghostly "who." Then a line of solidarity—the crucial identification for Berryman lies in how two ages inhospitable to poetry ignored these two poets, but the tie is far more universal than that, suggesting a constant in some separation both feel from the world. "Both our worlds unhanded us" throws the two back to the same mortal whelm of the past tense. Then the imperative mode breaks the declarative mode, with "stark" possibly suggesting "naked" and charging the poem at the outset with erotic dimensions, but also suggesting that the poem hopes its own methods are unveiled and unflinching. With the pause from one section to the next something uncanny again happens: The imperative prophesies her appearance, but the tonal authority of the voice breaks with the shift in address from a "you" to a "thy." A changing other evolves. "Useful and sweet, public and private, sacred and profane, intelligible and sensuous, transcendent and immanent, other and own, immortal and mortal, general and particular, archetype and anecdote, collective and individual participate in one another in the act of speech," Allen Grossman says of voice in poetry. It is just this sort of congeries that Berryman's radical syntax and radical use of pronouns try to provoke into being.

Suddenly it is Berryman's voice that seems mild, as mild as her eyes. He is able to reestablish a second-person, informal and therefore more intimate address by concentrating on what her body is made of, maize (suggesting, via the pun, the maze of her own sources in the physical, the familial, the natural, and the spiritual) and air (including song). With the body appearing and the speaker's apprehension becoming more attuned to the material and less to voice comes the recognition that the poet's efforts at summoning his source are going to face physical limitations. Hence, "I think you won't stay," a shrewd address that somehow also queries the speaker's self-doubt. What follows is a hydra-headed question wherein, at least at first, "I" and "you" join forces again as both an intimate and a public "we"—to "linger" is all that they have of each other by way of memory. "Lingering" is an intimate, even physical way to put how memory works. And for whom, or as the poem puts it, "*to* whom," in our poetry, in our love, do "we" linger? That pronoun couldn't be more open-ended: It summons present readers and future readers, it summons the openness of spirit and it summons it with the sharply felt longing that is the subtext of any such question: We don't ask questions, after all, in the expectation that they won't be answered. The question also questions itself, or whether we linger at all "or not." Then Berryman reestablishes his presence as "a long stranger," momentarily forgoing the hope of any intimate connection whatsoever, and the question finally comes round to asking how it is that, like the natural world itself, human relations must shimmer and disappear. No moment I can think of in poetry so scrupulously questions the depths of the simple hope for human connection, or so worries that hope into the open.

More and more frequently in the last half of the poem the possibility of mutuality emerges through recurring images of the soul, itself tangled and multitudinous and changing, mirroring the plurality of Bradstreet's own cares and responsibilities, or the "frenzy of *who* love me & who shine." This phrasing bears up under great pressure of pronominal indistinction—the capacity for loving and for shining defines and locates her loved ones better than their Christian names. In this line they are as "unutterable" as the "Mind" later "flashing through the universe one thought." That very frenzy opens Bradstreet up to the most direct expression both of her despair and of her hope:

> Vomitings, trots, rashes. Can be hope a cloak?

> **41**
> for the man with cropt ears glares. My fingers tighten
> my skirt. I pass. Alas! I pity all,
> Shy, shy, with mé, Dorothy.
> Moonrise, and frightening hoots. 'Mother,
> how *long* will I be dead?' Our friend the owl
> vanishes, darling, but your homing soul
> retires on Heaven, Mercy:
> not we one instant die, only our dark does lighten.

We hear dialogue within dialogue here, as voice opens up to Bradstreet's domestic intimacies, and her best loves. This poem couldn't be more insistent upon opening up the single voice to the various voices that inform it. The most unique trait of Berryman's craft is this ability to go transparent before voice at its most needful. "Not we one instant die, only our dark does lighten"—how could belief, how could the human voice, take on a more elegant embodiment? Such passages take voice to be an unremitting variousness. This variousness accounts for the "homing soul": In this poem the soul very nearly always figures as *the capacity for sourcing*, not to trace one's origin back to a single undivided creator but to acknowledge that the soul has its seat in plurality and in the "Mercy" that finds itself apposite to "Heaven." Wisdom, physicality, and the predatory in the form of an owl may vanish, but the soul is too plural to be mortal. The guarantee of immortality is community. This is to say, "I" must die but the "we" I also am to myself will somehow survive.

With that comfort Bradstreet now is seen seeking not unearthly union with an authoritative Other but simple proximity to loved ones:

> **42**
> When by me in the dusk my child sits down
> I am myself.

She is returned to herself by a sense of belonging, by nearness rather than by carnal or religious union. It may be her abiding sense of belonging, in contrast with the isolation of the speaker, that most accounts for the heartbreaking atmosphere of the poem. And none of these revelations unveil for long, for in this world hope only seems to produce more cloaking. Bradstreet's parting utterance, which seems almost to happen in a vacuum, refuses all and any finality:

> I am closed & coming. Somewhere! I defile
> wide as a cloud, in a cloud,
> unfit, desirous, glad—even the singings veil—

"I am closed & coming. Somewhere!" has some of the dislocated feel of the last line of "Song of Myself," "I stop somewhere waiting for you." But the voice here, finding itself at its vanishing point, seems at once less assured and somehow more ecstatic.

The hope for human connection is voiced in its fullest complexity by the poem's most caring and elegant eccentricities of phrasings. Eccentric phrasing is Berryman's way of getting at the mercurial nature of some inmost language. The precise qualifications of hope and of the possibility of eternity or the "forever" further ennoble the human voice. And the human voice turns out all at once to be patient and restless, existential yet part of history, vulnerable to the elements yet somehow free to be rescued and to continue to "run." Listen to the third line of the poem's last stanza—"so long as I happen"—and how the power of it resides in the way the apostrophic sentence, and the breathless optimism of it, breaks open to the acceptance of mortality and limitations on knowledge; and listen to the aposiopesis in the last line. That last unutterable pause is such that the force of love rejuvenates:

> O all your ages at the mercy of my loves
> together lie at once, forever or
> so long as I happen.
> In the rain of pain & departure, still
> Love has no body and presides the sun,
> and elfs from silence melody. I run.
> Hover, utter, still,
> a sourcing whom my lost candle like the firefly loves.

Let me try to extract a few things from all that is here. The speaker confronts primarily his own mortality—"so long as I happen"—but the mortality of poetry itself also seems implied in this phrase. In a vocal gesture that shimmers between the declarative and the imperative moods, he gathers up all the "ages" of Bradstreet with such obstinate delicacy that she seems not to exist as herself here but as possibility, as love, bodiless. In fact, the end of the poem virtually shakes loose from any direct address to Bradstreet—there is a sense with the imperative "hover, utter" that no personhood in particular is being summoned. Or is this self-address? In any case the voice is all faith, all belief, minus the hubris of confidence or the social skill of optimism. One *hovers* through *utterance* is the poem's final measure of its own accomplishment: that the promise it senses is not poetry, primarily, but the human voice. For that voice to be released, the imperative itself has to break at the moment the "sourcing" is evoked: and any remaining certitude the imperative has that it is actually being heard seems to dissolve, to have to dissolve, to the "whom"—enacting the acceptance of the uncertainty of whoever is listening. "Lost candle"—make what you will of the image, but consider this: The lost candle that has the capacity to kill with its flame now seeks with its flame. That flame is an echo of the soul, or Bradstreet's own "minute tangle of flame." The "whom"—on the most accessibly literal level Bradstreet herself—now can exist apart from any assignable identity, as a sourcing, as potential—as summoning.

All of Berryman's subsequent experiments with pronouns and with a fractured or polyphonic sense of speaker inhere in this last evocation of the changing other. This poem is Berryman at his most convincingly hopeful, and that hopefulness has the strength of belief, and no less a skeptic than Frost said "At bottom the world isn't a joke. ... Belief is better than anything else." Continuity—that's what exists in the enactment of the human voice in its fullest range of sources. The uncertainty about audience, about whether we are actually being heard, creates the possibility of an inner authority, or the consciousness of being right about nothing less than who and what we are. Berryman has "interpreted" Bradstreet forward by returning her from history to the myriad complexities of the human voice itself. Interpretation, after all, is prophecy. If you don't interpret what you read, you are leaving your heart at the door and your mind in the dark, you are remaining in the netherlands of appraisal and of enthusiasm and of hostility, you are refusing both close encounter and the strength and resilience of your own emotions, and you are discarding the live voice in the poem for some unreachable ideal, something that wouldn't want you to query it or reach out to it.

I would love to be able to codify the craft of this poem, but craft at its most effective and fascinating happens in ever novel turns. To appreciate craft you have to experience craft; in poetry this means you have to hear it done and learn how to hear it be done rather than learn handbooks and be content with their excerpts and principles: You have to encounter another poem, not the one you would write from your own life but one from another existence than yours. It is in this shared place that craft happens.

In *I and Thou*, Buber refers to an old Hindu folk tale that gets at how productive poetry can be if it speaks with the entirety of the human voice:

> Once upon a time, tells the Brahma of the Hundred Paths, gods and demons were at strife. The demons said: "To whom can we bring our offerings?" They set them all in their mouths. But the gods set the gift in each other's mouths. Then Prajapati, the primal spirit, gave himself to the gods.

It is not appropriation to have another voice speak through one's own voice, and it is not ventriloquism to locate the gift of one's own voice in another's voice. It is a matter of love, an offering, a gift that is literally a giving-over, and it is the most inspiriting purpose to which poetry can be put, far different than anyone had ever supposed, and luckier.

INCIDENTAL MUSIC:

The Grotesque, the Romantic, and the Retrenched

By Roger Weingarten

I remember speaking once on a very opaque and ornery aspect of contemporary poetry—and just when I was caught up in some thorny abstraction, a smirking, friendly genius in the back of the room piped up and asked, "Please, Herr Professor, what is a poem?" Like an egret with a pipe, bow tie, and shoelaces tied together, I flapped, fumbled, and tripped all over myself, all the time thinking *why not have something to say about the monistic, microscopic essence of the thing?* just as the defensive linebacker part of my mind blurted that there was no way to define exactly what a poem is, and if someone could come up with just the right container, no one with a creative bone in their body would want to write one ever again.

Well, I don't know the answer now and didn't then, but I did come up with a few ideas I thought might help both writer and reader of the contemporary free verse poem see the possibilities a little differently, see some of the elements that hold it together from a perspective that speaks to the elemental while not shortchanging some of the wild card complexities. Although my talk went well enough, there was something missing from it that has been gnawing at me all this time. I realize now what it was—I call it Incidental Music.

Webster's Dictionary says that Incidental Music is the "[m]usic played in connection with the presentation of a play, film, or poem in order to heighten the mood or effect on the audience." It defines *incidental* as "happening as a result of or in connection with something more important" and brings up the word *casual* in the same context, then *accidental* in the synonym department.

The base word *incident* is derived from the Latin *incidere*, which means "to fall upon." Music that falls upon its subject casually, almost accidentally.

Music originally meant "an art of the muses." The word *muse* is derived from the Greek word *mousa*, which means "muse, music, eloquence": The morpheme of that word means "to pay attention to, be lively." Music, according to Webster, is "the art and science of combining vocal or instrumental sounds or tones in varying melody, harmony, rhythm, and timbre, especially so as to form structurally complete and emotionally expressive compositions."

"Incidental Music" is not a term that has been in the forefront of anyone's critical vocabulary (a keyboard in the pit of a silent movie or bongo background to drown the onanistic words chanted into a coffeehouse microphone)—you won't find it in the *Princeton Encyclopedia of Poetry and Poetics* nor in the postmodernist *Dictionary of Poetic Terms*, so there isn't any reason, at this time, not to fall upon it, twist its arm a little, and bring it to bear on our understanding of how a free verse poem operates in the open market.

My perception of Incidental Music absorbs what Denise Levertov called "sonic structure"—meaning sound patterns and textures. Incidental Music is what compels or inspires the poet to fall upon the subject; it inspires or compels the reader to do the same; it holds the poem together, visibly, invisibly, subliminally, or bits of all three. Incidental Music integrates with, while staying slightly subordinate to, the subject, making the prose figure of the poem dance a jig in the ballroom of the poet/reader's imagination/ear/heart/sense of humor, what have you. When the music/structure of any poem calls more attention to itself than what it's talking about, like Tinkerbell doing the bump and grind in the lighthouse at the end of every other line, chances are you have the quack medicine that's being billed these days as the "New Formalism." To quote Mies van der Rohe, the modernist architect, "In architecture, the proportions that are important are not always the proportions of the things themselves. Often it is the proportions between the things that are important. There may be nothing there, but the proportions are still there."

Can Incidental Music, an artificially resuscitated term, like some new brand of super glue, help you, a writer and/or reader of poems, understand how free-verse poets make it all come together and stay afloat? Let's look at the historical background and mechanics of Incidental Music with a few illustrations.

In the late eighteenth, early nineteenth century, the German philosopher Georg Wilhelm Friedrich Hegel "held that every existent idea or fact belongs to an all-embracing mind in which each idea or situation (thesis) evokes its opposite (antithesis) and these two result in a unified whole (synthesis), which in turn becomes a new thesis." This dialectical reasoning was adopted by Karl Marx in the nineteenth century and expanded by Roger Weingarten in the late twentieth for very different purposes; Marx, in looking to remedy the social and economic woes of the world, kept the *ménage à trois* structure of the Hegelian dialectic, which explains why the radioactive iodine that covertly flew out of a Marxist reactor in Chernobyl (thesis) for a rendezvous with Capitalist acid rain (antithesis) is really (new thesis) good news. Weingarten, in trying to throw a little light on the inner and outer workings of free verse, upped the ante by two and developed what is now commonly called Weingarten's Dialectic. Components of the dialectic are:

1) The Elastic Sentence: like an earthworm, it can be short or long, begin or end where you least expect it, and have more than one heart: a relativist creature of the Einsteinian universe;

2) The Line: traditionally regarded as the basic unit of the poem, reflecting linear or, if you will, Newtonian thinking—the flat earth, the end of the line (pun intended) where we fall into the unknown of enjambed possibility;

3) The Stanza: a framing or staging mechanism;

4) The Incidental Music: how the poet composes and choreographs the first three elements and holds them in tension, the most mercurial, personal, and abstract of the four; maybe what Plato meant when he spoke of "That light substance, winged and sacred"; and

5) Synthesis: the effect of the fourth element (Incidental Music) on the first three (Elastic Sentence, Line, Stanza), what throws the results into the arena of "New Thesis."

Pattiann Rogers's love poem to the planet, "Geocentric," helps us see it all at work in a Romantic context.

> Indecent, self-soiled, bilious
> reek of turnip and toadstool
> decay, dribbling the black oil
> of wilted succulents, the brown
> fester of rotting orchids,
> in plain view, that stain
> of stinkhorn down your front,
> that looking oil of bracket
> fungi down your back, you
> purple-haired, grainy-fuzzed

smolder of refuse, fathering
fumes and boils and powdery
mildews, enduring the constant
interruption of sink-mire
flatulence, contagious
with ear wax, corn smut,
blister rust, backwash
and graveyard debris, rich
with manure bog and dry-rot,
harboring not only egg-addled
garbage and wrinkled lip
of orange-peel mold but also
the clotted breath of overripe
radish and burnt leek, bearing
every dank, malodorous rut
and scarp, all sulphur fissures
and fetid hillside seepages, old,
old, dependable, engendering
forever the stench and stretch
and warm seethe of inevitable
putrefaction, nobody
loves you as I do.

I used to think that the Romantic poet was one who believed that roses grew in garbage heaps; I accepted Isaac Babel's view of the Romantic as the near-sighted soldier who preferred to see the world without his spectacles. After reading "Geocentric," I will forever think of the Romantic poet as one who sees—with microscopic clarity—that roses *are* garbage heaps.

It's easy to see how the elastic sentence snakes its gaseous and oily way through the lines against the fairly short five- to nine-syllable lines, over half of which are downshifted into a lower gear by commas, the caesura of least resistance—a tenacious hard-driving sentence framed like a cameo brooch portrait of a loved one in the single stanza. You have to look a little closer and listen a little more carefully to catch the subliminal moves on your attention. Part and parcel of, and corollary to, Incidental Music, "music that falls upon its subject casually, almost accidentally," is what I call The Pinball Effect. Imagine the ricocheting steel ball making bells go off like surprises across the rectangular fantasy under glass, then peruse this poem's orchestrated alliterative and assonant topography: Indecent/succulents/flatulence; self-soiled/oiled/roil; black/bracket/back; reek/leek/seethe.

For all of you line-breaking, transition-hungry strategists and cool maneuverers, there are some extraordinary moves in this poem, but I'll pick just one: the line "old orange-peel mold but also." If you read down to it from a few lines above, then the next line after it, you'll see/hear how we are forced to take in the visual (orange peel mold) while the eye moves beyond, the "but also" carrying us forward into the next sensory delight. The name-calling thrust of each image and smell, like an alliterated, assonant canoe ride through the rapids of some muddy carp of river, is what carries your imagination, bilious and reeking, into The New Thesis, which is more than the resolution of the poem: that the author loves this perpetually decaying compost heap of a planet; and that we have enjoyed the piggyback ride on her trek through the personification/collage/sculpture of that thing. I'd shape The New Thesis as a rhetorical question: Can you, the reader, having been pleasured by the poem's trip, having turned away from putrefying nature, turn back and love the foul and gorgeous slippage into decay/new life? I hope you won't have to put the poem down because the fumes and boils are too strongly brewed from the everyday, garden-variety grounds of the grotesque. For my money, to bring Mies van der Rohe back into the act, "the proportions between the things" (the detailed imaginative particulars) are just right, though wonderfully intoxicated, because the force (as in *Star Wars*) of the Incidental Music, from start to finish, is energetic as hell or, as Webster would say, "lively," and what the hell, to stay with Webster for another moment, "structurally complete."

The following poem by Norman Dubie possesses certain features I think are worth considering in the light of the Weingarten Dialectic:

The Ugly Poem That Reluctantly Accepts
***Itself* as Its Only Title:**

It's that icy, blue, chain-dragging sincerity of ghosts just
Screaming out under the linden tree in a book
Written before Lincoln was born; and it's

Abraham Lincoln who slept alone and better than his wife did.
He who was once being entertained by a prince
Who had brought as a gift his celebrated Mongoose, Keise:
At first, the ochre and red eyes of the mongoose were closed;

He seemed wounded, and the snake swayed back,
At that instant, the mongoose sunk his teeth
Into the soft mauve jewel on the cobra's hood. The snake
Straightened like a wave, Lincoln said!

John Wilkes Booth thought sex was a preparation for death,
You read that letter of his to me in your farmhouse
By the creek in the steamy Iowa landscape:
                                        remembering the morning
By the railway depot where Lincoln had once waved
To the black-and-lavender Amish children: beside
That depot we watched an Angus bull that suddenly stood,
Balancing on the spotted rump of a young cow,
A huge violet artery crossed his square face, he sniffed
The air and looked with downcast eyes from the fields
To the willow trees that ran beside the river;
The cow cried out and the towering Angus bellowed back at her,
And the cow, then, looked
Over herself to the bull who was just finishing: large flies,

As in Tier's photograph of the dead in the South, were walking
Across his open eyes and into his nostrils and mouth!

The colon at the end of the poem's title turns it into a kind of prologue to the heightened poem that is both poem *and* title, something more than just the sum of its parts. This poem offers more than one kind of stanza to look at so the reader not only sees the *in media res* lines, such as lines one and three, bumping up against the elastic sentence framed by a stanza, but can also hear and see the stanzas themselves as distinct entities operating with (stanza two) or against (stanzas one and three) the sentence surging forward, though in this poem at a slightly more relaxed—though excited by exclamation marks and enthusiasm for the gossipy details—narrative pace. Stanzas one and three, like lines one and three, are in process, in the middle of things. A more conventional framing of the first stanza would be to include the first line of the second stanza as an end-stopped closure. There's a robust syntactical energy delivered setting up the break or tension between the open-ended stanza and the conclusion of the sentence kicking off the next. Also, Dubie is not giving in to any rote sentence-patterning here; you get them very long (the last sixteen lines of the poem) to very short: "The snake / straightened like a wave, Lincoln said!" What he *is* up to is starting, or moving forward, a lot of the action at line's end.

There is a tension between his manipulation of sentence, line, and stanza and the reader's expectations of what begins where: *where* conventionally begins at the beginning of the line and the stanza, but in this piece the title isn't the title, and the first three words of the poem demand an antecedent, which we are told is the poem itself. So, on the one hand, the poem reads like the serpent with a head at each end of its body; on the other, because of the Incidental Music—the author's eccentrically choreographed and sonically communicated passion for his subject—the reader can stay with it even if he's not sure the subject is an apocryphal string of Abe Lincoln/John Wilkes Booth anecdotes coupled with a little bovine coupling between an unwilling cow and the fly-ridden closeup of Mr. Steak.

Or, is all of this meant to somehow comment on the relationship between the author/narrator and the "you" in the poem made accessory to the grand finale via the "we" in line eighteen: "*You* [italics mine] read that letter of his to me in your farmhouse" (implicating the "you" in the poem's reason for being) and "*we* [italics mine] watched an Angus bull." So Booth kills Lincoln, the bull rapes the cow, the mongoose nails the snake, and if I were the "you" in the poem I'd have to call upon all the negative capability in Poughkeepsie as I studied the implications, though at the same time, I think I'd feel glad to participate in the hurly-burly of it all. Dubie has never been one to shy away from, if you'll pardon my French, what Marlon Brando called, in *Last Tango in Paris*, "the asshole of death." Maybe The New Thesis of this uniquely orchestrated argument among the bucolic, the historical, the personal, and the omnipresent "Ugly" is that the reader—though the reader is given the opportunity to see the poem at a self-contained distance—can't shy away from it, despite himself. Like what Ken Kesey said about vegetarians not being able to take their eyes from the sight of a cow being slaughtered.

When the word *retrenched* is brought up these days it usually refers to a lot of folks being fired from their jobs for purposes of corporate economy. What I mean by it is paring back to the essentials while still maintaining a compelling flow to the poem, while still permitting the subject its day in court, with its shirt hanging out, with its high and low ideals squabbling with each other. I am not talking about the "Language poem" that refuses to play upon the reader's intelligence, heart, imagination, and sense of humor.

Though there is, in contemporary poetry, a frightened, reactionary back-lash to the ambiguities of the new—not unlike the pro-life, new Republican, born-again movements—I am not talking about the Ivy League cynicism of the form-crazed yuppie poet, either. Here is a poem by Charles Simic that demonstrates, on all levels, what I am talking about:

The Lesson

It occurs to me now
that all these years
I have been
the idiot pupil
of a practical joker.

Diligently
and with foolish reverence
I wrote down
what I took to be
his wise pronouncements
concerning
my life on earth.
Like a parrot
I rattled off the dates
of wars and revolutions.
I rejoiced
at the death of my tormentors
I even became convinced
that their number
was diminishing.

It seemed to me
that gradually
my teacher was revealing to me
a pattern,
that what I was being told
was an intricate plot
of a picaresque novel
in installments,
the last pages of which

would be given over
entirely
to lyrical evocations
of nature.

Unfortunately,
with time,
I began to detect in myself
an inability
to forget even
the most trivial detail.
I lingered more and more
over the beginnings:
The haircut of a soldier
who was urinating
against our fence;
shadows of trees on the ceiling,
the day
my mother and I
had nothing to eat ...

Somehow,
I couldn't get past
that prison train
that kept waking me up
every night.
I couldn't get that whistle
that rumble
out of my head ...

In this classroom
austerely furnished
by my insomnia,
at the desk consisting
of my two knees,
for the first time
in this long and terrifying
apprenticeship,
I burst out laughing.

> Forgive me, all of you!
> At the memory of my uncle
> charging a barricade
> with a homemade bomb,
> I burst out laughing.

He makes one- and two-word lines work like no one else. Because the conversational push of the elastic sentence walks right through the short but varied (one to six words) line lengths that are framed by stanzas mostly working out an individual thought (look at one and three), the individual lines are important unto themselves, slowing the poem down so the reader participates in each delightfully agonizing accrual of detail and self-awareness, while contributing, like tracks in the sand, toward the laugh that will go on forever. He knows how to unveil his story: When he says, "Forgive me, all of you!"—one time when the second-person pronoun really earns its keep—he finesses the reader into a merger with the teacher/practical joker's, his own consciousness's late-night offerings of remembered sufferings, beauty, and loss on the installment plan, and having arrived there, like witness-accessories to the crime of not forgetting, we learn a lesson different from the elegiac survivor's outburst of laughter in the face of his uncle's "homemade" answer to the machine of horror. We don't laugh. We have been seated in the lecture hall of his memory's insomnia; we have been made aware of a rare and lifelong consciousness of hard ironies, and because of this soliloquy, this frank and generous one-man intimate theater, we have been allowed in, not unlike the witnesses to the victim of a dramatic irony, though here the victim is aware, and aware that we are seeing him in this dual role, and that—New Thesis—is our lesson.

STRIKING THE WRONG HOURS:

Poetry and Time

By Nancy Eimers

> *Nouns.* **Time**, tide, term, duration,
> date; lifetime, afterlife, eternity …
> —*Roget's Thesaurus*,
> beginning of entry for "Time"

It takes Roget only six synonyms, six commas, and one semicolon to get from *time* to *eternity*. Eternity, infinite time—after infinity, where else is there to go? So I stop quoting there and add ellipses, and on the page, those end ellipses *look* like time to me, mortal time, not eternity—elusive, soap-slippery, trailing off. Time may sometimes feel interminable, but for most of us who aren't mystics, time often occurs as nows and thens, befores and afters, moments or flecks or flicks of time or time looked back on or dreaded or time looked forward to, squares on a calendar, ticks or chimes or the opening monologue of David Letterman. For most of us, there's no getting over that semicolon to *lifetime*, let alone *afterlife, eternity*. We notice time when we watch the tide, turn our grades in, endure a stupid movie, circle a date on a monthly planner, unpack the Christmas ornaments that seemed to have just been packed up and stored away. Time is "the indefinite continued progress of existence, event, etc., in past, present, and future regarded as a whole," says *The Illustrated Oxford Dictionary*. There is, of course, no illustration of time, though on the next page, to illustrate time-lapse photography, there is a tiny picture of a curving, stringy river of lights, highway traffic at night. But we aren't really seeing the traffic, just the fact of its having passed, expressed (rather beautifully) as intertwinings of neon.

Time for me, much of the time, exists behind and in front of me. Sometimes it's what I'm stuck in. One way we commonly talk about time has to do with pace: *Time moves quickly. Time moves slowly.* Or no: let me rephrase that in past tense: *Time inched along. The hours flew.* For isn't one of the mysteries of time its ungraspability, how hard it is to perceive except in retrospect, or as a guess about possible outcomes, about what's unseeable around the next bend? You can't cup your hand around time, you can't arrest it as a virtual sticky note on your computer. And yet in a way time *is* physical, or let's say it manifests itself in us physiologically; in that we are not stones, in that our bodies physically undergo changes in time and thus record its passing, we are all unwitting clocks and we can't help it. Time ticks *within* us. The neurologist Oliver Sacks has, throughout his career, made a sort of study of bodily time in his patients. In his essay, "Speed: Aberrations of Time and Movement," he describes watching a man with Parkinson's disease who, to all appearances frozen for hours with an arm lifted near his face, explained to Sacks that he was wiping his nose:

> I wondered if he was putting me on. One morning, over a period
> of hours, I took a series of twenty or so photos and stapled them
> together to make a flick-book, like the ones I used to make to
> show the unfurling of fiddleheads [a species of fern]. With this, I
> could see that Miron actually *was* wiping his nose but was doing
> so a thousand times more slowly than normal.

Sacks's patients with Tourette's Syndrome, on the other hand, seem, some of them, to be living at warp-speed:

> Some people with Tourette's are able to catch flies on the wing.
> When I asked one man with Tourette's how he managed this, he
> said that he had no sense of moving especially fast, but, rather,
> that to him the flies moved slowly.

The fiddlehead "flick-books" Sacks remembers making were his way of recording the otherwise undetectable progress of time's unfurling; as a child he admired not-yet-opened ferns for being "tense with contained time, like watch springs, with the future all rolled up in them."

In the history of human measurements of time, there are shadow clocks, water clocks, sundials, sand-glasses. King Alfred burned four-hour candles to register intervals of time. The naturalist Linnaeas planted a clock: a garden of flowers each section of which bloomed at a different hour of the day. There were even sundial rings. Now there are stopwatches, marine chronometers, time-balls, wristwatches, watch-rings. Our computers have clocks, our cars have clocks, our alarm clocks buzz and sing and ring to mark a spot in time. In that alarm-clock instant, the first jolt of music, or buzzer sounding, or invisible clapper striking invisible bell, are we actually hearing what "now" is? How long does it last? Miroslav Holub suggests that the present moment lasts three seconds, which apparently is as long, according to certain psychological experiments, as we can mentally maintain an impression. "How long," he asks,

> are we happy? Using my well-tested and reproducible model of taking off tight shoes, I cannot say I was happy for ten minutes after taking them off. Maybe those few seconds, followed by a reflection in the way of—oh, great, and also, damn, those shoes are tight! And another couple of seconds …

I don't mean even to pretend to understand the nature of time or what Holub calls "the dimension of the present moment." I know that time neither slows down nor speeds up, it's not a carriage or racecar or a jet, it's not a road we are traveling. And yet often I can't help experiencing time as if there *were* some movement involved. Existing in time seems like being on one of those moving walkways in an airport; we can stand or we can walk or even run, but at whatever pace, dragging whatever baggage, we are being swept farther and farther away from the ticket counters, the Cinnabon, the loved ones waving goodbye. … Of course, simultaneously, we are rushing, or being rushed, forward—into what? We can think we know, we can only guess.

What happens to time when we aren't thinking about it? When, for example, on a good writing day, you forgot what time it was, it feels like time flew. Where did it go? A bad day: time stalls. The clock ticks thunderously. Is that time? On a day like that, when the hours have passed, I am glad, I can go to a movie; on a good day, time passes and I want it back and I can't have it. I have the poem instead. Like a tree that accumulates rings: a kind of time. There is, says Muriel Rukeyser in *The Life of Poetry*,

> in the growth of a tree, the story of those years which saw the rings being made: between those wooden rippled rings, we can

read the wetness or dryness of the years before the charts were kept. But the tree is in itself an image of adjustment to its surroundings. There are many kinds of growth: the inorganic shell or horn presents its past and present in the spiral; the crocus grows through minute pulsations, each at an interval of twenty seconds or so, each followed by a partial recoil.

Sacks's Parkinsonian patient was living at the speed of a fern. In an episode of *Star Trek* I once saw, on board the Enterprise there were creatures moving so fast they registered to the human crew—well, human except for one Vulcan—not as moving bodies but as buzzy flickers of light. We humans sit up in bed in comparatively infinitesimal increments (one of those aliens might have to photograph us for a flick-book to see what we're doing!), or roll back over at the sound of the alarm, we sit up, we put on our shoes, we wipe our noses, every "now" is already fugitive, a "then." Was there really a "now"? What was it? Maybe without memory and curiosity we *would* perpetually be on a moving airport walkway—like the brain-damaged patient Sacks called "the Lost Mariner" in *The Man Who Mistook His Wife for a Hat*, a man who, no longer having a short-term memory, would reintroduce himself to Dr. Sacks every few minutes. On his ceaseless walkway, every few minutes of his life he left behind everything but the distant past. But memory and curiosity deepen time, make us more complicated, nonlinear, in linear time. Forget the moving walkway—because of memory, time seems to move backwards and sideways too. The scene sliding backwards slides forward again and again. Memory makes us sadder, says long-dead Boethius: Nothing is sadder than the memory of past joy. Makes us happier? In *Moments of Being*, Virginia Woolf writes, "For the present when backed by the past is a thousand times deeper." "What then *is* time?" puzzles St. Augustine. "If no one asks me, I know; if I wish to explain it to one that asketh, I know not."

Of course all poems browse through time, but it occurs to me that what I am really talking about here, what I have really been leading up to, has to do with poems that reckon with passing of some kind, poems that structure and restructure time to undo the momentum of forward motion. The dead, lost items, earlier selves—like boats cut loose from shore, do they drift away from us? Do we drift away from them? In a way, poems *about* time are necessarily questions about—or questioning of—time and movement. In an elegy—in the act of expressing regret for, musing over, a loss—doesn't that walkway become a ribbon turning back on itself, past spooling forward, present (future?) spooling back? "First day of spring—" goes one Bashō haiku, "I keep thinking about / the end of autumn." If that poem were a ribbon, "first" would crisscross over "end," "spring" over "autumn." But is the ribbon folding forward or back? If spring exists in the present, is the speaker remembering last winter—and, if so, reflecting on the cyclical process of nature—or anticipating the fall-to-come, and endings, and mortality? There's a gentle self-parody, maybe, in that middle line: something obsessive in "I keep thinking about." Why think of autumn, for heaven's sake, on the first day of spring? (I've always thought Boethius must have been lousy company with his warnings against joy and his conscientious reminders of future misfortunes.) Still, the poem ends with "the end of autumn"; the shiver is irrepressible. The end of autumn—the beginning of winter—is in front of us, not behind us.

Elizabeth Bishop's "Sestina" takes place at the beginning of autumn. Its domestic scene has a frail, bygone quality to it—the poem's first title was "Early Sorrow"—yet the poem occurs in present tense. It begins with this:

> September rain falls on the house.
> In the failing light, the old grandmother
> sits in the kitchen with the child
> beside the Little Marvel Stove,
> reading the jokes from the almanac,
> laughing and talking to hide her tears.

The present progressive verb forms—*reading, laughing, talking*—reflect the grandmother's attempt to prolong the shelter of their present moment together, to keep some unnamed grief from the child. Yet this present belongs to the past, dated by the Little Marvel Stove and the almanac and the failing light, and even by the poem's dramatic irony, which allows us to know what the child and even her grandmother do not, cannot know: that their moment of comfort and safety will end. It is already ending. The sestina form with its circularity seems to act as a stay against passing time, yet glimmers of an adult narrator's perceptions ("equinoctial," "secretly," "marvelous," "inscrutable") testify that time has passed, contrasting with the poem's mostly simple diction and its storybook end-words—*house, grandmother, child, stove, almanac, tears*—in which are contained the story's unhappy ending, a loss the grandmother will be powerless to reverse or disguise. Paradoxically, the poem is sorrowful about the pastness of the present and the overpowering "present-ness" of the past. (Jean Valentine recently told of hearing that Bishop gave a public reading of this poem toward the end of her life with tears streaming down her face.)

That grief is "equinoctial"—inevitable—is what the grandmother must hope the child doesn't sense. The story is mainly told in simple present tense: The kettle *sings*, the grandmother *hangs* up the almanac, the child *draws*. The grandmother "shivers and says she thinks the house / feels chilly, and puts more wood in the stove." Simple present, yet the chill (*I keep thinking about / the end of autumn*) suggests an inner weather too. Because of it things in the present begin to complicate; presentness—its absences, sadnesses—begins to fold over or layer itself. The grandmother announces,

> It's *time for tea now*; but the child
> is watching the teakettle's small hard tears
> dance like mad on the hot black stove,
> the way the rain must dance on the house.

Multiple *now*s are beginning to emerge; the ritual of tea coexists with the strangeness of water droplets transformed in the child's mind into tears (she is picking up on something), alongside yet another ongoing present—real weather—outside the sheltering house. The assertion of a simple (eternal) present, of routine and order, in *It's time for tea now* is challenged by the word *foretold*—the gloomy weather, the very sadness foretold by the almanac—and by the Little Marvel Stove's *It was to be*; suddenly there is acknowledgment of a past, of inevitability: The grandmother's "now" would gladly obliterate "was," but can't. The room may be tidied, the too-portentous almanac may be hung back on its string, but equinoctial sadness will find a way in. It happens "secretly," in the child, unknown to her: The little moons in the almanac "fall down like tears" into the child's drawing of an orderly, well-tended house-and-garden scene. "*Time to plant tears*," says the almanac in the final stanza: The "now" of "time for tea" is gone. It is time now for grief; the child, still inside but unsheltered now, draws "another inscrutable house," her unaware grandmother singing all the while. "Inscrutable" house—who lives inside? Where is the mother? Can anyone get in or out? That man with the buttons like tears is the closest the poem comes to naming one source of its elegy (Bishop's father died before she was five); the other, the absent mother (institutionalized soon after, and never again seen by Bishop), is not in the picture at all. The simple present—the grandmother sings, the child draws—goes on inside a house on which, in the past, the rain perpetually falls.

In her essay "The Poem as Time Machine," Tess Gallagher writes,

> This conception of time as an atmosphere, as the "now" of the poem, which [Octavio] Paz calls "the Historical Now," or "the Archetypal Now," is what I would like to call "the point of all possibilities." By this I mean the point at which anything that has happened to me, or any past that I can encourage to enrich my own vision, is allowed to intersect with a present moment, as in a creation, as in a poem.

Isn't this "point of all possibilities" the sad, inscrutable moment on which Bishop's poem—a present looking back at a past—ends? The "now" has been complicated by "*It was to be*"; the sadness can't be contained—sadness *is* the "point of all possibilities."

I want to turn now from a memory poem by Elizabeth Bishop to one written in memory of her. The poem is Jean Valentine's "Snow Landscape, in a Glass Globe." The poet is looking at a snow globe. Nontime?

> A thumb's-length landscape: Snow, on a hill
> in China. I turn the glass ball over in my hand,
> and watch the snow
> blow around the Chinese woman,
> calm at her work,
> carrying her heavy yoke
> uphill, towards the distant house.
> Looking out through the thick glass ball
> she would see the lines of my hand,
> unearthly winter trees, unmoving, behind the snow ...
>
> No more elders.
> The Boston snow grays and softens
> the streets where you were ...
> Trees older than you, alive.

The snow is over and the sky is light.
Pale, pale blue distance …
Is there an east? A west? A river?
There, can we live right?

I look back in through the glass. You,
in China, I can talk to you.
The snow has settled; but it's cold
there, where you are.

What are you carrying?
For the sake of what? through such hard wind
and light.
    —And you look out to me,
and you say, "Only the same as everyone; your breath,
your words, move with mine,
under and over this glass; we who were born
and lived on the living earth."

The world inside the glass is untroubled: The woman climbing a snowy hill with a bundle is "calm at her work." The speaker describes the woman as if she were moving—"carrying" her yoke up a hill—but the tiny figure, of course, is frozen in the "act." Inside the globe, if the woman could see out, she would, the speaker fancies, see the lines on the speaker's hand as "unearthly winter trees, unmoving, behind the snow …" The hand holding the globe, the woman inside it poised, each winter landscape, each world, unreal to the other, is motionless. Only the snow—a kind of veil between them—moves.

This sets up—what? Stasis, as in pictures on Keats's Grecian Urn, where leaves don't fall off trees, lovers don't kiss and they don't age. Nothing can happen here, unless time gets set in motion. A tiny woman climbs perpetually up "towards the distant house." But once the poet tells us there are "No more elders"—shrubs, beloved mentors, both?—historical time has entered the poem. Now the snow becomes real snow, Boston snow that "grays and softens / the streets where you were." "Were" is the first instance of past tense in the poem. Once it occurs the poem has become an elegy; we get outside the timeless globe, and the past folds forward over the present moment. Loss, so plainly said: "the streets where you were. / Trees older than you, alive." What is not, laid over what is: *you/trees, you/alive*. And, too, for the first time the speaker addresses the "you"—forever-absent friend survived by those older trees—a "you" now superimposed on the figure in the snow globe, who in her uphill climb towards a "distant house" she will never reach, "moves" in the mind—becomes a version of Bishop in her lifelong attempt to travel back to the lost home in "Sestina."

The look of the sky, "pale, pale blue distance," has a disorienting effect on the speaker: "Is there an east? A west? A river?" Distance becomes as a place—for how can we understand a loved one as truly nowhere? Sky, blue distance, the heavens, eternity—"*There*, can we live right?" "There," a version of Hannah Arendt's "timeless region, an eternal presence in complete quiet, lying beyond the human clocks and calendars altogether." But it doesn't exist, out in the weather, out in the world. The speaker turns back to the globe: "You, / in China, I can talk to you." The pale blue "there" becomes another "there, where you are," the rhyme of *there/are* itself a folding of one present over another—"thereness" as awayness, not-here-ness, "are" as presence, immediacy. At the same time, "there, where you are" loops back to "the streets where you were." The tiny woman has become a way of addressing Bishop—if I may say it awkwardly, not a *were* but an *are*—a way of imagining response. The load carried against "such hard wind / and light" isn't identified, but we can't avoid connecting it to thoughts of the burdens in Bishop's difficult life, expressed once more as the forces of weather—wind, light. The speaker wants better to understand her lost friend's sorrows. The woman doesn't answer directly, or explain, but the poet has her offer some kind of return, a look, a reply, "Your breath, / your words." The snow-veil is lifted, the stillness is overcome. Words *move*. Poems move. The dead depart and the dead return. The woman says "we who were born / and lived," not "we who were born / and died." And maybe it's just me, but I hear in *lived/living* an echo of the last line of Bishop's "At the Fishhouses": "our knowledge is historical, *flowing*, and *flown*" (italics mine). *Lived*, past tense, *living*, verb transformed into adjective, but resembling a verb in present tense, a continuing, not of death but of life.

In "Jean Valentine: A Continuum of Turning," Philip Booth suggests that "the time that is primary in Jean Valentine's work is the moment of the poem itself: the moment through which the poet seeks to come to terms with experience, and the moment (all but coincidental) when the poet means *to make the experience present* for her reader." It's interesting to think of that comment in terms of another of Valentine's elegiac poems, "1945."

A year in the Pacific
watching his pilots
not come back to the ship

—they were nineteen, twenty,
they called him "Pop" ...

We lived
for the day he came back.
The day he came back

he raged like Achilles

the day   the year   years

we flew off

one off a bridge   one into a book
one a note
into a bottle

we never came back.

—Oh my dead father
—Ah Jeanie, you're still in words ...

The poem traces the looping of that first "not coming back" forward to moments
years later in which the poet and her siblings also fail, finally, to come back to
their father. The poem is in past tense until the final stanza, when, as Booth
says, the experience of loss is "made present" by way, as in her Bishop poem,
of an address: "—Oh my dead father / —Ah Jeanie, you're still in words . . ."
One of the ironies of this moment of "conversation" between two parallel times,
between living and dead, is the difference in tone between the first address and
the second, the first a lament, the second a reproach, the difference mocked
by the slant rhyme of *Oh/Ah*. The other irony resides in "still," meaning, here,
both "at this present time"—as in, *this is as far as you've come?*—and "silent."
The affectionate use of the nickname "Jeanie" makes the voice seem all the
more alive, more loving, more dismissive, less easily dismissed. It's a powerful,
unexpected moment of unrelieved presentness.

The first clocks, invented in the thirteenth century, weren't wholly accurate,
so one wishing to know the correct time had to consult the nearest sundial.
When in the twenty-first century things go according to schedule, we say they

went like clockwork. Clocks get us there on time, or if we arrive too late, or too early, we say they are *slow*, or *fast*. In British slang, a clock is a person's face. Birds pop out of some clocks and sing to us. Time, we say, is something clocks *tell*. Mechanical birdsong. Shadow. A passing face.

When clocks are off, or stopped, what happens to the telling of time?

"The clocks are sorry, the clocks are very sad. / One stops, one goes on striking the wrong hours," begins Donald Justice's elegy for his mother, "Psalm and Lament." Justice suggests that death moots all our measurements of time.

This poem begins (and ends) in a present tense whose present endures, a sort of meantime, a clock-less "now" in which nothing is happening; "now" and the "suddenly" are like signposts moving past a walkway that isn't going anywhere:

> And the grass burns terribly in the sun,
> The grass turns yellow secretly at the roots.
>
> Now suddenly the yard chairs look empty, the sky looks empty,
> The sky looks vast and empty.
>
> Out on Red Road the traffic continues; everything continues.
> Nor does memory sleep; it goes on.

There's progression without progress, forwardness without a plot. The poem is based on a simple fact: The past is past. And yet ... memory, like the present, goes on. What is—the ordinary details in this poem, Red Road, the scorched grass, the lawn chairs, the light on the patio—is made extraordinary, is ... *deepened* ... by what is not. *The present when backed by the past is a thousand times deeper*. Made sadder, made deeper. Quite simply, the spell of the mother's absence transforms everything in this poem:

> Out spring the butterflies of recollection,
> And I think that for the first time I understand
>
> The beautiful ordinary light of this patio
> And even perhaps the dark rich earth of a heart.

The painful fact of the death—or the discovery of the death—is neatly enclosed, but not finally contained, by parentheses.

> (The bedclothes, they say, had been pulled down.
> I will not describe it. I do not want to describe it.)

The speaker, desiring to hold this past moment off, cannot do so: The parentheses are too flimsy, the image too powerfully stark, that turning down the ghost of an actual gesture. And though he insists he won't describe it, he does, while protesting: "No, but the sheets were drenched and twisted." These aren't images from the past of *erstwhile* or *once upon a time* or *one fine morning*. If the facts are brutal, their metaphor is powerfully lyrical: "They were the very handkerchief of grief." Grief leaks outside the parentheses, where linear time exists, but grief just makes futurity seem beside the point. Summer will arrive, yes:

> Let summer come now with its schoolboy trumpets and fountains.
> But the years are gone, the years are finally over.
>
> And there is only
> This long desolation of flower-bordered sidewalks
>
> That runs to the corner, turns, and goes on,
> That disappears and goes on
>
> Into the black oblivion of a neighborhood and world
> Without billboards or yesterdays.

Living in a pastless present is, in a way, what our suburbs are all about—their ideal is that of safe living, of keeping out all dangerous elements and dangerous thoughts. But a present without a past, as in this Florida neighborhood, is a little like the chaotic scene in Bishop's "Over 2,000 Illustrations and a Complete Concordance"—"Everything only connected by 'and' and 'and.'" The sidewalk moves—and disappears—though without really moving, and

> Sometimes a sad moon comes and waters the roof tiles.
> But the years are gone. There are no more years.

That sad moon comes "sometimes": *at some indefinite time.* There remain lawn chairs and schoolboys and roof tiles, but "There are no more years." Real time turns and turns pointlessly into the motherless future; but, even so, the elegy itself runs back and forth and sideways, a clock of lost years.

> **I used to see** him daily. **I did see** him daily.
> —two sentences in my old grammar
> book, in a chapter on verb tense

I'll end with another Bashō poem. It's not strictly an elegy, but like the poems by Bishop, Valentine, and Justice, it refuses the notion that time moves ahead in an orderly fashion.

> Lime blossoms!
> Let's talk about the old days
> making dinner in the kitchen.

The collision of present and past, in a way, is incredibly simple. As Bashō explains, "The blossoms of a single potted lime tree in front of the bamboo are fragrant, and they inspired these verses." Out of presentness came the past, or a past called the present back—is that a looping forward or a looping back? "Blossoms" is laid over "old days"; "making dinner in the kitchen" could be an act in the present, ongoing while people talk; or it could be the everydayness remembered so vividly in talk it seems to be happening now. The poem leaves us in *a* present—not the simple present but the onwardness of the present progressive: in the dailiness of –*ing*.

NOTES ON NOTES,/:

Punctuation and Poetry

By Robin Behn

For some time, I've been obsessed by punctuation. Like many formal things I love, I came to this late, and had to forget the first way I learned. When I was ten I learned to play the flute from a saxophone player, then learned it all over from a real flutist who taught me not where to put my mouth and how to blow, but, rather, why it was worth doing, what effects—from forlorn bottle with prairie wind blowing across it, to viscous arguing bass—it could achieve. Likewise, I spent ten or so years of childhood summers being tossed into a freezing town pool at precisely eight a.m. with other children of my precise age while over us hovered the lifeguards, hulking or vivacious high school kids with dreamy tan lines and ardently fluorescent suits, drilling us in the Red Cross method of swimming. By the time I was in college, I was lucky if I could get across the pool once. It wasn't until—what possessed me to sign up, I will never know—I enrolled in Life Saving, that a great teacher taught me how to move my legs and what to do with flailing arms, mine or the drowning others', so I would be able to reach them, and, with a kind of feigned drowning myself, secure them and carry the lot of us, arms paired like some kind of elaborately drawn treble clef in the key of G, back to shore. The forms now had a purpose. But it was the forms I secretly loved, and the best days of the swimming class were the ones when we were videotaped through a window four feet down the pool's side, and watched, afterward, ourselves from underneath, the feeling of the form of swimming suddenly, startlingly, visible. The arm drawn down the length of the torso during the crawl, which, if done right, conveyed a feeling of massive, powerful propulsion, suddenly showed itself for what it was: a centered, flipped, question mark of a gesture.

The first time I learned question marks, commas, periods and other such devices, I cannot remember. I seem to remember enjoying them—like having a bottomless pocketful of bright or dull, shattered or perfectly round marbles to set out on the white ground at will. The game had rules, of course. And sometime after first shakily acquiring these rules by osmosis, I came across Mr. Rex, the seventh-grade grammar teacher. English wasn't books anymore, not Whodunit?, not How shall the children make their way back from the woods at the end of chapter three?, not even Pick the main idea from four possible choices. English, suddenly, was rules. Sentences were tacked up like laboratory insects to the blackboard with chalk marks like pins, and we all looked on, budding naturalists.

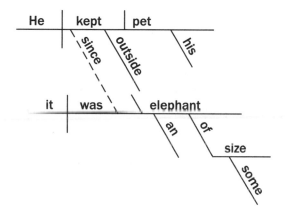

It is the first time my mind wandered Big Time (I know that shouldn't be capitalized, Mr. Rex, but I *wanted* to, it sounded like big letters!). By then we were all carrying around notebooks, and I took to analyzing the handwriting of the girls nearby. Suzi made the dot of her *i* into a globe. It occurred to me that one could be approved of—or not—for one's writing. One did it not to write something down but to show something off. I looked back up at the board: Where, in that scheme, the capturing of thought and the proffering up of the sentence as an object for our edification and further study, did language fit in? The sentence—but I must have needed glasses by then, and it must have been that no one had noticed, not even me, for all I can see when I look now is the spider's broken legs, the chalky lines and angles like a web drawn with an Etch A Sketch, the shape of the sentence—*diagrammed*. And, here and there, among the glistening lines and the illegible names that named the parts language had become, was the empty ache where the marks of punctuation no longer were. The beautiful, stately, gravity-defying architecture of the sentence existed without them. I penciled them into my notebook: dots, one or two, little lines, straight or curved, angled this way or that, to decorate the spider. Or was the spider making them, and, if so, did the marks record the spinning of what it wanted to show (I'd read about Charlotte's SOME PIG) or something internal, not meant to be seen or scene ... like twists of spinal fluid as it thought, if spiders thought, if they had spines ...

I emerged with the sense of language as a map, the map-making riddled with rules that might or might not coincide with what my ear wanted to hear, what the pen wanted to speak.

There was another place, though, several years later, when I was seventeen and lightheaded from the altitude at the Aspen Music School, that I was allowed—required!—to record with markings exactly what my ear heard. I still like the name of the class: *ear training*. First it was just rhythm. Dum dum da da da dum ... de dum. We'd listen to it once, twice, then transcribe it, using the absolute system of rhythmic notation we'd learned from our first music teachers. A quarter note lasts half as long as a half note: even their names could tell you that; an eighth note a half of that, a sixteenth, a half of that. There were notations for silence, too, which, like the notes' values, indicated precise duration: whole rest, half rest, quarter rest, sixteenth ... Oh, and a comforting time-grid to string it on: we are in 4/4 time, we are in 6/8: the whole thing a lovely puzzle. It had the allure of arithmetic. Measure by measure, we could check our work. Measure by measure, the things we heard, the things we tapped out on our own, could be recorded. Precise, checkable. I always had the feeling, taking this kind of dictation, that the proper transcribing of rhythm added to my hearing of it: It made me able to hear the form, the duration/relation where music doesn't just sound but transverses through time. Once recorded, the elegant, mathematical shapes would always be part of my hearing. The way, after I first saw an X-ray of my spine, I could feel and see its form bending precisely like a question mark each time I lifted a heavy box.

Of course music, and written music, had its other, murkier, sides. I was a flutist, not a snare drum player, so there was pitch, the up-and-down-edness of notes. But for this, too, there was a precise notation—notes on the staff, sharps and flats, and the orchestral instruments only capable, or only allowed—hours and hours in a little practice room with a box called a strobocon, trying to play a scale in tune—to produce notes coinciding with what could be notated. B, and b flat, but not b flat flat ... Did that limit the music? I didn't think about that then. And there *was* a kind of mark for how a slide trombone slides. This pitch transcription, the next phase of ear training, consisted first of intervals—"Here comes the bride," that's a major fourth—and eventually of chords and counterpoint. But here, too, there was a way to check: You could play back what you'd transcribed, and it either did or did not sound like what had been played. The system was finite and, at least at this level of training, devoid of emotion or intent, of thought of all but the most analytical kind, in reference to known schemes: clefs, note values, time signatures—I've always loved that, *time signature*, as if time could sign off with a flourish of approval once you'd notated it right!

These musical marks were not, in essence, open to question. Two flutists could "interpret" Mozart's Concerto in G however they liked, but if they were any good, the first note would indeed be a quarter note, the next a dotted eighth, then a sixteenth: Gee dee de dee dee: and anyone reading the score would have to agree about that.

One has to play the piece with those note values and pitches. If we were to translate our musical language into "English" on the board in Mr. Rex's class, what would we see? Is notation, at this level, the sentence of musical thought conveyed in the way it is actually, crucially imagined and heard by the composer? Or is it—listen again, hear how the two performers differently interpret another set of marks—mezzo forte—how loud? Adagio, what kind of overall-slow?—so that, for one, the opening bars make you feel a kind of steadfastness and hope, a guiding light even, whereas the other flutist is finding his way, never sure if the boat will right itself, if passenger A is meant to be reunited, on that distant shore of G, with her lover B?

How much of the music in the composer's mind does the score convey? And are the musical marks available to us up to the job? Are the possibilities of music limited by the visual marks? Does the composer "think" in these marks? The plethora of new musical notation in twentieth-century music suggests that new sounds do, indeed, require new notations. The score of George Crumb's flute piece "Voice of the Whale" contains a number of unconventional markings needed to make whale sounds, for example:

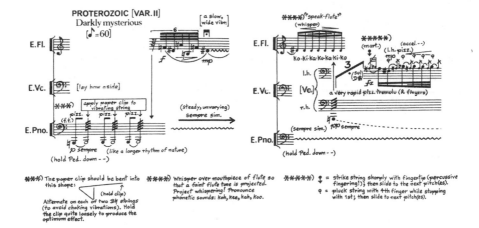

But what, if any, new notations are available to us who compose in the language of, well, language?

To the extent that a musical score can be variously interpreted, is it that the system of notation falls short, that there is no way to say how loud and what kind of loud that fourth forte should be? Or is the performer really meant to have this leeway? Did the composer intend to leave a mere suggestion of the form? Are sentences like that? Words, certainly, are both specific and slippery in their meanings. But I was thinking about the marks, not the words—the humble comma, the showy exclamation point, the beloved, flexible dash. Are they, like the notes' durations, clear-cut marks in an agreed-upon contractual system between writer and reader, so that everyone will hear the sentence's rhythm and pitch and meaning basically "right," basically the same? Or are they more "expressive" marks, the way, over the opening bar, the composer might write "andante" or "adagio"? Or are they the merest outline of form, the way, say, in the Bach cantatas that have come down to us, we have the note values and pitches only, and the phrasing—not one slur in sight!—and even *which* instruments, which tones of voice, will play the piece, are left completely up to us as we try to "read" the music? What should punctuation do? The books we had in Mr. Rex's class seemed to imply that punctuation marks had specific, definable jobs: Here is a page that explains the use of the comma, and here, the uses of the colon, and so on. It seemed complete, comprehensible, capable of showing whatever needs showing about the pacing and pitch and—gulp! music doesn't have to do this!—the *meaning* of the line or sentence!

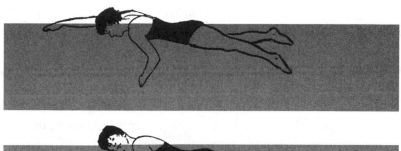

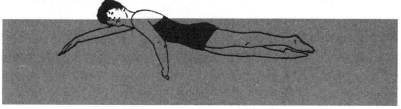

Back at the pool, I like to think of how Mrs. E interpreted the Red Cross Manual for us. She knew how to teach it—just keep this one thing in mind, your hairline meeting the line of air and water, this one time across the pool— and she had a performer's passion and vision of how, and whay, the strokes should be done. She never had us look at the diagrams in the book; the notation, it seemed, was insufficient or misleading. Nor did she ever, herself, enter the water, as if the very medium, however transparent, in which the form took place could not reveal the form. She adopted, instead, a kind of poolside grammar of talk and gesture, and coupled this with occasional transcriptions of our strokes themselves via the underwater video. And I knew when I had finally "got" the crawl, because instead of thinking about her formal tips, I began to hum underwater in hymn meter, verse after verse, lap after effortless lap, *lovely secret gardens grow / underneath the sea* (and a breath, and) …

But I was thinking about grammar. Just now. I've put an ellipsis (it always makes me think of *ellipse*, earth endlessly orbiting the sun) at the end of that breath. But really I wanted to leave it blank. Just the parenthesis floating at the end of the paragraph (and a breath, and)

Yes better

In most of the expository prose I wrote through most of school, I used a kind of ear training by which I transcribed what I heard and thought into a system of marks. The end of a thought was a dot: period. A pause, or lapping series, meant commas. An almost pause, with a kind of erudition soon to follow: a semicolon. Something that felt like breath taken in in order to blow out a candle: a colon. A dash, something—well—indeterminate, both a starting and a stopping, the ice-bound car rocked halfway up the wheel trough that falls back in and is rocked back up …

In my middle school years there was a fad of testing. If something was to be learned, we'd all take a "pre-test" to see what we already knew. Then they'd teach it to us. Then the "post-test" to see what we had learned. When it came to grammar, specifically, to punctuation, I aced the pre-test although I had no idea whatsoever about the names and rules governing the use of the various lines and hooks and dots. I was sent to the "resource center" for the duration of the lesson. And so I escaped, after that first day on sentence diagrams, learning the actual rules of punctuation. I did have a copy of the grammar book, but I never quite got around to reading it. And so for me, punctuation remained not so much a method of conveying meaning to a reader who knew the same rules, as a method of marking the way thought *sounded*. For this writer, anyway, biology recapitulated phylogeny: Unwittingly but unmistakably, I was retracing the history of punctuation in my own evolving understanding of it. Beginning as a sound-based punctuator, and only later, as a teacher of freshman comp, becoming a text-based punctuator, I seem to have revisited the history of punctuation.

Punctuation originally developed to record the sound of spoken language. In the earliest Western written tradition, *scripto continua*, like a kind of primitive children's writing, runswordstogethersothatitshardtoreadwithoutthespaces. Like a young beginning reader, one has to sound it out to get the meaning, which is just what you are supposed to do: High value was placed on oration, particularly of religious texts. A variety of punctuation marks arose over the centuries. The earliest, from Aristophanes of Byzantium in 200 B.C.E., consists of three dots of varying heights to mark a short, medium, or long pause. More elaborate systems, to capitalize a letter at the beginning of a verse, to mark beginnings and ends of passages, or to identify quotes from scriptures, began to come into use as Latin, a second, *written* language, was disseminated. (For a stunning exploration of the trials of St. Jerome, fourth-century biblical translator and inventor of many punctuation marks, see Maurya Simon's sequence "A Brief History of Punctuation.") And so punctuation begins its journey from the spoken to the written, from the elocutionary to the syntactical. But still, in England and especially Ireland, where few people were literate, basic speaking marks>>>such>>>as>>>several positura in a row or spaces between words harkened back to punctuation's elocutionary origins. By the eighth century, the period, semicolon, colon, and question mark appeared, and by the ninth century, most scribes were adding some form of punctuation to the texts they copied, though it is not until the fourteenth century that most authors punctuated their own works. The invention of the printing press both narrowed the options and regularized their uses, and Ben Jonson's *English Grammar* (1640) recommended syntactical punctuation. And so, by the seventeenth century, our basic punctuation practice was established. Punctuation exists to show us how to navigate the architecture of the written sentence. It consists, now, of marks of reading and understanding, not of how words are said or of how thought "feels." Or does it? In the poems that I will discuss in this essay, the writers seem to capture something of the exploratory sense the scribes and early authors may have felt, feeling their way with punctuation as a way to give voice, to get the sound of a passage heard by the reader, not for the purpose of syntactical understanding or clarity, but for something more elusive, something like music.

Compare the difference in the energies of consciousness (something like Coleridge's notion of a logic of the activity of thinking, of form as "proceeding") of these two poets in a moment of fresh grief:

> The clocks are sorry, the clocks are very sad.
> One stops, one goes on striking the wrong hours.
>> *(Donald Justice, from*
>> *"Psalm and Lament")*

> exactly half the phenomenal world is gone
> look you can see it take anything anything
> roses a half corona of petals red lush
> half black rot now the aching mountains Heidi
>> *(Paul Monette, from "Half Life")*

In Justice's world, things are endlessly doubled; in Monette's, endlessly halved. Time is slow for Justice, speeding for Monette. Justice's world is made up of a few familiar images; Monette's is littered almost indiscriminately with whatever things butt their way into consciousness. One is an excruciatingly ordered grief; the other an out-of-control free fall of a grief. And among the qualities of language that create, or record, these differing consciousnesses is punctuation. Justice needs a comma to divide almost every long line of his poem; the moment of each line, each experience of "now," is subdivided into two achingly similar halves: time is endless, repetitive, inescapable: the familiar world and its familiar punctuation stifle and comfort. In the passage from Monette, as the world is shattered, half of it gone, the other half crowded with images, punctuation is obliterated. It is as if the furious, uncomprehending speed of grief has wiped out all the stops and with it all the marks of consideration, pausing, ending: no punctuation: the text as a solid, uninterrupted block. He explains in the preface to *Love Alone: Eighteen Elegies for Rog*, from which this poem comes, "I wanted a form that would move with breathless speed, so I could scream if I wanted and rattle on and empty my Uzi into the air. The marbles of Greece kept coming back to mind. ... On the high bluff of ancient Thera, looking out across the southern Aegean toward Africa, my hand grazed a white marble block covered edge to edge with Greek characters, line after precise line. The marble was tilted face up to the weather, its message slowly eroding in the rain."

In these very different passages, the marks of punctuation seem to "happen"— or not happen—*as* the poem is written, not as an afterthought to elucidate the overall structure of thought. From the beginning, I always found myself tending to write this way; the marks of punctuation were a record of thinking, of writing at the speed of thought. They were (possibly, hopefully) discernible to a reader, but, at an early age, I sensed that their real value was in moving my own thought along as I wrote in ways not necessarily coherent.

It wasn't until much later, when, in my first, much-belated methods course, "Teaching Freshman Composition"—the whole subject intimidated me greatly, for I myself had no memory of ever having been taught how to write—I would finally keep my mind from wandering long enough to witness the elements of grammar, including punctuation, being reviewed (or, in my case, viewed for the first time). I found myself spirited back in time to Aristotle, to a rhetoric that displayed the coherence found in completed acts of thought. Marks of punctuation pointed out or even *created* various structures of elegant thought. This is what we were going to teach!

I warmed to the task. Why, it was like being back in beginning ear training and having someone finally analyze how, in each measure of 4/4 time, the rhythmic variations always add up to 4. I felt I was finally beginning to be an English teacher—a little more practice, and the uncertainty I'd always felt along with the rush of exhilaration at using a set of semicolons would be erased; a little more practice and I'd be ready to rub parenthetical shoulders with nuns!

Mr. Rex tried to teach us a system by which we could discover and create sentences whose architecture—and, therefore, whose meaning—would be discernible to readers. My music teachers—beginning with Mr. Miller's class for seven-year-olds in which the notes themselves wore jaunty hats—tried, in their way, to do the same. The systems of verbal and musical notations are taught as givens: Here is a comma, a slur, a clef—things the words or notes behave *according* to, as you, dear reader-writer-player, must behave. It is not my purpose here to trace the history of how these systems came to be. Nor will I chronicle the vital alternatives to these systems that exist and persist (I suspect that within a ten-mile radius of where I sit writing, someone is probably taking shorthand, or a group of someones is locked in the beautiful, visible fifths of Sacred Harp shape-note singing). Still, the basic systems of reading the notes involved in music and words are handed down to us as if there were a finished, final, and definable set of forms.

But in other fields, the accepted styles of notation are less codified, or have only recently been codified. The number of humans who can read the symbols that describe or proscribe, say, the movement through space or time or thought represented by the following dance notations is less than a grammar-school-full. Only one of the following systems, chronicled in Ann Hutchinson Guest's *Dance Notation: The Process of Recording Movement on Paper*, really caught on:

The Lilac Fairy Solo From Sleeping Beauty

Fig. 12.33 Sutton System: excerpts from classical ballet   (Courtesy Valerie Sutton)

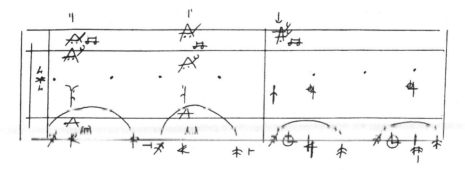

Fig. 12.5 Morris system: excerpt from Peer Gynt

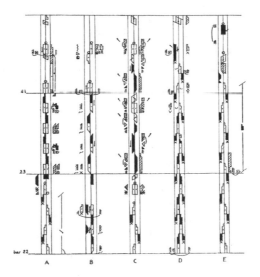

Fig. 12.10 Laban system: excerpt from "The Gentleman in Black" from the Ballet *The Green Table* by Kurt Jooss. Notated by Ann Hutchinson, 1939. (From *The New Ballet* by A. V. Coton, A. H. Guest Collection)

(The dominant system turned out to be *Laban*.)

I thought that the question of which system, which notes, to use was more or less settled with English—one does see a high degree of similarity among the notations carried on by otherwise competing freshman composition textbooks—but if we ask the "notes" to record or dictate something else about the language, say, the *spoken* language (and don't we sometimes talk about *voice* in poetry?) in a three-second sample of conversation (the length of an average line in a poem), we might need a radically different system. Here's one developed by a linguist, an anthropologist, and a psychiatrist in the 1960s to show exactly how spoken language sounds—a kind of visual tape recorder. It comes from a book called *The First Five Minutes*.

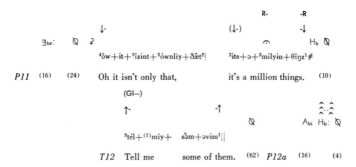

WORDS OVERFLOWN BY STARS

It turns out that this system, brilliantly thorough, was too difficult even for linguists to master and read, and so it fell out of use. Notes, it seems, not only must be accurate and suggestive, they must be readable, if not engaging. (But my poetry students were most engaged by *Sutton*, a loser system of dance notation. It was the "prettiest"; "it looks like dancers dancing!" The winning *Laban* notes seemed to them "cold"; "just a bunch of strung-out rests," one of the music-reading poets said.)

Like musical scores or the drawings of swimming strokes in the Red Cross Manual, dance notation and linguistic notation are probably just that: notes. Not the real thing. Not a form of art, or pleasure or satisfaction, in and of themselves. Those trained to read the signs read right through them—if they are done correctly, if the reader is sufficiently trained and motivated—to the thing signified. Each system contains certain elements that can be quite successfully conveyed: musical pitches and note durations, angles of arms. And each contains suggestions or approximations for interpretation: intensities, hesitancies, and, again, angles of arms. But what about the written notation we use to put a poem on paper or computer screen? Is it meant to be "read through" by the reader, taken in in that part of the brain that learned, if it was paying attention in Mr. Rex's class, just exactly what a comma means in a list, or preceding a coordinating conjunction? Learned it so well, so long ago, that we aren't even aware of reading them? Much, perhaps most, punctuation used in poems is of this type—part of a tacitly agreed-upon system known to both writer and reader, helpful in conveying "meaning" and in preventing misreading. The writer "means" this complete clause to be put as a question; we know this from the question mark that comes at the end. The question mark adds a quality of voice to the sentence—a slight rising of pitch.

A poem that uses standard punctuation in standard ways—a great many poems in the language—has a kind of outward pedigree of respectability. We come to it with certain expectations so familiar that we hardly notice having them. There are certain structures of thought likely to take place: lists made and marked with commas; questions posed and duly question-marked; ideas stated and then, after a comma, qualified; things described and (comma) re-described. The ordinary uses of punctuation—ordinary in terms of the type of marks used, their location relative to others, their overall frequency, their purpose in the syntax—are poetry's status quo.

I never noticed any of this until recently. I can still hear myself stating, restating, my worn-out maxim: "Use 'normal' punctuation unless you have a good reason to do otherwise. Don't do it just for effect." But what did I mean by "effect"? Sophomoric showiness, I suppose. The urge to imitate, to be different for the sake of it: the lowercase *i* student who reads cummings and forever after eschews capitals, was also prone, it seemed to me, to glomming on to some clever use of punctuation and doing it to death. I've never responded with much enthusiasm to form for form's own sake.

But recently, I've had to re-examine my prejudices. I came upon a writer who grabbed me by the dots: Her work led me (I see those dots on a column of dominoes, tripped, collapsing backward like a row of books, the bookend just removed, the first one tweaked) to re-examine poems by other writers, too, that show some original, or at least daring and effective uses of those familiar favorites—the comma, the period, the virgule, the dash—sometimes within a single poem or a handful of poems; sometimes in a whole body of work. In all of these poets, I have the sense that an adventurous method of using punctuation is part and parcel of a mode of thinking and speaking. It is as if, at the level of the writing, the writer is allowing some new mode, or speed, or application of feeling-to-thinking-to-music to take place, and transcribing it using familiar markings, but without self-consciousness about how the poem will look or read: After all, the marks of punctuation are just part of the "score," the visual notation, the crude written instrument to signify patterns of sound, thought, voice, pacing, time.

Although the poems that I will discuss shortly seem not to want to impress the reader with their unusual uses of standard punctuation marks, their surfaces come across as, indeed, unusual. Unlike dance or music, poems take place both in and out of time. We have the temporal poem heard at a poetry reading, but also the written poem in our hip pocket that occupies space independently of time. (I've always thought "Pocket Pals" was a perfect name for a poetry press, as if to stress the very chumminess of the visual, tactile poem.) Unlike dance notation, sheet music, or swimming diagrams, the visual event of the poem on the page is, indeed, an aspect of the art form—sometimes, *the* aspect. Whether the writer conceived of the poem in that manner or not, poems that contain unusual combinations or occurrences of punctuation *look* like they are breaking the rules. Mr. Rex is rolling his tyrannosaurus eyes. The nuns are ducking for cover. The dancer isn't sure what arm to move, the swimmer is floundering in, I hope, shallow water. No one has taught us how to read marks that do not behave like the models in our grammar books or the occurrences of daily conversation. The poems that follow do not resort to footnotes or stage directions to tell us what the marks are or how to read them. It is up to the poems themselves to bring us through and past the visual shock of new uses of old marks into some level of confidence about proceeding to read. It seems—unlike Crumb's musical score with its dense footnotes—we are meant to take the marks in as we read the poem. Perhaps that is one of the reasons these writers confine themselves to using standard marks, albeit for new purposes: The reader is already fluent in the reading of these marks, as, no doubt, the writer is already fluent. We don't need to study up. The player of Crumb's "Voice of the Whale" would have to set down the flute and memorize the footnotes, learn the piece a note or a bar at a time. Some weeks later, she might be able to play a reasonable rendition of the notation. But the reader of the poems that follow can actually sight-read these poems. The experience of the notation as a visual construct can take place simultaneously with the temporal reading. The look and the sound can "happen" in the brain at once.

But why confine ourselves to old marks? I think that if we writers were not all tied by the wrists to the finite number of buttons on our computer keyboards, and if there were a good, quick way to invent and publish our new marks, we'd see a revolution in punctuation, much like the outpouring of new symbols created to mark the new kinds of sounds, sometimes instrument-specific, in recent "art" music. I must admit, I invented a mark of punctuation. It happened many years ago, in seventh-grade social studies class. "Social studies," in "middle school," (I confess I am conscious of the quotation marks I have just put around each of those two-word phrases as conveying a kind of "wink" in the voice, and the commas I placed at the end of each dyad are also transcriptions, rather unconscious ones, of my actual voice dropping off, hesitating, sorting, before going on to the rest, but the fact that the commas are inside the quotation marks is because the grammar book says to do that: it's my acquiescence to the status quo, the invisible, hard-won agreement about symbols that is, precisely, that) (and, oh, says Mr. Rex, you'd best not put one extremely long aside inside parentheses inside this already too-long sentence, and goodness, don't put another such parenthesis after the first one or they'll lose you altogether, I am getting a B now, a C, the longer this parenthesis goes the worse the grade, I am down to the X now, the Y, the Z, those amazing interchangeables I loved in mathematics!)—and, indeed, my invented mark of punctuation, though it felt original to me, was something I would come across later, in "logic" class, and later yet, when I learned the notation secrets of chemical formulas. It was an arrow: → Oh, no key on this keyboard to type it with! (I've just had to execute the "Insert" pull-down menu, I've had to select *symbol*, click on "→," and click again on the box called *insert* (in the middle of which I had to do it all again to say what I just said, and on down the hall of mirrors into the screen—)!) I must have just come from the obligatory two-week archery unit in gym to the heat of the hourlong lecture on some particular battle of the Civil War. Mr. Peterson, I remember his name at least, had decided that "social studies," that year, would consist of a mapping, via the blackboard, and a lush accompanying description of every move in every battle in the Civil War. And we would be tested. So we had better take notes. So important was this taking of notes, of transcribing our new knowledge even as it was in the midst of entering our heads—ah, how like writing down a poem for the first time!—that he had the other teacher, Mr. O'Grady, model it for us one day by taking notes on an overhead projector as Mr. Peterson lectured. We got the idea that we'd better get it, get it *all*, down. There were things, things, things to know, but then sometime during the hour, there would be a dense passage of what had led to what: either what troop movement had caused what other troop movement, or, rarely but significantly, what had led the troops to do X or Y in the first place. These flashes of insight of historical importance would come to Mr. Peterson with such, well, speed! And one had to get it down, and one day I found myself penciling *blahblahblah → blahblahblah*. That's all I can remember. The excitement of the mark, but not the facts. The form, my form, in the heat of the moment, had outweighed the facts.

I forgot about the excitement of that moment for years, though I remembered the mark. My high school and college lecture notes are littered with it, and it means, variously, "leads to" or "because" or "for example" or, more crudely, "once you study this thing don't forget to go on to study this other thing." I think of it as notation for a kind of variable head nod, accompanied, sometimes, by a hand gesture I would later come to see as a conductor's way of moving the orchestra out of a *retard* and back, *a tempo*.

It has been my private mark for years, and I hope that my telling you about it now won't extinguish it. It won't hurt my poems, anyway, for I have never used it there, not even in first, rough, private drafts. I think that is because it is an unvoiced mark, one of head nod, hand gesture, whereas poems are so embedded, so occurring, in the language, that the kind of free-floating, fast, undetermined leading-forward thought my beloved arrow signifies cannot, finally, be written.

But isn't a lifetime of writing poems a lifetime of continually attempting to allow them to do the impossible? So I should have expected it: I came upon a poem that has my arrow in it. It accomplishes the arrow by means of an old standby, the colon—one, or a sequence of colons in a single line or sentence. The poem has an odd look: the sheer number of colons on the page, their dominance over other more commonly used marks. The poem is not punctuated in order to communicate familiar structures of syntax or ordered thought; it would not be possible to guess, just by looking at the unpunctuated text, what type of punctuation it contains, or where it goes. The poem is "Dead Doe" by Brigit Pegeen Kelly:

The doe lay dead on her back in a field of asters: no.

The doe lay dead on her back beside the school bus stop: yes.

Where we waited.
Her belly white as a cut pear. Where we waited: no: off

from where we waited: yes

at a distance: making a distance
we kept,
as we kept her dead run in sight, that we might see if she chose
to go skyward;
that we might run, too, turn tail
if she came near
and troubled our fear with presence: with ghostly blossoming: with
            the fountain's
                              unstoppable blossoming
                    and the black stain the algae makes when the water
                                            stays near.

We can take the gilt-edged strolling of the clouds: yes.
But the risen from the dead: no!

The haloey trouble-shooting of the goldfinches in the bush:
                    yes: but *in season*:

kept within bounds,

not in the pirated rows of corn,
not above the winter's pittance of river.

The doe lay dead: she lent
      her deadness to the morning, that the morning might have weight, that
            our waiting might matter: be upheld by significance: by light
                  on the rhododendron, by the ribbons the sucked mint
                                    loosed on the air.

by the treasonous gold-leaved passage of season, and you

from me/ child/ from me/

from ... not mother: no:
but the weather that would hold you: yes:

hothouse you to fattest blooms: keep you in mild unceasing rain, and
the fixed

stations of heat: like a pedaled note: or the held

breath sucked in, and stay: yes:

stay

but: no: not done: can't be:

the doe lay dead: she could
do nothing:

the dead can mother nothing ... nothing
but our sight: they mother that, whether they will or no:

they mother our looking, the gap the tongue prods when the tooth is
missing, when

fancy seeks the space.

The doe lay dead: yes: and at a distance, with her legs up and frozen,
she tricked

our vision: at a distance she was

for a moment no deer

at all

but two swans: we saw two swans
and they were fighting
or they were coupling
or they were stabbing the ground for some prize
worth nothing, but fought over, so worth *that*, worth
the fought-over glossiness: the morning's fragile-tubed glory.

And this is the soul: like it or not. Yes: the soul comes down: yes: comes
into the deer: yes: who dies: yes: and in her death twins herself into swans:
fools us with mist and accident into believing her newfound finery

and we are not afraid
though we should be

and we are not afraid as we watch her soul fly on: paired
as the soul always is: with itself:
with others.

Two swans. ...

Child. We are done for
in the most remarkable ways.

The punctuation in this poem is the marker of a kind and speed and color of thought, of shifting planes of attention, of self- and other-hood. Imagine this poem with the same appearance on the page except devoid of all punctuation. Hear the voice, the urgency, go out of it. Hear how its shifts become arbitrary, formality for its own sake. Then hear how the punctuation, restored, breathes the complicated life back in. I find particularly devastating the cadences that build up to the chopping block of "me/ child/ from me/" and then the visual silence of the stanza break and then the more articulated silence of the ellipsis— "from … not mother: no: / but the weather that would hold you: yes:"—, the free fall across these late colons now, how different from the speculative quality of the colon followed by "yes" or "no" at the poem's beginning.

There is, of course, a free use of the page here, the visual field. And the marks of punctuation have their role as visual elements in that field. And they surprise us, the obsessive use of the colon surprises us, and then we grow used to seeing it, and then we are shocked by new marks, by how the shifts turn the colons into quite something else.

This poem excites me with its freedom in using the old marks. It sends me thinking back to, or looking for, other poems that have similarly daring uses of punctuation, signature uses, for now I am afraid that after this poem I shall always think of Kelly as Queen of the Colon and I hope she won't mind that title as I mean it with all reverence. After all, it's worth a lot: the "colon" is a monetary unit in Costa Rica, worth 100 centimos. Or, if you prefer, the entrance to the Panama Canal. Among other . . .

For King of the Slash how about Etheridge Knight? Here are two approaches to his poem "Report to the Mother." Sample it first without punctuation and capitalization:

Well things be pretty bad now mother
got very little to eat
the kids got no shoes for their tiny feet
been fighting with my woman and one other
woe ain't got a cent to pay the rent

And now here's the real poem:

Well, things / be / pretty bad now, Mother—

Got very little to eat.
The kids got no shoes for their tiny feet.
Been fighting with my woman, and one / other
Woe: —Ain't got a cent to pay the rent.

Been oiling / up / my pistol too—
Tho I / be / down with the flu,
So What / are / You going to do … ?

O Mother don't sing me
To the Father to fix / it—
He will blow-it. He fails
        and kills
His sons—and / *you* / know it.

The slash (my grammar book says it is a "virgule," derived from the Latin for "small rod," but I like *slash*) sounds like a wall and a knife blade at once: something to get over / something to cut through to get the utterance out, to make sure it is heard. And it is also a kind of glue, more urgent than Bishop's "everything only connected by *and* and *and*," a kind of urgent glue as if to make sure no one seizes one word and tears it from the context of its brethren.

For the dash, Dickinson, of course. I think when I first read her I was so confused and enthralled by the density and beauty of the words that I failed to let the dashes have their way with me. Cristanne Miller's study *Emily Dickinson: A Poet's Grammar* elucidates what Miller calls a variety of "pointing marks," slanting lines that critics have divided into categories such as "angular slants, vertical slants, elongated periods, stress marks, and half-moon marks, differentiating them according to their position above, at, or below the writing line." Miller joins many editors and critics in deciding that no harm is done by reproducing all the slanting marks typographically as dashes—a notable exception being the scholar Edith Wylder, who argues in *The Last Face: Emily Dickinson's Manuscripts* that Dickinson's punctuation derives from the elocutionary marks she learned from her Amherst Academy text, Ebenezer Porter's *The Rhetorical Reader*. But when the punctuation in one line of "A Narrow Fellow in the Grass" was altered without her permission, Dickinson responded angrily: "Lest you meet my Snake and suppose I deceive it was robbed of me—defeated too of the third line by the punctuation. The third and fourth are one—I had told you I did not print—"

However she wrote them, adapting Porter's elocutionary marks or inventing her own private set of punctuation symbols, what has been lost by their standardization as a uniform dash? Her "dashes" allow the mind to move unfettered by standard logic. They show the mind at work with all its suspense and fragmentation, emphasizing the architecture of the sentence,

> Urging the feet—that would—not—fly—

or dislocating our ordinary sense of time,

> Pain—expands the Time—
> Ages coil within
> The minute Circumference
> Of a single Brain—

or breaking it altogether

> And yet—Existence—some way back—
> Stopped—struck—my ticking—through—

These dashes serve to stop the flow of time at the same time pain is said to expand it; time and pain become both large and still. In a letter, Dickinson mentions her habit of reading poems from bottom to top, so as to increase her enjoyment of them. Here is a poet concerned with time beyond, or instead of, sequence—what better mark than the dash, a kind of seesaw balanced at the very middle, equating, hesitating, balancing, disrupting the sense of the inevitable temporal? Things not normally equal can be—in eternity—aligned. Dickinson's language, in many ways predictable in its subjects, meters, and rhyme schemes, is infinitely flexible and uncertain as it addresses the infinite. Dashes are the mark of eternity, it seems—the punctuation best suited to nonsequential time. They don't move us forward to completion of an argument—how can one move forward when time itself has ceased to exist?—but hold us, shuttling, in a passionate hovering—

period. The period. The mark to end all marks. What else is there to say? You need a few to mark the ends of your several sentences. If your sentences are long, or if the poem is short, you will need only a few. If the sentences are short, or fragmentary, you'll end up with more. Squint. They make an elegant constellation on the page. Connect the dots and you will have something close to the most basic kind of map: an enunciation of the sentence-ends of the poem. But wait. More than that. I can think of poets who use a lot of them—Linda Gregg comes to mind with the sheer, fast-paced lurching out of silence of her many abrupt fragments bent like precise gymnasts over the horizontal bars of the line breaks. And look at C.D. Wright—even her name has two periods:

More Blues and the Abstract Truth

I back the car over a soft, large object;
hair appears on my chest in dreams.
The paper boy comes to collect
with a pitbull. Call Grandmother
and she says, Well you know
death is death and none other.

In the mornings we're in the dark;
even at the end of June
the zucchini keep on the sill.
Ring Grandmother for advice
and she says, O you know
I used to grow so many things.

Then there's the frequent bleeding,
the tender nipples and the rot
under the floormat. If I'm not seeing
a cold-eyed doctor it is
another gouging mechanic.
Grandmother says, Thanks to the blue rugs
and Eileen Briscoe's elms
the house stays cool.

Well. Then. You say Grandmother
let me just ask you this:
How does a body rise again and rinse
her mouth from the tap. And how
does a body put in a plum tree
or lie again on top of another body
or string a trellis. Or go on drying
the flatware. Fix rainbow trout. Grout the tile.

Buy a bag of onions. Beat an egg stiff. Yes,
how does the cat continue
to lick itself from toenail to tailhole.
And how does a body break
bread with the word when the word
has broken. Again. And. Again.
With the wine. And the loaf.
And the excellent glass
of the body. And she says,

Even. If. The. Sky. Is. Falling.
My. Peace. Rose. Is. In. Bloom.

The mark of punctuation that predominates, in this case, the period, means or expresses various things at various points. Words do this—we're used to it. But let us finally grant that the lowly dot transmogrifies according to its station. Like the dancer's, or the swimmer's, arm, its purpose depends upon the use. In the first stanza, for example, the three periods convey three different senses of closure.

The first period, concluding the two-part sentence that contains a semicolon (Horrors, Gertrude Stein would say; she railed against the semicolon, "It ties your shoes for you, it puts on your coat for you! You know perfectly well when you need to take a breath, even such a big breath!"), provides a kind of closing-down, know-it-all stop: it says that the implied cause and effect of the first two lines (something the semicolon tried to showboat) is something the speaker feels sure, final, about. The next period is more hesitant, run over by the continuation of the line into "Call Grandmother" and the sudden shift to this mode of speaking, as if Grandma backed up over the pitbull, paying him no heed. Her surety comes through even more by the time we arrive at—well, swallow down whole!—the stanza's last sentence. Here, as in all subsequent stanzas, Grandma gets the last word, and she takes for granted that she will get the last word, period. The speaker's own attempt to order and explain shows up as she repeats her last try at her own brand of a stay against confusion: her trusty logic of the simultaneous, argued for once again by the trusty but by now less trustworthy semicolon.

A little more of this back and forth between the speaker's non sequiturs in search of the sound, if not the logic, of common sense in their comfortable-length sentences, followed by Grandmother's last word, period. By stanza three, it seems that Grandma has gone into the zone where she knows it is the sound of her cadences, always rounded off with that line- and stanza-ending period, that are the real balm and compass for the speaker. "Thanks to the blue rugs / and Eileen Briscoe's elms / the house keeps cool" has nothing except the familiarity of its details and its comforting and final-sounding cadence to offer the bleeding, the tender, the gouged. And it starts to work. "Well. Then." The speaker's pattern of short, seemingly logical but disjointed reasoning gets off the track by almost mocking Grandma's use of the period. It sounds like both "Well, then!" and "Well, Then ..." at once.

As the speaker flails and yearns against the periodic elegance of Grandma's answers for everything, she whips herself into a pelting of advice that degenerates finally into "Again. And. Again." The only thing to comfort her now is for Grandma to pick up the pieces and lay them squarely on her own table with the precision of the deepest, most tested wisdom: "Even. If. The. Sky. Is. Falling. / My. Peace. Rose. Is. In. Bloom." Chicken Little meets Buddha. The sky may be falling but here is the period not to separate or conclude but to tack the roses to the page where we will have to see them. The pacing in this poem, accomplished largely by the use and placement of the period, raises that dot from the dead. I think I'll put it like a diadem in the center of my forehead until. it. is. in. bloom.

... and sing that next time I'm swimming. Every word won. Every thrust and splice of song pointed out. Or how about the opposite, Wright's "Woman Looking Through a Viewmaster," in which we get the beginnings of sentences but are denied the ends, the period made obvious by its absence, the woman eternally doomed to nothing but new starts:

> Then if the woman hadn't got off the bus
> she could be in Terrebonne Parish
> playing a squeezebox eating red peppers living
> in a stilt house learning to make gumbo praying
> to Saint Anne to get rid of her sty one night
> she'd go home with a trapper named Clothilde
> a fleet of children would pass in pirogues singing
> *nous sommes tout seul* and the song sends the girl
> mending mosquito nets to the *Holiday Magazine*
> that leaves her where she can cut a star into ice

Cut a star into the ice That makes me think of an asterisk. Cut a star/ into/ the ice: cut—a Star—

Not bad advice for how a hand enters the cold morning water before the laps begin. A dancer could do it. Or a flute. But if a poem did it, the record of doing it, the written marks that are the doing of it could, "old" and →new←, like *flowers* among f(±)lowers, be as variously beautiful as words.

ON VOICE AND REVISION

By Mark Cox

When we say a poet has a "strong voice" or has yet to "find" his or her voice, what we're really locating is a certain sense of, or lack of, authority. This authority is deeply related to style, but poets have been known to change radically in terms of their style and still display a strong, unique voice. This is because authority is related as much to vision as it is to style. No matter how conflicted the attitude or content in question, there is a multidimensional wholeness at the heart of authenticity, a relatively conscious synthesis of all the voices that make up the chorus of a person's being. We have intellectual selves, we have sexual and physical selves, we have emotional selves, we have spiritual selves; we carry with us each of the children we have been and each of the jobs we have labored at. And each "self" has its own language. When shaking the pastor's hand after church, we do not speak or carry ourselves as we would courting love at the neighborhood bar. Nor do we comport ourselves at job interviews in the same way we lean back with family or friends at the kitchen tables of our lives. So, since each self truly has its own way of speaking, its own way of emphasizing things about the world, perhaps style and authenticity are not such separate issues after all.

Voice in our lives, in our vision as writers, has to do with how we synthesize the various voices of which we are made. Voice in our writing has to do with making fictions seem real and consistent in light of our intentions. It has to do with appropriate diction, appropriate sentence structure and syntax, appropriate and well-modulated levels of emotion, and intensity between different psychological states. If the poem employs a speaker who is forty years old and who is at times during the poem looking back on something that happened when he was seven, it would be natural at points in the poem to vary perspectives and levels of diction, to seemingly get so close to that memory that the language lapses, becomes more childlike. Likewise, a harried or confused narrator might think in fragments or a dramatic, heightened tone we would not accept as direct speech.

Nor are these issues purely personal ones for a writer. Our beloved English language is itself a hybrid mongrel aching with tension and ambivalence. Our Anglo-Saxon heritage is extremely physical, offering harsh sounds and direct cadences of one- and two-syllable words: *meat* and *soul*, for instance. It is from the Anglo-Norman/Romance influence that we've been given words like *subsistence* and *ethereal*. Though one shouldn't over-generalize, it is no accident that the more intellectual diction of science and abstract thought is traced to Latin, while the diction of immediate feeling and dramatic imagery is often rooted in Old English. Our language is as comfortable with imagery, with physicality, with being grounded in the concrete world, as it is comfortable with abstract thought and reflection. Add to this the fierce desire of the American idiom to free itself from British influence, and the differences in formality that result, and you have a very volatile and energetic language. Most effective poets to one degree or another, consciously or unconsciously, use these tensions to their poems' advantage.

Revision, then, is not merely the act of shifting words around. These words and the ways in which they are arranged are the embodiment of how the author and her characters view the world. The sentence structure and syntax are actually reflections of how they exist within the flow of time. And as such, revision can lead us both into a sharpening focus of our visions and farther and farther into the unknown—into what we can't quite recognize about ourselves. Revision is the means by which we gradually gain perspective on the different facets of ourselves and by which we come to know all the many voices that must come together to create our one voice.

Another way to envision it: Revision, the experimentation with language and style, is the smoke in the bank that shows us the alarm system's laser beams. It allows us to see what is beyond us, particularly our personal limitations and patterns. Once we can see patterns of style, we can understand that they are reflections of patterns in our way of being, reflections of involuntary frames of reference so deeply ingrained in us that we don't even remember them, let alone recognize them. Viewed in this way, experimentation and revision offer us nothing less than the ability to change ourselves, to live consciously.

To my mind, my body of work is really one long poem. I see it as the record of my being in time. Sometimes I will approach that very lyrically, trying to absorb the subverbal feelings of a moment in time; other times I find myself trying to narratively pin that moment to my forensic bulletin board to understand the moment's relationship to other moments. Both modes are important to me, parts of who I am. Ultimately, on my good days, I resist my limits—I choose to take risks, to love the writing process more than what gets written, to love revision even more than the early bursts of self-expression that trigger poems. On my good days, occasionally, a voice coalesces for me and I write it down.

THE WRITER AS REVISIONARY

By Clare Rossini

The writer creates the universe of words that we call the rough draft. He or she then becomes its keeper, the little god whose task is to nudge the draft along until—how to say it? Until the burgeoning of thought and emotion are contained within language's form and music. That's a big job, because, like the big universe "out there," the rough draft has great pools of energy, complicated interconnections, and a seemingly ever-expansive form. Like the universe out there—itself a work-in-progress—a rough draft may seem craggy and obscure, its ultimate shape and meaning beyond the writer's grasp.

So often we get stuck in this process, one way or another. Successive drafts seem to be some smaller, impoverished version of the original, poor cousins to that initial fecund mass of words. Or our poems and stories and essays spin their wheels, so to speak; we work them over and over, not enlarging or deepening the material; not enlarging or deepening ourselves as writers. "It's not a work-in-progress, it's a work-in-regress," a poet friend recently complained. As for myself, for years I experienced what I'd call "final draft grief." Early versions would be full of energy, blustery and wayward—isn't that why they're called drafts? They're meant to be "inspired"—literally, "filled with wind." But my revising process at the time was essentially one of finding the vague shape of a poem in that initial outburst, and then whittling and whittling it until I was flipping commas around. The poems that resulted weren't terrible, don't get me wrong. But they seemed—how to say it—emaciated. Ghosts of the possible.

Part of the problem may be that we too soon come to think we know the poem—or at least, think we know it. "Uh-huh, I see where this one is going," we say to ourselves with relish for our authority, and then wield our pencils or delete buttons accordingly. After all, we bring to each new poem a clear sense of the poems we've written in the past as well as our assumptions about who we are as writers—that is, what a poem by _____ (fill in your name) looks like and is about. So we go about finding in the new draft a poem that's within our comfort range, one that formally or thematically covers familiar territory. In a piece about his revising process, Bill Matthews speaks of writing a first draft more "from habit" than from "a good negotiation between the poem's needs and mine." Ah—the poem's needs! Poems have needs, too! What Matthews points toward is the fact that every rough draft presents the opportunity for creating something extraordinary—a new poem that not only reinvents the poet but the human relationship with language itself. That sounds lofty, even presumptuous. But why not write large? Goodness knows there's enough comma-flipping going on.

Back to that issue of thinking we know the poem, that abortive "Eureka" that too soon turns the work-in-progress toward closure. What is needed is a drafting process that is more open-ended, one that perpetuates the sense of discovery and wonder we experience when we first begin a new piece of writing. I'd like to introduce here a term from literary history that might be of help: *defamiliarization*, a translation of the Russian word *ostranenie*, which can also be translated as "making strange." Viktor Shklovsky, one of the Russian Formalists whose writings profoundly influenced art criticism in the early twentieth century, coined the term. Along with fellow Formalists like Osip Brik and Roman Jakobson, Shklovsky was attempting to find ways to describe how the language of literature is different from more practical, day-to-day usage. In a particularly influential essay titled "Art as Technique," Shklovsky said that poems and stories use language in ways so fresh and unexpected that they break through our well-worn and habitual ways of seeing. Such language, Shklovsky said, has the ability to "defamiliarize" the objects or experiences found in literature, to make them strange, wonder-full.

Defamiliarization is a powerful concept, one that has continued to compel critics and writers alike. And I believe we can fruitfully apply the idea not just to finished works, but to the drafting process itself. It seems only sensible that, to produce poems or stories or essays that have the power of "making strange" to our readers, we must continually defamiliarize our drafts as we write them—must find strategies, or tricks, if you will, that will force us to see each successive draft freshly, to feel the same thrill of discovery that accompanied our initial foray into the work. To quote Mister Frost, "No surprise for the writer, no surprise for the reader." Such an approach may require a new way of thinking about our relationship to the work-in-progress. We are not seeking to "figure out" our drafts, to ferret out the poem or story or essay contained within the initial outpour. Instead, our task as revisionaries is to keep the drafts—and ourselves as their makers—porous, open to possibility, until the moment we pronounce the work "done." Not that I'm encouraging a writerly version of the Sisyphusian enterprise; I've suffered enough rocks up the hill not to wish such agony on another. But if we can come to each session of work wide open to "making strange," the work that results is more likely to be full-blooded, to retain the spark and vibrancy of its rough original.

What follows is a small compendium of reflections and strategies that may be helpful in thinking about the drafting process as one of "making strange." Some of the suggestions may seem to impose a prefab or overly rationalized strategy on a process which, in the Romantic view of inspiration, should be intuitive and organic. But I make these suggestions in the spirit of serious play, playful experimentation. And note that, while my remarks and examples from this point forward are especially aimed at poets and poetry (forgive my provincial view) I believe they may be generalized to any sort of writing that aspires to what we call "the lyrical."

WHEN IN DOUBT, GO FOR THE MUSIC

As part of their concentrated attention on "literariness"—that is, in what makes the language found in poems and stories different from more pragmatic uses of words—the Russian Formalists became particularly interested in the musical dimension of poetry. Shklovsky speaks of the "phonetic 'roughening' of poetic language," a quality, he notes, that Aristotle himself described as "strange and wonderful." A more contemporary thinker and critic, George Steiner, has reframed the dynamic between language and music in slightly different terms. In his *Errata: An Examined Life*, Steiner speaks of what he calls the "primal conflict" between music and language. The music of the lyric poem, the verbal libretto, the biblical passage, is meant merely to accompany the words, he says, "to ornament, to project, to underline and 'body forth' emotions, reflexes of sensibility, semantic contents ultimately linguistic." Yet, he says

> ... music and dance are of themselves primordial motions and figurations of the human spirit which declare an order of being nearer than is language to the unknown of creation. We hear, we

> perceive in them what today cosmology calls "the background noises," "the background radiation" of the primal burst out of nothingness. At the roots of grammar lies the fragmentations and, in a vital sense, diminutions of cerebral rationality, the fall of man into logic.

Therefore, Steiner asserts, music and language are "quintessentially conflictual," and when these two competing forces meet in language, the "'strangeness' or daimonia in music ... will out."

Using a vocabulary clearly influenced by Shklovsky's notion of *ostrenanie*, Steiner reminds us that, where the music is most pronounced in our drafts, the power of defamiliarization is equally pronounced, linking the work to the primordial forces that music projects. It's an assertion that takes some chutzpah, but one that nonetheless seems to explain the sway of the lyrical over us. Steiner's reflections suggest an imperative: We must reflexively prioritize music over sense, at least in the earliest version of a poem or lyrical piece of prose. For many of us, it's too easy to get caught up in the conceit, the blessed idea that precipitated the writing in the first place or emerged early on. But if Steiner—and before him, the Formalists—are right, we must hold that an insistent rhythm or compelling rhyme (whether true or slant) is a kind of sense unto itself; must see that the literal meaning of a line is often less important than the line's function as part of a larger musical passage; and revise accordingly. This is radical news indeed to the rational mind and the writers' group, both of which share the job of rooting out the inexplicable. But analyze any number of memorable poems, and you'll find that paraphrase often falters in places where the music—and the poem itself—accumulate the most power. Consider these lines of my first great poet-love, Yeats, from "Byzantium":

> Marbles of the dancing floor
> Break bitter furies of complexity,
> Those images that yet
> Fresh images beget,
> That dolphin-torn, that gong-tormented sea.

For years, I refrained from trying to figure out what these lines meant—I didn't want to reduce them to mere meaning. That same kind of delicious sensuous sound, the stuff that cries out to the viscera as much as the brain, is found in another favorite stanza, this in Heather McHugh's "A Few Licks":

Because I am lucky, I'm a glutton
for sea punishment this summer:
for the discipline of the current
    backlash, bondage

of the temporary.

"Bondage of the temporary" seems to me in the same league as Yeats's "bitter furies of complexity": It's not entirely explicable. Or at least, as we try to
reduce it to paraphrase, we discover an oxymoronic quality at the core of the
phrase. (If something is temporary, one might ask how it can be "bondage."
Doesn't bondage imply an ongoing condition? Otherwise, what is experienced
is not "bondage," but mere irritant . . .) When such an image arrives in a draft,
the brain is likely to click on: "'Bondage of the temporary' or 'bitter furies of
complexity'—what the heck is that??" It's too obscure, the brain says, it's too
abstract. And the line capsizes beneath the pressure of its interrogation.

And yet, we must trust the music in our drafts—must hear it and then
trust those lines as carrying something essential, even if it not be wholly articulated. Hear it: Sometimes that alone is difficult, we are so inclined toward
the sense-side of words. I've taken to humming my drafts aloud, at times, to
get into the musical infrastructure, or using the "ba-ba-ba" of the scat singer
to mouth the rhythms. Either tactic forces me to temporarily efface the grip
of meaning, and to experience in a physical way the musical infrastructure of
the sentences and lines.

And then what? Early in the drafting process—after draft one or two—I
often pause to extract the lines that strike my ear as having the most compelling
or insistent musicality and put them at the top of a blank page. I then examine
those lines for clues as to what seems to be the lyrical landscape of the emergent
draft—what sounds, rhythms, line-length seem most organic to it. The lines
then can be treated as paradigmatic for the work-in-progress, as carrying the
musical DNA of the embryonic poem, and the rest of the poem written to complement that music. Or the strongly lyrical passages might be woven together
to make a subsequent draft that is an utter stranger to the original. The point is
to use music as a compass for our works-in-progress, to recognize its forceful
eruption into a draft as a sign that the imagination has tapped into a rich vein.
And then, to be sure that "strangeness" is preserved as a form of content unto
itself, a "phonetic roughening," as Shklovsky says, that compels the reader's ear
and then mind into the unique vision of the story or poem.

PERSPECTIVE SHIFT

There's an apocryphal story about Picasso, one of the many anecdotes inspired by the life of this eccentric and difficult and, yes, brilliant artist. According to the story, a casual viewer asked Picasso why one of his portraits of Dora Maar looked so odd—the eyes skewed, the nose and mouth crooked. Had the great master been inspired by the principles of cubism? No, Picasso answered, this portrait was in fact quite realistic; he had painted Dora exactly as she looked when he was kissing her.

Picasso's remark implies another idea essential to Shklovsky and the Formalists: the way in which something is rendered, the "mode of expression," is critical. More specifically, Shklovsky asserts that one of the most important tools a writer has for "making strange" is to slow down, to linger over an image or effect by rendering it in complex detail, thereby allowing the reader to experience it fully. This technique of slowing down can be embodied quite literally in the scale of the poem's imagery; as in film, suddenly zooming in can break the apparent surface of the poem, startling the lines with unexpected imagery and (therefore) unexpected insight. Elizabeth Bishop is a master of such. Early on in "At the Fishhouses," she shifts away from a "big picture" image of the sea—"the heavy surface of the sea, / swelling slowly as if considering spilling over"—and then moves in close:

> The big fish tubs are completely lined
> with layers of beautiful herring scales
> and the wheelbarrows are similarly plastered
> with creamy iridescent coats of mail,
> with small iridescent flies crawling on them.

Oh my. Within a few lines, Bishop moves from the epic to the minute, from the bird's-eye view to the microscopic. And what strangeness resides in this perspective: We feel as if we have broken through to another universe of vision and meaning, a brave new world of fish scales and tiny flies, all a-glitter. The result is not only an exhilarating shift in scale, but in tempo; the poem slows down as the poet's eye renders the wheelbarrows and their decor. In Shklovsky's words, such "slowness of perception" creates a fuller experience of an object or experience: "it creates a 'vision' of the object [or experience] instead of serving as a means for knowing it." In Bishop's poem, the close-up of the wheelbarrows complements that of the sea, whose vastness is more fully experienced in contrast to the wheelbarrows' small, strange cargo.

Following Shklovsky, we might make a draft "strange" by homing in on an image, dissecting it like a specimen, in fastidious detail. In experimenting with this technique, I've learned to choose an image that doesn't seem important to what I conceive to be "the poem"—an image that the poem breezes over, that's part of the poem's wallpaper—just to keep the startle factor strong. I've gone the other direction, too, abandoning a close-up view by putting a frame around the poem and stepping outside. A poem about a character, a specific experience, or a private memory can suddenly yawn open to a bigger landscape, whether literal, historical, philosophical—you name it. In the ending to D.H. Lawrence's hermetic little poem "Elephants in the Circus," such a shift occurs. After describing in meticulous detail the delicate exertions of the circus elephants, Lawrence pulls back to the children watching the performance: "wispy, modern children, half-afraid / watch silent. The looming of the hoary, far-gone ages / is too much for them." The final lines throw into relief an insight implicit in the foregoing description: how profoundly the natural world can work on behalf of the human, and yet, how the human—"wispy," "modern," "half-afraid"—seems shrunken and small in its understanding. By suddenly enlarging the poem to include its audience, one that figuratively stands in for all of us, Lawrence "makes strange," casting the preceding details into a new light and enlarging the poem's breadth of vision.

It would be hard to pull off a poem written entirely at the level of the microcosmic or the cosmic. The fussiness of the minutiae becomes claustrophobic—we want to know what the pile-up of details points toward. And the monumental scale can quickly fade out into abstraction—our minds aren't capable or beholding Eternity or Death for long. But the interplay of perspectives—yes, in that dynamic, complexity is bred and truths are born.

A couple of revising techniques often mentioned in workshops are wholly Shklovskian in spirit and can, with a few keystrokes, enact profound changes in a poem. Readers of drafts will often suggest that a poem would work better if written in a different person, replacing the third-person *he*, for example, with the first-person *I*. It seems such an easy and obvious way to defamiliarize a work-in-progress that I now build such person-shifts into the revising process itself, and I'm often amazed at what new material erupts in the poem, how the tone changes, how my very relationship with the material shifts. To see how such pronoun shifts can play out, take a look at Yusef Komunyakaa's *Dien Cai Dau*, a book length sequence on the poet's experience of the Vietnam War. Poem to poem, Komunyakaa moves from first-person singular to second person to third person to first-person plural. These pronoun shifts give the sequence a jittery, unsettled quality, one appropriate to poems that depict a war whose enemy is elusive and whose lush tropical landscape is often as not seeded with mines. In *The Dream Songs*, John Berryman employs pronoun shifts not just poem to poem but line to line. These shifts are not merely an exhibition of poetic chutzpah but become part and parcel of Berryman's vision. By refusing to settle into a single voice or perspective, Berryman creates a poetic version of the fractured modern consciousness, one upbraided by its past, torn by competing thoughts and emotions, and riddled by external voices and realities.

Another revision technique that's familiar to experienced writers might be called "the Protean strategy," a phrase inspired by the ancient sea-deity Proteus, whose distinctive power was to regularly, willfully metamorphose. What's required here is a mechanical recasting of the poem's shape, so that one draft might be in short stanzas with long lines, another in syllabics, another in blank verse, another in stanzas of irregular length with lines of irregular length. I recommend this drafting strategy even to poets who are comfortable with a certain form—who regularly write long-lined free verse, for example, or in traditional forms. Such formal shifts quickly and easily can break the spell of the original draft and allow the writer to see the poem freshly. The power of this simple strategy was brought home again recently, as I read a new version of one of my advisee's poems. I remembered the first draft of the poem; it had a strong narrative element, which seemed to me muddy, difficult to follow. But in the new version, the poem's story was remarkably focused and clear. As I turned to my file to find the previous draft, I was taken aback; all the poet had done was to change the poem's form from longish stanzas with lines of irregular length to couplets of more regular length. Though almost nothing else in the poem had been altered, I had the uncanny feeling that I was reading a brand-new poem—and of course, I was.

I'll mention a final drafting technique in this section, another that seems in the spirit of Shklovskian perception shift. At any given time, most of us are working on groups of poems, families, so to speak, that share the same DNA or have deep, bone-level connections we may not be consciously aware of. When I'm feeling "stuck" in a draft, I have found it enormously interesting to graft stanzas from one draft to another, even to merge two such "cousin" poems together, and then to stand back and see what I've got. Talk about "making strange"! At times, the results are downright Frankensteinian. But I must say, I've always come back to the draft with a new sense of possibility, if not a few knockout lines.

BLESSED BE THE WEAK AND TRANSGRESSIVE

What do we choose to keep in a draft? What do we excise? So often we cross off the cliché, the vague, the general, the ambiguous—all aspects of language that might be harshly described as "primitive." But in the light of Shklovsky's notion of defamiliarization, perhaps the primitive is exactly what's needed. As we push our drafts toward original conceptions, toward the unfamiliar and wonderful, we should expect weak passages; they may occur exactly when we are writing beyond what we know, where we are challenged by the complexity of an emotion or trying something new, form- or subject-wise. Instead of cutting out those parts like the brown spots on an apple, we might read them more generously, see them as locating the gaps between what we are capable of saying and where our experience invites us to go. Stephen Spender once said that "Great poetry is always written by somebody straining to go beyond what he can do," a remark that segues nicely to T.S. Eliot's "Only those who will risk going too far can possibly find out how far one can go." The so-called "weak spots" in our drafts may in fact be the side effect of our testing the scope of our talent, stretching our imaginative horizons.

And sometimes, it's a matter of making the poem in which that abstraction, that cliché, works, and works beautifully. Think of Robert Lowell's "Skunk Hour":

> A car radio bleats,
> "Love, O careless Love. ..." I hear
> my ill-spirit sob in each blood cell,
> as if my hand were at its throat. ...
> I myself am hell;
> nobody's here—

"I myself am hell; / nobody's here—": "Come on, Cal," I can imagine Lowell's writers' group saying, "You're better than that." Lowell would no doubt remind his readers that his line echoes Milton's Satan, who makes the same remark when he, like Lowell, is spying on a pair of young lovers—in Satan's case, the pair is Adam and Eve. Even so, the exclamation has a melodramatic ring; it is anything but subtle. But at a crucial point in Lowell's poem, this direct, unvarnished, in-your-face declaration of alienation seems to balance perfectly the external landscape of the poem, with its strait laced imagery of "Queen Victoria's century" and the "chalk-dry and spar spire / of the Trinitarian Church."

I'm always taken by the fact that Lowell's passage begins with the car radio that "bleats." There's something transgressive about the moment, as if the poem has suddenly descended to the realm of the animal world; that verb of primitive annunciation seems to open the poem to the human bleat that follows. What I'm getting at here is that there's often a connection between what we perceive of as "weak" in our poems and what is, in fact, "transgressive," points where we cross imaginary lines in what we allow ourselves to feel, much less to write. I've always loved the notion of "the fortunate Fall," an idea that dates back to the fourth century A.C.E. According to this notion, we're darn lucky that Eve ate the forbidden fruit. Sure, Eve's act got us booted out of the Garden. But who really wanted to live in that pristine Disney World of Immortality? And the good thing about the expulsion is that it made us available, as a species, for redemption; we had to be lost in order to know the profundity of salvation.

There's a literary corollary to this that might help us as we think about our drafting process. As we write successive versions of our works, our transgressions—whether in "weak" or "clichéd" language, uncharacteristic shifts in form, outlandish experiments in voice or subject, anything that seems unnatural, or difficult, or nervy—are worth indulging, at least as a drafting strategy. Last year, I went through a phase when I took all the punctuation out of my poems—every last comma was deleted, every colon and period expunged. I'd always been a person who was big on the virtues of punctuation in ordering our poems, both for ourselves and our readers. But I was suddenly, inexplicably tired of all those little dots and curves and lines; it seemed they girdled and pressed and poked my lines and thoughts, and unnecessarily so. That transgressive phase helped me enormously. A different voice started to show up in my poems, one more distant from my literal self; she seems a personification of Shklovsky's *ostranenie*. I'm still getting to know this voice. I've also returned to the fold of punctuators, but now use the stuff more sparingly; I don't want to lose touch with this stranger, whose bleat has entered my *oeuvre*.

A few closing words. I feel I often come at my drafts full of myself, my knowledge, my experience, my ambitions, my feelings. Lately, I've tried to approach the drafting process with more of a sense of wonder and humility. The drafts are not just there to absorb and reflect who we think we are and what we think we ought to be writing about. They have lives of their own, instincts and intuitions we may be wholly ignorant of. In effect, our drafts beg us to revise ourselves—our sense of authority, our values, our beliefs about what poems are or should be, as well as their function within our culture. Each new draft is an invitation to risk and to play. Each is a stranger to us in its own way. We must learn from our drafts what they are up to, and give them free rein to become themselves, in spite of us.

"IF YOU HAVE TO BE SURE DON'T WRITE":

Poetry and Self-Doubt

By David Wojahn

Tattoos begin to lose their luster in middle age. After a couple of decades of wear and tear, even permanent ink begins to fade, and middle-aged flesh, more prone to flab and loss of muscle tone than the taut skin of youth, is apt to become a poor display case for your body art. The roses and the bluebirds and the prancing tigers sag, and soon you're wearing one of Dali's melted watches—now the incised skin shouts *tempus fugit*. A friend of mine, who has just passed the other side of fifty, has given up her habit of receiving an annual tattoo, opting for a yearly branding instead. Scarification tightens the skin, and therefore your brand will never sag. She tells me there's a wide array of designs available, should I ever want to try the procedure myself. But I'm not much interested in body art, neither tattoos nor brands, not even decals or henna. Yet I am very interested in a tattoo which my student J. has recently affixed to his left arm. He's a do-it-yourselfer, and I hadn't realized this particular pastime had many adherents outside the slammer. You could hardly liken J.'s latest creation to your average prison tattoo, however. Over the summer, for god knows how many hours, J. labored to ink into his inner arm the following passage from Paul Celan:

> A word—you know:
> a corpse.

The presentation of this is more elegant than you might think. The letters are fairly large, 14-point or thereabouts, with the *A* which begins the sentence larger still. As tattoos go, it's not really garish. But it's also unsettling. In some ways it makes sense for a tyro writer to adorn himself with verses, but J. chose a stanza from one of the most hermetic of poets, a passage that, like so much of Celan, laments the inadequacies of language. As my theorist colleagues would say, in their exasperating jargon, this "problematizes" J.'s gesture. And the more you think of it, the more curious it gets. The inner arm, you'll remember, was the place where concentration camp inmates had their numbers tattooed, the place where a sequence of digits was doubtless inked into the flesh of Celan's mother, Fritzi Antschel, and into that of his father, Leo Antschel. Did J. know about this grim ritual of the Nazis? He isn't Jewish. But how could J. *not* know, for he chose to mark himself with a passage by the most famous poet to have survived the Holocaust? I should have thought to ask about this, but seeing Celan reduced to body decoration left me too stunned. Instead, pedant that I am, I asked J. what translation of Celan he used. Hamburger? Felstiner? McHugh? And what does it mean to tattoo yourself with a translation rather than something in its original tongue? If, as Frost famously said, poetry is what gets lost in translation, is poetry then doubly lost if it is replicated in a foreign tongue, and then painstakingly etched into skin, maybe during nights of TV watching, the way other people knit? Or is something of poetry's essence even more insistently preserved in this bizarre transport? It could be argued that J. has rewritten Celan, offering up another form of translation; in a very literal sense he's made the poet's lines his own. And his version is a definitive one, a final draft; nothing short of laser surgery can remove the tattoo. J.'s text cannot be revised, only erased.

But does J. possess a text or something more akin to a trophy? "Body artists" often talk of their tattoos as souvenirs of the time and place of their execution, pointing to them in much the same way that hunters speak of the eight-point bucks they've mounted above their mantels. To think of the Celan tattoo in this manner makes J.'s decoration quite distressing. For the Nazis had their trophies too, some of them lampshades made from human skin. (And it's known that the Nazis especially valued tattooed skin; a "hide" with a tattoo embossed upon it made for a uniquely pleasing lampshade. Eichmann reportedly instructed his Auschwitz kapos to be on the lookout for inmates with interesting tattoos; they were then separated from the gas chamber-bound prisoners and executed by gunshot—Zyklon-B tended to discolor the skin and make it unsuitable for tanning.)

Of course J. will have a lot of time to consider the myriad ramifications of his Celan handiwork. And it makes me glad that I never went in for tattoos myself. But how brazen is the confidence that allowed J. his Celan. The doubts and regrets will come later: That's the way it is with youth, and the way it also is with tyro poets. But I am a middle-aged member of the middle class, and a poet in mid-career, and I must admit that something in me envies J.'s cavalier disregard for the long-term consequences of his body decoration. Yet I'm glad I'm not in my twenties anymore, glad as a writer that I'm no longer a candidate for those endlessly replicating anthologies of young, younger, or "new" poets, those monotonous gatherings of versifying by "the next genera-tion," many of whom are rarely heard of again. I can no longer decorate my body; I instead have to maintain it, following an intricate regimen of Lipitor and Wellbutrin, visits to the gym and to the shrink, annual readjustments of my bifocals, and encounters with M.D.s—or sometimes machines—skilled in the art of unpleasant probings of the lower tract. And everything is about consequences—am I making the right choices in my CREF account? How will my wife and children fare if I die in an accident? Can I really afford this Victorian white elephant of a house? As I write this I am staring at a bucket placed beneath the leak in my study ceiling. It's raining outside, and the water beats down a different sort of tattoo.

Consequences, doubts: Of these I now am made. Of course, if you're a middle-aged member of the middle class who is also a poet, such doubts are not supposed to affect your writing life. The conventional wisdom has it that literary expertise improves with age and practice. You step onto a marvelous Hegelian escalator—if you keep writing, you're supposed to get better all the time. Doubt shouldn't trouble you. I want to debunk that notion. More importantly, I want to give doubt its due, to see it not as a nagging (or relentless) occupational hazard of the writing life, but as a necessary, if unwelcome, writerly tool. And not a glamorous tool, not some garish and decorative thing engineered along the lines of Keats's negative capability, but something humbler—something versatile, functional. A doubt you must live with, put up with, and in the end learn to wield with a certain facility.

Naturally, there are various kinds of writerly doubts, some more profound than others, and ones which a writer who writes long enough will eventually learn to overcome. Call them the expected doubts, the ones to which you affix a small d. There's the doubt that assails you as you try to hammer out a first draft of a poem: As Anne Lamott bluntly asserts, you must understand that "all first drafts are shitty first drafts." It takes time to learn this lesson, but the fear that what you write is shitty attends you every time you sit down to write a poem, and it only goes away—in provisional fashion—as the drafts pile up and the poem resembles something like poetry. But over the years you learn to live with this sad fact.

There's the related but more terrifying condition of writer's block: William Stafford's cure for this was to counsel you to "lower your standards." I've always thought of Stafford as an avuncular windbag, Polonius in a cardigan sweater, but here his advice is sound, especially because Stafford insists that you cure the writer's block not simply by "lightening up" and doing free writing and improvisations, etc., but instead that you be wary of competing against "your last good poem." There is furthermore the doubt that comes from rejections—also a tough one. If you write long enough and invest the requisite emotional energy and time into the activity, you are apt to get better. You are apt to find your voice (whether that is a blessing or a curse is another question entirely). You've worked hard: Yet why are the editors and judges of the poetry book contests not recognizing your hard work? Why do the grants and book contracts and teaching jobs go to the less worthy? Perhaps it means you're not really that good after all. Your exasperation turns to envy, your envy to self-doubt and finally to self-laceration. Yesterday you felt OK about your career—the call from the Nobel committee may not have come on that particular morning, but at least you had a body of work you could take pride in. But today you're a deluded fool. You're not successful because you're not any good, and so on. It takes effort to remember that your contemporaries are all for the most part mediocre, no better and no worse than you are, that editors and grants-giving committees are schooled at best in preserving and replicating the blandest pieties of the period style, that your writing life is about your writing and not your career, that the cover of *APR* is not an indication of your arrival upon Parnassus. These are the daily doubts, the ongoing doubts, but ultimately they are trivial. You learn to write better by rewriting. You conquer writer's block by writing. You overcome careerism by attending to writing and not to career.

But you will write and write, and still it won't be good enough. You will write for years and for decades and it still won't be adequate. You fail from lack of character, you fail because the language itself may not be able to say what you want it to say, you fail from lack of talent—although lack of talent is the least likely thing to hobble a dedicated poet. For whatever the reasons, you feel that what you want to say can't be said, and what you've already said was never good enough. This condition is a crisis more profound and more terrible than writer's block or lack of recognition, and it afflicts both the most lowly and the most esteemed writers. This is the sort of doubt I want to speak of here, and try to demystify. This is not an easy task, as you will see.

I want to begin with Ivor Gurney, a figure almost wholly unread in America, but well regarded in his native Britain. As with Wilfred Owen, Siegfried
Sassoon, Robert Graves, and Edmund Blunden, Gurney served in the trenches,
and saw more than his share of horror. He was wounded in action, gassed at
Paschendale, and finally discharged after a mental breakdown—or "deferred
shell-shock," as it was called in those days. Like his fellow war poets, his aesthetic affinities are with the Georgians rather than the modernists, and even
within his most horrific descriptions of battlefield carnage he presents some
oddly bucolic interludes. The spirit of merrie olde England always prevails. In
"First Time In," a group of fresh recruits are met in the trenches by a welcoming
committee of crooning Welshmen:

> and there the boys gave us kind welcome,
> So that we looked out as from the edge of home.
> Sang us Welsh things, and changed all former notions
> To human hopeful things. And the next day's guns,
> Nor any line-pangs ever quite could blot out
> That strangely beautiful entry to war's rout;
> Candles they gave us, precious and shared-over rations—
> Ulysses found little more in his wanderings without doubt.
> "David of the White Rock" and the "Slumber Song" so soft, and
>   that
> Beautiful tune to which roguish words by Welsh pit boys
> Are sung—but never the more beautiful than there under the
>   guns' noise.

We can't help but wonder what those "roguish" lyrics might have been, but they
seem roughly equivalent to the "dirty" version of "Louie, Louie." Of course,
"roguish" words can only be alluded to rather than quoted in a poem such as
this. The tone is tender and consoling, but to contemporary readers it seems
a bit schmaltzy. Not schmaltzy at all, however, are many of the poems from
the later years of Gurney's career. Gurney's poetry and music compositions
brought him a brief period of success in the early twenties, but his mental illness worsened. From 1922 until his death in 1937, Gurney was an inmate at
the City of London Mental Hospital, and, following in the tradition of British
poets such as Christopher Smart and John Clare, the asylum became a kind of
writer's retreat for him. He wrote steadily, both music and poems, and penned
unsuccessful "appeals" for his release. Certain of these poems have a truncated

majesty reminiscent of Dickinson. They share, too, Dickinson's penchant for tonal reversals. The eight-line "Between the Boughs" begins with a bittersweet stanza that evokes all the watered-down Romanticism that makes the writings of the Georgians so dated. The speaker recalls two lovers staring at a night sky of "numberless stars" glimpsed among leaves "wonderful in blackness." We expect the rest of the poem to continue along these lines; soon the author will grow wistful and nostalgic, and doubtless will pine for his lost love. What, he asks, could possibly diminish the lovers' reveries? By line seven we have our answer, a telegraphic vision of dread: "The aloofness, the dread of starry majesties / The night-stilled trees." How puny these lovers seem beneath the vast impersonality of the stars. Why say anything more?

Gurney's later poems do not so much subvert our expectations as they deride them through their brusqueness. Familiar lyric premises are set forth, but the poet refuses to develop them. The initial couplet of "April Gale" seems to promise some predictable conceit-making, but the poem barely gets going before Gurney says to hell with it. We find the speaker and Rover on an amble through a spring field. The wind frightens poor Rover, but the speaker delights in the gale—that is, until the poem's fourth and final line. Suddenly Gurney confesses that "My coat's a demon, torturing like life." The awkwardness of this closing does not allow us to see it as a sudden insight: A haiku this is not. The end of the poem does not make what Robert Bly used to call an associative "leap"; instead it seems to bypass—out of impatience and exasperation—the methodologies of traditional conceit making. It's as if Gurney began to write a sonnet but by line four lost faith in his project. The fourth line, clumsy as it may be, has a certain abject bravery. "Why not dispel the lies of mere neat poetry?" it seems to say. Why take fourteen lines to tell you my life feels like torture? Read in this way, many of Gurney's poems look less like botched efforts at lyrics in the manner of Graves or Edward Thomas and more like harbingers of postmodernism. Fractured, often seeming to stutter, thanks to their syntactical inversions and belabored rhymes, and time and again lamenting the insufficiency of the lyric impulse and of language itself, certain of Gurney's later poems very much resemble those of Celan—although I doubt if "April Gale" will ever be etched into somebody's arm. Poems are repeatedly seen as "embers of a dream," "scrawls on a vain page," and "the sentimental fib of light and day." Lest my analogy seem far-fetched, let me turn my attention to "Moments," another eight-line poem, and one which has haunted me for years. Here the "loathed minutes" of daily life serve only to remind the speaker of his existential despair and mortality. They can do nothing but point to "that six-foot length I must lie in." Only death will bring him a kind of solace; only then will he not "grieve again / Because high autumn goes beyond my pen / And snow lies inexprest in the deep lane."

Unlike "April Gale," which ends before the writer can tell us the source of his suffering, Gurney here makes a very specific claim—*writing* is the cause of his problems. Upon first encountering "Moments," a reader is likely to misread its conclusion: Typing the poem just now, I wrote "unexpressed" for Gurney's oddly anachronistic "inexprest." But the difference between the two words is significant. "Unexpressed" can mean "unattempted," as in "I never tried to tell you what the snow looked like." "Inexprest" suggests inadequacy: "I tried many times, but I never got my descriptions to sound right," completing the trope that begins in the previous line. Failure is the issue here, not mere writer's block.

Like Hölderlin in his later poetry—work that also emerges from years of acute mental anguish—in the final phase of his career Gurney replaces lyric polish with writing that is fragmentary, piecemeal, stunted. Yet, these final unfinished efforts remain their writers' most interesting and resonant work. Is it their madness that speaks to us in their late poems, a force that prevents the authors from writing in the manner they once did? Perhaps to some degree it is. But along with their madness Gurney and Hölderlin were bestowed with the dubious gift of an acuity that sometimes comes with bereavement and self-doubt.

But neither poet was able to go beyond that acuity and wrest from his bereavement and doubt something larger, and even transformative. Gurney, like many writers of the past century, arrived at an aesthetic based upon permanent crisis. Confusion and uncertainty were never resolved over the course of his career; instead, the confusion and uncertainty intensified. But there are other writers who are able to face such traumas and learn to partially overcome them. Their doubts do not stunt their writing; in fact, their writing may be deepened by their doubts.

Often this deepening is the result of a poetic midlife crisis. In mid-career, "in the middle of life's journey," the author renounces his or her early work, and seeks to write from a totally new perspective. Dante famously ends *La Vita Nuova* with the statement that his praise of Beatrice has been inadequate, and that he cannot write of her again until he has relearned the craft of poetry. This knowledge, Dante tells us, comes literally in the form of a vision, one which arrives after he has written the highly self-questioning sonnet that appears in the penultimate section of the book. "A strange new understanding that sad Love / imparts" has occurred for Dante, but he "cannot understand the subtle words / it speaks." The final section gives us a Dante who is chastened and humbled, who tells us that Beatrice is the great subject of his writing, but that he is not yet capable of writing of her in the way that he must: "After this sonnet there appeared to me a vision in which I saw things that made me resolve to say no more about this blessed one until I would be capable of writing about her in a more worthy fashion. And to achieve this I am striving as hard as I can . . ." But a few lines later the tone shifts, suggesting ambition and even arrogance: "I hope to write of her that which has never been written of any woman." Beatrice may indeed be "inexprest" here, but the book ends with what Dante biographer R.W.B. Lewis calls "the foreshadowing of some enormous poetic endeavor." Yet Dante suggests that this new project can only be achieved through a total renunciation of his earlier poetic self. As if to make this point absolutely clear, early manuscripts of *La Vita Nuova* conclude with the medieval equivalent of a film's closing credits:

HERE ENDS

THE

NEW LIFE

OF

DANTE ALIGHIERI

The new life is in reality the old life, and it is over. Dante completed this book around 1295; the first cantos of the *Comedia* date from around 1309. Obviously the project of learning to write about Beatrice as no woman has ever been written of before took Dante a good bit of time. When Dante first encounters Beatrice in Canto XXX of *The Purgatorio*, she berates him about his failings of character, while at the same time slyly alluding to the inadequacies of *La Vita Nuova*:

> ... such, potentially, was this man
> in his new life, that every right disposition
> would have come to marvelous proof in him,

> but the more vigor there is in the ground
> the more rank and tangled grows the land
> if the seed is bad and tilling left undone.

Even on the threshold of paradise, Dante is reminded that he cannot leave his old selves and his old writings completely behind. Even in his renunciation of them, he understands that they must be grafted to his new self and new poetic project, grafted not in a fashion which bespeaks triumph, but instead with a sense of ongoing crisis and uncertainty. The transformation can never be complete.

American culture is of course reluctant to admit to the sorts of unease that the example of Dante suggests are inherent to writerly self-transformation. One of America's enduring myths is that you can truly make yourself over, that Gatsby will never be Jay Gatz again, nor John Wayne be Marion Morrison. This myth has become such a received truth that we even apply it to poets' careers, most egregiously to many of the poets who matured in the late 1950s and early 1960s: Robert Lowell, W.S. Merwin, Adrienne Rich, James Wright, and Hayden Carruth, to name the more obvious examples. Schooled in the impersonal academic formalism of the New Critics, these writers offered debut collections buffed to a glossy high modernist sheen, whether it is, in the case of Wright and Rich, a modernism deriving from Frost and Robinson, or in the case of Lowell a more cantankerous modernism following in the lines of Eliot and Hopkins. The conventional wisdom attests that this group soon left the frigidity of high modernism completely behind, Merwin and Wright making themselves over as Deep Image writers, Lowell and Rich as writers of a confessional mode, and so on. In reality, these changes were never the radical departures that critics saw them to be at the time, neither thematically nor formally. For example, Lowell in *Life Studies* and Rich in *Snapshots of a Daughter-in-Law* practice a kind of autobiographical poetry that had been already been published in the 1950s by writers as different from one another as Allen Ginsberg, W.D. Snodgrass, and Robert Penn Warren. Furthermore Lowell, Wright, and Carruth never entirely abandoned rhyme and meter for free verse. There are a fair number of poems in traditional form in every one of Wright's books, and Lowell's 1967 volume, *Near the Ocean*, is written largely in tetrameter couplets modeled on Marvell. In an interview published shortly after the publication of *Life Studies*, Lowell allowed that his new work did not represent a conversion to open forms: "I seesaw between something highly metrical and something free." More importantly, though, these writers changed their methods slowly, unmethodically, and often at significant personal cost. At certain points in the 1960s Wright and Carruth were unable to write at all. "My writing was at a dead end," says Carruth, "themes scrambled and uncertain, sense of a creative locus hopelessly lost." And Wright's now-legendary break with tradition between his second volume, *Saint Judas* (1959), and the Deep Image free verse of *The Branch Will Not Break* (1963) has been shown by the poet-critic Kevin Stein to be an exhausting process. Midway during the four years that passed between the publication of these two books, Wright submitted to his publisher a volume with a singularly unpromising title, *The Amenities of Stone* (he had earlier given the book an even more unfortunate title, *Now I Have Awakened*), containing a mixture of poems in his early formalist manner and efforts in his later Deep Image mode. But after the book was accepted Wright got cold feet and withdrew the manuscript. In examining Wright's papers, Stein gives us a portrait of a writer afflicted with grave uncertainties about his writing:

> Doubting a poem's worth was not uncommon for Wright. He was not easily satisfied with what he produced, be it a single poem or a collection of verse. Between 1959 and 1963 Wright did not work on *Amenities* alone; in fact, he tinkered with no less than six separate manuscripts in that period, placing side by side and in myriad combinations some 113 different poems in that four-year span. Various tables of contents reveal that twenty-eight of the forty-five poems in *Branch* originate as early as early as the previously mentioned 1960 manuscript *Now I Have Awakened*, and in the March 1961 draft of *Amenities*. Thus, it would seem that Wright's struggle was equally a matter of learning to write some new style, and a slow process of eliminating from his manuscript those poems that did not stylistically cohere with the Deep Image poems which later formed the crux of *Branch*.

Wright never fully abandoned his early style, and he continued to engage in an aesthetic and stylistic argument with his early manner throughout his career. "Saint Judas," the heretical retelling of the biblical story that is the title poem of Wright's second collection, is later alluded to and critiqued in Wright's 1972 volume, *Two Citizens*. Yet "Son of Judas" compares poorly with its predecessor. The earlier poem makes Judas a tragic figure, an existential hero in the manner of the outcasts and loners who populate Wright's other poems of the 1950s; it is also an impeccably written hybrid sonnet. "Son of Judas," by contrast, seems to grope for both a form and clear sense of purpose. Wright specifically alludes to several of his earlier poems—in addition to "Saint Judas," he references "A Blessing" and "To the Muse"—but the poem neither stands on its own nor enlarges our understanding of these earlier Wright efforts. But, as in the case of Dante's reappraisals of *La Vita Nuova*, we sense that Wright's project in the poem is an ambivalent one—he must deny the significance of his earlier writing while at the same time asserting that it predicts the directions his new work will take. Such a process does not always make for successful poetry, but it can frequently invest a new sort of urgency and a more rigorous self-appraisal in the career of a "writer of a certain age."

In the pages that follow, I want to examine some individual poems by three writers who in mid or late career address their self-doubt in a fashion similar to Wright's, but who do so in poems that are of greater interest than "Son of Judas." The three poems, by Robert Lowell, Larry Levis, and W.S. Merwin, have much in common. Each is a kind of *ars poetica*, explicitly or implicitly alluding to its writer's earlier poetry and aesthetic presuppositions—and often doing so in a decidedly harsh fashion. The poems do not seek to deny their writers' earlier productions as much as they hope to reconfigure the early work in the context of a new and considerably altered aesthetic. They are, like all *ars poeticas*, aesthetic credos, but in this case they are written not to articulate their authors' belief in poetry, but to *reassert* it. They are poems in the manner of Dante's "strange new understanding."

"I am tired. Everyone's tired of my turmoil." So ends "Eye and Tooth," a stark lyric from Lowell's 1964 volume, *For the Union Dead*. Unlike the often lapidary poems of childhood and family history found in Lowell's earlier and most famous collection, *Life Studies,* the poems of *For the Union Dead* are jagged and relentless—the lines are short and the writing lurches from baroquely intricate metaphors to bald statements such as the one above. But of course the turmoil in his life and writing continued onward through the various editions of his *Notebook* sonnets and into the frequently awkward efforts of his final volume, 1977's *Day by Day.* This collection, however, contains one of Lowell's most compelling individual lyrics, its final poem, "Epilogue."

The voice of the poem is plaintive. Lowell begins by asking why the "blessèd structures" of "plot and rhyme" can no longer serve him as he attempts to create "something imagined, not recalled." He seems to lament his entire oeuvre, bemoaning that it seems merely snapshot-like, "heightened from life / yet paralyzed by fact." He immediately retracts this statement, however. "Why not say what happened?" he asks. But factual truth is seen by the end of the poem as something far different from the often self-lacerating autobiographical writing we associate with Lowell:

> Pray for the grace of accuracy
> Vermeer gave to the sun's illumination

> stealing like the tide across a map
> to his girl solid with yearning.
> We are poor passing facts,
> warned by that to give
> each figure in the photograph
> his living name.

Day by Day is a valedictory collection, steeped in elegiac feeling; one senses that Lowell suspected this book would be his last. Lowell pays homage to friends and fellow writers, living and dead, among them John Berryman, Peter Taylor, and Robert Penn Warren, and mourns the collapse of his second marriage, to novelist Elizabeth Hardwick. He also paints a quietly turbulent picture of his marriage to Lady Caroline Blackwood, for whom he had left Hardwick. Lowell's previous two collections, *The Dolphin* and *For Lizzie and Harriet*, tell the tale of this triangle, but they are agonized and unseemly books; their tone is one of manic relentlessness. A more subdued ambivalence prevails in *Day by Day*. In writing of the collection, Richard Tillinghast astutely observes that "in poem after poem, [Lowell] says goodbye not only to friends but to old ideas—the ruling ideas of his time. He continues to feel ambivalent about the third of his troubled marriages. Ambivalence was Lowell's characteristic stance—a stance that positioned him to embody many of the conflicts of his period." This remark helps us to understand the curious unease with which most readers will likely approach "Epilogue." Lowell was a supreme rhetorician; a casual tonal authority prevails in the lines, as it does in so many of Lowell's other poems. But here the meditation bristles with anxiousness; contradictions abound. No sooner does the writer make a statement than he begins to nullify it. Like Yeats, whose mixture of rhetorical swagger and acutely self-conscious ambivalence colors so many of his lines, Lowell has an uncanny capacity to wrest memorable statement from conflictedness. As Tillinghast notes, "the sense of 'Epilogue' becomes problematic almost immediately." Within the space of scarcely a dozen lines the author announces his allegiance not to memory but to the imagination, ascribes a quotation to himself to illustrate what he means (*"the painter's vision is not a lens, / it trembles to caress the light"*), criticizes the Polaroid-like tendency of his previous work, but then reverses himself: "All's misalliance," the quasi-Shakespearean interjection that occurs in the middle of the poem, seems especially fitting commentary on Lowell's jittery shuffling between dichotomies. The poem also manages to allude to the various earlier poetic incarnations of Robert Lowell—the formalism of the early poems, the severely "plotted" monologues of *The Mills of the Kava-naughs*, the recollective verse of *Life Studies*, and the reportorially immediate *Notebook* sonnets—all with a rueful tenderness. He is weary of these earlier selves, but is not seeking to completely disown them now that he is, as he puts it in "Thanks-Offering for Recovery" (the poem which appears immediately before "Epilogue"), "free of the unshakable terror that made me write …" Yet how does Lowell resolve his divided feelings toward his work, and the similar conflicts that now so trouble him? Like Proust, another writer preoccupied with the seemingly insoluble division between recollection and imagination, Lowell turns to the painter Vermeer. The canvas to which Lowell alludes is one of the painter's most haunting and enigmatic ones, "Woman in Blue Reading a Letter," in which the light indeed appears to be "stealing like a tide across a map" behind its subject. *Plot* is "of no help" as we attempt to narrativize the painting—the girl, in profile and likely pregnant, holds a letter in her hand; on a table, atop the letter's envelope, glows a string of pearls. Richly implicit, the scene is, in the words of critic Edward Snow, "one of unresolved yet almost viscerally enforced contradictions." This rendering of delicate stasis may be the "grace of accuracy" that Lowell seeks in line seventeen of the poem, for the poet appears to regard the painting as a "snapshot" that avoids the pitfall of being "heightened from life but paralyzed by fact." (It is worth remembering that Vermeer likely painted with the aid of a *camera obscura*—the paintings were in this respect a kind of ur-Polaroid.) With this invocation of Vermeer, Lowell suggests he now must renew his artistry not by continuing the relentlessly personal writing for which he had become so justly famous, but by seeking a more intricate form of autobiography, one self-transcending but not self-negating. Despite the typically Lowellian agonies that prompt the poem, it ends on a note of quiet jubilation, a quality Alan Williamson finds in many of the poems of *Day by Day*: "A curious, joyful feeling of being—not in the ordinary sense—beside himself, beside his own life." One wonders if Lowell, who knew his century's literature better than almost anyone, had in mind as he reached the closing of his poem the famous reverie about Vermeer that Proust offers near the end of his novel:

> Thanks to art, instead of seeing one world only, our own, we see the world multiply itself and we have at our disposal as many worlds as there are original artists, worlds more different from the other than those which revolve in infinite space, worlds which, centuries after the extinction of the fire from which their light first

> emanated, whether it is called Rembrandt or Vermeer, send us
> still each one its special radiance.

The Lowell of "Epilogue," the writer who seeks to send us not his history but his "special radiance," is a Lowell we have not seen before, a Lowell who, as he puts it in "Thanks-Offering for Recovery," "was created to be given away." How regrettable it is that he was not permitted to live long enough to exercise this new understanding.

Larry Levis did not live long enough, either, and with his death in 1996 at the age of forty-nine, American poetry lost a writer who might well have grown to be a figure of Lowell's stature. Although Levis's aesthetic allegiances were to writers other than Lowell, most notably the European and Latin American poets of the surrealist tradition, to whom he pays homage in several of his poems, he shared with Lowell a capacity for unsparing self-examination, and the autobiography that emerges in his poems also seems to share something of the older poet's "turmoil." Like Lowell, Levis often writes in response to domestic trauma—divorce, the deaths of parents and loved ones. He shares Lowell's outrage at social injustice as well, and as a writer keenly aware of his rural working-class roots, he is blessedly free of Lowell's elitism. But the trait Levis most acutely shares with Lowell is a searing ability to convey the experience of personal apocalypse—of the tumult that characterizes Lowell's "Eye and Tooth" and "Skunk Hour." In "The Two Trees," the poem that opens his posthumously published *Elegy*, Levis describes a midlife crisis, a *noche oscura*, replete with rueful allusions to the opening of *The Inferno*:

> Friends, in the middle of this life, I was embraced
> By failure. It clung to me & did not let go.
> When I ran, brother limitation raced
>
> Beside me like a shadow ...

The poet's "only acquaintances" are a pair of trees, which come to seem emblematic of the breach that exists between the speaker and the world: They perform much the same function as the skunk and her young do in the conclusion of Lowell's poem. Here are Levis's concluding lines:

> One, that seemed frail, but was really
>
> Oblivious to everything. Simply oblivious to it,
> With the pale leaves climbing one side of it,

An obscure sheen in them,

And the other side, for some reason, black, bare,
The same, almost irresistible, carved indifference

In the shape of its limbs

As if someone's cries for help
Had been muffled by them once, concealed there,

Her white flesh just underneath the slowly peeling bark

—while the joggers swerved around me & I stared—

Still tempting me to step in, find her,

And possess her completely.

This is a devastating poem, but I am more interested in another effort from *Elegy*, a poem which more obliquely addresses the doubt that informs "The Two Trees" and so many of the rest of the collection's efforts. "The Poem Returning as an Invisible Wren to the World" is a strangely majestic meditation on poetry's power to transform consciousness and solace human tragedy. It makes these claims while at the same time acknowledging poetry's insignificance within history and its inability to cure injustice. Almost as significantly, it achieves all this by rewriting one of Levis's earliest published efforts, "The Poem You Asked For."

Let me begin with the latter poem, first published in 1972 and typical of the neo-surrealist mode so fashionable in the 1970s. "The poem you asked for" is personified, alternately, as a kind of fickle muse, a precious stone, a bird, or an animal: "My poem would eat nothing. / I tried giving it water / but it said no, / … I held it up to the light, / turning it over, / but it only pressed its lips / more tightly together. / / … I cupped it in / / my hands, and carried it gently / out into the soft air, into the / evening traffic, wondering how / / to end things between us." By the end of the piece the "poem" has grown more decisive and strong, but abandons the speaker, instead "going / over to your place." It's the sort of effort you can read in any number of Charles Simic or Gregory Orr poems of the period. The short lines are neatly parsed and only rarely enjambed, but the clarity of presentation is meant to counterpoint the poem's essential mystery. Levis is careful to make the conceit spacious, never letting his personified poem remain in any one of its incarnations for long. By the final lines, we well understand that Levis's personified poem is a metaphor for something, perhaps the essential ineffability of poetic creation; the poem is finally about the poet's surrender to meaning's changeability and precariousness. Yet ultimately the poem is arch and formulaic. Of course, we might expect to encounter such problems in the work of a poet barely out of his teens. Twenty or more years later, Levis employs nearly identical conceits and rhetorical strategies for "The Poem Returning as an Invisible Wren to the World." Again, poetry is personified as a mutable and shape-shifting force. Here are the opening stanzas:

> Once, there was a poem. No one read it & the poem
> Grew wise. It grew wise & then it grew thin,
> No one could see it perched on the woman's
> Small shoulders as she went on working beside
>
> The gray conveyer belt with the others.
> No one saw the poem take the shape of a wren,
> A wren you could look through like a window,
> And see all the bitterness of the world
>
> In the long line of shoulders & faces bending
> Over the gleaming, machined parts that passed
> Before them, the faces transformed by the grace
> And ferocity of a wren, a wren you could look
>
> Through, like a lens, to see them working there.

Levis replaces the surrealism of his earlier poem with a different approach to fantasy, with a fabular narration akin to magical realism. In contrast to the vapory imagistic transformations that "poetry" undergoes in "The Poem You Asked For," here it is seen as a force informed by paradox rather than by mystery. As it grows more insubstantial, it also grows wise, becoming the lens through which we may distinguish not only the woman factory worker and her partners on the assembly line, but "all the bitterness of the world." The force of poetry is thus sacrificial, destroying itself in the process of presenting the clarity it seeks to reveal. And this is not a clarity that aims to console us through a palliative Romanticism. The final stanzas of the poem are insistent upon this point:

This is not about how she threw herself into the river,
For she didn't, nor is it about the way her breasts
Looked in moonlight, nor about moonlight at all.

This is about the surviving curve of the bridge
Where she listened to the river whispering to her,
When the wren flew off & left her there,
With the knowledge of it singing in her blood.

By which the wind avenges. By which the rain avenges.
By which even the limb of a dead tree leaning
Above the white, swirling mouth of an eddy
In the river that once ran beside the factory window

Where she once worked, shall be remembered
When the dead come back, & take their places
Beside her on the line, & the gray conveyor belt
Starts up with its raspy hum again. Like a heaven's.

The metaphorical transformations the poem makes are complicated, partly because, like Lowell in "Epilogue," Levis seeks to divest himself and his readers of all of the conventionally Romantic preconceptions of poetry's mission. The factory worker does not throw herself into the river, and Levis refuses to traffic in the imagery of clichéd surrealist decoration—the poem is not "about moonlight at all." When the "invisible wren" of poetry departs from the poem, we are left with a scene of abjection. Moonlight does not survive, but the "curve of the bridge" and the "limb of a dead tree" do. The poem's final images describe a strangely desolate resurrection, a scene made visionary by the sheer intensity of its pitilessness. Yet it is this very quality that gives the poem its urgency, suggesting a perspective beyond uncertainty, of a curious imaginative triumph in its glimpse of *thanatos*. It's the stance we encounter in such late poems of Wallace Stevens as "The Plain Sense of Things," where the abandoned mansion, "the great pond and its waste of the lilies ... / Had to be imagined as an inevitable knowledge, / Required, as a necessity requires." Levis refuses to charm us, refuses to offer the tidy blandishments we might have expected from his earlier self.

But this is not to imply that the cure for our doubts is merely to reconcile ourselves with mortality. Perhaps doubt is also mitigated by a reconciliation with our past selves, and "Poem Returning as an Invisible Wren to the World" implies this as well: It is not a recapitulation of one of Levis's early poems as much as a reconstitution, and therefore an act of acceptance—the prodigal poem returning, forgiven and renewed. In "mid-career" and beyond, such perspectives are now possible for a poet, and a new kind of self-integration may arise in one's writing as a result. While attempts to correct or improve one's earlier selves are likely to fail—think of the aged Wordsworth's disastrous attempts to rewrite the poems of his youth—perhaps it is possible to glimpse as never before the multiplicity of selves that make up a writing career: and possible to write for all of those selves, past and present both. This seems to be the task W.S. Merwin sets for himself in his astonishing "Berryman," a poem which manages to be a kind of Horatian *ars poetica*, a memoir of Berryman as teacher and mentor, and a retrospective self-portrait. And as for doubt, Merwin speaks of it straightforwardly and eloquently.

Merwin invokes Berryman "in the days before the beard / and the drink," when he was Merwin's teacher at Princeton. The portrait is a mixture of affection and awe. The advice Berryman offers the youthful Merwin about his poetic aspirations is sometimes grandiose, sometime merely eccentric. He counsels Merwin to "never lose [his] arrogance," and to "paper his wall" with rejection slips. He suggests that Merwin pray to the muse for guidance "and he / said he meant it literally." But the closing of the poem offers some chilling advice:

> I had hardly begun to read
> I asked him how can you ever be sure
> that what you write is really
> any good at all and he said you can't
>
> you can't you never can be sure
> you die without knowing
> whether anything you wrote was any good
> if you have to be sure don't write

All morning the page was blank. Yesterday, too, the notebook leaves were empty, and the day before that as well. But as morning turned to afternoon, I was able to put down onto the page a few lines that seemed to me interesting enough to return to later. Now it is later, and I've spent the afternoon telling graduate students why their poems worked or didn't work. Outside the streetlights have come on, and the snow predicted all week is finally upon us. The grimly intractable pewter of the sky is now going dark. I open the notebook to this morning's lines—or are they this *week's* lines? or the lines that the years and decades have always been leading me toward?—and they seem to me dull, static, derivative. Tomorrow I will have to start again. And it occurs to me that for weeks I have written about doubt while avoiding any discussion of my own doubts. How could I show you these mornings of silence, culminating in these paltry few lines, and the panic or fear or self-loathing that is this moment? And what point would there be in sharing this with you? Neither the lines nor the sharing are poetry, although perhaps at some point the mornings and the silences and the gracelessly stuttering lines will coalesce into something that might become poetry, and be worthy enough to present to you. But how do I know they will coalesce? Perhaps I have no new poems to write, and can present to you only shards and fragments, glinting pieces of the vessels which once were my poetry, but which neither you nor I can hope to reconstruct. For one thing I do know about verse is that it is perishable, friable, and sometimes made precious because of this, whether it is written on paper or with pixels on glowing screens, or inked into human skin. That it can be written at all is astonishing, and that it can survive its writing is astonishing as well.

NOTES ON THE ESSAYS

BEFORE WE GET STARTED, by Bret Lott

Baxter, Charles. "Kiss Away." In *Believers* (New York: Pantheon, 1997).

Carver, Raymond. "Where I'm Calling From." In *Where I'm Calling From: Selected Stories* (New York: Vintage, 1989).

James, Henry. *The Art of the Novel* (New York: Scribner's, 1962).

O'Connor, Flannery. "A Good Man Is Hard to Find." In *The Complete Stories* (New York: Farrar, Straus and Giroux, 1981).

_____, "The Nature and Aim of Fiction." In *Mystery and Manners* (New York: Farrar, Straus and Giroux, 1969).

THE GIRL I WAS, THE WOMAN I HAVE BECOME: FICTION'S REMINISCENT NARRATORS, by Ellen Lesser

Ishiguro, Kazuo. *The Remains of the Day* (New York: Knopf, 1989).

McDermott, Alice. *That Night* (New York: Harper & Row, 1988).

O'Brien, Edna. "The Connor Girls." In *A Fanatic Heart: Selected Stories of Edna O'Brien* (New York: Farrar, Straus, and Giroux, 1984).

Schwartz, Lynne Sharon. *Leaving Brooklyn* (Boston: Houghton Mifflin, 1989).

Smiley, Jane. *Ordinary Love & Good Will* (New York: Knopf, 1989).

Wetherell, W.D. "What Peter Saw." *In Hyannis Boat and Other Stories* (New York: Little, Brown, 1989).

FROM LONG SHOTS TO X-RAYS: DISTANCE AND POINT OF VIEW IN FICTION, by David Jauss

Baxter, Charles. "Media Event." In *Through the Safety Net* (New York: Penguin, 1986).

Booth, Wayne C. *The Rhetoric of Fiction* (Chicago: The University of Chicago Press, 1961).

Bowen, Elizabeth. "The Demon Lover." In *The Collected Stories of Elizabeth Bowen* (New York: Vintage, 1982).

Brockmeier, Kevin. "These Hands." In *Things That Fall From the Sky* (New York: Vintage, 2002).

Burroway, Janet. *Writing Fiction: A Guide to Narrative Craft*, 5th ed. (New York: Longman, 2000).

Casparis, Christian Paul. *Tense Without Time: The Present Tense in Narration* (Bern: A. Francke, 1975).

Chekov, Anton. "A Trifle From Real Life." In *Russian Silhouettes: More Stories of Russian Life by Anton Tchekoff*, translated by Marian Fell (New York: Scribner, 1915).

Cohen, Richard. *Writer's Mind: Crafting Fiction* (Lincolnwood, IL: NTC Publishing Group, 1995).

Cohn, Dorrit. *Transparent Minds: Narrative Modes for Presenting Consciousness in Fiction* (Princeton, NJ: Princeton University Press, 1978).

Conrad, Joseph. "Heart of Darkness," In *The Portable Conrad*, edited by Morton Dawen Zabel (New York: Penguin, 1978).

Dostoevsky, Fyodor. *Crime and Punishment*, translated by Constance Garnett (New York: Modern Library, 1950).

Eliot, T.S. "Hamlet and His Problems." In *The Sacred Wood: Essays on Poetry and Criticism* (London: Methuen, 1983)

Eugenides, Jeffrey. *Middlesex* (New York: Picador, 2002).

Faulkner, William. *Light in August* (New York: Random House, 1959)

_____. *The Sound and the Fury*, edited by David Minter (New York: Norton, 1987).

Fitzgerald, F. Scott. *The Great Gatsby* (New York: Collier Books, 1986).

Flaubert, Gustave. *Madame Bovary*, translated by Mildred Marmur (New York: Signet, 2001).

Hemingway, Ernest. *A Farewell to Arms* (New York: Scribner, 1995).

_____. "Hills Like White Elephants" and "The Light of the World." In *The Short Stories of Ernest Hemingway* (New York: Scribner, 1966).

James, Henry. "Preface to *The Wings of the Dove*." In *The Art of Criticism: Henry James on the Theory and Practice of Fiction*, edited by William Veeder and Susan M. Griffin (Chicago: The University of Chicago Press, 1986).

James, William. *The Principles of Psychology*, vol. 1 (Cambridge, MA: Harvard University Press, 1981).

James Joyce, *A Portrait of the Artist as a Young Man* (New York: Signet, 1991).

_____. *Ulysses* (New York: Vintage, 1990).

Rosenthal, Chuck. E-mail to the author, April 22, 2002.

Rushdie, Salman. *Midnight's Children* (New York: Avon Books, 1982).

Sartre, Jean-Paul. "Intimacy," cited in Dorrit Cohn, *Transparent Minds: Narrative Modes for Presenting Consciousness in Fiction* (Princeton, NJ: Princeton University Press, 1978).

Schwartz, Delmore. "In Dreams Begin Responsibilities." In *In Dreams Begin Responsibilities and Other Stories* (New York: New Directions, 1978).

Tolstoy, Leo. *War and Peace*, translated by Anthony Briggs (London: Penguin, 2005).

Vargas Llosa, Mario. *Letters to a Young Novelist*, translated by Natasha Wimmer (New York: Farrar, Straus and Giroux, 1997).

_____. *The Perpetual Orgy: Flaubert and Madame Bovary*, translated by Helen Lane (New York: Farrar, Straus and Giroux, 1986).

BREAKING THE "RULES" OF STORY STRUCTURE, by Diane Lefer

Braverman, Kate. "Winter Blues," *Squandering the Blue* (New York: Fawcett Columbine, 1990).

Cisneros, Sandra. *Woman Hollering Creek and Other Stories* (New York: Random House, 1991).

Hempel, Amy. "In the Cemetery Where Al Jolson is Buried." In *Reasons to Live* (New York: Knopf, 1985).

Jen, Gish. "The Water-Faucet Vision." In *Best American Short Stories 1988* (Boston: Houghton Mifflin, 1988).

Kafka, Franz. "The Metamorphosis." In *The Complete Stories*, edited by Nahum N. Glatzer (New York: Schocken Books, 1971).

Kelly, Robert. "Russian Tales." In *Cat Scratch Fever* (Kingston, NY: McPherson & Co., 1991).

Lefer, Diane. "What She Stood For." In *The Circles I Move In* (Cambridge, MA: Zoland Books, 1994).

Le Guin, Ursula K. "Conflict." In *Dancing at the Edge of the World: Thoughts on Words, Women, Places* (New York: Grove/Atlantic, 1989).

O'Brien, Tim. "How to Tell a True War Story." In *The Things They Carried* (Boston: Houghton Mifflin/Seymour Lawrence, 1990).

Philip, M. NourbeSe. "Burn Sugar." In *International Feminist Fiction* (Freedom, CA: Crossing Press, 1992).

Phillips, Robert. "William Goyen: The Art of Fiction, 63." In *The Paris Review*, 68 (Winter 1976).

Williams, Diane. *Some Sexual Success Stories and Other Stories in Which God Might Choose to Appear* (New York: Grove Weidenfeld, 1992).

NOTES ON NOVEL STRUCTURE, by Douglas Glover

Amis, Kingsley. *Lucky Jim* (New York: Viking, 1953).

Atwood, Margaret. *Cat's Eye* (New York: Doubleday, 1988).

Bellow, Saul. *Henderson the Rain King* (New York: Viking, 1959).

Brontë, Emily. *Wuthering Heights*, edited by William M. Sale, Jr. (New York: Norton, 1963).

Carey, Joyce. *The Horse's Mouth* (London: M. Joseph, 1944).

Cervantes, Miguel de. *Don Quixote*, translated by Tobias Smollett (New York: Modern Library, 2001).

Conrad, Joseph. *Heart of Darkness* (New York: Penguin, 1995).

Fitzgerald, F. Scott. *The Great Gatsby* (New York: Scribner, 1958).

Fowles, John. *The French Lieutenant's Woman* (New York: Little, Brown, 1969).

Glover, Douglas. *Elle* (Fredericton, New Brunswick: Goose Lane Editions, 2003).

———. *Precious* (Fredericton, New Brunswick: Goose Lane Editions, 2005).

———. *The Life and Times of Captain N.* (New York: Knopf, 1993).

Huxley, Aldous. *Point Counter Point* (Normal, IL: Dalkey Archive Press, 1996).

James, Henry. "Preface to *The Golden Bowl*." In *Prefaces to the New York Edition* (New York: Viking, 1984).

Kundera, Milan. *The Unbearable Lightness of Being* (New York: Harper & Row, 1984).

le Carré, John. *The Russia House* (New York: Knopf, 1989).

McCarthy, Mary. *The Group* (New York: Harcourt, Brace and World, 1963).

O'Brien, Tim. *In the Lake of the Woods* (Boston: Houghton Mifflin, 1994).

Smollett, Tobias. *The Expedition of Humphry Clinker* (New York: Oxford University Press, 1998).

Tolstoy, Leo. *Anna Karenina*, translated by Richard Pevear and Larissa Volokhonsky (New York: Penguin, 2004).

Tyler, Anne. *The Accidental Tourist* (New York: Knopf, 1985).

Wolf, Christa. *The Quest for Christa T.* (New York: Farrar, Straus and Giroux, 1979).

Yeats, W.B. "Emotion of Multitude." In *Essays and Introductions* (New York: Macmillan, 1961).

WAKE UP AND GO TO SLEEP: DREAMS AND WRITING FICTION, by Philip Graham

Allegretti, Andrew. "From the short novel *A Fool's Game*." In *F Magazine*, no. 4 (1999).

Caughey, John L. *Imaginary Social Worlds* (Lincoln: University of Nebraska Press, 1984).

Chaon, Dan. "Big Me." In *Among the Missing* (New York: Ballantine Books, 2002).

Couto, Mia. *Sleepwalking Land*, translated by David Brookshaw (London: Serpents Tail Press, 2006).

Epel, Naomi, ed. *Writers Dreaming* (New York: Carol Southern Books, 1993).

Hilts, Philip J. "Listening to the Conversation of Neurons." In *The New York Times*, March 27, 1997.

Léon-Portilla, Miguel. *Aztec Thought and Culture: A Study of the Ancient Nahuatl Mind*, translated by Jack Emory Davis (Norman: University of Oklahoma Press, 1990).

Lohmann, Roger Ivar, ed. *Dream Travelers: Sleep Experiences and Culture in the Western Pacific* (New York: Palgrave Macmillan, 2003).

Murch, Walter. *In the Blink of an Eye: A Perspective on Film Editing*, 2nd ed. (Los Angeles: Silman-James Press, 2001).

Pessoa, Fernando. *The Book of Disquiet*, translated by Richard Zenith (New York: Penguin Books, 2003).

States, Bert O. *Dreaming and Storytelling* (Ithaca, NY: Cornell University Press, 1993).

Tedlock, Barbara, ed. *Dreaming: Anthropological and Psychological Interpretations* (Santa Fe, NM: School of American Research Press, 1992).

Tolstoy, Leo. *Anna Karenina*, translated by Louise and Aylmer Maude (Hertfordshire, UK: Wordsworth Editions, 1995).

Updike, John. *Couples* (New York: Knopf, 1968).

KEEPING OPEN THE WOUNDS OF POSSIBILITY: THE MARVELOUS, THE UNCANNY, AND THE FANTASTIC IN FICTION, by Christopher Noël

Alexander, Lloyd. "Wishful Thinking—Or Hopeful Dreaming." In *The Horn Book Magazine*, vol. XLIV, no. 4 (August 1968).

Cameron, Eleanor. *The Green and Burning Tree: On the Writing and Enjoyment of Children's Books* (New York: Little, Brown, 1985).

Dickinson, Emily. *Emily Dickinson. Selected Letters,* edited by Thomas H. Johnson (Cambridge, MA. Belknap Press, 2006).

Emerson, Ralph Waldo. "Experience." In *Ralph Waldo Emerson: Essays and Lectures* (New York: Library of America, 1983).

Freud, Sigmund. "The Uncanny." In *On Creativity and the Unconscious* (New York: Harper Colophon, 1958).

Márquez, Gabriel García. "A Very Old Man with Enormous Wings." In *Collected Stories* (New York: Harper Perennial, 1999).

———. Interview with Peter Stone. In *Writers at Work: The Paris Review Interviews: Sixth Series*, edited by George Plimpton (New York: Viking, 1984).

Gilman, Charlotte Perkins. "The Yellow Wallpaper." In *Herland, The Yellow Wallpaper, and Selected Writings* (New York: Penguin, 1999).

Hansen, Ron. *Mariette in Ecstasy* (New York: Harper Perennial, 1992).

Howard, Elizabeth Jane. *Three Miles Up* (Yorkshire, UK: Tartarus Press, 2003).

Jarrell, Randall. *The Bat-Poet* (New York: HarperCollins, 1997).

Kafka, Franz. *The Diaries of Franz Kafka* (New York: Schocken, 1988).

———. "The Metamorphosis." In *The Complete Stories* (New York: Schocken, 1995).

Kierkegaard, Sören, cited in Karen Lang, "The Dialectic of Decay: Rereading the Kantian Subject." In *The Art Bulletin* (Sept. 1997).

Lewis, C.S. "On Science Fiction" and "Sometimes Fairy Stories May Say Best What's to Be Said." In *Of Other World: Essays and Stories* (New York: Harvest Books, 2002).

———. *Perelandra* (New York: Scribner, 1996).

———. *Surprised by Joy: The Shape of My Early Life* (New York: Harvest Books, 1966).

Long, David. "Making the Stone Stony." In *Poets & Writers Magazine* , vol. 26, no. 2 (March/April 1998).

Shklovsky, Viktor. "Art as Device." In *Theory of Prose* (Normal, IL: Dalkey Archive Press, 1991).

Todorov, Tzvetan. *The Fantastic: A Structural Approach to a Literary Genre* (Ithaca, NY: Cornell University Press, 1975).

Tolkien, J.R.R. "On Fairy-Stories." In *The Tolkien Reader* (New York: Ballantine, 2001).

Van Doren Stern, Philip. *Travelers in Time* (Garden City, NY: Doubleday, 1948).

HOW DO WE MEAN WHAT WE DO NOT SAY: THE USES OF OMISSION IN FICTION, by Victoria Redel

Goodman, Nelson. *Ways of Worldmaking* (New York: Hackett Publishing Co., 1978).

Hempel, Amy. "In the Cemetery Where Al Jolson Is Buried." *In Reasons to Live* (New York: Harper Perennial, 1995).

Jackson, Shirley. "The Lottery." In *The Lottery and Other Stories* (New York: Farrar, Straus and Giroux, 1982).

Schutt, Christine. "You Drive." In *Nightwork* (New York: Random House, 1997).

***MULTI-CULTI LITERATI*: OR, WAYS OF WRITING FICTION BEYOND "PC,"** by Xu Xi

Cohen, Warren I. *The Asian American Century* (Cambridge, MA: Harvard University Press, 2002).

Elliott, Stuart. "The Media Business: Advertising." In *The New York Times*, C-1, April 21, 2003.

Goode, Erica. "How Culture Molds Habits of Thoughts." In *The New York Times*, F-1,4, August 8, 2000.

Hijuelos, Oscar. *The Mambo Kings Play Songs of Love* (New York: Farrar, Straus and Giroux, 1989).

Jen, Gish. *Who's Irish?: Stories* (New York: Vintage, 1999).

Jin, Ha. *In the Pond* (New York: Vintage International, 2000).

Nisbett, Richard E. "The Anticreativity Letters." In *American Psychologist*, no. 45 (1990).

———. *The Geography of Thought* (New York: Free Press, 2003).

Suri, Manil. *The Death of Vishnu* (New York: Norton, 2001).

Thien, Madeleine. "Four Days from Oregon." In *Simple Recipes: Stories* (Toronto: McClelland & Stewart, 2001).

Tolstoy, Leo. *Anna Karenina*, translated by Constance Garnett, edited by Leonard J. Kent and Nina Berberova (New York: Modern Library, 1965).

U. S. Census Bureau. *DP-1: Profile of General Demographic Characteristics: 2000 vs. 1980*.

———. *H15G.: Tenure by Household Size (Two or More Races Householder): 2000*.

———. *QT-H1: General Housing Characteristics: 2000*.

———. *QT-P16: Language Spoken at Home: 2000*.

Yeats, W.B. "The Fisherman." In *Yeats's Poetry, Drama, and Prose*, edited by James Pethica (New York: Norton, 2000).

THE TEXTURES OF FICTION: AN INQUIRY, by François Camoin

Barthes, Roland. *Image, Music, Text* (New York: Noonday Press, 1988).

Borges, Jorge Luis. *Otras Inquisiciones* (Madrid: Alianza, 1976).

Malraux, André. *Man's Fate* (New York: Vintage, 1990).

Robbe-Grillet, Alain. *For a New Novel* (Evanston, IL.: Northwestern University Press, 1992).

Whorf, Benjamin Lee. *Language, Thought, and Reality*, edited by John B. Carroll (Cambridge, MA: MIT Press, 1956).

SHOWING *AND* TELLING, by Laurie Alberts

Burroway, Janet. *Writing Fiction* (New York: HarperCollins, 1996).

Cheever, John. "Artemis the Honest Well Digger." In *The Short Stories of John Cheever* (New York: Ballantine Books, 1980).

Kingston, Maxine Hong. *The Woman Warrior* (New York: Vintage Books, 1975).

Macauley, Robie. "Handling the Problems of Time and Pace." In *What If?: Writing Exercises for Fiction Writers*, edited by Anne Bernays and Pamela Painter (New York: HarperCollins, 1995).

Marrazzo, Carol-Lynn. "Show and Tell: There's a Reason It's Called Storytelling." In *What If?: Writing Exercises for Fiction Writers*, edited by Anne Bernays and Pamela Painter (New York: HarperCollins, 1995).

O'Brien, Tim. "The Things They Carried." In *The Things They Carried* (Boston: Houghton Mifflin/Seymour Lawrence, 1990).

Savic, Sally. *Elysian Fields* (New York: Charles Scribner Sons, 1988).

Silverman, Sue William. *Because I Remember Terror, Father, I Remember You* (Athens: University of Georgia Press, 1999).

Stern, Jerome, cited in Janet Burroway, *Writing Fiction* (New York: HarperCollins, 1996).

Wolff, Tobias. *This Boy's Life* (New York: Harper and Row, 1989).

PAINFUL HOWLS FROM PLACES THAT UNDOUBTEDLY EXIST:
A PRIMER OF DECEIT, by Robin Hemley

Capote, Truman. *Answered Prayers* (New York: Vintage, 1994).

Carter, Forrest. *The Education of Little Tree* (New York: Delacorte, 1976).

Coetzee, J.M. *Elizabeth Costello* (New York: Viking, 2003).

Faulkner, William. Feb. 11, 1949, letter to Malcolm Cowley, cited in Joseph Blotner, *Faulkner* (New York: Random House, 1974).

Frey, James. *A Million Little Pieces* (New York: Anchor Books, 2005).

Hellman, Lillian. *An Unfinished Woman* (Boston: Little, Brown, 1969).

_____ *Pentimento* (Boston: Little, Brown, 1973).

_____ *Scoundrel Time* (Boston: Little, Brown, 1976).

Least Heat-Moon, William. *Blue Highways* (Boston: Back Bay Books, 1999).

LeRoy, J.T. *The Heart is Deceitful Above All Things* (London: Bloomsbury Publishing, 2001).

Maechler, Stefan. *The Wilkomirski Affair: A Study in Biographical Truth* (New York: Schocken Books, 2001).

McCarthy, Mary. From an interview on *The Dick Cavett Show*, 1980.

Nasdijj. *The Blood Runs Like a River Through My Dreams* (Boston: Houghton Mifflin, 2000).

Psalmanazar, George. *An Historical and Geographical Description of Formosa ...* (London: R. Holden, 1926).

Slater, Lauren. *Lying: A Metaphorical Memoir* (New York: Penguin, 2001).

Trilling, Lionel. *Sincerity and Authenticity* (Cambridge, MA: Harvard University Press, 19772).

Wilkomirski, Binjamin. *Fragments: Memories of a Wartime Childhood*, translated by Carol Brown Janeway (New York: Schocken Books, 1996).

Wolfe, Thomas. *Look Homeward, Angel* (New York: Modern Library, 1934).

Wolff, Tobias. *This Boy's Life* (New York: Harper and Row, 1989).

THE FICTIONAL "I" IN NONFICTION, by Phyllis Barber

Alberts, Laurie. *Fault Line* (Lincoln: University of Nebraska Press, 2004).

Cather, Willa. *The Song of the Lark* (New York: Penguin, 1915).

Hafiz. "Someone Should Start Laughing." In *I Heard God Laughing: Renderings of Hafiz*, translated by Daniel Ladinsky (Walnut Creek, CA: Sufism Reoriented, 1996).

Hanh, Thich Nhat. *Zen Keys* (New York: Doubleday, 1974).

Hengst, Carolyn. "The Stories We Tell Ourselves." In *Mandala Magazine* (June 2001).

Mallarmé, Stephane. *Crisis in Poetry,* cited in Alice Kaplan, *French Lessons* (Chicago: The University of Chicago Press, 1993).

McCormick, John S. and John R. Sillito, eds. *A World We Thought We Knew: Readings in Utah History* (Salt Lake City: University of Utah Press, 1995).

Nicoll, Maurice. *Psychological Commentaries on the Teaching of Gurdjieff and Ouspensky* (York Beach, ME: Samuel Weiser, Inc., 1980).

THE MEANDERING RIVER: AN OVERVIEW OF THE SUBGENRES
OF CREATIVE NONFICTION, by Sue William Silverman

Chavez, Lisa D. "Independence Day, Manley Hot Springs, Alaska." In *Fourth Genre: Explorations in Nonfiction* (Spring 2000).

Clinton, Bill. *My Life* (New York: Vintage Books, 2005).

D'Agata, John. "Finding Love at Thirty." In *Seneca Review* (Spring 2000).

_____. "Hall of Fame of Us/Hall of Fame of Them." In *Fourth Genre: Explorations in Nonfiction* (Spring 2000).

Dillard, Annie. *Pilgrim at Tinker Creek* (New York: Harper Perennial, 1998).

Ehrenreich, Barbara. *Nickel and Dimed: On (Not) Getting By in America* (New York: Metropolitan Books, 2001).

Frost, Robert. *Selected Prose of Robert Frost*, edited by Hyde Cox and Edward Connery Lathem (New York: Collier Books, 1949).

Hampl, Patricia. "We Were Such a Generation—Memoir, Truthfulness, and History." In *River Teeth* (Spring 2004).

Hemley, Robin. *Nola: A Memoir of Faith, Art, and Madness* (St. Paul, MN: Graywolf Press, 1998).

Hochschild, Adam. "Isle of Flowers, House of Slaves." In *Finding the Trapdoor* (Syracuse, NY: Syracuse University Press, 1997).

_____. *King Leopold's Ghost: A Story of Greed, Terror, and Heroism in Colonial Africa* (Boston: Houghton Mifflin, 1998).

Kirkpatrick, Melanie. "*Robert Frost: A Life*," *Pif Magazine* (August 1, 1999) http://www.Pifmagazine.com/SID/235/.

Mora, Pat. *House of Houses* (Boston: Beacon Press, 1998).

Morris, Edmund. *Dutch: A Memoir of Ronald Reagan* (New York: Random House, 1999).

Parini, Jay, cited in Paul Holler, "An Interview with Jay Parini," *Bookslut* (April, 2006) http://www.bookslut.com/features/2006_04_008406.php.

_____. *Robert Frost: A Life* (New York: Henry Holt, 1999).

Pekar, Harvey. *American Splendor* (New York: Ballantine, 2003).

Plimpton, George. *Paper Lion: Confessions of a Last-String Quarterback* (New York: Pocket Books, 1967).

Satrapi, Marjane. *Persepolis: The Story of a Childhood* (New York: Pantheon, 2004).

Sutin, Lawrence. *A Postcard Memoir* (St. Paul, MN: Graywolf Press, 2003).

Thompson, Lawrence. *Robert Frost* (New York: Henry Holt, 1966).

Vivian, Robert. "Light Calling to Other Light." In *Cold Snap as Yearning* (Lincoln: University of Nebraska Press, 2001).

"I RECOGNIZE THY GLORY": ON THE AMERICAN NATURE ESSAY AND LYRIC POETRY, by Sydney Lea

Abbey, Edward. *Desert Solitaire* (New York: Ballantine Books, 1985).

Bass, Rick. *The Ninemile Wolves* (New York: Ballantine Books, 1992).

Dillard, Annie. *Pilgrim at Tinker Creek* (New York: Harper & Row, 1974).

Fritzell, Peter. *Nature Writing and America: Essays Upon a Cultural Type* (Ames: Iowa State University Press, 1990).

Galvin, Brendan. "The Contemporary Poet and the Natural World." In *The Georgia Review* (Spring 1993), 130-144.

Hall, Donald. "Granite and Grass." In *White Apples and the Taste of Stone: Selected Poems, 1946-2006* (Boston: Houghton Mifflin, 2006).

Holden, Jonathan. *The Rhetoric of the Contemporary Lyric* (Bloomington: Indiana University Press, 1980).

Lea, Sydney. "On the Bubble." In *Hunting the Whole Way Home* (Hanover, NH: University Press of New England, 1994).

Stevens, Wallace. "On Modern Poetry." In *Wallace Stevens: Collected Poetry and Prose* (New York: Library of America, 1997).

Thoreau, Henry David. *Walden* (Princeton, NJ: Princeton University Press, 1971).

Wordsworth, William. *The Prelude* (Oxford: Clarendon Press, 1959).

POETIC TECHNIQUE IN NONFICTION WRITING, by Cynthia Huntington

Frazier, Ian. "Crazy Horse." Excerpt from *Great Plains* (New York: Farrar, Straus and Giroux, 1989). Reprinted as an individual essay in *In Short: A Collection of Brief Creative Nonfiction*, edited by Judith Kitchen and Mary Paumier Jones (New York: W.W. Norton, 1996).

Gerard, Philip. *Creative Nonfiction: Researching and Crafting Stories of Real Life* (Long Grove, IL: Waveland Press, 2004).

O'Brien, Tim. "The Vietnam in Me." In *The New York Times Magazine* (Oct. 2, 1994).

Shelton, Richard. In *The Other Side of the Story* (Lewiston, ID: Confluence Press, 1987).

COLLABORATING WITH CHAOS: NOT KNOWING AND THE CREATIVE PROCESS, by Jack Myers

Hall, Donald. "Poetry and Ambition." In *Poetry and Ambition: Essays 1982-1988* (Ann Arbor: University of Michigan Press, 1988).

Richards, I.A. *The Philosophy of Rhetoric* (New York: Oxford University Press, 1965).

STAKING THE CLAIM TO THE TITLE, by Nance Van Winckel

Ashbery, John. "Out Over the Bay the Rattle of Firecrackers." In *As We Know* (New York: Viking, 1979).

Bennerstrom, Susan. *Waiter*, Davidson Gallery, Seattle, WA, 2001.

Cedrins, Inara. "Inward." In *New Letters*, vol. 68, no. 1.

Dobyns, Stephen. *Best Words, Best Order* (New York: St. Martin's, 1997).

Gregg, Linda. "Twelve Years After the Marriage She Tries to Explain How She Loves Him Now." In *Alma* (New York: Random House, 1985).

Lensing, George S. *Wallace Stevens: A Poet's Growth* (Baton Rouge: Louisiana State University Press, 1986).

Lux, Thomas. "A Man Gets Off Work Early." In *House of Clocks* (Boston: Houghton Mifflin, 2001).

Meuris, Jacques. *Magritte* (Cologne, Germany: Benedikt Taschen Verlag BambH, 1992).

Ruefle, Mary. "Surprised Girl of the North." In *The Adamant* (Iowa City: University of Iowa Press, 1989).

Stevens, Wallace. "No Possum, No Sop, No Taters." In *The Collected Poems of Wallace Stevens* (New York: Knopf, 1955).

Tate, James. "A Tattered Bible Stuffed With Memos." In *Memoir of the Hawk: Poems* (Hopewell, NJ: Ecco, 2001).

Vendler, Helen. "The Hunting of Wallace Stevens." In *The New York Times Book Review,* Nov. 20, 1986.

Wright, Franz. "The Forties." In *Ill Lit: Selected & New Poems* (Oberlin, OH: Oberlin College Press, 1998).

Wright, James. "A Message Hidden in an Empty Wine Bottle That I Threw Into a Gully of Maple Trees One Night at an Indecent Hour." In *Collected Poems* (Middletown, CT: Wesleyan University Press, 1977).

ON BEGINNINGS, by Mary Ruefle

Bachelard, Gaston. *The Poetics of Space* (Boston: Beacon Press, 1969).

Dickinson, Emily. *Selected Letters*, edited by Thomas H. Johnson (Cambridge, MA: Harvard University Press, 1986).

Fenollosa, Ernest. *The Chinese Written Character as a Medium for Poetry* (San Francisco: City Lights Books, 1964).

Herrnstein Smith, Barbara. *Poetic Closure: A Study of How Poems End* (Chicago: The University of Chicago Press, 1968).

Valéry, Paul. *The Art of Poetry* (New York: Vintage Books, 1961).

SOULS ON ICE, by Mark Doty

Doty, Mark. "A Display of Mackerel." In *Atlantis: Poems* (New York: HarperCollins, 1995).

ROOTS IN OUR THROATS: A CASE FOR USING ETYMOLOGY, by Natasha Sajé

Alexander, Elizabeth. "Affirmative Action Blues." In *Body of Life* (Chicago: Tia Chucha Press, 1996).

Barrett, Conrad. "Keys to Language and Cultural Awareness," http.//www.bolchazy.com/al/whylatin

Carver, Raymond. "What We Talk About When We Talk About Love." In *The Story and Its Writer*, edited by Ann Charters (New York: St. Martin's, 1999).

Derrida, Jacques. *Spurs* (Chicago: The University of Chicago Press, 1979).

Emerson, Ralph Waldo. "The Poet." In *Essays and Lectures* (New York: Library of America, 1983).

Forsyth, Neil. "Of Man's First Dis." In *Milton in Italy: Contexts, Images, Contradictions*, edited by Mario A. Di Cesare (Binghampton, NY: Medieval & Renaissance Texts and Studies, 1981).

Grossman, Allen. "Sentinel Yellowwoods." In *Of the Great House: A Book of Poems* (New York: New Directions, 1982).

Heidegger, Martin. "Building, Thinking, Dwelling." In *Poetry, Language, Thought* (New York: Harper & Row, 1971).

Hopkins, Gerard Manley. *The Journals and Papers of Gerard Manley Hopkins*, edited by Humphrey House (Oxford: Oxford University Press, 1959).

Jacobsen, Josephine. "The Monosyllable." In *The Chinese Insomniacs* (Philadelphia: University of Pennsylvania Press, 1981).

James, Henry. "Paste." In *The Story and Its Writer*, edited by Ann Charters (New York: St. Martin's, 1999).

Kronich, Joseph. "On the Border of History: Whitman and the American Sublime." In *The American Sublime* (Albany, NY: SUNY-Albany University Press, 1986).

McHugh, Heather. "Etymological Dirge." In *The Father of the Predicaments* (Middletown, CT: Wesleyan University Press, 1999).

Metcalf, Allen and David Barnhart. *America in So Many Words: Words That Shaped America* (New York: Houghton Mifflin, 1997).

Mitchell, Susan. "The False Etymologies of Isidore of Seville." In *Rapture* (New York: HarperCollins, 1992).

Mysko, Madeleine. "Out of Blue." In *Out of Blue* (Medina, OH: Rager Media Press, 2007).

Nietzsche, Friedrich, cited in Jacques Derrida, *Spurs* (Chicago: The University of Chicago Press, 1979).

Rekdahl, Paisley. "Stupid." In *Six Girls Without Pants* (Spokane: Eastern Washington University Press, 2002).

Sajé, Natasha. "Creation Story." In *Red Under the Skin* (Pittsburgh, PA: University of Pittsburgh Press, 1994).

Schnackenberg, Gjertrud. "Supernatural Love." In *The Lamplit Answer* (New York: Farrar, Straus, and Giroux, 1985).

Snyder, Gary. "Earrings Dangling and Miles of Desert." *Mountains and Rivers Without End* (Washington, DC: Counterpoint, 1996).

West, Paul. *The Secret Lives of Words* (New York: Farrar, Straus, and Giroux, 1985).

Whitman, Walt. *Prose Works 1892: Specimen Days*, vol. II, edited by Floyd Stovall (New York: NYU Press, 1963).

MIND THE GAP, by Betsy Sholl

Bialoszewski, Miron. "A Ballad of Going Down to the Store." In *Postwar Polish Poetry: An Anthology*, edited and translated by Czeslaw Milosz (Garden City, NY: Doubleday & Co., 1965).

Bishop, Elizabeth. "Brazil, January 1, 1502." In *The Complete Poems, 1927-1979* (New York: Farrar, Straus and Giroux, 1983).

Bobrick, Benson. *Knotted Tongues: Stuttering in History and the Quest for a Cure* (New York: Kodansha International, 1996).

Creeley, Robert. "I Know a Man." In *The Collected Poems of Robert Creeley, 1947-1975* (Berkeley: University of California Press, 1985).

Deleuze, Gilles. *Anti-Oedipus: Capitalism and Schizophrenia*, translated by Robert Hurley, Mark Seem and Helen Lane (London: Athlone Press, 1984).

Ferris, Jim. "The Enjambed Body: A Step Toward a Crippled Poetics." In *Georgia Review*, vol. LVIII, no. 2 (Summer 2004).

Milosz, Czeslaw. *The Witness of Poetry* (Cambridge, MA: Harvard University Press, 1983).

Mitchell, Susan. "Self Portrait With Young Eros." In *The American Poetry Review*, vol. 33, no. 4 (July/August 2004).

Muldoon, Paul. "Incantata." In *Poems 1968-1998* (New York: Farrar, Straus and Giroux, 2001).

Sappho. "I Am Awed by Your Beauty." In *The Love Songs of Sappho*, translated by Paul Roche (Amherst, NY: Prometheus Books, 1998).

_____. *If Not, Winter: Fragments of Sappho*, translated by Anne Carson (New York: Vintage, 2003).

Tranströmer, Tomas. "The Scattered Congregation." In *The Half-Finished Heaven: The Best Poems of Tomas Tranströmer*, translated by Robert Bly (St. Paul, MN: Graywolf Press, 2001).

Updike, John. *Self-Consciousness: Memoirs* (New York: Fawcett Crest, 1989).

Vallejo, César. "The Black Riders." In *Neruda and Vallejo: Selected Poems*, translated by Robert Bly (Boston: Beacon Press, 1971).

Whitman, Walt. "After the Supper and Talk." In *Leaves of Grass* (New York: Norton, 1973).

Williams, William Carlos. "A Unison" and "Spring and All." In *The Collected Poems of William Carlos Williams* (New York: New Directions, 1991).

Wright, Charles. *Half-Life: Impovisations and Interview, 1977-1987* (Ann Arbor: University of Michigan Press, 1989).

TOWARDS A POETICS OF PULL-AND-RELEASE:
SOME THOUGHTS ON SILENCE IN POEMS, by Leslie Ullman

Bachelard, Gaston. *On Poetic Imagination and Reverie*, edited by Colette Gaudin (New York: Bobbs-Merrill, 1971).

Bly, Robert. *Leaping Poetry* (Boston: Beacon Press, 1975).

_____. "What the Image Can Do." In *Claims for Poetry*, edited by Donald Hall (Ann Arbor: University of Michigan Press, 1982).

Gilbert, Jack. "In Dispraise of Poetry." In *Monolithos* (New York: Knopf, 1982).

McPherson, Sandra. "On a Picture of My Parents Together in Second Grade." In *The Year of Our Birth* (New York: Ecco Press, 1978).

Ruefle, Mary. "From Memory." In *Life Without Speaking* (Tuscaloosa: University of Alabama Press, 1987).

Sontag, Susan. "On Style." In *Against Interpretation* (New York: Farrar, Straus and Giroux, 1966).

THE WORD OVERFLOWN BY STARS: SAYING THE UNSAYABLE, by Richard Jackson

Alighieri, Dante. *The Divine Comedy*, translated by John Ciardi (New York: New American Library, 2003).

Anonymous, chapter 51, *The Cloud of Unknowing* (New York: Doubleday, 1966).

Ashbery, John. "My Philosophy of Life." In *Can You Hear, Bird* (New York: Farrar, Straus and Giroux, 1997).

Bachelard, Gaston. *The Poetics of Space*, translated by Maria Jolas (Boston: Beacon Press, 1994).

Cassirer, Ernst. *Language and Myth*, translated by Susanne Langer (New York: Dover, 1953).

Celan, Paul. "Argumentum e Silencio," "Landscape with urn beings," "A Rumbling," "Solve," "Speak You Too," and "Where the word." In *Selected Poems and Prose*, translated by John Felstiner (New York: Norton, 2001).

Derrida, Jacques. *Writing and Difference*, translated by Alan Bass (Chicago: The University of Chicago Press, 1980).

Dickinson, Emily. Poem 465. In *The Complete Poems of Emily Dickinson*, edited by Thomas H. Johnson (Boston: Little, Brown, 1960).

Eckhart, Meister, cited in Bruce Milem, *The Unspoken Word: Negative Theology in Meister Eckhart's German Sermons* (Washington, DC: Catholic University of America, 2002).

Emerson, Ralph Waldo. *Selections from Ralph Waldo Emerson*, edited by S. Whicher (Boston: Houghton Mifflin, 1957).

Frost, Robert. "For Once, Then, Something." In *The Poetry of Robert Frost* (New York: Holt, Rinehart and Winston, 1967).

González, Ángel. "Useless Words." In *Astonishing World: Selected Poems of Ángel González*, edited by Steven Ford Brown, translated by Gutierrez Revuelta (Minneapolis, MN: Milkweed Editions, 1993).

Gregg, Linda. "The Unknowing." In *Things and Flesh* (St. Paul, MN: Graywolf Press, 1999).

Hass, Robert. "Meditation at Lagunitas." In *Praise* (Hopewell, NJ: Ecco, 1990).

Heidegger, Martin. *On the Way to Language*, translated by Peter Hertz (New York: Harper Collins, 1971).

———. *Poetry Language Thought*, translated by Albert Hofstadter (New York: HarperCollins, 1971).

Kierkegaard, Sören. *Either/Or*, translated by Howard V. Hong and Edna H. Hong (Princeton, NJ: Princeton University Press, 1987).

———. *Fear and Trembling*, translated by Alastair Hannay (New York: Penguin Books, 1985).

Koch, Kenneth. "One Train May Hide Another." In *One Train* (New York: Knopf, 1994).

Lacan, Jacques. *Ecrits*, translated by Alan Sheridan (New York: Norton, 1977).

Lakoff, George and Mark Johnson. *Philosophy in the Flesh: The Embodied Mind and Its Challenge to Western Thought* (New York: HarperCollins, 1999).

Levertov, Denise. "A Common Ground." In *The Jacob's Ladder* (New York: New Directions, 1961).

———. "I learned that her name was Proverb." In *Breathing the Water* (New York: New Directions, 1987).

———. "Immersion." In *This Great Unknowing* (New York: New Directions, 2000).

———. *The Poet in the World* (New York: New Directions, 1974).

———. "Tree Telling of Orpheus." In *Relearning the Alphabet* (New York: Norton, 1970).

Levine, Philip. "Call It Music." In *Breath* (New York: Knopf, 2004).

Levis, Larry. "Elegy Ending in the Sound of a Skipping Rope." In *Elegy* (Pittsburgh, PA: University of Pittsburgh Press, 1997).

Longinus. "On the Sublime." In *Classical Literary Criticism* (Oxford: Oxford University Press, 1989).

MacEwen, Gwendolyn. "The Red Bird You Wait For." In *Volume One: The Early Years* (Toronto: Exile Editions, 1993).

———. "Poems in Braille." In *A Breakfast for Barbarians* (Toronto: Ryerson Press, 1966).

McHugh, Heather. "A Stranger's Way of Looking." In *Broken English* (Hanover, NH: Wesleyan University Press, 1993).

_____. "What He Thought." In *Hinge & Sign: Poems, 1968-1993* (Hanover, NH: Wesleyan University Press and University Press of New England, 1994).

Nietzsche, Friedrich. "On Truth and Lies in an Extra-Moral Sense." In *The Portable Nietzsche*, translated by Walter Kaufmann (New York: Penguin, 1977).

Pavese, Cesare. "Poetical." In *Cesare Pavese: Le Poesie* (Torino, Italy: Ein Audi, 1998).

Paz, Octavio. *The Bow and the Lyre*, translated by Ruth Sims (Austin: University of Texas Press, 1991).

Plath, Sylvia. "The Courage of Shutting-Up," "The Moon and the Yew-Tree," and "Morning Song." In *The Collected Poems* (New York: HarperCollins, 1992).

Rich, Adrienne. "Diving Into the Wreck." In *The Fact of a Doorframe: Poems Selected and New, 1950-1984* (New York: Norton, 1984).

Rilke, Rainer Maria. *Duino Elegies*. In *The Selected Poetry of Rainer Maria Rilke*, translated by Stephen Mitchell (New York: Vintage, 1982).

Ríos, Alberto. "The Cities Inside Us." In *The Smallest Muscle in the Human Body* (Port Townsend, WA: Copper Canyon Press, 2002).

Schopenhauer, Arthur. *World as Will and Representation*, translated by E.F. J. Payne (Toronto: Dover, 1958).

Shelley, Percy Bysshe. "Mont Blanc." In *The Complete Poems of Percy Bysshe Shelley* (New York: Modern Library, 1994).

Simic, Charles. "Evening Talk." In *The Book of Gods and Devils* (New York: Harcourt Brace Jovanovich, 1990).

_____. "Notes on Poetry and Philosophy." In *Wonderful Words, Silent Truth* (Ann Arbor: University of Michigan Press, 1990).

_____. *The Uncertain Certainty* (Ann Arbor: University of Michigan Press, 1986).

Stevens, Wallace. "Adagia," "Connoisseur of Chaos," "An Ordinary Evening in New Haven," "Prologues to What Is Possible," and "The Snow Man." In *The Collected Poems of Wallace Stevens* (New York: Knopf, 1955).

Szymborska, Wislawa. "The Three Oddest Words." In *Poems, New and Collected, 1957-1997*, translated by Stanislaw Baranczak and Clare Cavanagh (New York: Harcourt Brace, 1998).

Tate, James. "Constant Defender." In *Constant Defender* (Hopewell, NJ: Ecco, 1983).

Trakl, Georg. "De Profundis" and "On the Way." In *Autumn Sonata: Selected Poems of Georg Trakl*, translated by Daniel Simko (London: Asphodel Press, 1998).

Tranströmer, Tomas. "April and Silence." In *The Great Enigma: New Collected Poems*, translated by Robin Fulton (New York: New Directions, 2003).

Unamuno, Miguel de. *The Tragic Sense of Life*, translated by J. E. Crawford Flitch (New York: Dover, 1954).

Ungaretti, Giuseppe. "Envoi" and "Variations on Nothing." In *Selected Poems*, translated by Andrew Frisardi (New York: Farrar, Straus and Giroux, 2002).

Van Duyn, Mona. "Earth Tremors Felt in Missouri." In *If It Be Not I: Collected Poems 1959-1982* (New York: Knopf, 1993).

Warren, Robert Penn. *Audubon: A Vision* (New York: Random House, 1969).

Wittgenstein, Ludwig. *The Blue and Brown Books* (New York: Harper Perennial, 1942).

_____. *Tractatus Logico Philosophicus* (London: Routledge, 2001).

THE POEM, AS AND OF ADDRESS, by Ralph Angel

Appolinaire, Guillaume. "Zone." In *Alcools*, translated by Donald Revell (Hanover, NH: Wesleyan University Press, 1995.

Benveniste, Emile. "Subjectivity in Language." *Contemporary Theory Since 1965*, edited by Hazard Adams and Leroy Searle (Tallahassee: Florida State University, 1986).

Buber, Martin. *I and Thou*, translated by Walter Kaufman and S.G. Smith (New York: Scribner, 1974).

Celan, Paul. *Collected Prose*, translated by Rosemarie Waldrop (Riverdale-on-Hudson, NY: Sheep Meadow Press, 1986).

———. "With all my thought I went." In *Poems of Paul Celan*, translated by Michael Hamburger (New York: Persea Books, 1988).

Dickinson, Emily. Poem 667. In *The Complete Poems of Emily Dickinson*, edited by Thomas H. Johnson (Boston: Little, Brown, 1960).

Heidegger, Martin. *Existence and Being*, translated by D. Scott (London: Vision Press, 1956).

Kafka, Franz. "In the Penal Colony." In *The Complete Stories* (New York: Schocken Books, 1995).

Levertov, Denise. *The Poet in the World* (New York: New Directions Books, 1973).

Montale, Eugenio. "In Sleep." In *The Storm and Other Poems*, translated by Charles Wright (Oberlin, OH: Oberlin College Press, 1978).

O'Hara, Frank. "For Grace, After a Party." In *Meditations in an Emergency* (New York: Grove/Atlantic, 1957).

Plath, Sylvia. "Poppies in July." In *The Collected Poems* (New York: HarperCollins, 1992).

Sappho, cited in Anne Carson, *Eros the Bittersweet* (Normal, IL: Dalkey Archive Press, 1998).

Schauss, Hayyim. *The Lifetime of a Jew* (New York: Union of American Hebrew Congregations, 1950).

Schuyler, James. "Watching You." In *Collected Poems* (New York: Farrar, Straus and Giroux, 1993).

Simic, Charles, preface to Ales Debeljak, *Anxious Moments* (Fredonia, NY: White Pine Press, 1994).

Syme, Daniel B. *The Jewish Home* (New York: Union of American Hebrew Congregations, 1988).

Vallejo, César. "The Weary Circles." In *Neruda and Vallejo: Selected Poems*, translated by John Knoepfle, edited by Robert Bly (Boston: Beacon Press, 1993).

THE CHANGING OTHER, by William Olsen

Auden, W.H. *The Dyer's Hand* (New York: Vintage, 1968).

Berryman, John. "The Art of Poetry: An Interview With John Berryman," conducted by Peter Stitt. In *Berryman's Understanding: Reflections on the Poetry of John Berryman*, edited by Harry Thomas (Boston: Northeastern University Press, 1988).

———. *The Freedom of the Poet* (New York: Farrar, Straus and Giroux, 1976).

———. *Homage to Mistress Bradstreet and Other Poems* (New York: Noonday Press, 1973).

Bradstreet, Anne. *Early American Writings*, edited by Carlo Mulford, Angela Vietto, and Amy E. Winans (New York: Oxford University Press, 2001).

Buber, Martin. *I and Thou*, translated by Ronald Gregor Smith (New York: Scribner, 2000).

Creeley, Robert. "On the Road: Notes on Artists and Poets, 1950-1965." In *Claims for Poetry*, edited by Donald Hall (Ann Arbor: University of Michigan Press, 1982).

Eliot, T.S. *The Sacred Wood* (London: Faber and Faber, 1997).

Frost, Robert. *The Letters of Robert Frost to Louis Untermeyer* (New York: Holt, Rinehart & Winston, 1963).

Ginsberg, Allen. "America" and "Howl." In *Collected Poems 1947-1980* (New York: Harper Perennial, 1988).

Graham, Jorie, introduction to *The Best American Poetry 1990* (New York: Scribner, 1990).

Grossman, Alan. "Summa Lyrica. A Primer of the Commonplaces in Speculative Poetics." In *The Sighted Singer: Two Works on Poetry for Readers and Writers* (Baltimore: The Johns Hopkins University Press, 1992).

Heidegger, Martin. *Poetry, Language, and Thought*, translated by Albert Hofstadter (New York: Harper Perennial, 2001).

Hirshfield, Jane. "Thoreau's Hound: On Hiddenness," *The American Poetry Review* (June 2002).

Keats, John. Letter to George and Tom Keats, Dec. 21 (27?), 1817. In *The Letters of John Keats, 1814-1821*, vol. 1, edited by Edward D. McDonald (New York: Viking, 1936).

Mandelstam, Osip. *The Noise of Time: Selected Prose*, translated by Clarence Brown (Chicago: Northwestern University Press, 2002).

Neruda, Pablo. *Elemental Odes*, translated by Margaret Sayers Peden (London: Libris, 1991).

Pomus, Doc. "The Journals of Doc Pomus (1978-91)," *Antaeus*, no. 71/72 (1993).

Pound, Ezra. "The Audience," *Poetry* (1914), cited in Michael Ryan, *A Difficult Grace* (Athens: University of Georgia Press, 2000).

Revell, Donald. *There Are Three: Poems* (Hanover, NH: Wesleyan University Press, 1998).

Ryan, Michael. "Poetry and Audience." In *A Difficult Grace* (Athens: University of Georgia Press, 2000).

Simpson, Eileen. *Poets in Their Youth* (New York: Random House, 1982).

Stevens, Wallace. "Adagia." In *Wallace Stevens: Collected Poetry and Prose* (New York: Library of America, 1997).

Vallejo, César. *Trilce*, translated by Clayton Eshleman (Hanover, NH: Wesleyan University Press, 2000).

Welty, Eudora. *On Writing* (New York: Modern Library, 2002).

Whitman, Walt. "Preface 1855," "Song of Myself," and "When Lilacs Last in the Dooryard Bloom'd." In *Leaves of Grass*, edited by Sculley Bradley and Harold W. Blodgett (New York: Norton, 1973).

Wordsworth, William. "Preface to *Lyrical Ballads*" and *The Prelude*. In *William Wordsworth: The Major Works*, edited by Stephen Gill (Cambridge: Oxford University Press, 2000).

Wright, James. "Ars Poetica: Some Recent Criticism." In *Above the River: Complete Poems* (New York and Hanover, NH: Farrar, Straus and Giroux and University Press of New England, 1990).

Yeats, W.B. *A Vision* (New York: Colliers, 1966).

INCIDENTAL MUSIC: THE GROTESQUE, THE ROMANTIC, AND THE RETRENCHED, by Roger Weingarten

Dubie, Norman. "The Ugly Poem That Reluctantly Accepts *Itself* as Its Only Title." In *The Illustrations* (New York: George Braziller, 1977).

"Hegel." *Webster's New World Dictionary of American English*, edited by Victoria E. Neufeldt (New York: Prentice-Hall, 1988).

Levertov, Denise, cited in Jack Myers and Michael Simms, *The Longman Dictionary and Handbook of Poetry* (New York: Longman, 1985).

Mies van der Rohe, Ludwig, cited in Martin Filler, "Building & Nothingness," *The New York Review of Books*, vol. 33, no. 10 (June 12, 1986).

Plato, cited in Shlomy Mualem, "The Imminence of Revelation: Aesthetics and Poetic Expression in Early Wittgenstein and Borges," *Variaciones Borges*, no. 18 (2004).

Rogers, Pattiann. "Geocentric." In *Firekeeper: New and Selected Poems* (Minneapolis, MN: Milkweed Editions, 1994).

Simic, Charles. "The Lesson." In *Selected Poems* (New York: George Braziller, 1985).

STRIKING THE WRONG HOURS: POETRY AND TIME, by Nancy Eimers

Arendt, Hannah. *The Life of the Mind* (New York: Harcourt, Brace, 1978).

Augustine. *The Confessions of St. Augustine* (Grand Rapids, MI: Revell, 2005).

Bashō, Matsuo. *The Essential Haiku: Versions of Bashō, Buson, and Issa*, edited and translated by Robert Hass (Hopewell, NJ: Ecco Press, 1994).

Bishop, Elizabeth. "At the Fishhouses," "Over 2,000 Illustrations and a Complete Concordance," and "Sestina." In *The Complete Poems: 1927-1979* (New York: Farrar, Straus and Giroux, 1983).

Boethius. *The Consolation of Philosophy*, edited by P.G. Walsh (New York: Oxford University Press, 2000).

Booth, Philip. "Jean Valentine: A Continuum of Turning," *The American Poetry Review* (Jan/Feb. 1980).

Coleman, Lesley. *A Book of Time* (London: Longman Group, 1971).

Gallagher, Tess. "The Poem as Time Machine." In *Claims for Poetry*, edited by Donald Hall (Ann Arbor: University of Michigan Press, 1982).

Holub, Miroslav. *The Dimension of the Present Moment and Other Essays*, edited by David Young (London: Faber and Faber, 1990).

Hood, Peter. *How Time Is Measured* (London: Oxford University Press, 1955).

Justice, Donald. "Psalm and Lament." In *New and Selected Poems* (New York: Knopf, 1995).

Lewis, Norman. *The New Roget's Thesaurus* (New York: Putnam, 1978).

Rukeyser, Muriel. *The Life of Poetry* (Ashfield, MA: Paris Press, 1996).

Sacks, Oliver. *The Man Who Mistook His Wife for a Hat* (New York: Summit Books, 1985).

———. "Speed: Aberrations of Time and Movement," *The New Yorker* (Aug. 23, 2004).

"Time." *DK Illustrated Oxford Dictionary* (New York: Oxford University Press, 1998).

Valentine, Jean. "1945" and "Snow Landscape, in a Glass Globe." In *Door in the Mountain: New and Collected Poems, 1965-2003* (Middletown, CT: Wesleyan University Press, 2004).

Woolf, Virginia. *Moments of Being*, 2nd ed. (New York: Harvest Books, 1985).

NOTES ON NOTES,/: PUNCTUATION AND POETRY, by Robin Behn

American National Red Cross. *Swimming and Water Safety* (Washington, DC: American National Red Cross, 1968).

Bishop, Elizabeth. "Over 2,000 Illustrations and a Complete Concordance." In *The Complete Poems 1927-1979* (New York: Farrar, Straus and Giroux, 1983).

Cameron, Sharon. *Lyric Time: Dickinson and the Limits of Genre* (Baltimore: The Johns Hopkins University Press, 1979).

Crumb, George. "Voice of the Whale." In *Vox Balaenae for Three Masked Players*. (New York: C.F. Peters Corp., 1971).

Dickinson, Emily. Poems 443, 503, and 967. In *The Complete Poems of Emily Dickinson*, edited by Thomas H. Johnson (Boston: Little, Brown, 1960).

———. Letter 316. In *The Letters of Emily Dickinson*, edited by Thomas H. Johnson (Cambridge, MA: Harvard University Press, 1965).

Guest, Ann Hutchinson. *Dance Notation: The Process of Recording Movement on Paper* (New York: Dance Horizons, 1984).

Justice, Donald. "Psalm and Lament." In *The Sunset Maker* (New York: Atheneum, 1987).

Kelly, Brigit Pegeen. "Dead Doe." In *Song* (Brockport, NY: BOA Editions, 1995).

Knight, Etheridge. "Report to the Mother." In *The Essential Etheridge Knight* (Pittsburgh: University of Pittsburgh Press, 1986).

Miller, Cristanne. *Emily Dickinson: A Poet's Grammar* (Cambridge, MA: Harvard University Press, 1987).

Monette, Paul. "Half Life." In *Love Alone: Eighteen Elegies for Rog* (New York: St. Martin's Press, 1988).

Mozart, Wolfgang Amadeus. Concerto No. 1 in G major, K. 313

Pittenger, Robert E., Charles F. Hockett and John J. Danehy. *The First Five Minutes: A Sample of Microscopic Interview Analysis* (Ithaca, NY: Paul Martineau, Publisher, 1960)

Simon, Maurya. *A Brief History of Punctuation* (Winona, MN: Sutton Hoo Press, 2002).

Stein, Gertrude. "Poetry and Grammar." In *Lectures in America* (Boston: Beacon Press, 1985).

Sutton, Valerie. Illustration from The Lilac Fairy Solo from *Sleeping Beau*ty. In *A Collection of Classical Ballet Variations*, available for download in the DanceWritingLibrary at http://www.dancewriting.org/library.

Werner, Marta L. *Emily Dickinson's Open Folios: Scenes of Reading, Surfaces of Writing* (Ann Arbor: University of Michigan Press, 1995).

Wesling, Donald. *The New Poetries: Poetic Form Since Coleridge and Wordsworth* (Lewisburg, PA: Bucknell University Press, 1985).

Wright, C.D. "More Blues and the Abstract Truth." In *Steal Away. Selected and New Poems* (Port Townsend, WA: Copper Canyon, 2002).

_____. "Woman Looking Through a Viewmaster." In *Room Rented by a Single Woman*. (Fayetteville, AR: Lost Road Publishers, 1977).

Wylder, Edith. *The Last Face: Emily Dickinson's Manuscripts* (Albuquerque: University of New Mexico Press, 1971).

THE WRITER AS REVISIONARY, by Clare Rossini

Berryman, John. *John Berryman: Collected Poems 1937-1971*, edited by Charles Thornbury (New York: Farrar, Straus, and Giroux, 1989).

Bishop, Elizabeth. "At the Fishhouses." In *The Complete Poems, 1927-1979* (New York: Farrar, Straus, and Giroux, 1985).

Eliot, T.S., preface to Harry Crosby, *Transit of Venus: Poems* (Paris: Black Sun Press, 1931).

Frost, Robert. "The Figure a Poem Makes." In *Robert Frost: Collected Poems, Prose and Plays* (New York: Library of America, 1985).

Komunyakaa, Yusef. *Dien Cai Dau* (Middletown, CT: Wesleyan University Press, 1988).

Lawrence, D.H. "Elephants in the Circus." In *The Complete Poems of D. H. Lawrence* (Ware, UK: Wordsworth Editions Limited, 1994).

Lowell, Robert. "Skunk Hour." In *Collected Poems*, edited by Frank Bidart and David Gewanter (New York: Farrar, Straus, and Giroux, 2003).

Matthews, William. "Nurse Sharks." In *50 Contemporary Poets: The Creative Process*, edited by Alberta T. Turner (New York: David McKay Company, 1977).

McHugh, Heather. "A Few Licks." In *Hinge & Sign: Poems, 1968-1993* (Hanover, NH: Wesleyan University Press and University Press of New England, 1994).

Milton, John. *Paradise Lost*, edited by John Leonard (New York: Penguin Classics, 2003).

Shklovsky, Viktor. "Art as Technique," translated by Lee T. Lemon and Marion J. Reis. In *Modern Criticism and Theory: A Reader*, edited by David Lodge (London: Longman, 1988).

Spender, Stephen. "There's Very Little Room for Gretchen," *The New York Times Book Review* (March 26, 1961).

Steiner, George. *Errata: An Examined Life* (New Haven, CT: Yale University Press, 1997).

Yeats, William Butler. "Byzantium." In *The Collected Works of William Butler Yeats*, vol. I, edited by Richard J. Finneran (New York: Scribner, 1997).

"IF YOU HAVE TO BE SURE DON'T WRITE": POETRY AND SELF-DOUBT, by David Wojahn

Alighieri, Dante. *La Vita Nuova*, translated by Mark Musa (Oxford: Oxford University Press, 1992).

_____. *Purgatorio*, translated by W.S. Merwin (New York: Knopf, 2000).

Bly, Robert. *Leaping Poetry* (Boston: Beacon Press, 2004).

Carruth, Hayden. *Selected Essays and Reviews* (Port Townsend, WA: Copper Canyon Press, 1986).

Celan, Paul. "Nocturnal Pouting." In *Paul Celan: Poems*, translated by Michael Hamburger (New York: Persea Books, 1980).

Frost, Robert. "Conversations on the Craft of Poetry." In *Robert Frost: Collected Poems, Prose and Plays*, edited by Richard Poirier and Mark Richardson (New York: Library of America, 1995).

Gurney, Ivor. "April Gale," "Between the Boughs," "First Time In," and "Moments." In *Selected Poems*, edited by P.J. Kavanagh (Oxford: Oxford University Press, 1990).

Keats, John. Letter to George and Tom Keats, Dec. 21 (27?), 1817. In *The Letters of John Keats, 1814-1821*, vol. 1, edited by Edward D. McDonald (New York: Viking, 1936).

Lamott, Anne. *Bird by Bird* (New York: Anchor Books, 1995).

Levis, Larry. "The Poem Returning as an Invisible Wren to the World" and "The Two Trees." In *Elegy*, edited by Philip Levine (Pittsburgh, PA: University of Pittsburgh Press, 1997).

_____, "The Poem You Asked For." In *The Selected Levis*, edited by David St. John (Pittsburgh, PA: University of Pittsburgh Press, 2000).

Lewis, R.W.B. *Dante* (New York: Penguin, 2001).

Lowell, Robert. "An Interview with Frederick Seidel." In *Collected Prose*, edited by Robert Giroux (New York: Farrar, Straus and Giroux, 1987)

_____. "Epilogue" and "Thanks Offering for Recovery." In *Day by Day* (New York: Farrar, Straus and Giroux, 1977).

_____. "Eye and Tooth" and "Skunk Hour." In *Collected Poems* (New York: Farrar, Straus and Giroux, 2003).

Merwin, W.S. "Berryman," *Selected Poems* (New York: Atheneum, 1988).

Proust, Marcel. *Remembrance of Things Past*, vol. III, translated by C.K. Scott Moncrieff and Terence Kilmartin (New York: Vintage Books, 1982)

Snow, Edward. *A Study of Vermeer* (Berkeley: University of California Press, 1994).

Stafford, William. *Writing the Australian Crawl: Views on the Writer's Vocation* (Ann Arbor: University of Michigan Press, 1978).

Stein, Kevin. *James Wright: The Poetry of a Grown Man* (Athens: Ohio University Press, 1989).

Stevens, Wallace. "The Plain Sense of Things." In *The Collected Poems of Wallace Stevens* (New York: Knopf, 1955).

Tillinghast, Richard. *Robert Lowell's Life and Work: Damaged Grandeur* (Ann Arbor: University of Michigan Press, 1995).

Williamson, Alan. *Eloquence and Mere Life: Essays on the Art of Poetry* (Ann Arbor: University of Michigan Press, 1994).

Wright, James. "A Blessing," "Saint Judas," "Son of Judas," and "To the Muse." In *Above the River: The Complete Poems* (New York: Farrar, Straus and Giroux and the University Press of New England, 1994).

ABOUT THE AUTHORS

LAURIE ALBERTS has taught fiction and creative nonfiction in the Vermont College of Fine Arts M.F.A. in Writing Program since 1999. She is the author of six books, including the memoir *Fault Line* and the novel *The Price of Land in Shelby*. She has received the Katherine Anne Porter Prize, the Pirates Alley Faulkner Society Prize, and a James A. Michener Award, among others. She lives on a farm in southern Vermont with her family.

RALPH ANGEL is the author of four books of poetry, most recently *Exceptions and Melancholies: Poems 1986-2006*, winner of the 2007 PEN USA Poetry Award, as well as a translation of Federico García Lorca's *Poem of the Deep Song*. Other awards include the James Laughlin Award of the Academy of American Poets, the Willis Barnstone Translation Prize, a Fulbright Fellowship, a gift from the Elgin Cox Trust, and the Bess Hokin Prize of the Modern Poetry Association. He is Edith R. White Distinguished Professor at the University of Redlands and has also taught at Vermont College of Fine Arts since 1998.

PHYLLIS BARBER is the author of seven books, the latest, *Raw Edges*, a memoir to be published by the University of Nevada Press in fall 2009. Another of her books, *How I Got Cultured: A Nevada Memoir*, was the winner of the Associated Writers & Writing Programs Award for Creative Nonfiction. A graduate of the Vermont College M.F.A. in Writing Program, she has taught in the program since 1991. In 2005 she was inducted into the Nevada Writers' Hall of Fame. She was also a co-founder of the Writers at Work Conference in Park City, Utah. She's also an accomplished classical pianist, a wannabe jazz artist, and the mother of three rock and roll sons.

ROBIN BEHN is the author of three collections of poetry, *Paper Bird*, *The Red Hour*, and *Horizon Note*, and co-author, with Chase Twichell, of *The Practice of Poetry: Writing Exercises From Poets Who Teach*. Her awards include the Associated Writers & Writing Programs Award for Poetry, the Brittingham Prize, and fellowships from the Guggenheim Foundation and the National Endowment for the Arts. She teaches at the University of Alabama and has been on the Vermont College of Fine Arts M.F.A. faculty since 1994.

FRANÇOIS CAMOIN was born in Nice, France, and came to the U.S. in 1951. He has published five books of fiction: *Benbow and Paradise*; *The End of the World Is Los Angeles*; *Why Men Are Afraid of Women*; *Deadly Virtues*; and *Like Love But Not Exactly*. He taught at Vermont College of Fine Arts from 1990 to 2004 and currently teaches in the Creative Writing Program of the University of Utah.

MARK COX, a professor in the Department of Creative Writing at the University of North Carolina-Wilmington, received his M.F.A. from Vermont College in 1985 and began teaching in the program in 1987. He also directed the program from 1997-2000. His honors include a Whiting Writers' Award, a Pushcart Prize, the Oklahoma Book Award, and The Society of Midland Authors Poetry Prize. The most recent of his four books of poetry are *Thirty-Seven Years From the Stone* and *Natural Causes*.

MARK DOTY writes, "I graduated as part of the last M.F.A. class from Goddard in 1980, and began teaching at Vermont College in the program's second residency, in 1982. I stayed for eleven years, and consider my time teaching in the program to have been my own second graduate education." He has published nine books of poems, including *Fire to Fire: New and Selected Poems*, and four volumes of nonfiction, most recently *Dog Years*, a memoir that was a *New York Times* bestseller in 2007. Two more books are forthcoming: *Theories and Apparitions*, a collection of poems, and *The Art of Description*, a craft book. Doty's work has been honored by the National Book Critics Circle Award, the *Los Angeles Times* Book Prize, and the T.S. Eliot Prize, as well as by fellowships from the Guggenheim, Whiting, and Ingram-Merrill Foundations. Since 1998, he has taught in the graduate creative writing program at the University of Houston.

NANCY EIMERS is the author of three collections of poetry: *A Grammar to Waking*, *No Moon*, winner of the Verna Emery Prize, and *Destroying Angel*. She has been the recipient of a *Nation*/"Discovery" Award, two National Endowment for the Arts Creative Writing Fellowships, and a Whiting Writers' Award. She is on the Creative Writing faculty at Western Michigan University and has taught in the Vermont College of Fine Arts M.F.A. in Writing Program since 1995.

DOUGLAS GLOVER has been teaching at Vermont College of Fine Arts since the spring of 1995. He has published eleven books, including the novel *Elle*, which won the 2003 Governor General's Award for Fiction in Canada and was a finalist for the IMPAC Dublin International Literary Award. His short fiction is frequently anthologized, notably in *Best American Short Stories, Best Canadian Stories*, and *The New Oxford Book of Canadian Short Stories*. His nonfiction includes a collection of essays and memoir, *Notes Home From a Prodigal Son*, and *The Enamoured Knight*, a study of *Don Quixote* and novel form.

PHILIP GRAHAM is the author of two story collections, *The Art of the Knock* and *Interior Design,* and a novel, *How to Read an Unwritten Language.* He is the co-author (with Alma Gottlieb) of two memoirs of Africa, *Parallel Worlds,* winner of the Victor Turner Prize, and the forthcoming *Braided Worlds.* Graham is the recipient of a National Endowment for the Arts Creative Writing Fellowship, a grant from the National Endowment for the Humanities, and the William Peden Prize in Fiction. He is also the recipient of three campus teaching awards at the University of Illinois, Urbana-Champaign, where he is a professor of English and the fiction editor of the literary/arts journal *Ninth Letter.* He has taught in the M.F.A. in Writing Program at Vermont College of Fine Arts since 2003.

ROBIN HEMLEY, who joined the Vermont College of Fine Arts M.F.A. in Writing faculty in 1999 and served as Faculty Chair from 2002-2005, is the author of seven books of fiction and nonfiction. He has published his stories and essays widely in such places as *The New York Times, New York Magazine, The Chicago Tribune, The Southern Review, Conjunctions, Boulevard, Prairie Schooner, Creative Nonfiction, Fourth Genre, Ploughshares, Shenandoah,* and many other literary magazines and anthologies, including *Sudden Fiction (Continued), The Best American Fantasy, The Best American Humor,* and *The Touchstone Anthology of Creative Nonfiction.* His latest book, *Do Over: A Middle-Aged Man Takes a Second Shot at Youth's Disappointments,* will be published by Little, Brown in 2009. He is Director of the Nonfiction Writing Program at the University of Iowa and founder of the biennial NonfictioNOW Conference.

CYNTHIA HUNTINGTON is the author of three books of poems, most recently *The Radiant,* and a work of nonfiction, *The Salt House.* A former Poet Laureate of New Hampshire, she has received the Larry Levis Prize, a National Endowment for the Arts Fellowship, and numerous other grants and awards. She teaches at Dartmouth College and taught at Vermont College of Fine Arts from 1994 until 2008.

RICHARD JACKSON has taught in the Vermont College of Fine Arts M.F.A. in Writing Program since 1988. He is the author of nine books of poems, including *Unauthorized Autobiography: New and Selected Poems* and *Heartwall,* as well as a *Selected Poems* translated into Slovene, two books of criticism, a translation of a Slovene poet, and several chapbooks of translations from Italian poets. His poems have been translated into over fifteen languages. He is the winner of Guggenheim, Fulbright, Witter-Bynner, National Endowment for the Arts, and National Endowment for the Humanities Fellowships and five Pushcart Prizes, and was awarded the Order of Freedom Medal from the President of Slovenia for his literary and humanitarian work in the Balkans.

DAVID JAUSS is the author of two collections of fiction, including *Black Maps,* which won the Associated Writers & Writing Programs Award for Short Fiction; two collections of poetry, including *You Are Not Here,* which won the Fleur de Lis Press Poetry Competition; and a collection of essays on the craft of fiction writing, *Alone With All That Could Happen.* His stories have appeared in numerous journals and in the O. Henry Prize and Pushcart Prize anthologies, *Best American Short Stories,* and *The Pushcart Book of Short Stories: The Best of the First 25 Years of the Pushcart Prize.* He has edited two previous anthologies, *The Best of Crazyhorse: 30 Years of Poetry and Prose* and, with Philip Dacey, *Strong Measures: Contemporary American Poetry in Traditional Forms.* He teaches at the University of Arkansas at Little Rock and has taught since 1999 at Vermont College of Fine Arts, where he has served as faculty chair since 2004.

SYDNEY LEA taught in the Vermont College of Fine Arts M.F.A. in Writing Program from 1989 to 2001 and currently serves on the college's Board of Trustees. He has published a dozen books, primarily of poetry. His most recent books are *Ghost Pain,* a collection of poems, and *A Little Wildness: Some Notes on Rambling,* his second naturalist memoir. Lea founded and for thirteen years edited *New England Review.* He has received fellowships from the Guggenheim, Rockefeller, and Fulbright Foundations. His 1996 selected poems, *To the Bone,* was co-winner of the Poets' Prize, and his 2000 collection, *Pursuit of a Wound,* was a Pulitzer Prize finalist. Lea teaches graduate students at Dartmouth College and is active in conservation and literacy endeavors in upper New England.

DIANE LEFER is the author of eight books, including the short fiction collections *Very Much Like Desire, The Circles I Move In,* and, most recently, *California Transit,* which was awarded the Mary McCarthy Prize. Her recent play, *Nightwind,* created in collaboration with exiled Colombian theatre artist Hector Aristizábal, dramatizes the true story of his arrest and torture by the U.S.-trained military and has been performed at theatres, colleges, houses of worship, and human rights conferences around the country. She has received literary grants and fellowships from the National Endowment for the Arts, the New York Foundation for the Arts, and the City of Los Angeles, as well as recognition from the Library of Congress and five PEN Syndicated Fiction Prizes. She joined the faculty of the M.F.A. in Writing Program at Vermont College of Fine Arts in 1987.

ELLEN LESSER graduated from the Vermont College M.F.A. in Writing Program in 1985 and has been teaching in the program since 1989. She is the author of the short story collection *The Shoplifter's Apprentice* and the novels *The Other Woman* and *The Blue Streak*. She has two other novels in progress and is also working on a new collection of stories about mothers and teenage daughters in crisis. She lives in East Montpelier, Vermont.

BRET LOTT is the author of twelve books, most recently the novel *Ancient Highways*; others include the best-selling novels *Jewel* (an Oprah's Book Club selection in 1999) and *A Song I Knew by Heart*, and the memoir *Fathers, Sons, and Brothers*. The essay in this anthology is from his book *Before We Get Started: A Practical Memoir of the Writer's Life*. From 2003 to 2007, he edited *The Southern Review*. He currently teaches at the College of Charleston. He taught at Vermont College of Fine Arts from 1994 to 2003.

JACK MYERS taught in the Vermont College of Fine Arts M.F.A. in Writing Program from its inception in 1981 to 2004. The 2003-04 Poet Laureate of Texas, he is the author of seventeen books of and about poetry, including *The Glowing River: New and Selected Poems, Routine Heaven*, and *The Portable Poetry Workshop*. He is the recipient of two National Endowment for the Arts Fellowships, two Texas Institute of Letters Awards, and the Violet Crown Award, and he was the winner of the 1985 National Poetry Series Open Competition. He teaches at Southern Methodist University and is on the board of The Writer's Garret, a Dallas literary center.

CHRISTOPHER NOËL is the author of the novel *Hazard and the Five Delights*, the memoir *In the Unlikely Event of a Water Landing*, and the story collection *A Frail House*. He has taught at Vermont College of Fine Arts since 1989, and he lives in East Calais, Vermont.

WILLIAM OLSEN has taught in the Vermont College of Fine Arts M.F.A. in Writing Program since 1995. He has published four collections of poetry, most recently *Trouble Lights* and *Avenue of Vanishing*. His awards include fellowships from the Guggenheim Foundation and the National Endowment for the Arts. He lives in Kalamazoo, Michigan, and teaches at Western Michigan University.

VICTORIA REDEL is a poet and fiction writer who taught at Vermont College of Fine Arts from 1997 to 2003. She has published three books of fiction, including the novels *Loverboy*, which won the S. Mariella Gable Award and was adapted for film, and *The Border of Truth*, which was a Barnes & Noble *Discover Great New Writers* selection. She has also published two collections of poems, most recently *Swoon*, which was a finalist for the James Laughlin Prize. She is on the faculty of Sarah Lawrence College and Columbia University's Graduate Writing Program.

CLARE ROSSINI is the author of three collections of poems: *Selections from the Claudia Poems, Winter Morning With Crow*, which received the Akron Poetry Prize, and *Lingo*. Her poems have appeared in numerous journals and anthologies, including *Manthology, Poets for the New Century, An Introduction to Poetry*, and *Best American Poetry*. Her awards include fellowships from the Connecticut Commission on the Arts, the Minnesota State Arts Board, the Bush Foundation, and the Maxwell Shepherd Foundation. She teaches at Trinity College in Hartford, Connecticut, and has been on the faculty of Vermont College of Fine Arts since 1996.

MARY RUEFLE is the author of ten books of poetry, most recently *Indeed I Was Pleased With the World*, and a collection of prose, *Most of It*. Her poems and prose appear in many anthologies, including *Best American Poetry, Great American Prose Poems*, and *The Next American Essay*, and she is the recipient of numerous awards, including a Whiting Writer's Award and National Endowment for the Arts and Guggenheim Foundation Fellowships. She has taught at Vermont College of Fine Arts since 1994.

NATASHA SAJÉ is the author of two books of poems, *Red Under the Skin* and *Bend*, and numerous essays. Her work has been honored with the Robert Winner Award, a Fulbright Fellowship, the Campbell Corner Poetry Prize, and the Utah Book Award. She is an associate professor of English at Westminster College in Salt Lake City and has been teaching in the Vermont College of Fine Arts M.F.A. in Writing Program since 1996.

BETSY SHOLL graduated from the Vermont College M.F.A. in Writing Program in 1989 and began teaching there in 1993. She also teaches at the University of Southern Maine. Sholl is the author of seven collections of poetry, including *The Red Line* (winner of the Associated Wrting Programs Prize), *Don't Explain* (winner of the Felix Pollak Prize), *Late Psalm*, and *Rough Cradle*, which is forthcoming in 2009. She has received fellowships from the National Endowment for the Arts and the Maine Arts Commission. In 2006 she was named Poet Laureate of Maine.

SUE WILLIAM SILVERMAN has published two memoirs: *Because I Remember Terror, Father, I Remember You*, which won the Association of Writers & Writing Programs Award for Creative Nonfiction, and *Love Sick: One Woman's Journey Through Sexual Addiction*, which was made into a Lifetime Television original movie. She is also the author of the poetry collection *Hieroglyphics in Neon*. Her essays have won the Brenda Euland Prose Prize from *Water~Stone Review* and the literary competitions sponsored by the journals *Hotel Amerika* and *Mid-American Review*. Another essay was included in Simon & Schuster's *Touchstone Anthology of Contemporary Creative Nonfiction: Work from 1970 to the Present*. She is associate editor of *Fourth Genre: Explorations in Nonfiction* and has taught at Vermont College of Fine Arts since 2003. For more information please visit www.suewilliamsilverman.com.

LESLIE ULLMAN has been teaching for the Vermont College of Fine Arts M.F.A. in Writing Program since its inception in 1981. She recently retired from teaching at the University of Texas-El Paso, where she founded the country's only bilingual M.F.A. program and taught for twenty-five years. She is the author of three books of poetry, *Dreams by No One's Daughter, Natural Histories*, and *Slow Work Through Sand*, and her awards include the Yale Younger Poets Prize, the Iowa Poetry Prize, and two National Endowment for the Arts Fellowships.

NANCE VAN WINCKEL is the author of five collections of poetry, including *Beside Ourselves* and *No Starling*, and her poems have received a Pushcart Prize, *Poetry* magazine's Friends of Literature Award, and two National Endowment for the Arts Fellowships. She has also published three books of short fiction, the most recent of which is *Curtain Creek Farm*, and is the recipient of a Christopher Isherwood Fiction Fellowship and the Patterson Fiction Award. She teaches in the M.F.A. programs at Eastern Washington University and, since 2000, Vermont College of Fine Arts.

ROGER WEINGARTEN taught in the Vermont College M.F.A. in Writing Program—which he founded in 1980 and directed until 1997—from 1981 until 2008. For many years he directed the Vermont College Postgraduate Summer Writers' Conference, which he also founded, along with the M.F.A. in Writing for Children and Young Adults Program, in 1995. He is the author of ten collections of poetry, including *Premature Elegy by Firelight* and *Ghost Wrestling*; co-editor of six poetry anthologies, including *Stranger at Home: American Poetry With an Accent, New American Poets*, and *Manthology: Poems on the Male Experience*; editor of a short story collection, *Ghost Writing: Haunted Tales by Contemporary Writers*; and co-editor of *Open Book: Essays from the Vermont College Postgraduate Writers' Conference*. His awards include a Pushcart Prize, a *Louisville Review* Poetry Prize, a National Endowment for the Arts Fellowship, and an Ingram-Merrill Foundation Award in Literature.

DAVID WOJAHN is the author of seven collections of poetry, most recently *Interrogation Palace: New and Selected Poems 1982-2004*, which received the O.B. Hardison Prize and was a finalist for the Pulitzer Prize. He has also published a collection of essays on contemporary poetry, *Strange Good Fortune*, and edited (with Jack Myers) *A Profile of 20th-Century American Poetry*. He has also edited *The Only World*, a posthumous collection of Lynda Hull's poetry, and (with Mark Doty) Hull's *Collected Poems*. His awards include the Yale Series of Younger Poets Prize, the Poetry Society of America's William Carlos Williams Book Award, the Society of Midland Authors Award, and fellowships from the Guggenheim Foundation and the National Endowment for the Arts. In 1987-88 he was the Amy Lowell Traveling Poetry Scholar. He teaches at Virginia Commonwealth University and has also taught in the M.F.A. in Writing Program of Vermont College of Fine Arts since 1983.

XU XI is the author of seven books of fiction and essays, most recently *Evanescent Isles: From My City Village* (essay collection), *Overleaf Hong Kong: Stories and Essays of the Chinese, Overseas* (collection), and *The Unwalled City* (novel). She is also editor of *Fifty-Fifty*, an anthology of new Hong Kong writing in English, co-editor of the first comprehensive anthologies of Hong Kong literature in English, *City Stage* and *City Voices*, and a contributing editor for the *Asian Literary Review*. She was shortlisted for the inaugural Man Asian Literary Prize, and she has received an O. Henry Prize, a NYFA Fiction Fellowship, and *Ploughshares'* Cohen Award for Fiction. She teaches writing internationally, including at Stockholm University, Hong Kong University, Syracuse University in Hong Kong, and Sun Yat-Sen University in Guangzhou, and also lectures and writes regularly on globalized culture. In 2008, she was the first English-language writer-in-residence at Lingnan University, Hong Kong, and she will be the Bedell Distinguished Visiting Writer at the University of Iowa's Nonfiction Writing Program in 2009. She has been on the M.F.A. in Writing faculty at Vermont College of Fine Arts since 2002.

ACKNOWLEDGMENTS

On behalf of the faculty of the M.F.A. in Writing Program of Vermont College of Fine Arts, I would like to express our gratitude to the graduating classes of spring and fall 2006, and especially to Wayne Lindeman, for their generous support for this anthology. I would also like to thank Bret Lott for his invaluable assistance in the early stages of the compilation of this book, and past and present VCFA staff members Melissa Fisher, Katie Gustafson, Caroline Mercurio, and Betsy Rode for their exceptional work for the program. And finally, all of us are especially grateful to the incomparable Louise Crowley, who has served as the M.F.A. in Writing Program's administrative director and guiding spirit since 1981.

"Showing *and* Telling" by Laurie Alberts is reprinted from *Open Book: Essays from the Vermont College Postgraduate Writers Conference*, edited by Kate Fetherston and Roger Weingarten, by permission of the author.

Illustrations from *Swimming and Water Safety* are reprinted courtesy of the American National Red Cross. All rights reserved in all countries.

"The Poem, As and Of Address" by Ralph Angel is printed by permission of the author.

"Out Over the Bay the Rattle of Firecrackers" by John Ashbery are reprinted from *As We Know* by permission of Georges Borchardt, Inc., on behalf of the author, and by Carcanet Press, Ltd. Copyright © 1979 by John Ashbery.

"The Fictional 'I' in Nonfiction" by Phyllis Barber is printed by permission of the author.

"First day of spring" and "Lime blossoms!" by Matsuo Bashō is reprinted from *The Essential Haiku: Versions of Bashō, Buson & Issa,* edited and with an introduction by Robert Hass, by permission of HarperCollins Publishers. Copyright © 1994 by Robert Hass. Translations copyright © 1994 by Robert Hass.

"Notes on Notes,/: Punctuation and Poetry" by Robin Behn is reprinted from *Open Book: Essays from the Vermont College Postgraduate Writers Conference*, edited by Kate Fetherston and Roger Weingarten, by permission of the author.

"A Ballad of Going Down to the Store" by Miron Bialoszewski is reprinted from *Postwar Polish Poetry* by Czeslaw Milosz, translation copyright © 1965 by Czeslaw Milosz, by permission of Doubleday, a division of Random House, Inc.

"Brazil, January 1, 1502" by Elizabeth Bishop is reprinted from *The Complete Poems 1927–1979* by Elizabeth Bishop by permission of Farrar, Straus and Giroux, LLC. Copyright © 1979 by Alice Helen Methfessel.

"The Textures of Fiction: An Inquiry" by François Camoin is printed by permission of the author.

"Inward" by Inara Cedrins is reprinted from *New Letters* by permission of *New Letters* and the Curators of the University of Missouri-Kansas City. Copyright © 2001 by Inara Cedrins.

"A Rumbling" by Paul Celan is reprinted from *Selected Poems and Prose of Paul Celan*, translated by John Felstiner, by permission of W.W. Norton and Company and Suhrkamp Verlag.

"Where the Word" by Paul Celan is reprinted from *Selected Poems and Prose of Paul Celan*, translated by John Felstiner, by permission of W.W. Norton and Company and S. Fischer Verlag. The original poem, "Wohin mir das Wort," appears in Paul Celan, *Sprachgitter. Die Niemandsrose. Gedichte.* Copyright © 1986 by S. Fischer Verlag GmbH, Frankfurt am Main.

"With All My Thoughts I Went" by Paul Celan is reprinted from *Poems of Paul Celan*, translated by Michael Hamburger, by permission of Persea Books.

"On Voice and Revision" by Mark Cox is reprinted from *The Contemporary Review* and *Show and Tell* by permission of the author.

"I Know a Man" by Robert Creeley is reprinted from *The Collected Poems of Robert Creeley, 1945-1975* by permission of the University of California Press. Copyright © 2006 by Regents of the University of California.

Excerpt from "Voice of the Whale" by George Crumb is reprinted from *Vox Balaenae for Three Masked Players* by permission of C.F. Peters Corporation.

"A Display of Mackerel" by Mark Doty is reprinted from *Atlantis* by Mark Doty by permission of HarperCollins Publishers. Copyright © 1995 by Mark Doty.

"Souls on Ice" by Mark Doty is reprinted from *Introspections: American Poets on One of Their Own Poems*, edited by Robert Pack and Jay Parini, by permission of the author. Copyright © 1997 by Mark Doty. All rights reserved.

"The Ugly Poem That Reluctantly Accepts *Itself* as Its Only Title" by Norman Dubie is reprinted from *The Illustrations* by permission of the author.

"Striking the Wrong Hours: Poetry and Time" by Nancy Eimers is printed by permission of the author.

"Crazy Horse" by Ian Frazier is reprinted from *Great Plains* by permission of Farrar, Straus and Giroux, LLC. Copyright © 1989 by Ian Frazier.

"In Dispraise of Poetry" by Jack Gilbert is reprinted from *Monolithos* by Jack Gilbert, copyright © 1982 by Jack Gilbert, by permission of Alfred A. Knopf, a division of Random House, Inc.

"Notes on Novel Structure" by Douglas Glover is reprinted from *The New Quarterly* by permission of the author.

"Wake Up and Go to Sleep: Dreams and Writing Fiction" by Philip Graham is printed by permission of the author.

"Twelve Years After the Marriage She Tries to Explain How She Loves Him Now" by Linda Gregg is reprinted from *Alma* by Linda Gregg, copyright © 1979, 1983, 1984, 1985 by Linda Gregg, by permission of Random House, Inc.

"Meditation at Lagunitas" by Robert Hass is reprinted from *Praise* by Robert Hass by permission of HarperCollins Publishers and the author. Copyright ©1979 by Robert Hass.

"Fig. 12.5: Morris system" and "Fig. 12.19: Laban system" from *Dance Notation* by Ann Hutchinson Guest are reprinted by permission of Ann Hutchinson Guest. Copyright © 1984 by Ann Hutchinson Guest.

"Someone Should Start Laughing" by Hafiz is reprinted from *I Heard God Laughing: Renderings of Hafiz*, translated by Daniel Ladinsky, by permission of Daniel Ladinsky. Copyright © 1996 by Daniel Ladinsky.

"Painful Howls From Places That Undoubtedly Exist: A Primer of Deceit" by Robin Hemley is reprinted from *The Writer's Chronicle* by permission of the author.

"Poetic Technique in Nonfiction Writing" by Cynthia Huntington is printed by permission of the author.

"The Word Overflown by Stars: Saying the Unsayable" by Richard Jackson is printed by permission of the author.

"The Monosyllable" by Josephine Jacobsen is reprinted from *The Chinese Insomniacs* by permission of the University of Pennsylvania Press. Copyright © 1981.

"From Long Shots to X-Rays: Distance and Point of View in Fiction" by David Jauss is reprinted from *The Writer's Chronicle* by permission of the author.

"Dead Doe" by Brigit Pegeen Kelly is reprinted from *Song* by permission of BOA Editions, Ltd., www.boaeditions.org. Copyright © 1995 by Brigit Pegeen Kelly.

"Report to the Mother" by Etheridge Knight is reprinted from *The Essential Etheridge Knight* by permission of the University of Pittsburgh Press. Copyright © 1986 by Etheridge Knight.

"'I Recognize Thy Glory': On the American Nature Essay and Lyric Poetry" by Sydney Lea is reprinted from *Hunting the Whole Way Home* by permission of the author. Originally published in *Sewanee Review*.

"Breaking the 'Rules' of Story Structure" by Diane Lefer is reprinted from *Novel & Short Story Writer's Market*, edited by Robin Gee, and *Best Writing on Writing*, edited by Jack Heffron, by permission of the author.

"The Girl I Was, The Woman I Have Become: Fiction's Reminiscent Narrators" by Ellen Lesser is reprinted from *The Writer's Chronicle* by permission of the author.

"Nostalgia" by Richard Shelton is reprinted from *The Other Side of the Story* by permission of the author. Copyright © 1987 by Richard Shelton.

"Mind the Gap" by Betsy Sholl is printed by permission of the author.

"The Meandering River: An Overview of the Subgenres of Creative Nonfiction" by Sue William Silverman is reprinted from *The Writer's Chronicle* by permission of the author.

"The Lesson" by Charles Simic is reprinted from *Selected Poems* by permission of George Braziller, Inc. and the author.

"No Possum, No Sop, No Taters" and "The Snow Man" by Wallace Stevens are reprinted from *The Collected Poems of Wallace Stevens*, copyright © 1954 by Wallace Stevens and renewed 1982 by Holly Stevens, by permission of Faber and Faber, Ltd., and Alfred A. Knopf, a division of Random House, Inc.

"Fig. 12:33 Sutton system" by Valerie Sutton is reprinted from *A Collection of Classical Ballet Variations*, available for download in the DanceWriting Library at http://www.dancewriting.org/library, by permission of the author.

"The Three Oddest Words" by Wislawa Szymborska is reprinted from *Poems, New and Collected: 1957-1997*, translated by Stanislaw Baranczak and Clare Cavanaugh, by permission of Harcourt, Inc., Faber and Faber, Ltd., and Stanislaw Baranczak. Copyright © 1998 by Harcourt, Inc.

"A Tattered Bible Stuffed with Memos" by James Tate is reprinted from *Memoir of the Hawk: Poems* by James Tate by permission of HarperCollins Publishers. Copyright © 2001 by James Tate.

"Towards a Poetics of Pull-and-Release: Some Thoughts on Silence in Poems" by Leslie Ullman is reprinted from *The Writer's Chronicle* by permission of the author.

"Envoi" by Giuseppe Ungaretti is printed by permission of Richard Jackson, who translated it from the original Italian in *Selected Poems* by Giuseppe Ungaretti, translated by Andrew Frisardi, and by permission of Farrar, Straus and Giroux, LLC, and Carcanet Press, Ltd.

"The Weary Circles" by Cesar Vallejo, translated by John Knoepfle, is reprinted from *Neruda and Vallejo: Selected Poems*, edited by Robert Bly, by permission of Robert Bly and John Knoepfle. Copyright © 1971 by Robert Bly.

"1945" and "Snow Landscape, in a Glass Globe" by Jean Valentine are reprinted from *Door in the Mountain: New and Collected Poems, 1965-2004* by permission of Wesleyan University Press. Copyright © 2004 by Jean Valentine.

"Staking the Claim to the Title" by Nance Van Winckel is reprinted from *The Writer's Chronicle* by permission of the author.

"Incidental Music: The Grotesque, the Romantic, and the Retrenched" by Roger Weingarten is reprinted from *Poetry East* and *The Contemporary Review* by permission of the author.

"A Unison" and "Spring and All" by William Carlos Williams are reprinted from *The Collected Poems of William Carlos Williams* by permission of New Directions Publishing Corp.

"'If You Have to Be Sure Don't Write': Poetry and Self-Doubt" by David Wojahn is reprinted from *The Writer's Chronicle* by permission of the author.

"More Blues and the Abstract Truth" by C.D. Wright is reprinted from *Steal Away: Selected and New Poems* by permission of Copper Canyon Press, www.coppercanyonpress.org. Copyright © 2002 by C.D. Wright.

"Woman Looking Through a Viewmaster" by C.D. Wright is reprinted from *Room Rented by a Single Woman* by permission of the author.

"The Forties" by Franz Wright is reprinted from *Ill Lit: Selected & New Poems* by permission of Oberlin College Press.

"A Message Hidden in an Empty Wine Bottle That I Threw Into a Gully of Maple Trees One Night at an Indecent Hour" by James Wright is reprinted from *Collected Poems* by permission of Wesleyan University Press. Copyright © 1971 by James Wright.

"*Multi-Culti Literati*: Or, Ways of Writing Fiction Beyond 'PC'" by Xu Xi is printed by permission of the author.

INDEX

WORDS OVERFLOWN BY STARS